NEW DIRECTIONS IN GERMAN STUDIES
Vol. 41

Series Editor:
IMKE MEYER
Professor of Germanic Studies, University of Illinois at Chicago

Editorial Board:

KATHERINE ARENS
Professor of Germanic Studies, University of Texas at Austin

ROSWITHA BURWICK
Distinguished Chair of Modern Foreign Languages Emerita,
Scripps College

RICHARD ELDRIDGE
Charles and Harriett Cox McDowell Professor of Philosophy,
Swarthmore College

ERIKA FISCHER-LICHTE
Professor Emerita of Theater Studies, Freie Universität Berlin

CATRIONA MACLEOD
Frank Curtis Springer and Gertrude Melcher Springer
Professor in the College and the Department of Germanic Studies,
University of Chicago

STEPHAN SCHINDLER
Professor of German and Chair, University of South Florida

HEIDI SCHLIPPHACKE
Professor of Germanic Studies, University of Illinois at Chicago

ANDREW J. WEBBER
Professor of Modern German and Comparative Culture,
Cambridge University

SILKE-MARIA WEINECK
Grace Lee Boggs Collegiate Professor of Comparative Literature and German Studies, University of Michigan

DAVID WELLBERY
LeRoy T. and Margaret Deffenbaugh Carlson University Professor, University of Chicago

SABINE WILKE
Joff Hanauer Distinguished Professor for Western Civilization and Professor of German, University of Washington

JOHN ZILCOSKY
Professor of German and Comparative Literature, University of Toronto

A list of volumes in the series appears at the end of this book.

Interwar Salzburg

Austrian Culture Beyond Vienna

Edited by
Robert Dassanowsky and
Katherine Arens

BLOOMSBURY ACADEMIC
NEW YORK • LONDON • OXFORD • NEW DELHI • SYDNEY

BLOOMSBURY ACADEMIC

Bloomsbury Publishing Inc, 1359 Broadway, New York, NY 10018, USA
Bloomsbury Publishing Plc, 50 Bedford Square, London, WC1B 3DP, UK
Bloomsbury Publishing Ireland, 29 Earlsfort Terrace, Dublin 2, D02 AY28, Ireland

BLOOMSBURY, BLOOMSBURY ACADEMIC and the Diana logo
are trademarks of Bloomsbury Publishing Plc

First published in the United States of America 2024
Paperback edition published 2025

Copyright © Robert Dassanowsky and Katherine Arens, 2024
Each chapter © by the contributor, 2024

For legal purposes the List of Figures and Acknowledgments on p. ix
constitute an extension of this copyright page.

Cover design: Andrea F. Busci
Cover image: The City of Salzburg, Austria. Photograph by Thomas Pintaric

All rights reserved. No part of this publication may be: i) reproduced or transmitted in any form, electronic or mechanical, including photocopying, recording or by means of any information storage or retrieval system without prior permission in writing from the publishers; or ii) used or reproduced in any way for the training, development or operation of artificial intelligence (AI) technologies, including generative AI technologies. The rights holders expressly reserve this publication from the text and data mining exception as per Article 4(3) of the Digital Single Market Directive (EU) 2019/790.

Bloomsbury Publishing Inc does not have any control over, or responsibility for, any third-party websites referred to or in this book. All internet addresses given in this book were correct at the time of going to press. The author and publisher regret any inconvenience caused if addresses have changed or sites have ceased to exist, but can accept no responsibility for any such changes.

Library of Congress Cataloging-in-Publication Data
Names: Dassanowsky, Robert, editor. | Arens, Katherine, 1953- editor.
Title: Interwar Salzburg : Austrian culture beyond Vienna / edited by Robert
  Dassanowsky and Katherine Arens.
Other titles: Austrian culture beyond Vienna
Description: New York, NY : Bloomsbury Academic, 2024. |
  Series: New directions in German studies | Includes bibliographical
  references and index. | Summary: "A long-overdue reassessment of post-1918
  Salzburg as a distinct Austrian cultural hub that experimented in moving beyond
  war and empire into a modern, self-consciously inclusive, and international center
  for European Culture"– Provided by publisher.
Identifiers: LCCN 2023031925 (print) | LCCN 2023031926 (ebook) |
  ISBN 9798765112588 (hardback) | ISBN 9798765112571 (paperback) |
  ISBN 9798765112595 (epub) | ISBN 9798765112601 (pdf) | ISBN 9798765112618
Subjects: LCSH: Arts–Austria–Salzburg–History–20th century. | Salzburg
  (Austria)–Civilization–20th century. | Austria–Civilization–20th century.
Classification: LCC DB879.S18 I584 2024 (print) | LCC DB879.S18 (ebook) |
  DDC 943.6/3200904–dc23/eng/20230826
LC record available at https://lccn.loc.gov/2023031925
LC ebook record available at https://lccn.loc.gov/2023031926

ISBN:	HB:	979-8-7651-1258-8
	PB:	979-8-7651-1257-1
	ePDF:	979-8-7651-1260-1
	eBook:	979-8-7651-1259-5

Series: New Directions in German Studies

Typeset by Integra Software Services Pvt. Ltd.

For product safety related questions contact productsafety@bloomsbury.com.

To find out more about our authors and books visit www.bloomsbury.com
and sign up for our newsletters.

Contents

List of Figures	vii
Acknowledgments	ix
Introduction Katherine Arens, with Robert Dassanowsky	1

I   DREAMING SALZBURG: HOPING FOR HOPE, GRASPING AT WHAT IT WAS AND MIGHT HAVE BEEN ... 31

1 Fantasy as Parody?: Hermann Bahr's Salzburg Dialogue
   Vincent Kling   33

2 The Capital of Europe (1900): "A Fantasy in Salzburg"
   Hermann Bahr   39

3 Salzburg's Age of Aquarius: Der Wassermann as an Austrian Sonderweg in the European Arts   *Katherine Arens*   44

4 Notes on Salzburg and Cinema 1911–1938
   Robert Dassanowsky   99

II CHOOSING SALZBURG: COSMOPOLITAN REFUGE AND THE SEARCH FOR A THIRD WAY   137

5 The "World of Doomed Enchantment": Carl Zuckmayer and the "Henndorf Circle"   *Christopher Dietz*   139

III BEING SALZBURG: CULTURES FOUND AND LOST   175

6 Sport Cultures in Salzburg Between State and Dictatorship
   Andreas Praher   177

7 Everyman and the New Man: Festival Culture in Interwar Austria   *Alys X. George*   201

8 In the Shadow of the Salzburg Festival?: The Mozarteum
   Foundation and Conservatory as Protagonists in Salzburg
   Music Culture Between the Wars   *Julia Hinterberger*   222

9 Shadow Sides of Modernism: Poldi Wojtek's Designs
   for the Salzburg Festival and Austria's Conservative
   Modernity   *Julia Secklehner*   259

IV EYES ON SALZBURG: SALZBURG AS OTHER   279

10 Jewish Identities and Antisemitism in Salzburg
   after 1918   *Helga Embacher*   281

11 Hungarian Salzburgs: Salzburg and the Salzburg Idea
   as Inspiration for Mozart Concerts, Urban Tourism
   Development, and Festivals in Interwar Hungary
   Alexander Vari   299

Notes on Contributors   331
Index   334
In Memory of Robert Dassanowsky   344

Figures

Frontispiece Salzburg (2011), © K. Arens — x

4.1 The famous theater director Prof. Max Reinhardt (*right*) signing his first US sound-film contract, together with the German-American film producer, director, and press representative Curt (Curtis) Melnitz. Photo by Georg Pahl (May 1930) — 101

4.2 Max Reinhardt, actor and director, with Lady Diana Manners (actress, later Lady Diana Cooper) in the Park of Schloss Leopoldskon, Salzburg, 1905. Photo by ullstein bild Dtl.via Getty Images — 102

8.1 Number of students at the Mozarteum Conservatory, 1909/10–1945/46 — 233

8.2 Visitors to the Mozart Museum and the *Zauberflötenhäuschen*, 1923–1935. Source: Hummel (1936), 50 — 242

8.3 Visitors to the Mozart Museum and the *Zauberflötenhäuschen*, 1936–1949: by number of tickets sold (excluding group tours at special events). Source: Hummel (1951), 60 — 242

8.4 Concert attendance figures, 1925/26–1935/36. Source: Hummel (1936), 43 — 244

8.5 Students and teachers at the Mozarteum summer courses, 1929–1935. Source: Hummel (1936), 69 — 252

8.6 Students at the Mozarteum summer courses, country of origin, 1932–1939. Source: Hummel (1951), 81 — 254

Figures

9.1 Poldi Wojtek, *Salzburger Festspiele 1928*, poster. Archive of the Salzburg Festival, © Salzburg Museum, Salzburg. Leopoldine Wojtek © OOA-S 2023. Photo: Salzburg Museum   261

9.2 Karl Springenschmied and Poldi Mühlmann, *Eine wahre Geschichte. Worte und Bilder von zwei Deutschen aus dem Auslande.* Stuttgart: Frank'sche Verlagsbuchhandlung, 1937. Austrian National Library. Karl Springenschmied and Leopldine Wojtek-Mühlmann © OOA-S 2023   263

9.3 Erika Giovanna Klien, *Kleßheim Courier: Skandal-Nachrichten, Salzburg, 12 February 1927.* © Wien Museum, Vienna. Photo: Birgit and Peter Kainz   269

9.4 Kajetan Mühlmann and Poldi Wojtek, *Salzburger Festspielführer.* Salzburg: Salzburger Festspielhausgemeinde, 1928. Austrian National Library. Karl Springenschmied and Leopldine Wojtek-Mühlmann © OOA-S 2023   272

Acknowledgments

The inspiration for this collection was provided by Robert Dassanowsky, who assembled a team of authors for whom both he and Katie Arens are incredibly grateful. The essays they provided are models of scholarship, in form, content, and research. Thanks to them all for their impeccable work, their support, and their patience in working with us through a difficult period in world academics. We hope they find the results worth the wait!

Thanks are due to Deborah Holmes, editor of *Austrian Studies*, for permission to reprint Alys X. George's article, "Everyman and the New Man: Festival Culture in Interwar Austria," originally published in *Austrian Studies* 25 (2017), 198–214.

Robert Dassanowsky would like to acknowledge the University of Colorado, Colorado Springs, for a sabbatical that provided released time critical for this project. Katherine Arens gratefully acknowledges the support of the College of Liberal Arts at the University of Texas at Austin which made her contributions to this volume possible: a Spring 2021 College Research Fellowship (a research leave) and a 2019–2022 Humanities Research Award for support for yearly short stays at the *Österreichishe Nationalbibliothek* in Vienna and other incidentals. Early phases of her research also benefited from the wit of Professor Madeline Maxwell in a writing group facilitated by UT.

Rupert Indinger, Librarian at the Paris Lodron Universität Salzburg, deserves special note for making the catalog of the 1919 Wasserman exhibition available to Arens as a scan in mid-2020, in an unparalleled act of scholarly camaraderie for a complete stranger, in the midst of the many 2020 shutdowns.

Our series editor, Imke Meyer, and our editor at Bloomsbury Academic, Haaris Naqvi, are to be thanked for their support of the project, with special thanks to Hali Han, for her expedient and kind handling of all the manuscript logistics. Finally, we acknowledge our anonymous press reader for suggestions that only made the volume stronger.

Salzburg (2011). © K. Arens.

Introduction Katherine Arens, with Robert Dassanowsky

The Case for Salzburg

Why a volume on Salzburg between two world wars? The contributors to this collection each provide their own answers, but they share a central conviction: Salzburg in the era was more than the Mozart-city and the city of the fabled Salzburg Festival, it remains critical for understanding the Austrian culture of the First Republic, the new Austrian nation that grew out of the ruins of the Empire after 1918. The essays that follow, in consequence, were undertaken with greater goals in mind than simply providing vignettes of a cultural center trying to recover its identity in the wake of the Great War, in an era where Europe was realigning its borders, struggling against economic collapses, and uncertain about how its past would lead to a viable future.

This volume's interwar Salzburg is more than a city seeking to reestablish its life and to reconnect with its historical legacies. This Salzburg is a crucible of plans and experiments designed to help the city and its citizens to chart a path forward within the fragile First Republic to which it had been consigned. To again become a center of "Austrian" culture, as it had been for most of the long millennium of Habsburg rule, would require it to reconnect with the Europe that had dismembered Austria-Hungary and the lifelines of Salzburg itself.

Our Salzburg, then, is a city at pains to find its way into a future and out of the shadows of the wreck of the Empire. It hoped not just to survive what would stretch into almost two decades of struggle with the eddies of politics, economics, and history itself—Salzburg, as we shall see, saw itself as having the wherewithal to reclaim its identity within the emerging realignments of Europe (at least until the Second World War).

Such hopes seem fantastic to those accustomed to seeing Austria's historic tragedies from the point of view of Vienna and the Austrian successor states of Central Europe. But the facts of infrastructure and consciousness underpinning Salzburg's post-First World War conditions reveal the city's hopes as optimistic but not improbable.

Vienna was, in fact, a "loser" of the First World War in many ways that Salzburg was not. Between 1910 and the start of the Second World War, Vienna lost about 10 percent of its population,[1] while Salzburg grew by about the same amount.[2] Salzburg was the only city outside of Vienna featured on the First Republic's new banknotes. An old song insists "Wien is'ne Weltstadt": Vienna had indeed been a world city on the eve of the First World War, with two million inhabitants (a figure only recently matched again, a century later). However, after 1918, the population of Vienna was being radically redefined, as ex-citizens of a region vaguely definable as *Habsburgia* flooded in and out of the city, a mass of people migrating internally through the ex-empire's regions to find stable harbors and to reestablish their lives.

Those internal migrations brought with them dislocations of the kind associated with the Partition of India, where individuals were forced out of traditional homes and into choices of identity and identity politics that left them no place for their memories, their experiences, their home languages, and (all too often) their traditional social roles. People were forced out of some regions of the former Austria-Hungary simply because they were and wished to remain German speakers (even if they were functionally bilingual with the "new" nations' languages). Food chains between Austria and its one-time breadbasket in the Czech crown lands (and Ukraine) were broken and needed to be reestablished by treaty. Vienna became a city greatly in need: "Red Vienna," with its social welfare programs (for housing, childcare and education, and health services) was a necessity as much as a choice.

Salzburg would also house these refugees from historical change (explaining its growth in the era), but it was differently situated than was Vienna. Now, as it had in 1918, the new states in "Austria"—the First Republic—aligned geographically along a strict east–west axis, with its commerce and transportation stretched between Vienna in the east, as gateway to Central Europe, and Salzburg in the west, close to

---

1 For a summary of the problems of Austrian devolution, see Pelinka, *Die gescheiterte Republik*. The city went from just over two million inhabitants to about 1.86 million. See the *Statistisches Jahrbuch der Stadt Wien* online, which has detailed the demographic data for the city and its various *Bezirke* (by year, downloadable at https://www.digital.wienbibliothek.at/wbrobv/periodical/titleinfo/2057276).
2 Statistics for Salzburg available through ANNO at the Austrian national library; for a summary of Salzburg's population statistics, see https://de.wikipedia.org/wiki/Salzburg.

Munich, Switzerland, and Italy through mountain passes. Habsburgia's north–south axis, stretching down to the Adriatic, had been largely lost to struggles about borders between Italy and what would become Yugoslavia—it would not be part of the new Austria.[3] The axis of trade, transportation, and political connections of the Austrian Republic had necessarily shifted toward the west, as the Empire's Slavic territories sought their own national identities within Central Europe. Yet at the end of the Empire, Salzburg was not only on that east–west axis, it also still functioned as a major rail hub to the south, as well.

By twentieth-century standards that equate industrialization with progress, Salzburg seemed to have resisted the modernization that is defined that way. Yet precisely that difference, Salzburg's limited industrialization, worked in its favor just after the First World War. As a small city, it was never an urban desert: it remained closer to farms and natural landscapes. It also offered options for easy international travel to the west that Vienna did not have, and it was much less vulnerable to in-migration because it lacked industrial jobs. While housing its own contingent of war veterans, displaced persons, widows, and orphans, Salzburg simply was not as vulnerable to the kind of chaos in the streets that led to the July Revolt of 1927 and the Vienna Palace of Justice fire. In the first decade after the end of the First World War, Salzburg's connections with Munich also were reestablished on similar terms, when a new set of refugees from the *Freikorps* and Munich's own political shifts arrived.

Still, Salzburg had always been different to Austria-Hungary's other regional cities. Salzburg had long been limited in size and reach by its position in the mountains and along the rivers which had made it rich in the seventeenth century (as a mainline in Europe's salt trade), but which constrained its physical growth in the nineteenth (there was little or no room for expansive industrial development, as had happened particularly in Linz in the era). Even in the early twentieth century, Austria's other regional centers, Graz and Klagenfurt, had long been larger and had participated more fully in modernization. Graz and Innsbruck could also offer universities with several faculties, where Salzburg's university had been closed in 1810 (and efforts to reopen it failed in 1918, so it was not until 1962 that the city would again see the opening of its university).

Nonetheless, Salzburg's long history also tended to work against its own attempts to re-cast itself as looking forward—one of the original goals of the Salzburg Festival. Its upper class was formed two centuries

---

3   See Jennings, *Flashpoint Trieste* for an account of these politics.

earlier using the profits of its salt monopoly. It trafficked in culture in ways that marked it as an upper bourgeoisie and set it apart from the clerical and Habsburg aristocracy nominally "ruling" it as a city-state. Mozart's scorn for Salzburg's culture-consuming classes was formed at the moment when Salzburg's material conditions did not make as great a differentiation between these two groups as would exist later; but even at that point, the city offered him enough of a world stage to make him visible and his work possible. Still, Mozart needed and wanted a larger stage: Vienna's aristocratic collectors held rare copies of Bach manuscripts and had the ballrooms that could host recitals for the paying publics among which Mozart hoped to make his career. In the subsequent two centuries, visual artists also gravitated toward Vienna's wealthy art patrons, such as those who supported society painters like Hans Makart and Gustav Klimt. Nonetheless, Salzburg's independent cultural sensibilities retained a credible enough arts scene to make the Salzburg Festival not just plausible, but also possible—even in the much-reduced economy of the interwar era.

The political dislocations of 1918 actually gave Salzburg a moment where it could emerge as a significant center over and against the *Wasserkopf* (swelled or encephalitic head) that rump Austria, seen from a Viennese point of view, had become. In the minds of those who chose to move there and swell its population, Salzburg still had the advantage of being, not unlike Chicago, a "second city" on the major trainlines to the east, west, and south, and close enough to both Munich and Vienna to get there when needed, but far enough away to avoid many of the postwar depredations and political unrest that beset both cities. Politically, Salzburg didn't have an imperial *Reichstag* to burn, as happened in Berlin under the aegis of the Nazi far right (but blamed on the left), or a *Justizpalast*, like the one destroyed by Vienna's socialist leftists of the working classes, or a *Bierhallputsch* staged by Munich's rightist SA hooligans.

Interwar Salzburg thus hosted a community fleeing from metropolitan unrest, especially for refugee artists and intellectuals who, after the war, were seeking peace in which to work, food for their families, solace for the losses of the influenza pandemic of 1919, and a public, however small, that understood the arts because of a long tradition of cosmopolitanism which included not only Habsburg territories, but also Bavaria and northern Italy.

Still, European politics in the interwar era revolved around national identities and hegemonies rather than regional ones or international connections. From such perspectives, Salzburg seemed to those in national capitals a poor candidate as the foundation for a national identity—and the new "Austrian" politicians trying to reestablish a state were claiming Vienna as central to Austria's existence (as they would again between 1945 and 1955, as the city remained under Four-Power occupation like Berlin and under the threat of being divided).[4] Vienna's postwar political and social chaos led the ruling Socialists in Vienna to claim their own legacy as grounding the future, resisting the coalition of Black Christian Socialists and other conservatives who controlled the federal government, claiming a control that, between 1920 and 1934, they never relinquished. Salzburg, in contrast, had a smaller segment of its population identifiable as the working-class culture that Viennese Socialists saw as the future. Salzburg's arts communities, especially in its music scene (from Mozart through the Salzburg Festival and embodied in its *Mozarteum* conservatory) echoed that of Vienna in quality. Those who wished to further the myth of a Salzburg with an identity diametrically opposed to urban Vienna could also point to Salzburg's somewhat more bourgeois art scene, also as opposed to the old order elites that dominated Vienna's and Munich's culture markets—it was not rich, but it was perhaps more differentiated, less exclusionary.

That Salzburg myth became increasingly more conservative as the 1920s gave way to the 1930s. The Salzburg Festival was coopted by the old orders (not all from Salzburg) who wished to use the land of Mozart as their cultural masthead (as it remains today)—a city far off the beaten path of both of Austria's economies, new and failing alike. The example of Mozart and the city-state's clerical history was also straightforwardly adaptable to Austrofascism, when, somehow, Salzburg emerged as more truly "German-Austrian" than the ethnically mixed populations of Vienna that began to threaten Germanness with newly formed non-German (but still Habsburg) nations. (Remember, too, that both Prague and Berlin actually lie to the *west* of Vienna.)

The Austrofascists of the last moments of the First Republic, like the Christian Social opponents of Red Vienna, could thus use Salzburg to represent *their* vision of Austria's "authentic" soul, just as it is today represented in the *Sound of Music*: a city driven by art and nourished by religious piety and folk music, somehow impervious to the depredations of modernity and the military industrial complex. In reality, as in that film, the forces that took over the Salzburg Festival as a counterpoint to Vienna's established art markets and inherited patterns of arts patronage blunted Salzburg's own art scene. What in 1919 had seemed an opportunity for many artists, an Austrian place still at the crossroads

---

4   This situation is reflected in a 1951 Swiss film, *Four in a Jeep* (*Die Vier im Jeep*), with memorable Vienna footage.

of Europe, all too easily turned into an extension of the Nazi party which had established itself in Munich, in opposition to the Prussian Germany that had lost the First World War and was, through its commitment to the military industrial complex and the proletariat, working its way forward toward the Second World War. The world economy also worked against Salzburg, which was not large enough to have a resilient economy that could maintain its visibility in the interwar era or reclaim it after 1945.

The Salzburg introduced by this volume's contributors is the center that did not hold as fascism washed over Central Europe. It remained a refuge for working artists and their families, but they often ultimately withdrew out of the city into the smaller villages in the state. The public face of Salzburg could not sustain itself as something *different* in and beyond the Second World War because of Europe's nationalist and nation-state-centered politics. Nonetheless, it had already established projects and colonies (work groups or institutions) that would be important to the reestablishment of Europe's modern culture after the Second World War, and of international art and performance networks—there was enough of the Salzburg we present here left to serve as "seed stock" for the artistic movements that the Nazis had suppressed or disposed of. That remnant of interwar Salzburg preserved essential elements of historic cultures that Vienna did not know, but not necessarily a memory of Salzburg's own political identity on the new map of Europe—a large part of its legacies was coopted by the cultural memories of Munich and Berlin or repressed in the Vienna of historical scholarship.

Salzburg as a New Optic on Austrian History

The thumbnail just provided documents how Europe's history and politics have not always been favorable to cities like Salzburg, which are both significant parts of Europe's networks of finance, culture, and politics, and at the same time vulnerable to the streams of European history. Most particularly, the conventions of history-writing established in Europe and North America after two world wars all too often betray other signs of having been written by the victors, who tend to overlook "regional" centers of culture, outside the political capitals of nation-states. The case for Salzburg as "different" from what is seen as "Austrian" culture would not, in general, be made, and especially not as we recover it here.

Immediately after the First World War and the fall and dismemberment of both Austria-Hungary and the German Empire, history-writing about Austria-Hungary was focused on recovering some vague "German" culture from behind that political endgame.[5] The decline and fall of the Habsburg empire became a morality fable for a nation that had not embraced "modern" democracy, as the Weimar Republic experiment had done.[6] The Habsburg successor states rewrote their histories in the region to justify their own political existences, often with revanchist undertones, and the many individuals displaced by newly emerging borders that did not accommodate their own heritages or financial futures led to a generation of emigrees. They and their descendants too often either espoused these revisionary histories (especially of Slavic territories) or waxed nostalgic for lost homelands, often in more folkloric tones.[7]

For germanophone Austrians and those studying them, tendentious texts like Stefan Zweig's *The World of Yesterday* (1944) became popular, propagating what Claudio Magris would in 1963 call the "Habsburg mythos" as it looked backwards at a Vienna he only knew from his youth as a kind of lost paradise—and one that, in retrospect, may have had very little to do with the rest of the "lost Habsburgia" of the interwar era. Historians working on new forms of "Germany" both outside and inside germanophone regions after the First World War discovered in more contemporary political contexts new reasons to overlook the Austro-Hungarian Empire: the one-time successor states were now identified as hostages of the Cold War, which ensconced Habsburg rule as an occupation, the first of the region's multiple moments of victimhood—first by the Habsburgs, then the Nazis, and finally by Stalin.[8]

---

5   See West, *Black Lamb and Grey Falcon* for the classic travelogue that solidified images of the decline of Habsburg culture in the Balkans. The classic *A History of the Habsburg Empire 1526–1918* by Robert A. Kann was a standard until virtually the millennium; it is a magisterial history of wars, treaties, and rulers. Kann was a refugee from Austria, leaving in 1938.
6   "Red Vienna" and its extraordinary commitment to working-class citizens was a particular casualty of that historiography. See Gruber, *Red Vienna* and McFarland et al., *The Red Vienna Sourcebook* for work that has begun to remedy this lacuna. For a selection of histories stressing decline and fall, see Jászi, *The Dissolution of the Habsburg Monarchy*, Sked, *The Decline and Fall of the Habsburg Empire, 1815–1918*, and Wawro, *A Mad Catastrophe*. See the introduction to Arens, *Vienna's Dreams of Europe* for an argument that even Vienna referenced itself to Europe throughout this era.
7   One of the most notable popular books in this vein is Fehr's *Fernkurs in Bömisch*.
8   It is noteworthy in this context that the German Historical Museum in Berlin still takes a nationalist approach, for instance almost effacing the Holy Roman Empire and downplaying the existence of both the Nazi regimes and the German Democratic Republic. A typical treatment of imperial Prussia is found in the excellent *Iron Kingdom* by Christopher Clark.

Leading into our own era, a half century or more of power-bloc politics under one framework or another also played into two well-known historiographic conventions that determined the fate of "Austrian" histories. First, as noted above: history is written by the winners—in the case of Central Europe, the western allies of the First and Second World War and the western Cold Warriors from the major western nation-states. Historians in Austria were rarely part of those discussions, which remained in the hands of the refugees or their descendants.[9]

A more persistent barrier to a more encompassing history of "Austria" lies in the conventions of historiography established in the era of high nationalism and dominance since the latter nineteenth century. History, particularly for English-language readers, has tacitly or overtly assumed that nation-states, their rises and falls, and those playing key roles in their often triumphalist or tragic narratives (as heroes and villains) would be the appropriate models for visible, prize-winning histories of the near-present. Moreover, such histories are often written causal-genetically, usually tracking the politics of the nation-states in their march toward successful resistance against the predatory decadence of empire and the depredations of fascisms and totalitarianisms. We need not remind readers that Salzburg and its economy were neither large enough nor memorably enough engaged in politics to count on that stage.

That "history written by the winners" persists today has all too often translated into history written from voices placed on the Anglo-American-German axis and with direct access of its politics (or by those "liberated" by these states that promised democratic futures to the world). Until volumes were translated, sometimes decades after they were written, English-language history-readers had not been aware of significant alternative approaches to historiography that revisionist

---

9   Later histories retain this focus on historians connecting with their own heritages and working through remnants of the unconquered past, not in the "German" or "Austrian" politics that features so prominently in the earlier generations. Important histories of the successor states written under these conditions include (on Poland) Reddaway et al., *The Cambridge History of Poland* and *The Cambridge History of Poland*, Davies, *God's Playground: A History of Poland*; (on Hungary) Sugar and Hanák, *A History of Hungary*, Hanák, *The Garden and the Workshop* (which includes Vienna); (on Bohemia/Czech lands) Agnew, *The Czechs and the Lands of the Bohemian Crown*, Judson, *Guardians of the Nation*, Zahra, *Kidnapped Souls*, and especially Luft, *The Austrian Dimension in German Intellectual History*. On "Austria," see especially Judson, *Exclusive Revolutionaries*: and *The Habsburg Empire* and Beller, *Vienna and the Jews, 1867–1938*. A regional literary history of the Balkans was offered by Cornis-Pope and Neubauer, *History of the Literary Cultures of East-Central Europe*.

historians on the continent were introducing to their own readerships. European history-writing comprised not only the great political histories of the triumphant European nation-states (focusing on statesmen, revolutions, wars, treaties, and legislative processes), through specialized histories of disciplines, professions, institutions, individual social or political groups, and projects defining the identities and indirect power imposed by these states.

It is not our place here to provide a history of historiography in and of Europe, but it is worth underscoring how other forms of history-writing can illuminate the history of networks, entities, problems, and regions, not just as micro-histories, as we turn to in the last section of this introduction. What is most important here is that the historiographic landscape on which many of the essays in our collection were conceived and executed lies both within and beyond the nation-state model. For this reason, as well, the very grammar of our title was chosen to resist the historiography most visibly important for historians of the European nation-states in the nineteenth and twentieth centuries. Many of our readers will read "Interwar Salzburg" as a simple indicator of a slice of time and a place—the twenty years between two world wars, and the city of Salzburg.

What we offer here is not simply a documentation of two decades of regional Austrian history—to assume that is to misread our intent of correcting a historical blindness about how cultures of forgetting are all too often imposed on "regions" that are not "official" political entities. The Salzburg case is particularly instructive as a corrective in this direction: Salzburg was for the greatest part of its attested history *Stadt und Land Salzburg* (the city and state of Salzburg)—a self-governing country or city-state. The case studies we present here point very clearly to the need for a more critical and nuanced vision of an entity like Salzburg that has appeared repeatedly as a significant node in Europe's culture, economics, and history. Those historians interested in conventional "national" history, many of whom consider Salzburg "provincial" or a "minor culture" or a "periphery," speak from within an optic that focuses on the idea that Habsburg history centers on Vienna or Habsburg hegemony in Western and Central Europe. In contrast, the essays presented in the following pages argue that there is no single framework for writing history, but rather *frameworks* that need to be chosen with respect to their intended audiences. The essays that follow, then, should help pull us back from a Vienna-centered history that replicates national-political focuses, and onto a city that requires us to attend to the bottom-up forces that shape any top-down politics at specific sites.

The contributions in the first section of the present collection reflect and try to correct the acts of forgetting that have all too often subordinated Salzburg to Vienna within Habsburg history and that have rendered *improbable* the very narrative that we have just pointed out was *probable*—the idea that Salzburg might contribute to the identity of the First Republic by looking beyond the urban chaos and politics that Vienna saw in the 1920s and 1930s. They challenge fundamentally the value of considering Vienna and Salzburg as engaging in a stable center-periphery relationship that would automatically render Vienna-centered histories as authoritative, while marginalizing "provincial" histories, and highlight instead a dynamic, shifting relationship between two cultural capitals each with legitimate claims to representing central moments in "Austrian" culture.

Vincent Kling introduces us to Salzburg in the early twentieth century through the lens of a 1900 essay by the author and culture critic Hermann Bahr (which Kling has also translated into English for the first time), an essay that takes up Salzburg's traditional reputation, as seen from Vienna. Kling is interested in Bahr's essay as cultural politics (not as a particular landmark in his own literary production). In his reading, Bahr's essay is a parody representing the Viennese point of view where civil servants and other "cultured" peoples were at pains to assert their preeminence over that small city in the west. Vienna was self-interested in portraying Salzburg as stuck in the picturesque rather than offering a set of different visions of what "Austrian" culture might mean. Bahr, of course, was offering both a relentless skewering of Salzburg and a challenge to those Viennese who did not see the logic of investing in Salzburg's culture—he manipulates stereotypes on both sides of that geographic axis, in firm recognition of "what people think" about Austria's second city.

Katherine Arens's essay opens out the other side of that dialogue between Vienna and Salzburg as centers for "Austrian" history. She tracks Salzburg's claims to having an independent culture and mission more as locals might have understood it. This *Stadt und Land* (city and state) had evolved out of an independent late medieval Prince-Bishopric that was the home for an Elector of the Holy Roman Empires—an honor probably gained because of the city's position in the lucrative salt trade of Europe. Later Prince-Bishops (like the Paris Lodron after whom the city's university is named) would establish the city as a force for intellectual work beyond the reach of a Vienna under Habsburg jurisdiction, even as it lay apart from Hapsburg political control (Mozart was *not* a Habsburg subject by birth).

In the latter nineteenth century, a cadet line of the Habsburg family again marked the city as a different Habsburg culture after it had become part of the Empire. Arens tracks how, almost up to the dawn of the Nazi era, this history is reflected in how Salzburg supported an arts community, led by an upper-middle class with its own sensibilities, next to the more familiar patronage models (church and civic) more familiar from Vienna. The Wassermann arts collective exemplified the potentials in that model. It was a short-lived project, almost a pop-up, that nonetheless offered a vision of a retooled Austrian cosmopolitan identity, on an internationalist trajectory aimed at stemming the tide against German National sympathies, even as refugees from growing political unrest in Munich and the world depression undermined these hopes.

Our second group of essays follows up on these initial expositions about what was at stake in Salzburg's culture and history for those who *chose* it for its potential—its economic advantages and its advantages in quality of life after the Great War. Focusing on interfaces between art and commerce (person or group), they highlight how networks all too often identified with Vienna alone actually extended to or found their origins in Salzburg, revealing very clearly how artistic networks respond to economics and infrastructure rather than politics and national identity alone, given their documented willingness to work between nation-states and national traditions.[10]

Robert Dassanowsky's "Notes on Salzburg and Cinema 1911–1938" shows how early documentary and narrative film might have made Salzburg a unique second cultural center for the First Republic. The city had the artistic and theatrical talent to cultivate a film industry, and a limited number of new technically advanced studio spaces were built, in the hopes of producing a new high-art cinema. It might have become the third prong of a cinema based on co-productions and promotions between Vienna and Hollywood, not just for prestige cinema, but also anti-Nazi films. By 1934, the budding industry was reabsorbing talent from neighboring Munich's politicized entertainment sector. As politics caught up with Salzburg's potential, the city was engaged with Vienna's planned dual industry: one branch producing "Aryanized" films aimed at distribution in Germany, and another, an independent co-production industry employing Austrian/Central European talent who could ground an *Emigrantenfilm*.

Christopher Dietz tracks a group of literary artists that formed in the village of Henndorf near Salzburg, congregating around Carl Zuckmayer, since 1926 the occupant of an estate (the *Wiesmühl*) on the village's outskirts. Greats such as Stefan Zweig, Max Reinhardt, Alexander Lernet-Holenia, Emil Jannings, Werner Krauß, Franz Theodor Csokor, Ödön von Horváth, and others crossed paths as locals, drop-ins, and

---

10 A fine case for how Vienna's professional interests were augmented by summers in the Salzkammergut is made by Deborah Coen in her *Vienna in the Age of Uncertainty*, focusing on the Exner family.

house guests, in a set of artistic crossings scarcely remembered today and that offer insight into connections between arts communities from across the German-speaking arts communities, especially to crossover moments between theater and film.

Questions of class-bound social-political identities define our third group of essays, especially from the perspectives of the institutions that fostered various identity groups in the city-state. As Salzburg was recovering its identities after the First World War, a new world order was reconfiguring what resources the city brought to popular and local cultures alike. That "new" order, however, revealed growing gaps between classes and interest group in identity politics and public identities. The essays in this section show the role of institutions as formal and informal networks of sociability create a diversity in sameness that needs to be accounted for very carefully in analyses. Not *classes* in the abstract, but *interest and professional groups*, were significant entry points for nationalist and Nazi politics into Salzburg's public sphere. Accounting for filiation, affiliation, and institutions of sociability reveals dimensions of political processes than official politics. Together, they reveal much about how cherished local cultural institutions gradually succumbed to aspects of Nazi ideology and repression—cultures found and lost in conflicts fueled by connections with both Munich and Vienna.

Andreas Praher offers a striking analysis of how sports clubs contributed to Salzburg's identity, both reifying and crossing class lines in various ways, depending on the sport and how their economics interfaced with shifting political currents. A second example of the different "Austrian" cultures across class lines is offered in Alys X. George's extended comparison of cultural festivals in Vienna and Salzburg. By contrasting the more upper-class approach to the Salzburg Festival with a mass festival held in Vienna on July 19–26, 1931, in honor of the Second International Workers' Socialist Olympiad, George not only distinguishes between the local cultures of Vienna and Salzburg, but also shows precisely how.

Turning to arts institutions and art networks proper, Julia Hinterberger discusses Salzburg's long-standing cultural jewel, the Mozarteum, and how it brought itself (both its students and faculty) through the interwar period through compromise and repression alike. The essay offers a significant diachronic perspective on what it means to be a working artist in an era of political transformation. In a careful tracing of how an individual artist's career was shaped by the era, Julia Secklehner introduces Poldi Wojtek, an artist known for book design who designed the famous drama mask logo for the 1928 Salzburg festival, and her career in both contemporary design and more popular art styles extended into the Nazi era. Both essays show how thin the lines between political victim and perpetrator could be, and how they need to be considered as part of larger cultural contexts. Our volume's final collection of essays shows how regional identities were both fragmented and mobilized in the gradual Nazi takeover of Europe, bringing to the fore local versions of stereotypes often attributed to Austria in general. These essays again set Salzburg apart from the identity politics at play in the Second Republic as known in Vienna and shows the necessity to broaden the optics we use to understand social and political stereotyping alike. In the early interwar period, Salzburg had worked at retooling its internalized stereotypes about itself, not least to present a new face to tourists and others—an image consciously cast in opposition to the Viennese. With a municipal government precariously balanced throughout the 1920s, however, Salzburg struggled to recover and maintain various its regional and international visibility.

Helga Embacher addresses the little-known Jewish community of Salzburg after 1918, charting a social landscape quite different from the more familiar Jewish communities in Vienna, showing the problems these business leaders faced and how those stresses destabilized Salzburg's public sphere. Finally, Alexander Vari tracks a connection between far-flung regions of the one-time Empire that joins problems of commerce and image: how postwar Hungary used Salzburg's cultural policies as a model for cultivating its own image as a nation with a capital worth visiting by tourists.

Taken together, these essays point the way to new considerations of how "Austria" needs to be rethought, moving it away from too-simple historiographic models that juxtapose "the provinces" with "the capital" and assess the politics of the First Republic, the Ostmark, a potential Deutsch-Österreich, and the Second Republic as a contestation of memory politics and identity politics. Austria in that brief historical moment between the end of Empire and its descent into the *Reich* cannot be seen from Vienna alone. Salzburg's stories tell much about an Austria that was moving far beyond Vienna 1900 to seek a future that it never found. It is a story of a resilient culture that needs to be seen in its own voice, on its own right.

Salzburg as a Challenge to Austrian and Habsburg History and Historiography

As already suggested, many of the essays in this volume come from the broader, more critical, and socially and political aware approaches to writing history than those often used in English-language history-writing for dealing with Austria and the Austrian successor states in all their historical forms. How such "different" history-writing affects what we understand about networks in play at certain times and places is critical. Where political histories all too often focus on Vienna (or, in the US, differentiate between "inside the Beltway" or beyond), they tend to essentialize assumptions of primacy or force that may or may not always be the case. Thus we entered into this collection with the idea that the whole concept of a "national culture" is an artifact of nineteenth-century nationalism that persists throughout the twentieth century, used in grand narrative histories popular in the era of nationalism, and posits (tacitly) the existence of some kind of national essence.

The essays that follow take up instead Salzburg as an "Austrian" culture only in the sense that it part of a *glocal* network under various political administrations (including its own independent history) that has been essentialized as part of the Austria that emerged after the First World War. "Glocal" is a term now used in some discussions to diffuse traditional center-periphery models. It refers to *local* sites within various networks of culture, history, economics, religion, and the like; it also acknowledges the existence what Saskia Sassen (2001) terms *global cities*, which underscores power in influence functions as an artifact of size and the local accumulation of capital (there are lists of global cities on Wikipedia). But in the cultural domain, many smaller places can function as "glocal cities," judged not just by their size or their absolute fiscal power, but in terms of their positions in various global flows of capital that transcend nations and regions.

We stress here that such glocal cities and sites have impact because of their salience within global flows, not just their absolute value or financial clout. An example would be the container ship that got stuck in the Suez Canal in 2021: a very small city that was providing technical support for the Canal emerged as a central node and controller for a huge portion of the global supply chains—its failure first disrupted, then redirected global capital (when shipping companies realized the Canal needed re-dredging, larger tugboats, and more specialized pilots). Current fears about the rare metals needed for semiconductors have created variants on such networks: many of the mines producing the world's major supplies of various minerals are fraught in conflict zones that "require" political interventions as well as fiscal ones.

Glocalized historical accounts about Central Europe, then, need to reach beyond the dominant political histories largely centered on Vienna or on tensions between Vienna and Prague, Budapest, the Balkans, or northern Italy/Yugoslavia/the Habsburg Littoral. Salzburg's history, like that of many other sites within the regions, was not a history that could be told by the winners, or even by the losers as a victim narrative. It remains to be reconstructed as a landscape of lost opportunities: artists and collectors who learned from art and observation rather than from patronage and contracts (the situation in Vienna); film studios built but not sustainable politically; and the need to survive and practice one's art and professions when profitability and politics achieved different roles.

There are models, particularly in Europe, for capturing history around sites or networks. The most prominent of these in the second half of the twentieth century rose in France. French historiography is often traced back to the "history of the people," associated not only with historians like Fustel de Coulanges, but also with the novels of Victor Hugo. It becomes in the twentieth century a history of *mentalités*—of the attitudes and strategies that people and groups use in dealing with experience, and in crafting their own futures. This is more than a history from below, recapturing the place of classes and groups who left little direct documentary evidence of their ways of being in the world—except traces which can be captured in what is called "the history of private life"[11] or history from below. The historians of and around the *Annales* School (a name drawing from their journal, *Annales d'histoire économique et sociale*) find it critical to write history not as the history of ideas or politics, but as a product of the materialist bases of the lives of groups and societies.[12]

Around the *Annales* school, for instance, we find the geographic history famous from Fernande Braudel's *Mediterranean* (1972 [1949 in French]), who highlights the need for looking at history not just as a series of events, but as reflecting how political and social history can depend heavily on their locations, the longue durée which give global ideas and events their local character, over longer periods of time.[13] Other historians of that generation dedicate themselves to the history of the book (often used as a control mechanism over culture),[14] or to studies of regional identities as they contest the centralized nation.[15]

---

11 The concept was popularized in the great series of five volumes entitled *History of Private Life* (1987–1991) (*Histoire de la vie privée* (1985–1987)).
12 See Dosse, *New History in France* and Burke, *The French Historical Revolution* for readable histories of the *Annales* school. Marc Bloch and Lucien Febvre are important founding members of the group.
13 Some examples: the Suez Canal disaster has rewritten how we understand world geographic and economic supply-chain networks; New Orleans, always a relatively small city, has always been an outsized force because of its position on the Mississippi River trade—which also allowed it to maintain its own long-term identity as based in Napoleonic law (rather than British common law).
14 Most familiar in this context is Chartier, *The Order of Books*.
15 E.g., Braudel's *The Identity of France* (two vols.). The Low Countries have also focused on cultural histories based on longer-term cultural identities and the mentalities that hold them in place. See for example Huizinga, *The Autumn of the Middle Ages*.

Salzburg, as we shall see, has retained an identity that has long been determined by its own geographic particularities that have defied the abilities of empires and nation-states to subsume it.

British historians of the latter twentieth century also took up materialist analyses, albeit different from those in France, with more Marxist overtones (and often focusing on the eighteenth century), stressing issues of hegemony and dominance associated with the Empire and its economies.[16] Their most famous heritors are probably the Birmingham School—the Centre for Contemporary Cultural Studies (CCCS) at the University of Birmingham, founded in 1964 by Stuart Hall and Richard Hoggart, and dedicated to what would become known as cultural studies. Again, they show a focus on histories from below, especially on "subcultures" who resist dominant ideologies ("resistant consumption" of dominant norms).[17]

Academic historiography in Austria itself also has a commitment to a materialist base, echoing the analyses of social structures and power that have interested their French and British peers, yet ultimately of a different, distinctive sort. Historians trained in Austria are likely to be cross-trained in what are called *geschichtliche Hilfswissenschaften* (auxiliary or ancillary sciences of history) which require the historian to assess the contents of their material source for interpretations that lead to history-writing[18]—in general, to look at both the *Wahrheitswert* and the *Wirklichkeitswert* of sources (their truth-value and value as representing reality). The "truth value" includes what is *taken as truth* in a document or situation, as well as its value as documentation.[19] Thus, this history *starts* by collecting data *and* the narratives that rest on it, understanding from the first that ethics and power relations are inherent to "material facts."[20]

---

16 The most familiar of these histories is probably Williams, *The Country and the City*.
17 Put forth in Hall and Jefferson, *Resistance Through Rituals*.
18 These include not only obvious candidates like paleology, genealogy, and heraldry, but also archival science (what the organization of archives does to data and how), diplomatics (the analysis, material and textual, of historical documents), philately, numismatics, onomastics, and fields with other specialized tools.
19 The classic case is the Donation of Constantine, which is and was from the first known as a forgery; it was, however, *taken as real* for centuries because of its pragmatic value.
20 It is worth noting, in addition, that many of these innovations yielded school textbooks. For Austria, an equivalent for teaching how to read material history is Dusak's *Alltagsfaschismus in Österreich*; for re-reading documents, see Thurich and Endlich, *Zweimal Deutschland*.

Salzburg presents a particularly interesting site for such materialist interpretations, given that so much of the body of "facts" that render it intelligible are simply unknown outside specialized circles.[21] The city-state's historical forms of organization are structured differently than those in other parts of historical "Austria" (and here it is important to note that Austria-Hungary had a uniform administrative code, but left the historical law codes of its regions largely intact). Thus to research *Salzburg* is to open visions about strategies of social and political organization that were understood as functional in various eras, but which can all too easily be elided in "national" history-writing, as well as tying specific events, assumptions, and actions to materially recoverable situations, data, and narratives that fall outside of "national" rationales.

These more materialist-based concepts of historiography echo throughout "Austrian" histories written in Austria, but often are undervalued in those written in English. The reason, again, rests in assumptions about national history-writing. One must not forget that even Carl Schorske was a historian who worked on Prussian history, yet with essays that became his legendary book on *Fin de siècle Vienna* (1981) that became almost a cult phenomenon, as it rescued Austria from charges of decadence in its art (while not in its politics).[22] It was one in a series of equally prominent books like Janik and Toulmin's *Wittgenstein's Vienna* (1973) which set the philosopher's work into its broader intellectual and social contexts, and William Johnston's *The Austrian Mind* (1972), an exceptional introduction to the names, projects, and achievements associated with the last decades of the Austrian Empire).[23]

On the one hand, Schorske's work signaled a disjuncture between the kinds of history of culture just sketched, and the focus on political and military history that is required in a history of Prussia and the forms of "Germany" arising from it, or the modernized *Geistesgeschichte*

---

21 The history faculties at Austrian universities are organized to represent this focus on evaluation of historical data *before* a narrative history is presented (see for example https://www.plus.ac.at/geschichte/forschung/forschungsfelder/oesterreichische-geschichte/ for Salzburg's broad focus, and the very unique history of faculties at Vienna, https://geschichte.univie.ac.at/de/themen/die-entwicklung-der-fakultaeten-der-universitaet-wien), which have differentiated between a *Historisch-Kulturwissenschaftliche Fakultät* that includes social science and the *Philologisch-Kulturwissenschaftliche Fakultät*.
22 See Arens, "Building the Habsburg Subject" for a more complete discussion of Schorske's work.
23 That volume has been called out for its focus on germanophone Austria; Johnston countered that in 2015 with an extensive review of Hungary's contributions, *Zur Kulturgeschichte Österreichs und Ungarns 1890–1938*, which he published in German (anticipating that the Anglophone world would not be interested).

represented in Gordon Craig's magisterial *Germany 1866–1945* (1978).[24] Yet it still presented Vienna as *the* Austrian city, thereby helping elide the presence of the multiple cultural and urban centers of Habsburgia. No surprise, then, that it was rapidly followed up on by titles like Lukacs's *Budapest 1900* (1988) and Hanák's *The Garden and the Workshop* (1998).

The last decades have seen a further set of revisions to "Austria's" histories, paying stricter attention to the particulars of its history and social structures—and each has been countered by revisions by perspective "from below" that pay broader attention to the material bases of history.[25]

For instance, Pieter Judson has offered significant correctives to the political landscapes, yet with distinct limitations inherited from the earlier Habsburg historians trained on that grid of Prussian history (including Schorske) that emphasized the emergence of Berlin as *the* modern germanophone culture. Such historians again favor histories around nation-states, often defined ethnically, with central capitals and based on economic and social models derived from Britain.[26] Judson follows Schorske in taking up the idea that modernization implicates liberalism, ultimately conflating modernization with the literary/artistic term *modernism*—overtly addressing the ideologies of "the modern" as somehow superior to "the old" or "the conservative,"[27] rather than looking at how change is effected glocally (as happened in Salzburg, along distinctive lines).[28]

---

24 In this context, one also ought to consider the visibility of the mainline of German historiography that rose in Imperial Germany, associated most familiarly with Leopold von Ranke—a different way of dealing with primary sources and history as narratives, one that tried to counter some aspects of Hegelian teleological histories while being the primary source of modern models for the history of nations. See Sältzer, *German Essays on History* for an overview of that historiography. Scherer, *Geschichte der deutschen Literatur* is the equivalent of this historiography for literary history.
25 See Hebenstreit, *Die Zeitschrift "PLAN"* which tracks the purportedly national identity politics of Vienna's interwar era and how they need to be factored into readings of institutions and arts production. Also increasingly important are online platforms, such as Kakanien revisited (dealing with the Balkans, perhaps the oldest of such networks).
26 The most salient critique of that approach is offered in Hardt and Negri's *Empire*, which cautions historians from using models drawn from the British or French states and empires to explain other states.
27 See Arens, "Hofmannsthal's Essays: Conservation as Revolution" for an argument for a revolutionary conservatism.
28 An equivalent for literary cultural histories would be Marjorie Perloff's *Edge of Irony*.

Steven Beller's edited volume on *Rethinking Vienna 1900* (2012) offers a direct refutation of Schorske in a smart series of essays updating issues raised. Yet Beller's collection still functions without questioning the nature of what "Vienna 1900" means as a historiographic construct, just as his *Vienna and the Jews, 1867–1938* (1991) reifies "Judaism" rather than addressing the various strands of Judaism present in Central Europe as predicating *widely varying* social cultures.[29] In a similar vein, Scott Spector has offered significant work on Prague, in *Prague Territories* (2000), without offering much discussion on Bohemia as a traditionally multiethnic and religiously diverse territory.[30] His more recent work on sexualities in Berlin and Vienna (*Violent Sensations* [2016]) assumes equivalencies between the two urban centers with little discussion of the differences between the patterns of in-migration that affected the ethnic mixes of each in different ways. Here again, a more recent book by Nancy Wingfield, *The World of Prostitution in Late Imperial Austria* (2017), amplifies how different sexual stereotypes were across the empire; her work models the careful work that needs to be done in comparing regions within the Habsburg territories.

These revisions that focus on rethinking "Austrian" politics and society have, to be sure, been important in renovating older historiographic visions of Habsburgia, especially for Anglophone history-writing, yet overall, they have not answered the conceptual challenges posed by the kinds of materialist historiography sketched above.

Salzburg as seen in a version of a global city based on culture rather than money, with ample culture capital if not fiscally dominant, requires a historiography not based on empire or nation-states. The various essays that follow argue for more materialist analyses of "Austrian" culture, wherein specific aspects of a local culture help it to emerge as a significant node within larger assemblages or networks of geopolitical connections, some of which are regional (or which can be designated as "national" in that they are conditioned by legal and real-existing political-economic-infrastructure connections), some of which are decentered and even geographically discontinuous or dislocating (such as alignments of Munich and Salzburg across national lines in the period we cover, over and against Vienna and Berlin). The same might be said for Vienna, Budapest, Innsbruck, Graz, or Prague—albeit at different points in their development and historical circumstances.

---

29 For correctives, see Lisa Silverman's *Becoming Jewish in Interwar Vienna* and most importantly, Caroline Kita's *Jewish Difference and the Arts in Vienna*.
30 Brodbeck, *Defining Deutschtum* offers an example of how to nuance ethnicities within accounts of music criticism in Vienna (he treats Carl Goldmark, a Jewish composer from German West Hungary, and the Czechs Smetana and Antonín Dvořák).

As our readers will encounter in the essays collected here, Salzburg in the interwar era not infrequently has more in common with interwar Bavaria than either has with "Austria" or the "Weimar Republic," and it exists in arguably long-term oscillating relationships with the larger entities that later absorbed them—political debates *in* and *about* Salzburg are made against a rather different political and social canvas than those in Vienna. For this reason, each of the sections of *Interwar Salzburg* thus open out *different* visions of what it meant to be in Salzburg and Habsburgia alike—what it might mean to be in Salzburg, of Salzburg, from Salzburg, or in its sphere of influence, however defined.

Why is it important to ask if history/ies might be written differently? Because significant new interpretations of what is history-making need to be entertained. Our classical historiographic inheritances of thinking in political and social hegemonies (and their opponents), national histories, and the treaties, battles, and matters of taste that define them still limit our vision about what lessons "Central Europe" and the cities within it bring to us today—in a new era of geopolitical mixing, ethnic diversity, and a nationalism that rarely should claim a monocultural inheritance. Different optics uncover a variety of credible "stories" that had *Wahrheitswert* for those living within a region, and they may show different ways forward into dealings with contemporary problems.

One may then ask, for example, if Salzburg might provide a different model for "modernization," one which makes it more than an aesthetic novelty for the modernist era (which is all too often an economic-propaganda move). A different Salzburg could offer visions of sustainability and survivability—a way to conserve and improve, not "modernize" for the sake of an ideology that essentializes a ruling class as "the nation." One might recover different reasons for Hitler's plans of making *Linz* the cultural capital of his benighted state: it might, for example, have been an attempt to defang not only the Viennese and Berlin upper classes, but also to appeal to a newly emerging working-class culture in Linz—a move already modeled when the First Republic tried to move Salzburg under Linz's administration.

Interwar Salzburg: Beyond Revisionisms

Let us be very clear: what we are arguing, and what the essays collected here demonstrate is that *Europe* and its *nations* have been historiographical constructs for a particular historiographic strategy that essentializes "national" classes and projects in ways that marginalize loci like Salzburg, ignore persistent (longue durée) flows of resources, expectations, and opportunities, and occlude larger Habsburg networks extending between regions, ethnic cultures, and groups. Recent advertising for Vienna noted "Wien ist anders," a point that also applies to

Salzburg—these concepts are overdue being redrawn to accommodate new glocal analyses.

The stories told in this volume open doors to these new networks and to new material optics based not on the "regions" under a "center," but as nodes in new kinds of networks emerging at specific moments, for the most elemental of material reasons—for example, the problems of food and cost of living that emerged after Austria-Hungary's political collapse and economic collapse, but which also implicate Munich and parts of Switzerland. Or when artists "start" working with political forces or entities not yet officially "Nazi." What does one do, moreover, when markets are interpenetrating: the Berlin and Vienna theater scenes of the interwar era were deeply intertwined (and both Schnitzler and Hofmannsthal wrote works that they knew would appeal to one city or the other, not necessarily both[31]). Perhaps the biggest gesture in that direction was Hitler's plan to develop Linz as a cultural center—something that was tried in tying Salzburg to Linz's administration, but which did not work. Hitler was being less a "hometown patriot" in that gesture than seeking a working-class cultural center with its own economy, which industrialized Linz offered in the era.

These case studies, moreover, reveal how important it is to question how particular historical narratives have essentialized or coopted particular terminology as having *Wirklichkeitswert*, not only *Wahrheitswert* within certain analytic contexts, thereby essentializing visions of a state, nation, region, or people that may have originated from particular ideological contexts. Narratives about "Austria" often include words like supranational, multiethnic, multilingual, colonial, or diasporic. Each such term posits a kind of real existence: "supranational" subscribes to the ideology of nations; "multiethnic" and "multilingual" create the illusion that languages and ethnicities actually exist and that each "nation" can only have one dominant (DNA evidence calls single ethnicity into question; the old joke is that a language is a dialect with an army[32]); "colonial" prescribes a certain structure for dominance/subservience relations;[33] "diasporic" ignores the differences in attitude

---

31 Dassanowsky makes the case for such regional sensitivities in the film world, as well, in both *Austrian Cinema* and *Screening Transcendence*. Janke's *Politische Massenfestspiele in Österreich zwischen 1918 und 1938* argues for a broader view of "local" innovations within larger cultural realms.
32 Michaela Wolf in *Die vielsprachige Seele Kakaniens* and *The Habsburg Monarchy's Many-Languaged Soul* makes the case for real-existing apparatuses helping Habsburgia function as a multi-lingual region.
33 See Clemens Ruthner, *Habsburgs "Dark Continent"* for a sophisticated set of rereadings of theories of colonialism as applied to Central Europe. Anna Babka's *postcolonial-queer* does similar pathbreaking work in understanding representations and performances of gender identities.

between leaving willingly or being driven out, well-received or poorly so—to say nothing of the question of what migration studies refers to as "circular migrants" who spend part of each year in different places, or sites where particular classes congregate during known seasons (like the *Salzkammergut*, where artists mixed with scientists, physicians, and politicians in summer).

Cognitive styles and research paradigms can also be "national" and artificial. When intellectual work, art, or literature crosses a "national" border and finds a new audience, for instance, it often gets a new name and a new reputation. The "Austrian Expressionism" that is sometimes used in reference to some of the Wassermann artists, for example, shares many connections to *Die Brücke* and *der blaue Reiter* in germanophone circles (terms with greater publicity, due to their victim status in Nazi "degenerate art" propaganda)—and even to the postwar Vienna School of Fantastic Realism. Nonetheless, these "schools" or "styles" are posited as *different* because they have not been recognized as *glocal* voices (often, for reasons of influence and power), which art historians are beginning to recognize in re-addressing issues like periodization.[34]

When disciplines move across borders of any sort, they can also be willfully or unwittingly detached from their networks by new "standard accounts." The "Chicago School of Economics," for instance, renowned for the number of Nobel Prizes it has in it, draws on the economic theories of Red Vienna, especially Carl Menger, whose *Principles of Economics* (1871) focused not on capital but on value. Freud's work has only recently been recovered as having a significant social welfare component in its original settings—in clinics for social workers and teachers in Vienna,[35] and in the Berlin's theorizations of the social

---

34 Rampley, *The Vienna School of Art History* discusses the politics of art history. Shona Kallestrup et al.'s recent collection, *Periodization in the Art Historiographies of Central and Eastern Europe* tracks how descriptions of periods reinforce the (often artificial) identity construction of nations. In Austrian literary history, that question has been raised with regard to "Austrian" literary histories implicated with nationalism (e.g., Nagl et al., *Deutsch-Österreichische Literaturgeschichte*) and especially the Nazi period (Nadler, *Literaturgeschichte der deutschen Stämme und Landschaften*), with a heavily redacted version published between 1938 and 1941 in Berlin]); see Sauer, *Literaturgeschichte und Volkskunde* for an exemplary speech outlining the problem delivered in Prague. Note too the significant work done since the mid-1970s by Austrian historians and archivists on the Nazi legacies in archives, universities, and teaching curricula (e.g., Grabenweger, *Germanistik in Wien; Österreichs Archive unter dem Hakenkreuz* (2010), and Giannini et al., *Eine Institution zwischen Repräsentation und Macht* on every aspect of the *Universität für Musik und darstellende Kunst*, from curricula, performances, staffing, and archives).
35 See Danto, *Freud's Free Clinics* for an account of social welfare in interwar Vienna.

origins of neuroses (they are predicable according to class experience, not only individual creations). And there are disturbing parallels to the "treatment" of socially neglected children at the "Spiegelgrund clinic" at the Steinhof psychiatric hospital that has direct connections not only to the Nazi T4 project, but also to the abuse cultures purportedly fostered by Bruno Bettelheim at the Orthogenic School in Chicago, or by Viktor Frankl, the latter known for his work on Auschwitz survivor trauma.[36] All too many narratives use terms like "protofascist" which make Nazism a necessary outcome of ethnic nationalism—a dangerous exculpatory narrative that occludes individual choice.

The essays in this volume do not complete a remapping of a future "Austrian" history. Nor are they the product of naive historicism or the simple geographic or "regional" histories that have proliferated as grand narrative histories recede in importance for the reading public. Their insights are cast more broadly, in awareness of Salzburg as part of various regional networks that often transcend both regional and national lines—or that redefine regions. In this, they have potential significance in decentering inherited narratives about centers and peripheries.

They offer challenges in new voices. They fall in the tradition of David Luft's *The Austrian Dimension in German Intellectual History* (2021), which maps Bohemia onto the map of Austria, and they amplify the sketch of Habsburgia best represented by William Johnston's work (not only the *Austrian Mind* (1972), but also his subsequent project on the Hungarian intellectual landscape *Zur Kulturgeschichte Österreichs und Ungarns 1890–1938* (2015) in tracking significant nodes within intellectual networks, rather than the status of the cities or institutions where they were situated.

Yet other impetuses related to geography and history are not represented here, and not generally used outside of popular or extreme professionalized history-writing.[37] Whole clutches of work on the Danube written for general audiences by historians are ignored,[38] as is work

---

36 On the *Spiegelgrund* clinic, see Sheffer, *Asperger's Children* (and a 2004 documentary, *Gray Matter*); on Bettelhem, see Pollak, *The Creation of Dr. B*; on Viktor Frankl, see Pytell, *Viktor Frankl's Search for Meaning*. All three volumes rely on witness testimony; the Bettelheim and Frankl cases remain highly contested by professionals.
37 History written about is generally sourced back to Henri Lefebvre, *Production of Space*.
38 The Danube has spawned its own raft of literature. See Bozovic and Miller, *Watersheds*, for an overview of the many different histories possible, and in it, especially Arens, "Danube *Limes*," for an overview of noteworthy Danube literature, including not only Claudio Magris's *Danubio*, but also especially Beattie, *The Danube*, Hoffman, *The Spell of the Vienna Woods*, Kaplan, *Balkan Ghosts*, Taylor, *The Habsburg Monarchy 1809–1918*, and Winder, *Danubia*.

on specific disciplines,[39] cultural groups and their networks (outside sports),[40] or institutions not factored into either the grand narrative histories or their revisions. Technical or specialized histories that extend beyond Salzburg are also absent (projects like Tait Keller's *Apostles of the Alps* (2015) that move from "Germany" into "Austria" and Switzerland), as are works like Desiree Hebenstreit's *Die Zeitschrift "PLAN"* (2022) that track histories and networks of publications, and a new generation of "memory studies" that are starting to look beyond testimony to monuments.[41]

Salzburg read as we do here requires us to reimagine Habsburgia as an entity based on such networks and built around many sites of importance, as a large (multi)regional entity that is identified as Central Europe, but which has for a thousand years actually extended across the globe (the Austrian Empire was, after all, the first empire on which the "sun never set" when it "owned" parts of the Americas through Habsburg Spain). We must still investigate the roles of global religion (especially beyond Catholicism), for example, or of filiation among elites and plutocrats. And we must teach "German" studies that Schiller's great political plays actually implicate Habsburg-controlled Spain (*Don Carlos*) or Italy (*Die Verschwörung des Fiesco zu Genua*); Lessing's *Emilia Galotti* and Goethe's *Götz von Berlichingen* comment on the Holy Roman Empire, under Habsburg control. Salzburg was *part* of such Habsburgian networks for a comparatively brief period of its attested history, but it remained a conscious node in that network, not a periphery to Vienna nor a footnote in Arctic exploration, economics theory, physics, meteorology, surrealist art, and other fields.

Overall, then, we hope that this volume makes the case for Salzburg and the formidable scholarship that exists on it as opening our eyes to a *different* Austrian history, not only affirming the "diversity of scholarly voices" and mixes of disciplines that have engaged with the

---

39 Deborah Coen on *Climate in Motion* provides the best argued explanation of Stifter's "sanfter Gesetz" that there is (for a discussion on how the collection of ecological data within the Habsburg empire allowed for the emergence of the modern discipline of meteorology out of an attempt to chart how regions worked together to explain global weather flows—an innovation of a collective within a profession more than at one specific site).
40 Work on social networks today often derives from either Latour's "actor-network theory" from *Reassembling the Social* or Luhmann's *Social Systems*.
41 For instance, Norbert Christian Wolf's book *Eine Triumphpforte österreichischer Kunst*, which is actually about the memory culture of the *Festspiel* that makes it a nationalist project (not Hofmannsthal's original intent). Work on memory cultures is generally sourced back to the projects of Jan and Aleida Assmann in Germany.

post-Habsburg map of Europe especially to tie it to the emergence of genocidal nationalisms, but also to argue the need for a non-national (or conditionally national) approach for scholarship on the era and region. In recognizing that, we can see how the tradition of national scholarship has *occluded* the depth and breadth of the cultural churn that the dismemberment of Austria-Hungary unleashed and that Hitler and Stalin continued.[42] By taking up issues and putting them back in empirical frames of reference that would have been recognized when they were formed, the essays point out how Salzburg was well-positioned to flourish among the ashes, as an ecosystem of weirdly collaborative innovation, all of which looks locally aberrant but which in connection argues for modernizing forces that were able to be transformative when hegemonic cultures receded in their dominance.

Salzburg, therefore, will teach us to track what kinds of alternative historiographic narratives have been provided by our case studies, and how they might help us better understand Europe's "peripheries" which actually constitute the ground on which hegemonic Europe stands or falls—they are coterminous and embody incompossible accounts of power, offering different "morals of the story" of that space between the two world wars and beyond.

Bibliography

Agnew, Hugh. *The Czechs and the Lands of the Bohemian Crown*. Stanford, CA: Hoover Institution Press, 2004.

Arens, Katherine. "Building the Habsburg Subject: Scholarly Historical Fictions." Special Issue: Festschrift for David Luft, ed. Donald Wallace. *Journal of Austrian Studies*, 54(4) (Winter 2021), 37–71.

Arens, Katherine. "Danube *Limes*: The Limits of the Geographic-Cultural Imaginary." In Marijeta Bozovic and Matthew D. Miller, eds., *Watersheds: Poetics and Politics of the Danube River*, 1–24. Brighton, MA: Academic Studies Press, 2016.

Arens, Katherine. "Hofmannsthal's Essays: Conservation as Revolution." In Thomas A. Kovach, ed., *A Companion to the Works of Hugo von Hofmannsthal*, 181–202. Rochester, NY: Camden House, 2002.

Arens, Katherine. "Introduction: Austria as a Challenge to Europe." In *Vienna's Dreams of Europe: Thinking Beyond the Nation State*, 1–22. London and New York: Bloomsbury, 2015.

---

42 There are, for example, no essays on politics proper, nor revisionist texts like those of Sean McMeekin for the First World War era in Germany that reevaluate the balance of the great powers (often hotly contested), or that invalidate claims rising from the ashes of the First World War (see for instance Timothy Snyder's *Bloodlands*).

Babka, Anna. *postcolonial-queer: Erkundungen in Theorie und Literatur*. Berlin: Verlag Turia + Kant, 2019.
Beattie, Andrew. *The Danube: A Cultural History*. New York: Oxford UP, 2011.
Beller, Steven, ed. *Rethinking Vienna 1900*. New York: Berghahn Books, 2001.
Beller, Steven. *Vienna and the Jews, 1867–1938: A Cultural History*. Cambridge: Cambridge UP, 1991.
Bozovic, Marijeta, and Matthew D. Miller. *Watersheds: Poetics and Politics of the Danube River*. Brighton, MA: Academic Studies Press, 2016.
Braudel, Fernand. *The Identity of France*, vol. 1, *History and Environment*, and vol. 2, *People and Production*. Trans. Siân Reynolds. New York: Harper Collins, 1989 and 1991.
Braudel, Fernand. *The Mediterranean and the Mediterranean World in the Age of Philip II*. Trans. Siân Reynolds. New York: Harper & Row, 1972 = *La Méditerrané et la Monde Méditerranéen à l'Époque de Philippe II*, 3 vols. Paris: Librairie Armand Colin, 2nd rev. ed., 1966 [1949].
Brodbeck, David. *Defining Deutschtum: Political Ideology, German Identity, and Music-Critical Discourse in Liberal Vienna*. Berkeley: U of California P, 2014.
Burke, Peter. *The French Historical Revolution: The Annales School, 1929–2014*. 2nd ed. Stanford: Stanford UP, 2015.
Chartier, Roger. *The Order of Books: Readers, Authors, and Libraries in Europe Between the 14th and 18th Centuries*. Trans. Lydia D. Cochrane. Stanford: Stanford UP, 1994 (1992 in French).
Clark, Christopher. *Iron Kingdom: The Rise and Downfall of Prussia, 1600–1947*. Cambridge, MA: Belknap Press/Harvard UP, 2006.
Coen, Deborah R. *Climate in Motion: Science, Empire, and the Problem of Scale*. Chicago: U of Chicago P, 2018.
Coen, Deborah R. *Vienna in the Age of Uncertainty: Science, Liberalism, and Private Life*. Chicago: U of Chicago P, 2007.
Cornis-Pope, Marcel, and John Neubauer, eds. *History of the Literary Cultures of East-Central Europe: Junctures and Disjunctures in the 19th and 20th Centuries*. Vol. 2. Amsterdam: John Benjamins Publishing, 2006.
Craig, Gordon. *Germany 1866–1945*. Oxford: Oxford UP, 1978.
Danto, Elizabeth Ann. *Freud's Free Clinics: Psychoanalysis and Social Justice, 1918–1938*. New York: Columbia UP, 2007.
Dassanowsky, Robert. *Austrian Cinema: A History*. Jefferson, NC, and London: McFarland & Company, 2005.
Dassanowsky, Robert. *Screening Transcendence: Film under Austrofascism and the Hollywood Hope, 1933–1938*. Bloomington: Indiana UP, 2018.
Davies, Norman. *God's Playground: A History of Poland*. 2 vols, rev. ed. New York: Columbia UP, 2005 [1982].
Dosse, François. *New History in France: The Triumph of the "Annales."* Champaign: University of Illinois Press, 1994.
Dusak, Peter. *Alltagsfaschismus in Österreich*. Mediathek der Zeitgeschichte, 1. St. Pölten: Verlag Niederösterreichisches Pressehaus, 1979 [book + 4 cassette tapes].
Fehr, Götz. *Fernkurs in Böhmisch*. Frankfurt/M: Insel Verlag, 1991.
Four in a Jeep [German: *Die Vier im Jeep*] [drama film]. Dir. Leopold Lindtberg and Elizabeth Montagu, 1951.
Giannini, Juri, Maximilian Haas, and Erwin Strouhal, eds. *Eine Institution zwischen Repräsentation und Macht: Die Universität für Musik und darstellende Kunst im Kulturleben des Nationalsozialismus*. Vienna: Mille Tre Verlag, 2014.

Grabenweger, Elisabeth. *Germanistik in Wien: Das Seminar für Deutsche Philologie und seine Privatdozentinnen (1897–1933)*. Series: Quellen und Forschungen zur Literatur- und Kulturgeschichte 85 (319). Berlin & Boston: De Gruyter, 2016.

Gray Matter [documentary]. Dir. Joe Berlinger, 2004.

Gruber, Helmut. *Red Vienna: Experiment in Working-Class Culture, 1919–1934*. Oxford: Oxford UP, 1991.

Hall, Stuart, and Tony Jefferson, eds. *Resistance Through Rituals: Youth Subcultures in Post-War Britain*. 2nd ed. London: Routledge, 2006 [original ed. 1975].

Hanák, Peter. *The Garden and the Workshop: Essays on the Cultural History of Vienna and Budapest*. Princeton, NJ: Princeton UP, 1998.

Hardt, Michael, and Antonio Negri. *Empire*. Cambridge, MA: Harvard UP, 2000.

Hebenstreit, Desiree. *Die Zeitschrift "PLAN": Österreichischer Identitätsdiskurs, individuelles und kollektives Gedächtnis in der Nachkriegszeit*. Vienna: Vienna UP/V&R UP, 2022.

History of Private Life. Trans. Arthur Goldhammer, 5 vols. Cambridge, MA: Belknap Press of Harvard UP, 1987–1991 = *Histoire de la vie Privée* (Paris: Seuil, 1985–1987).

Hofmann, Paul. *The Spell of the Vienna Woods: Inspiration and Influence from Beethoven to Kafka*. New York: Henry Holt & Co., 1994.

Huizinga, Johan. *The Autumn of the Middle Ages*. Trans. Rodney J. Payton and Ulrich Mammitzsch. Chicago: U of Chicago P, 1996.

Janik, Allan, and Stephen E. Toulmin. *Wittgenstein's Vienna*. Chicago: Ivan R. Dee, 1996 [1973].

Janke, Pia. *Politische Massenfestspiele in Österreich zwischen 1918 und 1938*. Wien: Böhlau Verlag, 2010.

Jászi, Oszkár (Oskar). *The Dissolution of the Habsburg Monarchy*. Chicago, U of Chicago P, 1929 (available in print into the 1980s).

Jennings, Christian. *Flashpoint Trieste: The First Battle of the Cold War*. Lebanon, NH: ForeEdge/UP of New England, 2017,

Johnston, William M. *The Austrian Mind: An Intellectual and Social History, 1848–1938*. Berkeley: U of California P, 1972.

Johnston, William M. *Zur Kulturgeschichte Österreichs und Ungarns 1890–1938: Auf der Suche nach verborgenen Gemeinsamkeiten*. Wien: Böhlau Verlag, 2015.

Judson, Pieter. *Exclusive Revolutionaries: Liberal Politics, Social Experience, and National Identity in the Austrian Empire 1848–1914*. Ann Arbor: U of Michigan P, 1996.

Judson, Pieter. *Guardians of the Nation: Activists on the Language Frontiers of Imperial Austria*. Cambridge, MA: Harvard UP, 2006.

Judson, Pieter. *The Habsburg Empire: A New History*. Cambridge, MA/London: Harvard UP, 2016.

Kakanien revisited (research platform). Available online: http://www.kakanien-revisited.at/, 2001–date (accessed June 11, 2023).

Kallestrup, Shona, Magdalena Kunińska, Mihnea Alexandru Mihail, Anna Adashinskaya, and Cosmin Minea, eds. *Periodization in the Art Historiographies of Central and Eastern Europe*. London: Routledge, 2022. Available online: https://library.oapen.org/bitstream/20.500.12657/56647/1/9781000602005.pdf (accessed July 26, 2023).

Kann, Robert A. *A History of the Habsburg Empire, 1526–1918*. Berkeley: U of California P, 1980.

Kaplan, Robert D. *Balkan Ghosts: A Journey Through History*. New York: St. Martin's Press, 2005.

Keller, Tait. *Apostles of the Alps: Mountaineering and Nation Building in Germany and Austria, 1860–1939*. Chapel Hill: U of North Carolina P, 2015.

Kita, Caroline A. *Jewish Difference and the Arts in Vienna: Composing Compassion in Music and Biblical Theater*. Bloomington: Indiana UP, 2019.

Latour, Bruno. *Reassembling the Social: An Introduction to Actor-Network Theory*. Harvard: Harvard UP, 2005.

Lefebvre, Henri. *Production of Space*. Trans. Donald Nicholson-Smith. Oxford: Blackwell, 1991 (1974 in French).

Luft, David S. *The Austrian Dimension in German Intellectual History: From the Enlightenment to Anschluss*. London/New York: Bloomsbury Academic Press, 2021.

Luhmann, Niklas. *Social Systems*. Trans. Bednarz, Jr. with Dirk Becker. Stanford: Stanford UP, 1995.

Lukacs, John. *Budapest 1900: A Historical Portrait of a City and Its Culture*. New York: Grove Press, 1988.

Magris, Claudio. *Danube*. Trans. Patrick Creagh. New York: Farrer Straus Giroux, 1989 = *Danubio*. Milano: Garzanti, 1986.

Magris, Claudio. *Der habsburgische Mythos in der modernen österreichischen Literatur*. Trans. Madeleine von Pásztory. Salzburg: Müller, 1966; rev. ed., Vienna: Zsolnay, 2000 = *Il mito absburgico nella letteratura austriaca moderna*. Torino: Einaudi, 1963; Nuova edizione e prefazione dell'Autore, Einaudi, 1988.

McFarland, Rob, Georg Spitaler, and Ingo Zechner, eds. *The Red Vienna Sourcebook*. Rochester, NY: Camden House/Boydell& Brewer, 2020

McMeekin, Sean. *The Russian Origins of the First World War*. Cambridge, MA: Belknap Press of Harvard UP, 2011.

McMeekin, Sean. *The Berlin-Baghdad Express: The Ottoman Empire and Germany's Bid for World Power*. Cambridge, MA: Belknap Press of Harvard UP, 2010.

Menger, Carl. *Principles of Economics*. Trans. James Dingwall and Bert F. Hoselitz. New York: New York UP, 1976 [1871] = *Grundsätze der Volkswirtschaftslehre*. Wien: Braumüller, 1871.

Nadler, Josef. *Literaturgeschichte der deutschen Stämme und Landschaften*. 4 vols. Regensburg: J. Habbel, 1912–1928; 4th ed. Berlin: Propyläen Verlag, 1938–1941.

Nagl, J[ohann] W[illibald], Jakob Zeidler, and Eduard Castle, eds. *Deutsch-Österreichische Literaturgeschichte*, vol. 1, *Von der Kolonisation bis 1750*. Vienna and Leipzig: Carl Fromme, 1898.

Österreichs Archive unter dem Hakenkreuz. Hrsg. von der Generaldirektion (Sabine Bohmann). Mitteilungen des Österreichischen Staatsarchivs, 54. Innsbruck: Studienverlag, 2010.

Pelinka, Anton. *Die gescheiterte Republik: Kultur und Politik in Österreich 1918–1938*. Wien; Böhlau Verlag, 2017.

Perloff, Marjorie. *Edge of Irony: Modernism in the Shadow of the Habsburg Empire*. Chicago: U of Chicago P, 2016.

Pollak, Richard. *The Creation of Dr. B: A Biography of Bruno Bettelheim*. New York: Simon & Schuster, 1997.

Pytell, Timothy E. *Viktor Frankl's Search for Meaning: An Emblematic 20th-Century Life*. Oxford/New York: Berghahn Books, 2020.

Rampley, Matthew. *The Vienna School of Art History: Empire and the Politics of Scholarship, 1847–1918*. University Park: Pennsylvania State UP, 2013.

Reddaway, W. F. [William Fiddian], J. H. Penson, O. Halecki, and R. Dyboski, eds. *The Cambridge History of Poland: From the Origins to Sobieski (to 1696)*. Cambridge: Cambridge UP, 1950.

Reddaway, W. F. [William Fiddian], J. H. Penson, O. Halecki, and R. Dyboski, eds. *The Cambridge History of Poland: From August II to Pilsudski (1697–1935)*. Cambridge: Cambridge UP, 1941.

Ruthner, Clemens. *Habsburgs "Dark Continent": Postkoloniale Lektüren zur österreichischen Literatur und Kultur im langen 19. Jahrhundert*. Tübingen: Narr Francke Attempto Verlag, 2018.

Sältzer, Rolf, ed. *German Essays on History: Hegel, Ranke, Spengler, and Others*. New York: Continuum/Bloomsbury, 1991.

Sassen, Saskia. *The Global City: New York, London, Tokyo*. Rev. ed. Princeton, NJ: Princeton UP, 2001.

Sauer, August. *Literaturgeschichte und Volkskunde: Rektoratsrede gehalten in der Aula der k.k. deutschen Karl-Ferdinands-Universität in Prag am 18. November 1907*. Prague; J.J. Calve'sche k.u.k. Hof- und Universitäts-Buchhandlung, 1907.

Scherer, Wilhelm. *Geschichte der deutschen Literatur*. 11th ed. Berlin: Weidmannsche Buchhandlung, 1908 [1st ed., 1883].

Schorske, Carl E. *Fin de siècle Vienna: Politics and Culture*. New York: Vintage Books, 1981.

Sheffer, Edith. *Asperger's Children: The Origin of Autism in Nazi Vienna*. New York: W. W. Norton & Company, 2018.

Silverman, Lisa. *Becoming Austrians: Jews and Culture Between the World Wars*. New York: Oxford UP, 2012.

Sked, Alan. *The Decline and Fall of the Habsburg Empire, 1815–1918*. London: Longman, 1989.

Snyder, Timothy. *Bloodlands: Europe Between Hitler and Stalin*. New York: Basic Books 2010

Spector, Scott. *Prague Territories: National Conflict and Cultural Innovation in Franz Kafka's Fin de Siècle*. Berkeley: U of California P, 2002.

Statistisches Jahrbuch der Stadt Wien. Wien: Magistrat der Stadt Wien, 1885. Available online by year: https://www.digital.wienbibliothek.at/wbrobv/periodical/titleinfo/2057276 (accessed July 26, 2023).

Sugar, Peter F., and Péter Hanák. *A History of Hungary*. Bloomington: Indiana UP, 1990.

Taylor, A. J. P. *The Habsburg Monarchy 1809–1918: A History of the Austrian Empire and Austria-Hungary*. 2nd ed. Chicago: U of Chicago P, 1964 (original, 1941, rev. ed., 1948).

Thurich, Eckart, and Hans Endlich. *Zweimal Deutschland: Lehrbuch für Politik und Zeitgeschichte*. Frankfurt/M: Diesterweg, 1970.

Wawro, Geoffrey. *A Mad Catastrophe: The Outbreak of World War I and the Collapse of the Habsburg Empire*. New York: Basic Books, 2014.

West, Rebecca. *Black Lamb and Grey Falcon: A Journey through Yugoslavia*. London: Macmillan London Ltd, 1942 [rpt. Penguin, 2007].

Williams, Raymond. *The Country and the City*. Oxford and New York: Oxford UP, 1973.

Winder, Simon. *Danubia: A Personal History of Habsburg Europe*. New York: Farrar, Straus and Giroux, 2013.

Wingfield, Nancy M. *The World of Prostitution in Late Imperial Austria*. Oxford: Oxford UP, 2017.

Wolf, Michaela. *The Habsburg Monarchy's Many-Languaged Soul: Translating and Interpreting, 1848–1918.* Trans. Kate Sturge. Amsterdam/Philadelphia: John Benjamins, 2015.

Wolf, Michaela. *Die vielsprachige Seele Kakaniens: Übersetzen und Dolmetschen in der Habsburgermonarchie 1848–1918.* Wien/Köln/Weimar: Böhlau, 2012.

Wolf, Norbert Christian. *Eine Triumphpforte österreichischer Kunst: Hugo von Hofmannsthals Gründung der Salzburger Festspiele.* Salzburg: Jung und Jung Verlag, 2014.

Zahra, Tara. *Kidnapped Souls: National Indifference and the Battle for Children in the Bohemian Lands.* Ithaca, NY: Cornell UP, 2008.

Zweig, Stefan. *Die Welt von Gestern: Erinnerungen eines Europäers.* Berlin: Suhrkamp, 1949 (original: Stockholm: Bermann-Fischer Verlag, 1944) = *The World of Yesterday: Memoires of a European.* London: Cassell, 1943.

Part I

Dreaming Salzburg: Hoping for hope, grasping at what it was and might have been ...

One   Fantasy as Parody?: Hermann Bahr's Salzburg Dialogue

Vincent Kling

When Hermann Bahr published his "Fantasy in Salzburg" in July 1900 ("Die Hauptstadt von Europa: Eine Phantasie in Salzburg"), no one visualized the city developing into the major festival center it later became, presenting opera, concert, and theater on a level that attracts visitors from all over the world. Under the auspices of the International Mozarteum Foundation, music festivals, limited in scope, had been held at irregular intervals since 1877, motivated partly in answer to the Bayreuth Festival, whose first season had taken place the year before, but which the First World War brought a halt. Bahr lived to see the Festival established by Max Reinhardt, Richard Strauss, and Hugo von Hofmannsthal, surely gratifying because the cosmopolitan center of culture he romanticized in his article was little more than a whimsy when he composed it.

A prolific and versatile playwright, novelist, critic, theoretician, and overall cultural commentator involved on virtually every artistic front, Bahr was a prime example of what would come to be called a public intellectual, a preeminent "influencer" admired and derided by turns. His Salzburg fantasy is typically energetic, flinging out ideas for their power to provoke while advancing a kind of agenda.

"Kind of" only, to be sure, because Bahr's piece is a *feuilleton*, a genre part journalism, part literature, at home in the features section of newspapers. These are color pieces, often brilliantly composed. Paradox, wit, play of language, imaginative projection, and subjective, semi-playful reaction to issues of the day were hallmarks of the *feuilleton* in Bahr's Vienna. Readers would not have been happy with anything less than a *jeu d'esprit*, deftly composed prose that the author could nonetheless pretend was an improvisation or throwaway. The *feuilleton* would never have been the right framework for serious proposals, complete with rationale, polemic, and practical planning, of the kind the organizers of the Salzburg Festival began publishing around 1917.[1] Though Bahr would have been expected to give his imagination free rein in 1900, he could have had good reason, when the Festival was actually launched in 1920, to feel that his pipedream might have made some contribution after all.

Droll reversals mark every aspect of Bahr's fantasy in its play with genre conventions. The partners in this lopsided dialogue have come down a mountain, and a holy one, judging by its name, "Monks' Mountain" (Mönchsberg). From before Moses to after Martin Luther King, the trope of having been to the mountaintop involves a descent in which the sublime revelation imparted on high is arduously adapted to mundane reality. Here, however, the rapturous vision first occurs when they are on level ground, and any thought of implementing it is dismissed to the point of parody, the rhapsodic idealist airily brushing aside any question of how to pay for it. The genre of literary dialogue, presenting antithetical viewpoints with equal apportionment of time, also reaches back to the ancients, but Bahr amusingly parodies its conventions as well on two counts. The partner who seems realistic and grounded in practicalities is the one who triggers off the idealist by sketching a scene rich with painterly Baroque or Rococo elaboration, but then he suddenly turns pragmatic, as a result of which he can hardly get in a word edgewise from then on, the lopsided proportions creating a comic effect as against the usual balance of evenly involved partners.

Bahr's image of Salzburg as the capital city of all Europe at a time when it was little more than a provincial town arose from his respect for its amalgamation of disparate cultural strains. Calling on geography as well as his understanding of the Baroque era as one that reconciled opposites to create new unities, Bahr's arguments anticipated the formulations of literary historian Josef Nadler;[2] Hofmannsthal in turn, who rejoiced in balancing antinomies, explicitly acknowledged Nadler as an important source. To Bahr and Hofmannsthal, Salzburg, far from the noise and bustle of the imperial capital, embodied as no other place the harmonious blend of Teutonic North and Latin South, of Bach and Buxtehude meeting Haydn and Mozart, of artistic subtlety and cosmopolitanism receptive to folk plays and rustic art, of high artifice and unassuming naturalness, of architectural elaboration with structural simplicity.

---

1 The main rationales and mission statements were written by Hofmannsthal, "Die Salzburger Festspiele," here 233–4, and "Deutsche Festspiele zu Salzburg," here 230.
2 Nadler, *Literaturgeschichte der deutschen Stämme und Landschaften*. [Editors' note: Nadler's work is hotly contended as Nazi-ethnic-nationalist in implication; see Arens, "Danube *Limes*" (2016) for a broader discussion of the issues involved.]

These values are implicit in Bahr's piece, but his designating it as a fantasy gave him—or his two characters—the quick escape, if challenged by anyone so pedantic as to raise objections, that it was a thought experiment or flight of fancy after all. And objections or misgivings abound once the oddities and imbalances are studied more closely. In his various mission statements, Hofmannsthal made a point of stressing the Festival as a way to foster peace after war, to reconcile cultures and provide art as a vehicle for social and political amity. Often (and always wrongly) chided as the ultimate aesthete, Hofmannsthal ceaselessly insisted on the fusion of art with social responsibility, on the impossibility of separating aesthetics from ethics.

Almost comic by contrast, Bahr's self-designated fantasy illustrates what happens when the aesthetic in isolation deteriorates into escapism and elitism, when *l'art pour l'art* is lived out in its full implications. Ethics is distorted into justifying a mere ethos of smug self-indulgence. There is no sense of communal or social obligation in this fantasy, or rather, the communal vision is of a self-sufficient coterie of self-appointed superior spirits who will unhesitatingly escort to the border those who don't think and feel as they do. This is exactly the kind of sterile community, declaring itself a bulwark to fend off the great unwashed, from which Hofmannsthal's Gianino in *Der Tod des Tizian* (1892) and the Empress in *Die Frau ohne Schatten* (1919) find the courage to escape, from which Joseph Knecht of Hesse's *Das Glasperlenspiel* (1943) abdicates, and which Prospero in Shakespeare's *The Tempest* must relinquish to reclaim his humanity.

Bahr is lampooning the practice widespread in his day of requisitioning its ideas in one mode and twisting them to justify political and social movements that the original writings cannot support. Darwin never envisioned social Darwinism, for example, but the misapplication of his insights provided a convenient rationale for the callous disregard of others. Bahr's loquacious rhapsodist wants to select the fittest by separating the strong from the weak—or the cultivated few from the throng—along lines he never clarifies, except that "we" have exquisite taste and "they" have none. Bahr is also presenting in his characters' vision of an elite society a garbled, reductivist Nietzscheianism, shrewdly but unwittingly prefiguring the ideologies Nietzsche would later be distorted to serve. When the more talkative partner speaks of "superior humans," he is using Nietzsche's famous term *Übermenschen*, but it is notable as parody that neither partner advances any actual trait or quality to substantiate the privileged status of the exalted ones. They are purportedly refined, but as to what exactly?

Similarly, the speaker's appeal to the "third empire" draws on a term, *das dritte Reich* or Third Reich, that would take on the notorious meaning it acquired only after being given an explicit political application in 1923 by Moeller van den Bruck. At the turn of the twentieth century, the Third Reich was a philosophical conceit derived from Hegel's dialectics and positing that the medieval German empire and then the Prussian empire of 1870–1918 were stages in the emergence of a new and stronger imperial entity. Once again, our interlocutors never ground the abstraction; it does not occur to them that they have no idea how to bring this new empire about except to banish the vulgarians—but what if they refuse to leave?

Our partners realize at least fleetingly that their dream will cost money, and plenty of it, but the rhapsodist keeps saying, like Dickens's Mr. Micawber, that it will just turn up on its own somehow. Proposing to buy the whole city of Salzburg(!) and taking for granted that the town fathers would be willing to sell, he keeps dismissing all financial considerations as distractions. Here again Bahr rightly spoofs any quixotic belief that finances will take care of themselves. The actual founders were able to bring the Festival into being not only through their enormous prestige but also through their enormous labor, tirelessly writing pamphlets and giving speeches and receptions to raise funds, calling alike on Church and state for approval and financial support.

In keeping with Hofmannsthal's ideal of inclusion, the Salzburg Festival has worked almost from the start to enable wide attendance and participation. The founding of Bayreuth by royal decree lives on in the constricting, reverent atmosphere of art for the select few, who even have to ascend a mountain, or at least a hill, to partake of the sacred revelation. Part of its mystique, featured in its marketing, is the need for mere mortals often to spend years on a waiting list for tickets. The Salzburg Festival, on the other hand, offers reduced-price tickets to students, children's programs, and music camps, among other initiatives, and has financed programs for developing and supporting conductors and other artists through subsidies and grants.

All of which needs to be paid for, creating the paradox that the Festival—purposely upholding traditional high culture, after all—can only fulfill its democratic and inclusive mission of making great art accessible and of training young artists through major sponsorship. It is the way of the ironist or parodist to direct attention to a major problem and then not address it; Bahr adroitly evokes financial babes in the woods who couldn't address the practicalities of their own time, let alone imagine today's mixed configuration, with corporations and foundations underwriting ever greater sums to make up for dwindling budgets from government sources, and shows how to expand the Festival's mission. It persists: Audi, Siemens, Rolex, Nestlé, Roche, Swarovski, Uniqa, Bank of America, Merrill Lynch, and other corporations with deep pockets have been instrumental in supporting the Festival and its aims.

Fantasy as Parody?: Hermann Bahr's Salzburg Dialogue

For what in return? Do sponsors influence policy? Management consistently answers with reassuring negatives,[3] but capitalists are investors and usually look for something in exchange. At least two outcries over the last years make official statements appear disingenuous. In 2011, the Festival cancelled the opening address by Jean Ziegler, ostensibly for his close ties to Libya's Muammar Gaddafi, but perhaps in reality because of intervention by sponsors Credit Suisse and Nestlé on the basis of Ziegler's outspoken environmental and ecological activism.[4] Strong objections also arose in 2019, when the Festival accepted sponsorship from Gazprom in seeming contravention of its own environmental concerns.[5]

We are admittedly far distant from Bahr's idyllic Mirabell Garden in 1900, but it was there that he planted a seed for this consideration of Mammon through his tactic of bringing up the subject and then so amusingly dismissing it. We could ask, too, if Bahr's very framework of newspaper publication might not have played some inadvertently prefiguring part in the media circus often accompanying the Festival. There is as much a performance aspect about what dignitaries arrived in what limousines, what gowns fashion-minded women were wearing, who was seen entertaining crowned heads, what parties were thrown by Many (the Princess Marianne) Sayn-Wittgenstein-Sayn and Eliette von Karajan, who is playing *Buhlschaft* in *Jedermann* and how provocatively she dresses as a strumpet, as much as there is about anything presented on stage or in the concert hall. And perhaps all that hoopla is the best possible corrective to the airy-fairy, cloud-cuckoo-land, Shangri-La atmosphere so archly projected by Bahr's interlocutors. They would have certainly have shunned all the vulgar media publicity in horror, but its flourishing alongside the actual mission of the Festival may just ratify how robust Salzburg is.

Bibliography

Arens, Katherine. "Danube *Limes*: The Limits of the Geographic-Cultural Imaginary." In Marijeta Bozovic and Matthew D. Miller, eds., *Watersheds: Poetics and Politics of the Danube River*, 1–24. Brighton, MA: Academic Studies Press, 2016.

Bahr, Hermann. "Die Hauptstadt von Europa: Eine Phantasie in Salzburg." *Neues Wiener Tagblatt*, 34(202) (July 25, 1900): 1–3. Reprinted in Hermann Bahr, *Bildung*: Essays, 116–22. Berlin, Leipzig: Insel-Verlag, 1900. Available online: https://anno.onb.ac.at/cgi-content/anno-buch?apm=0&aid=56 (accessed June 15, 2023).

---

3 Salzburg Festival Archive, "Project Sponsors."
4 "Salzburger Festspiele laden Festredner aus."
5 Marshall, "The Arts Are Shunning Big Oil: The Salzburg Festival Isn't."

Hofmannsthal, Hugo von. "Deutsche Festspiele zu Salzburg" (1919a). In Klaus E. Bohnenkamp, Katja Kaluga, and Klaus-Dieter Krabiel, eds., *Sämtliche Werke 34: Reden und Aufsätze 3 [1909–1911]*, 229–30. Frankfurt: S. Fischer, 2011.

Hofmannsthal, Hugo von. "Die Salzburger Festspiele" (1919b). In Klaus E. Bohnenkamp, Katja Kaluga, and Klaus-Dieter Krabiel, eds., *Sämtliche Werke 34: Reden und Aufsätze 3 [1909–1911]*, 231–5. Frankfurt: S. Fischer, 2011.

Marshall, Alex. "The Arts Are Shunning Big Oil: The Salzburg Festival Isn't." *New York Times*, October 21, 2019. Available online: https://www.nytimes.com/2019/10/21/arts/music/salzburg-festival-gazprom.html (accessed June 15, 2023).

Nadler, Josef. *Literaturgeschichte der deutschen Stämme und Landschaften*. 4 vols. Regensburg: J. Habbel, 1912–1928.

"Project Sponsors." Salzburg Festival Archive. Available online: https://archive.salzburgerfestspiele.at/en/project-sponsors (accessed June 15, 2023).

"Salzburger Festspiele laden Festredner aus." *Der Standard*, March 31, 2011. Available online: https://www.derstandard.at/story/1297821929901/salzburger-festspiele-laden-festredner-aus (accessed June 15, 2023).

van den Bruck, Moeller. *Das dritte Reich*. Berlin: Ring-Verlag, 1923.

Two The Capital of Europe (1900): "A Fantasy in Salzburg"

Hermann Bahr, translated by Vincent Kling

Making our way down from the Mönchsberg, the "Monks' Mountain," we'd gone strolling through the old section of the city and were now standing on the bridge, looking by turns toward the rushing Salzach River, the Hohensalzburg Fortress, and the tower of the yellow church in the mountains. Then we turned away to stroll over to the other bank and entered the Mirabell Garden by the theater. There are two old gray statues standing here, in front of them greenery all in bloom, flanked by a balustrade with urns from which red, red flowers were hanging. The castle closes off this most delightful picture in brightness. It made me exclaim spontaneously, "Put on plays here! Imagine it! On the gravel, among the flower beds, a line of slender women twined with roses; in front of the fountain, under those heavy yellow blossoms, a page reciting verses, and in the tree-lined promenade farther off, a rapt, enchanted and happy audience leaning against the marble. And there would be rustling in the leaves and the purling of water. Wouldn't that be beautiful?"

My friend nodded. The he said, simply, "You'd have to buy the whole city of Salzburg!"

I laughed. But he continued imperturbably: "What could such a town cost, after all? You go to the mayor, find out the price, and lay the money on the table. Everyone would be happy at making such a deal."

"What then?" I asked, just to provoke my fantasy-spinning friend.

"Then?" he said as we were stepping under the old trees, "well, we move here and end up founding the capital city of Europe. The time is right. It's really a crying shame! There are good Europeans everywhere—at least that's what they always say. But now some place finally has to be arranged for them to live." "An idea for a humorist," I said. "Watch the good Europeans arrive and march in while the people of Salzburg form rows and look on."

He shook his head, however. He was back to dreaming with his eyes open, which is just like him. He pressed on: "It's no joke. I'm totally serious. Look here, haven't you ever noticed that a new nation has gradually come into being in Europe but has yet to find a home? You and I and a hundred more, or perhaps—I don't know—a thousand or twenty thousand people in Europe have through their cultural attainments so fully detached and separated themselves from their own people that they are hardly connected by a common language to those others any longer except on a makeshift basis. What are they even doing among those others? All those others do is inhibit them, and they are inhibited in turn—rapport or agreement is no longer possible. What do they really have in common with the broad masses into which we happen to be born? What they like is hateful to us, what they hanker for, we scorn; what they want, what they're struggling for, what they're suffering over strikes us as vapid and petty, but what we ourselves desire with the highest passion of our whole nature as the genuine meaning and purpose of existence—as its sole justification and rationale, for that matter—we can't even name, because they wouldn't so much as understand the words that are so precious and sacred to us. But the whole time we're eating our hearts out as we turn in a narrow circle among people to whom we are fools and they to us barbarians, with not the faintest hope of ever understanding them or being understood by them—since we consider what they call the serious side of life to be ridiculous, whereas they look on what we require with our whole souls as a silly game—while we are withering away in unbearably empty loneliness, there are those in Brittany or the Caucasus Mountains who have the same yearnings we do and who, like us, reach out with trembling hands when the sun sets in the evening, who lean forward breathlessly and grasp the very air, anxious and confused by achingly blissful intimations. These men and women scattered through the world and filled with great longing, feeling what we feel, hoping what we hope, fearing what we fear—they are our true fatherland. With those who are by mere chance born next to us but with their whole being deny what we hold true and insult what we consider beautiful we live as if in exile. We have grown to be strangers in our own dwellings and must create a new home from within ourselves. Have you never had the experience of sitting with a stranger on a large steamship between Tangier and Marseille or at a *table d'hôte* in Naples and after half an hour finding him a closer companion than your neighbor or even your brother, because the stranger thinks and feels as you do and wants the same things, while you can't even say to your neighbor or your brother what's weighing you down or elating you? Why should I live with people whom I can give nothing to, whom I can be nothing to? Why wouldn't I prefer to live with those who are like me? These are my people, these and these alone."

The Capital of Europe (1900): "A Fantasy in Salzburg"   41

"Good friend," I said, "everyone's had such whims and fancies from time to time. But in the long run you have to be careful. If you think and feel differently from the people around you, that's your fault. In such cases the people are always right, and never the individual, unless he were so strong as to reshape the others in his own image. If you can't do that, if you're not a prophet or a great artist, then you're wrong and the people are right. There can be no disputing about desires, and feelings are not subject to proof—what's decisive here is power, and since there are at most a few thousand of us but millions of the others, they will overrule us. You will never convert them."

My hopeless dreamer grew impatient. "I don't wish to convert anyone," he exclaimed vehemently. "That's exactly the point: all should be free to live as they see fit, whereas today a lone individual is always unsettling the rest—we them and they us, but nothing comes out of it but rancor and strife. Those who feel with the masses can stay put. We feel differently; we need to move onward! Let those who feel as we do come to us until there are so many of us that we too form a mass. That's what I have in mind—with my city! The mass is already here, the new nation is already here, but for the time being they're only drifting on the wide lakes, dispersed throughout the large hotels—let's gather them together, let's give them a homeland, let's allow them to take root. Let's create a colony within—that's what I have in mind! And look here—I'm certainly not biased, not claiming that our opinions and our wishes and our feelings are the only valid ones; I don't know that, and indeed no one *can* know that; I don't want to repress the others in any way, either; let them continue to live as they see fit; I ask only that they don't repress us any longer; we should finally be permitted to live as *we* see fit, according to the ideas *we* have formed, rightly or wrongly, about the good and the beautiful, according to the way *we* think life should be. That's something granted to everyone, just not to us. Arrangements are made everywhere to cater to the lowest taste, and if you say these appalling kinds of crude entertainment are bound to brutalize people, the answer you hear will be that well there are unrefined people after all, sorry to say, who crave this kind of entertainment, and that's supposed to excuse everything. But if you expect provision to be made for your refined taste as well—no, can't be done! Concession to taste moves only downward, never upward. What good does it do us to speak of 'superior humans' and the 'third empire' and from 'life lived in beauty'—what of it? Where does it all lead? There's never anything but talk, talk, talk—let's finally carry it out! When a few people want to go bowling, they form a club and rent an alley. All right, we have the thought of living in a new spirit. What are we doing, though? Writing books. All we ever do is write books. All we ever do is talk. But what if we had the same passion for our idea as the others do for bowling?

Then we would form a club, a club of the new spirit, and rent an alley, as they do! Here—in Salzburg!"

I had to laugh at the way he pointed toward the garden with a lordly gesture; in his fantasy he was already seeing himself as master of all he surveyed. "The third empire," I said, "founded on shares in a corporation—at least I have to admit you're modern. But I'm curious what we would actually do here. This spot is really lovely, but beyond taking walks and playing cards, I don't know—I'm afraid your good Europeans would soon look like retired generals."

My friend stayed silent for a while. Then he said pensively, "What would we do, you ask. We'd finally get serious. No more than that is required. We'd finally take action. We'd finally carry out what we've only talked and written about for so long. Imagine one of our grandchildren taking down one of our books a hundred years from now and comparing what's in it to the way we really lived; what's he supposed to think about us? What's in our books is one thing, but how we live is another! I don't believe there's ever been a time like ours. At all other times people had a definite feeling that life should be this way or that way, and that's how they organized themselves; later on, only after they had made things happen did they seek out explanations and write them down. All we ever do, though, is write about how life should be, but nobody has the strength or the courage to organize it accordingly. We need to take out our books and turn into a living force what's merely written in them."

"I'd like to request a more exact agenda, with more detail; otherwise, your shares won't have any takers."

"Detail? Nothing easier. First, we found an academy. Then matters will become clear. We will call upon anyone who's ever spoken or written to deplore the ugly life of our times or to rhapsodize about heroic existence and will say, 'Let your actions show what you have in mind; live the way you think you should—this is the place to fulfill your dream.'"

"That will be quite amusing; I know so many who will make total fools of themselves; I'm looking forward to it."

"So many—absolutely! So many—perhaps even most! But if there's even one, one only among thousands who can live up to what he promised! The others we'll lead to the border with all due commiseration. But that one will be our king."

"And then?" I persisted.

"Then we will place a notice in the newspapers, a notice to the young. Just think of the thousands of young people today stagnating without teachers, without advice, without friends—all the cheerful high spirits and lively passion being extinguished! They run from school to school, knocking on every door: 'I want to know the truth, want to see beauty, want to become fully human!' And in every school and from behind every door the same refrain: 'Here you can become a civil servant or a scholar, but we ourselves don't have what you're craving!' We will say to them, however: 'Come to us; live among us! Here is your school, a school of life. We set no store by rote knowledge; to each will be given here only what he is capable of acquiring and fully absorbing until it is as much a part of him as his hand or his foot. Our wise men will show you whatever truth they have found, our artists whatever beauty they have seen, and then all of you—wise men and artists and young people together, all upholding one another in close bonds, all following and leading at the same time—will strive to recognize how each and every one is developing to its highest and in just the right place what nature has bestowed on him. And so it is that each of you will impart the highest of teachings to one another, the wise men and artists to the young, the young to the artists and wise men—teaching how to be joyous! For it is our law and our belief that mankind has been sent out into life by higher powers in order to be happy. We enjoin what helps mankind to that goal; we reject whatever hinders it. We toss away everything else and hold fast to this as the highest truth, the highest beauty: joy!'"

My friend was now standing like a visionary against the glow of the setting sun. For a moment I had a feeling he might be able to fly away all of a sudden, borne by inner wings. I gently plucked at his sleeve and to calm him down said, "But you don't have the money yet!"

He looked at me as if coming awake. Then he said dismissively, "Oh, the money's the least of it. You can always get hold of outward things like that if only you decide to. A strong will attracts everything, draws everything to itself. All you have to do is want it!"

"I'll have to give that a try sometime soon," I said, "all that about the strong will that draws money—quite an idea!"

And we went out onto the street and back into the city, which hadn't yet been purchased by the Europeans.

Three   Salzburg's Age of Aquarius: Der Wassermann as an Austrian *Sonderweg* in the European Arts

Katherine Arens

The visual art scene in Salzburg (*Land und Stadt*, state and city) evolved in step with the region's history, evidence of a commitment to the arts and humanities that was long considered central to its existence. This essay will address the identity and impulses implicated in this commitment to the arts in their varied form, first, by situating the Salzburger Kunstverein (founded 1844, housed in its own building since 1885, the Salzburger Künstlerhaus) as a significant challenge to its era's academy art. Salzburg's "official" art establishment stressed art as more than *Bildung* for the bourgeoisie, conceiving all facets of art production and circulation as a more encompassing civic project, central to the very existence of local culture. After setting that scene, I will turn to the last great bloom of that distinctive art scene in the interwar period, the oppositional artist's group (Künstlerverein). The most visible of the individual artist groups associated with the Kunstverein in the interwar period was Der Wassermann, founded on January 8, 1919, a name referring to its birth month's zodiac sign. It was presumably named by Munich author Oskar A. H. Schmitz, who also wanted to refer to Salzburg's astrological position, which purportedly was associated with concepts of tolerance, transparency, departure, dynamics, or revolt.

Through three exhibits (1919–1921), Der Wassermann (Aquarius) embraced an aesthetic inspired by international trends but local in inspiration and execution, responsive to and responsible for local audiences and to their experiences rather than simply to the art markets, collectors, and academies that served capitals like Vienna.[1] In setting itself into an international context of influence, Salzburg's art scene cast itself as a counterpoint to the elite art scene and its patronage in Vienna, as it also functioned as a kind of international lifeboat for the art markets in Munich and Vienna that faltered with the First World War and then gave their last gasps as Munich politics turned National Socialist immediately after the war's end (Hitler would announce his party program there in a speech on February 24, 1920).

That brief resurgence of art in Salzburg brought at least three strands of Europe's art-making together. In one sense, it was a continuation of Die Brücke (founded 1905 in Dresden), the Neue Künstlervereinigung München (NKVM, with three exhibits that traveled through Germany between 1909 and 1911), and Der blaue Reiter (founded between 1911 and 1912 with an almanac and exhibitions, but not surviving the First World War). In another framing, it was a new center for an extended group of artists that Wassermann shared with these groups and predecessors in Salzburg. This Wassermann grew out of a local variant of Impressionism (called Stimmungsimpressionismus, an impressionism of mood rather than optics) to create a different Expressionist aesthetic (a Farbenexpressionismus, an expressionism through color). This program, as we shall see, firmly opposes the Expressionism that has been preserved in art-historical memory as German and not European. The third context for Der Wassemann is embodied in the two most important of its founding members: Anton Faistauer (1887–1930, born in *Land* Salzburg) and Felix Albrecht Harta (1884 in Budapest–1967 in Salzburg), a portrait and landscape painter.[2] The former is remembered today principally for the murals he contributed to the Salzburger Festspielhaus and for a controversial book of aesthetics; the latter, and to his contribution to the founding of the Wassermann and the evolution of the Festspiele.

This essay will thus make the case for the visual arts of *Stadt und Land Salzburg* as a scarcely acknowledged connection between French, international, and Viennese Secessionisms/Impressionisms, and German Expressionism that set the ground for much postwar art in germanophone Europe—a strand of art history hardly remembered in the shift of the field to nationalisms, and of European history into forgetting about Central Europe as a region of cultural projection. The Wassermann, as we shall see, was very much a piece with Salzburg, as it

---

1   For the best introduction to the group, see Jandl-Jörg, "'Der Wassermann': Ein europäisches Forum für die lebendige Kunst."
2   For the most detailed information on Harta and Faistauer, see "Faustauer, Schiele, Harta – Biografien" for timelines of their activities, and Jandl-Jörg, "Nachmittag Schieles bei uns" for a narrative history.

represented an aesthetic that claimed the relevance of art to the everyday lives and experience of individuals, not just to a narrow tranche of the elite public, just as the city itself had done for a half-century in establishing its commitment to visual arts.

To illuminate the implications of these claims, the Wassermann will be treated both externally and internally—as part of a long tradition of art in a Salzburg that was politically and socially quite different from the rest of the Habsburg regions, and as a very conscious attempt to move art beyond Expressionism and the traumas of the Great War. Der Wassermann was a nodal event that showed a constellation of European aesthetic-social thought and practice emerging from the ruins of nationalism, and that was again lost in the depredations of the Second World War.

Part 1 Salzburg as Austria's *Other*

Salzburg International

Art in Salzburg between the wars is inextricably linked to Salzburg's special history—it is a city and official region (*Stadt und Land*) long tied to political centers, and one that has at times been rich or influential enough to be a factor in history, while rarely driving that politics beyond securing itself and its ongoing identity. It is critical, I believe, to see the different allegiances and identities forced onto and accepted by *Stadt und Land Salzburg*, in order to see how it did *not* define itself simply in respect to the ruling Habsburgs. Instead, Salzburg had a consistent identity rooted in the basin of the Salzach River, as its political and personal ties reflected international trade and commerce.

The city, like so many in the region, had international roots: its earliest documented form was a Celtic settlement taken over by the Romans in 15 BCE, then turned into an important transport hub (*Iuvavum*, after the Roman name for the Salzach River, *Iuvarus*). Three major Roman roads converged in the Salzach basin, important enough to be mentioned by Pliny the Elder in his natural history (*c.* 150 CE), but that settlement was largely destroyed by the influx of Germanic tribes in the migration age (171 CE). Ultimately the site was evacuated by force by Odoaker (in 488), when the inhabitants fled to a fortress on the Nonnberg. Nonetheless, locals never entirely abandoned the Salzach basin and its natural commercial advantages. Already in 696 CE, then, Salzburg was reestablished as an episcopal see and then raised to be an archbishop's seat in 798. This rise was supported by the local salt mining industry, some gold mining, and trade related to these important commodities.

Salzburg was politically part of the evolving late medieval and early modern political landscape, as reflected in the construction of the

Salzburg Fortress, whose oldest sections date from 1077, when Archbishop Gebhard built it as his residence. In this era, the region was often aligned under or with Bavaria, but a 1322 battle ("die Schlacht bei Mühldorf") led to their estrangement and to the establishment of the territory as an independent Prince-Bishopric (Fürstbistum, and later Fürsterzbistum) within the Holy Roman Empire. That independence led to a fifteenth-century economic boom, and to the city's entanglement with the Protestant Reformation. That participation is probably best understood as a gesture toward local control, as it was in so many German territories, rather than a strictly doctrinal stance; it culminated with the farmers and local mercenary soldiers taking over the Fortress in 1525. In consequence of these disruptions, Protestants were banned from the city until 1590; the locals raised charges of local authoritarianism. Nonetheless, the central authorities prevailed. By 1600, the region was one of the richest principalities in the Holy Roman Empire, and a center for the Counter-Reformation.

Salzburg's consistently prominent role in the latter part of the second millennium CE is reflected in the city architecture, still visible today. From the seventeenth century onward, the city visibly became a Residenzstadt: the seat of a powerful Prince-Bishop ruling the region. The early hallmark for that prominence was the investment in Schloss Hellbrunn, with its park, waterworks, and allées—all now part of a UNESCO World Heritage Site that includes the old city. Hellbrunn reflects the era's cosmopolitan outlook: laid out between 1614–1615 by Santino Solari as a villa in the Italian-Roman style popular in northern Italy, it is modeled after the Villa d'Este in Tivoli and other Roman parks, with a prominent Festsaal (large reception/ballroom), an Octagon Room, and famous "Theater of the Waterworks" (*Theatrun der Wasserspiele*) in the garden.

The city itself was also expanded in that era, as befitted its association with the Counter-Reformation. Paris Graf von Lodron is the name associated with this investment in the region's municipal face. Elected Roman Catholic archbishop in 1619, right after the outbreak of the Thirty Years' War, Lodron tasked Solari with adding five large, fortified bastions (in the Italian style) around the then-new parts of the city[3] and had the Mönchsberg rock shaved and smoothed to act as natural protection for the older parts of Salzburg, thus creating a fortified city on both sides of the river. Within those fortifications, the population participated heavily in lay piety, including organized brotherhoods, and a considerable number of Baroque churches were built. After a wave of

---

3   He has new city gates built, expands the Festung and its defenses; Lodron's family crest is evident on many of these projects.

the plague, the moors in the region were even drained to improve living conditions.

Even more important is that, in 1617, Lodron founded a Gymnasium (academic secondary school), which evolved into the University of Salzburg by 1622; Pope Urban VIII granted its official charter in 1625. The Cathedral (Dom) was rebuilt by Solari into something like today's form, and it was consecrated in 1628; three monasteries were also founded. In a very real sense, Lodron saved the city from the Thirty Years' war, for which he has been remembered as *pater patria* (father of the fatherland). Notably, Salzburg's rebirth was political, as well as architectural: in 1620, Lodron also reinstated the Landtafel, Salzburg's estates general assembly as an official government.[4] After keeping his principality happily at the margins of the Thirty Years' War, Lodron died in 1655; he is the only Salzburg Prince in Ludwig I's *Walhalla*, the commemorative hall of the Bavarian nation, near Regensburg.

Salzburg's geopolitical position slowly deteriorated past that high point, but never disappeared. Between 1675 and 1690, the city initiated a series of witch trials, which seem to have been an attempt to control beggars (the victims were almost entirely male vagabond youths and children), signaling some kind of economic strain (see Felix Mitterer's 1989 play, *Kinder des Teufels*). In 1732, the reigning archbishop again banned all remaining Protestants from Salzburg and forced them into exile. Toward the end of the eighteenth century, roads were built in the *Land* which helped Salzburg to become a tourist destination because of its natural and civic beauties.

In 1803, the principality was secularized, amidst repeated plundering by Napoleonic troops (1800, 1805, 1809). During those disruptions, the Duke of Salzburg (Ferdinand III of Tuscany, a Habsburg) received the title of Elector of the Holy Roman Empire (when votes were being rearranged in light of the shifts in European ruling houses). Yet the 1805 Treaty of Pressburg granted Salzburg to his elder brother, Emperor Franz II, as Holy Roman Emperor,[5] at which point the Duke moved to

---

4   What is informally called the Landtafel was formally called the Hohe Salzburger Landschaft or landschaftliches Collegium; the estates were representatives from the clergy (Prälatenstand), the nobility (Adelsstand), and citizens "of the cities and markets" (Bürgerstand), as compiled according to the Landtafel, the list of the Duchy's representatives originally compiled in the twelfth century. It was actually only called to assemble twice during the Thirty Years' War (1620 and 1637), and once again in 1797, at the start of the French wars; it was formally dissolved in 1811, as Salzburg was assigned to Bavaria (https://www.sn.at/wiki/Salzburger_Landtafel).

5   Emperor Franz II became Franz I of the Austrian Empire once the HRE was formally abolished in 1806.

the Grand Duchy of Würzburg, taking his Electoral title with him into that newly secularized bishopric—he never cast a vote as Elector, and his title was never actually ratified by the Emperor (he was deposed by Napoleon). However, Salzburg's political peregrinations continued: the land was assigned "back" to Bavaria in 1810 with the Treaty of Schönbrunn, to be ruled by the Bavarian Crown Prince as the governor general of the Inn- und Salzachkreis (he lived officially in both Salzburg and Innsbruck). This solution was short-lived: the Congress of Vienna assigned the "province" (minus Berchtesgaden and a number of other villages) to Austria as part of Upper Austria (Oberösterreich), in the 1816 Treaty of Munich. As a side result, the university was also closed at that time.

But the Salzburg that came "back" to Austria was stressed and depleted. The city had lost its court (it was no longer a Residenz), and its population had dropped from sixteen thousand to twelve thousand; many elite dwellings were abandoned: "On the streets and in the squares of the city, which are plentiful and beautiful, grass is growing, they so seldom see anyone walking on them," wrote Franz Schubert about his 1825 Salzburg visit (https://www.sn.at/wiki/Herzogtum_Salzburg).[6]

And the city's material situation only got worse: bad harvests between 1814 and 1818 led the region to famine and general poverty, and a great fire broke out on April 20, 1818, destroying a hundred buildings in four days, including the Mirabell Palace. Finally, the Austrian politics initiated by the Congress of Vienna and lasting through the Vormärz (the "pre-March" or Biedermeier era, 1815–1848) brought surveillance and police repression.

Only in 1850 did Salzburg regain its status as an independent part of the Austrian Empire (a Kronland[7]) as the Herzogtum Salzburg (Duchy), but it was still administered from Linz for the better part of a decade

---

6   All translations from German-language courses are by the present author.
7   The titles for Salzburg's political status are complicated: it was earlier the Fürsterzbistum Salzburg ("Prince-Archbishopric," to 1803) and Kurfürstentum Salzburg ("Prince-Electorate," 1803–1806). Note that the term Herzogtum ("duchy") was used only as a title within imperial bureaucracy; it was not in common use as a political designation, nor did it have any particular legal force. Kronland ("crown land") was the term used after August 4, 1849 for the archduchies, duchies, counties, etc. that belonged to the Austrian Empire and that were recognized constitutionally as independent entities within the Empire (meaning they had local legislative bodies). Before that date, they were Erbländer (hereditary lands of the Habsburg dynasty), which, until 1806, was also used to differentiate them from the lands ruled by the Holy Roman Empire.

(the Landesregierung stayed in Linz until 1860[8]). Salzburg recovered enough to move forward significantly only in the second half of the nineteenth century, a recovery again signaled by a building boom: it tore down the city walls in 1860, as it became a new kind of travel hub, when railroad lines from Salzburg to Munich and Vienna were built. This is the boom that sponsored a whole new bourgeois culture in the city, and a new art scene, to which we will turn in in a moment.

The framework for that art revival did not seem favorable. The First World War was another terrible setback for *Stadt und Land*,[9] bringing Russian POWs, the Spanish flu, and general political confusion, as the Austrian *Crown Lands* were reorganized into something like today's Republic of Austria, as states of the union (Bundesländer). Nonetheless the city's cultural momentum in the latter nineteenth century was not lost in the twentieth. A film studio was opened in 1920, in a collaboration between a producer and a local brewer. And similar collaborations between the fine arts and the local population also were upheld, allowing a bloom of the artworld in *Stadt und Land Salzburg*. Between 1935 and 1939, the municipality extended its jurisdiction over other nearby towns that had grown together (the terms are Stadterweiterung and Eingemeindung)—its last significant act before the Nazi period.

The endgames of these evolutions are worth noting as well. It took until 1951 for the title of Fürsterzbischof to be retired (by Archbishop Andreas Rorhracher), a title of nobility which had been retained since 1824, in reaction to the secularization of the state. Pope Pius XII prohibited the use of such secular titles within the church, and so the archbishop was no longer entitled to wear a crown or princely regalia. The Second World War came close to ending Salzburg. While the city was bombed in 1944/45, it was ultimately saved by an unlikely hero, the Wehrmacht officer in command of Salzburg, Oberst Hans Lepperdinger, who defied orders from the Nazi high command and surrendered the city to the Americans with no resistance, once he heard they were ready to continue bombing the city out of existence. Yet the damage in status was done, institutionally: the university that had existed from 1622 to 1810 was only refounded in 1962, again named after Paris von Lodron.

Since it had come into modernity under Lodron in 1619, then, Salzburg was repeatedly challenged to reassert and reclaim its identity.

---

8   Salzburg's own state legislature (Landtag) met for the first time in 1861, in the Landhaus. Its representation was constituted according to the hereditary estates (*ständische Vertretung*) of Salzburg; see note 7 above. In 1861, only twenty-six families were still attested in Salzburg's Landtafel.
9   See Dohle and Mitterecker, *Salzburg 1918–1919*, for extensive overviews of the challenges and transformations.

Astonishing nonetheless is how that identity persisted in including the arts in all its forms, keeping its Baroque legacy intact as it adapted to the times. Mozart's Salzburg in the eighteenth century gave the city a modern identity in music; its visual arts, however, needed to wait until the nineteenth century to make that leap to the heart of the city.

Contexts for Art in Salzburg

What distinguished the visual arts that emerged in nineteenth-century Salzburg is not so much any particular style or excellence, but rather how it was positioned within the community of its *Stadt und Land*. As the nineteenth century's thirst for travel and tourism grew, the city knew it had an advantage in its setting and heritage. But it had work to do to rectify the damages inflicted on its sovereignty by Napoleon and the Congress of Vienna.

The first move in this direction was a conscious modernization of the public sphere. In 1834, the first variant of today's Salzburg Museum was founded as a history collection like many others in the region, out of a municipal arsenal (Städtisches Arsenal in Salzburg), used to document and claim local history: a collection of weapons, books, documents, coins, and minerals that was opened to the general public the year after its establishment. That move was not disinterested: the collection in the Städtisches Arsenal was established in no small part as a stoploss. The Salzburg recovered from Bavaria had lost its government to Linz, the administrative center of what would become Oberösterreich, and it was a particular threat to Salzburg's existence because it was on a transportation hub with the Danube and was installed as the state capital of the northwest regions of Austria. Salzburg was included until it became the Kreisstadt des Salzachkreises, a district administrative center, restoring its autonomy to a degree.

The presence of visual arts in Salzburg grew throughout the next decades. From 1836 to 1844, the museum was supported by public donations, under the direction of its founder and director Vinzenz Maria Süß (a local historian and history-writer, whose great-aunt was Nannerl Mozart). On March 5, 1849, the Arsenal was taken as property of the city, and on November 11 of that year, it acquired a permanent patroness who resided in the city, Karoline Auguste von Bayern, the widow of Emperor Franz I, after whom the museum was named: the Museum Carolinum Augusteum. Significantly, however, it did not have a permanent or purpose-built home but had temporary housing in various buildings through the city center as the collections grew.

That war for space marked the growth of civic awareness about the visual arts, even before a specific role for them evolved. How that narrative plays out helps to explain *why* the arts were sponsored in

Salzburg, so it is worth tracking it as an issue of resources. On the 100th Anniversary Celebration of Salzburg's belonging to Austria (1916), there were hopes that the museum could move into the Fortress, but the First World War dashed those hopes. The natural history collections from the original Arsenal, now augmented, were moved to the Haus der Natur in 1922. The Salzburg Museum displayed its *Volkskunde* (ethnographic) collections in a building in the part of Schloss Hellbrunn (1923). The Nazis had planned that the collections would be moved to one of their buildings in the city, or to the Stift St. Peter (which they had taken possession of), but on October 16, 1944, Salzburg was heavily bombed, and the Nazi building was destroyed. Fortunately, many of the collections were in safe repositories in the salt mines and in castles and churches outside of the city, but some were destroyed (the gold coin collection vanished when the US troops were guarding the salt mines). The museum would not find a permanent home until 2007, when it was installed in the Neue Residenz am Mozartplatz and focused in new ways, especially looking for special exhibits.

Nonetheless, although the Museum Salzburg contains the city's historic collections, that entity did not drive the art scene in Salzburg, despite over a century of local support for its activities. Up until the Second World War, Salzburg's public debates about art stemmed from a different institution, the Salzburger Kunstverein (KV), the "Art Association" that dedicated itself to art in a completely different way, not just as relevant to the *Vaterland* or patriotic causes. To set up its significance requires a bit more attention to contextualizing the Salzburg art scene in general, because, again, the material circumstances of art production and circulation come to the fore in explaining Salzburg's unique approach.

In speaking of Austrian art, art historians customarily make the history of art *in Vienna* determining of their narratives. Christa Svoboda summarizes that bias:

> The reason for the metropolis' dominance [in art history] lies in the *a priori* of the city's leading position as capital of the Danube Monarchy: as the seat of the ruling house, the center of its administrative apparatus, and finally also of the collection point for its cultural institutions. At the start of the 19th century, Vienna was the largest German-speaking Catholic center for the philosophers, writers, and painters who travelled to it, and its Academy of Arts (*Kunstakademie*) was one of the most famous. This Academy of Arts, in a position without competition, drew in the artists from all the *Kronländer* of the monarchy, as well as from neighboring Germany.[10]

---

10 Svoboda, "Zur Geschichte des Salzburger Kunstvereins," 9.

Vienna was indeed the place in the monarchy where the most art was exhibited and sold, but it did not only "draw in" artists from within imperial borders. Munich always figures prominently in "Vienna's" art circuit, and other Austro-Hungarian cities had significant investments in the arts; Salzburg's art market and populations of collectors rarely emerge except as implicating an Austrian *Farbexpressionismus* ("color Expressionism," usually defined with respect to the work of Anton Kolig) or *Stimmungsimpressionismus* ("mood Impressionism").[11] Yet from Salzburg's point of view (also echoed at other sites outside of Salzburg), Vienna's art establishment often looked stylistically antiquated or behind the times in responding to current tastes and circumstances (it was still heavily invested in history painting).

That charge was not new. Early resistors were the Nazarene Movement painters, often remembered in art history as being German, but two were Austrian (Joseph Anton Koch and Joseph von Führich), and the group (most notably Julius Schnorr von Carolsfeld and Johann Friedrich Overbeck) founded its program in 1804, when they were studying at Vienna's Imperial Academy of the Visual Arts (Kaiserliche Akademie der bildenden Künste). Taking cues from German Romantic theorists Wilhelm Heinrich Wackenroder, Friedrich Schlegel, Novalis, and Ludwig Tieck, they worked out their new program. Yet they were retaliated against: after the Academy cut its student numbers, they were expelled. Their response was to go to Rome in 1810, where they found instead a world like that familiar from Winckelmann, stuck in the worship of the Classics and needing renewal.

The name "Nazarene" came from seventeenth-century Rome, referring to the clothing and long-flowing hair familiar from portraits of Jesus or Dürer's self-portraits—a retrospective creation of art historians. They called themselves the Lukasbund, after St. Luke, the Evangelist and patron saint of painters. After a time in Rome, these Romantic, Catholic painters decided that their goal was to reestablish religious art—a different kind of genre work, if you will, opposing history painting and its antiquated appeal to the audience (the art they had learned in the Academy). Instead, the art should address the Napoleonic era and restore spirituality to a society in an age of disruption, bearing witness to a true Christian and contemporary German sentiment. Today, that decision is decried as German nationalist. The politics of that movement were also antithetical to their own moment—Austrian Chancellor Metternich apparently hated their work. On the other hand,

---

11 "Mood impressionism" is better established as a term, coined to express an impressionism focused on experience rather than exteriority of vision. See https://de.wikipedia.org/wiki/Stimmungsimpressionismus.

their complaint about training at the Vienna Academy had already been made by others and would continue to be. Famous Viennese painter Ferdinand Georg Waldmüller (1793–1865), for example, complained still at mid-century that reforms in the Academy were, indeed, still needed and suggested a return to nature and a turn away from Academy norms.[12]

Such a move against the Academy was much more than simply a political move or shift in aesthetics. Any artist leaving the Academy would also lose the important privilege of exhibiting with them, which would impact their sales. But between the Congress of Vienna (1815) and the Revolutions of 1848, that call might have been less worrisome than it had been, because the art market was shifting:

> From the side of those commissioning art, the ruling house, the nobility, and the Church no longer were the sole sources of commissions or collectors of art objects. A tranche of the bourgeoisie that had achieved prosperity in the early stages of industrialization wanted to do as the noble art patrons (*Kunstmäzen*) did. The financial means to do so were present in sufficiency, as was the interest in art.
>
> (10)

An "upper crust" of the bourgeoisie in that era did indeed take over the role of art patrons from nobles and upper clerics. Yet the nobility was still in charge of the public galleries, and patronage support for artists (rather than just purchases of individual works) was still guaranteed by the crown. Thus, along with these new art patrons, a new art market arose: "Der Bürger trat entweder einzeln aus Auftraggeber in Erscheinung – meist für Portraits – oder als Kollektivmäzen und Käufer im Rahmen der neu gegründeten Kunstvereine" ("The burghers made themselves felt as those who commissioned art – mostly portraits –, either individually or as collective patronages or buyers in the newly founded Art Associations" [10]).

Such a transition was grounded on a graduate historical change: a number of European galleries had been open to the public since the eighteenth century. In Austria, that was the case by the early nineteenth century for some local museums (for instance, Graz's museum was founded in 1811). Even the provinces started to collect their own local histories, handcrafts, and art (*Heimatkunde*). The change in viewership was so evident that artists in Vienna complained about the

---

12 Svoboda, "Zur Geschichte," 10. Subsequent references to this essay are in parentheses in the text.

rabble visiting the galleries ("Kellnerburschen, Wäschermenscher mit ihren Galanen sowie die gemeinsten Weiber störten die geräuschlose Betrachtung der Kunstwerke" ("Busboys, washerwomen and -men with their lovers, and the most common of women disturbed the soundless viewing of the artworks") [11]). Throughout the region, new collective forms of sociality emerged to solidify these new identities, particularly associations (*Gesellschaften*), aimed at refining manners and *mores* (*Verfeinerung der Sitten* [11]). Art Associations (Kunstvereine), for instance, had become popular since the French Revolution (Germany had a hundred by 1871) (15). Just as critically, the Habsburg central government took up its responsibility for inventorying and maintaining the artwork of their realm in its totality (1856, which has its echoes in Adalbert Stifter's *Nachsommer* [1857]).

With this shift in the demographics of art consumers and in the forms of art exhibition, we also reach Salzburg's own movement. With the support of Salzburg patrons, the Salzburg Museum was founded in 1834, a direct response to the establishment of the *Musealverein* in Linz in 1833. As Svoboda summarizes the moment:

> Patriots were loath to consider that this traditional clerical territory, that had its own historical tradition [as part of the HRE], would be abandoned without resistance to a "foreign" museum directorship or a foreign museum association. [...] It was an issue of preserving one's art-historical independence, despite belonging to another country politically.
>
> (11)

In this sense, as already noted, the competition was as much Linz as it was Vienna, especially given the loss of its university in 1810.

Despite this cultural "threat," Salzburg had profited from the general rejection of Viennese art education since the Nazarenes or Waldmüller and from a general call for painting to go to go "back to nature," since there was a tradition of landscape painting around the Salzach, not surprisingly, given the growing tourism industry in Europe. Salzburg was as good as Italy as a place to paint, said any number of "Academy refugees" (*Akademie-Flüchtlinge*) in the 1830s who preferred the city over Vienna.[13]

---

13 Landscape painting and *Vedutenmaler* (landscape or view painters) came to the fore when the popularity of the Grand Tour brought a genre that came out of Flanders into new popularity in Italy (Venice was the new center of these artists as the famous paintings of Vienna by Bernardo Bellotto attest). Exact reproductions soon competed with fantasy landscapes (*veduta ideale*, or *cappricci*, associated with Giambattista Piranesi, and later with Hubert Robert).

If the Salzburg Museum was a collection based on a historical panorama that became a symbol of local art patriotism, then, it was thus almost inevitable that a Kunstverein (KV) would be founded in this era of new social partnerships. Salzburg saw a collaboration between friends of the art (*Kunstfreunde*) and artists in order to capitalize on the rejection of academic historicist modes and a turn toward the local. The KV founders understood that a great part of their job was to keep local art and artists alive (rather than preserving the past), thus simply functioning differently than the museums and public art galleries.

In the typical association, artists who were members could exhibit with no cost to themselves; landscape and genre paintings that could not be shown in the Academy were accepted, as was work in the applied arts. A Kunstverein, therefore, was itself often an act of local patriotism, focused on the active life of art in its city, not history. They encouraged local art lovers to look at and buy art locally, as "der Brückenschlag vom Akademie- und Auktionswesen zum Verkaufs - und Galeriewesen im 20. Jahrhundert" ("bridge-builders between the academy and gallery entities in the twentieth century"). They also relied on local tastes as they "became the object of general small-talk and trade goods for the public markets" ("zum allgemeinen Gegenstand des Geschwätzes und zur Handelsware eines öffentlichen Marktes"[14]).

The first such Kunstverein in Austria had been opened in Vienna in 1830, an initiative started by *Kardinal Fürst* Schwarzenberg. However, where its ultimate success might have rested with the bourgeoisie and with collaborating artists, its demographic ultimately comprised a comparatively conservative demographic (the old nobility). Salzburg, in contrast, began its planning with a debate about what the scope of its activity would be: would it be, for example, a *Salzburger Verein für Kunst*, or a *Verein for Salzburger Kunst*—an academy for art from Salzburg, or one for Salzburg's art (the decision that had motivated the foundation of the Salzburg Museum)? Such deliberations were broadminded, if not utopian. If Vienna had founded its Association to support artists and thus limited itself to Austrian artists, Salzburg also wished to educate taste, and so extended its reach through the monarchy and beyond, while also setting up conditions for sales of locally produced art.

The final result was the Salzburger Kunstverein (KV), which would exist in more or less continuous form from 1844 until 1922, and then would be resuscitated after the Second World War. Its founding moment was one of geopolitical peace and relative prosperity, and it understood that tourism and a cosmopolitical look would serve it better than insularity. *Fürstbischof* Friedrich Schwarzenburg went to Rome to

---

14 Svoboda, "Zur Geschichte," 15.

get his cardinal's hat, and there he met a Salzburg artist who served as his guide to Rome.[15] Upon his return, he helped float the KV idea, even holding planning meetings in his rooms. Nonetheless, the final paperwork did not bear his name: the founding statutes and correspondence were attributed to a committee of prominent citizens of the city. Their Kunstverein zu Salzburg (Art Association in Salzburg) set as one of their most prominent goals the desire to bring the status of the visual arts in their region up to the standards of its music culture. Permission to establish the institution was granted by the Hofkanzelei and the Emperor in Vienna on December 2, 1844.

What emerged in Salzburg was thus an institution rather different from many histories of the arts in Central Europe would have it. "Raising taste" suggests to our ears today British ideals of normative taste based on a vision of the ruling classes; the act of educating the viewing public sounds initially like the *Bildungsideal* of German Classicism and Romanticism. Yet as we shall see, the KV in Salzburg took up that mission according to its own traditions, focusing on the integration of art into what we would today call the public sphere—as a way of having art and its public come into dialogue about what art was to mean for both artists and their audiences.

The Mission of the Salzburger Kunstverein

The goal of setting artists and audiences into a relationship fostering growth led to the Kunstverein's distinct plan for its schedule and use of space. The KV planned to sponsor regularly changing exhibitions rather than holding a marquee event once or twice a year or installing a permanent collection of historically important works.[16] Support for this activity would come from two principal sources: membership (defined as share- or stockholders), and raffles for and sales of works displayed. This decision was practical, as well. This schedule also removed any suspicion that the KV would be in competition with the Museum: the KV stressed art as practiced, not historical legacies or masterpieces.

By March 1, 1844, the Kunstverein already had six hundred member-shareholders (727 shares) that constituted the project's startup capital, with members from Vienna (including Habsburgs), citizens, nobles, and clerics from Salzburg who bought shares and donated works. The membership in that first year was heavily weighted to

---

15 The information on Schwarzenberg and the founding of the KV is from Svoboda, "Zur Geschichte," 18–19.
16 Svoboda, "Zur Geschichte," is the authoritative source for the KV; subsequent references to this essay are in parentheses in the text. Here, 16.

Salzburg (405), but it had substantial contributions from Bavaria (29), Vienna (156), and several from Italy. Those external memberships were often from other art associations or nobles who were associated with Austria-Hungary who lived abroad. Buying a membership share worked much like today's museum memberships: it allowed free entry to the exhibits for the member and family and the right to compete in the yearly raffles by purchasing five Gulden chances (in any quantity), to win art that had been exhibited and donated to or bought by the Verein for the purpose. Artist-members paid nothing to exhibit their works. The KV also shared reciprocal memberships with other Art Associations, in country and abroad. In this way, art was cast not just as a luxury item, but as part of life.

The KV's first exhibit was actually held in a hall in Linz, put at the Verein's disposal by Schwarzenburg. It is perhaps noteworthy that the Salzburg newspapers reported on the exhibit, but not on the actual founding of the Kunstverein (21). The exhibited art came from many places, since Austria purportedly lacked exhibiting artists at that time (24). That internationalism, however, was considered a positive, as it contributed to raising standards for local artists. Also not surprisingly, there were no history paintings worth mentioning in that first exhibit: the KV resisted academy painting, favoring local tastes for genre painting, still lifes, and landscape painting (19). The exhibitions helped the membership to stay relatively stable until the 1848 revolutions. If a year was bad, the organizing committee would offer a retrospective of recent art that included loans of the raffled pieces (25).

The selection of art exhibited in Salzburg was broadened when the Imperial Academy in Vienna sent out their call for participation to its own artists and students; response was quick because artists did not have as many opportunities to exhibit in the capital (there was greater competition). Art came in from other German lands, as well. In the first year of exhibiting, the *Kunstverein* showed over a hundred pictures (sixty-seven landscapes, twenty-six genre paintings, and six history paintings), and twenty sculptures. In the next years, prominent Austrian names like Johann Ranftl and Friederich Amerling were represented, and forty works (some of which were contributions) were raffled one year. The image arose of what Svoboda called a *Kollektiv-Kunstmäzen*, a collective patronage (15).

As time passed, the art scene in the Austrian Empire itself was evolving. In 1851, Vienna created a mechanism to circulate paintings among the monarchy's art associations in 1851, to present international and contemporary work in ways that did not require too much funding from individual entities. By 1852, the first complaints were raised in Salzburg that there were too many landscapes being shown, and not enough work with contemporary content. Despite the fact that the KV did not have its own permanent collection until 1914, it even did its own outreach, supporting the Mozartstiftung's first music festival in 1877, organizing a special retrospective exhibit and borrowing works from abbeys, churches, and private donors. Money remained problematic: the KV had hoped to open an art school, but without funding, they settled for opening a library (26). And on January 14, 1876, a city vocational school (Staatsgewerbeschule) opened under the supervision of the architect Camillo Sitte, dedicated to the applied arts. In a city of 21,000 inhabitants, the school soon acquired 1,150 students. But the Kunstverein had a turn of fortune in 1882, when Sigmund Graf Thun-Hohenstein had the idea of building a gallery building, a Künstlerhaus, a house for artists. Ground was broken in 1884, and the finished building was turned over to the Kunstverein on August 1, 1885. Again, local donations were critical: even local banks lowered their loan rates to facilitate funding, a sure signal of support by the local elites. Not surprisingly, the Künstlerhaus's first exhibit (1885) combined fine arts with arts and crafts (*Kunstgewerbe*), a combination different from Vienna's art school.

The haste with which the building was erected brought one unintended consequence: the exhibit rooms were not configured in the right way to exhibit both fine and applied art, and so there was a movement (never realized) to found an Association for Arts and Crafts, such as Munich and Innsbruck had already done. Nonetheless, the fact that the KV now owned its space allowed them to schedule more freely (they'd been using borrowed spaces). Their role in the city was also transformed: the KV started moving their most important exhibitions to the "good season" when summer tourists were present, while reserving exhibits for local artists and audiences for the "bad season" (*schlechte Monate*). More importantly, toward the end of the century, the KV rented out studio space to artists, so that art exhibits could show *artists* as well as their works (they could sell out of their studios during opening hours); the main space was also used for some music and theater performances.

Money and subventions were still insufficient for the KV's reputation to keep pace with Munich and Vienna. Over the years, local parties did help: artists donated pieces to the raffles, and private collectors lent to exhibits. And the Kunstverein generally ranked fourth in its overall sales compared to its peers in Austro-Hungary, Germany, and Switzerland. As another sign of maturity, the KV started to issue catalogs in 1891 and repeatedly showed important artists from the Biedermeier and Gründerzeit, like Peter Fendi, Hans Makart, and Carl Spitzweg. It upped its publicity and heightened the visibility of its artists when it started issuing gold and silver medals in 1900. (Strategy was involved: gold-medal winners were not allowed to receive the prize again, only silver ones.)

To be sure, there were setbacks: the Künstlerhaus flooded heavily in 1899, and the Kaiser-Jubiläums-Festzug for 1908 hit them hard financially. Ultimately, the costs were covered by donations, including some by the Emperor's brother, the Archduke Ludwig Viktor, who resided in Salzburg (after being banned from Vienna). There were other hopes for the KV's next steps: there was talk of a *Landesbildersammlung*, a permanent collection that would belong to the *Land Salzburg*. But the First World War scuttled such plans: many prominent voices in art and many promising artists died. After the Second World War, records of the Künstlerhaus become scarce; and the Kunstverein was suspended in 1959.

Roman Höllbacher noted that: "In Salzburg, the terms *Künstlerhaus* and *Kunstverein* were practically synonymous in use."[17] Nonetheless, it was the building that was the quixotic move, a decision that served its day but also the future. That building, perversely, may also have hastened the demise of the Kunstverein, even as it was the concrete example of its hope. The building had been built hastily, which meant that it at times became a maintenance nightmare—its bad moments (like the flood) damaged the Kunstverein. Moreover, the institution was built to compete with "art cities" of the time like Düsseldorf or Munich, but also to a quality standard that hoped to raise tiny Salzburg's art culture to reach par with its music culture. Unfortunately, such planning was unrealistic: the city had limits on its growth, especially geographical ones. It could be a transportation hub but did not have the space for full-scale industrial development.

Nonetheless, it is clear that the KV and its exhibition building together embodied a different ethic from many official art spaces at the start of the twentieth century in Europe. As we have seen, the Künstlerhaus had a history very much like that of the modern museum, dependent on donors. The attendance at the openings in mid-century were good, but then they fell (and there was an economic downturn after the great stock market crash of 1873). At such times, the KV and the Künstlerhaus gave free entrance tickets to schools and workers unions, and they catered more and more to tourists. That trend had already led them to build the building close to the railroad on the south side of the river rather than in the heart of the city on the north. And the management never thought to appeal directly to the proletariat. But that is hindsight, correlated with latter twentieth-century experience—it was a set of new calculations for the nineteenth, as a public-private cooperative.

The project was also notable as the first to include women artists as artists, not just as members of arts and crafts guilds. In 1823, its first year of existence, the Munich Kunstverein had seriously discussed

---

17 Höllbacher, "Das Künstlerhaus als Denkmal des Kunstvereins," 47.

whether women should even be allowed to visit its premises (purity, decorum, and good taste had to be preserved, and history-paintings violated these standards).[18] In 1824, the compromise was struck that women might visit with their families, and only in 1829 were they allowed to become members themselves—because the city's art students demanded that right.

It seems that Salzburg understood the number of women involved in art as careers, given that their numbers had been growing since the eighteenth century in situations where local morality police did not interfere with worries about their fragility and dilettantism. Linda Nochlin pointed out long ago how the curricula at art schools associated with art academics kept women out: to paint in the historicist mode meant learning to paint nudes, and women could not, after all, have their sensibilities offended by having to paint models from life. In consequence, in Vienna and other great cities, women were not part of academy painting, and so were most often given arts and crafts educations. But in Salzburg, the women exhibited alongside the men, even as sculptors, and crafts and other "applied arts" (*angewandte Kunst*), not stigmatized as arts and crafts (*Kunstgewerbe*), were often exhibited alongside easel paintings.[19]

Such distinctive moments of inclusivity would not have been possible without the ideology that the Künsterhaus was designed to serve. The first hint of that is in its style: it was built in Baroque classical style (Vienna's equivalent was more modern and bourgeois), to suit Salzburg's own era of greatness: it was designed for the city. At the same time, the designers designed a space not to look at art, but to foster a climate of discussion about the arts (Höllbacher says it filled the community's need for communication, its *Kommunikationsbedürfnisse*[20]): its

---

18 See Fraueneder, "Weiblichkeit und Kunst," for the most complete statistics on women's participation.
19 See Habsburg-Halbgebauer, "Aufbruch zu neuen Ufern," for an extended discussion of women in the Salzburg art scene. Women were well-placed in applied arts in Salzburg, in no small part because they were allowed into the Academy until 1919 in Munich, 1921 in Vienna (although they could attend the School for Applied Arts in Vienna, as did Emma Schlangenhausen, Maria Cyrenius, Luise Spannring, Hilde Heger, and Hilde Exner). Women artists tended to be local, and often worked side jobs (teaching) to support themselves, if they didn't come from rich families. They all had extensive careers, including Salzburg natives Luise Spannring, Christine Pöschl, Hilde Heger, and Hilde Exner, who were sculptors. Spannring and Exner were both members of the Wassermann, and about a third of the artists in their first exhibition were female. For the women with the Wassermann proper, see Smola, "Partnerinnen und Künstlerinnen im Umkreis von Anton Faistauer, Egon Schiele und Felix Albrecht Harta."
20 Höllbacher, "Das Künstlerhaus als Denkmal," 58–9.

programming combined ideas of education (*Bildung*), continuing education in its utopian sense (*Weiterbildung*), and social contact. It was to be a forum for the *people* to interact in, a public space where the public was brought together with artists, and for artists to come out of their private ateliers as *Mitspieler* (player-partners) in all facets of culture production and consumption.

To this end, the Künstlerhaus's atelier space was built to include artist studios for rent on its perimeter, and it had storerooms where they could stow the bric-a-brac that artists of the time used to "paint realistically," including stuffed animals (and occasionally live ones, for which provisions were also made). The private studios of the era's famous painters (e.g., Hans Makart) are always portrayed as stuffed to the gills with plants, throws, small statues, and furniture—those who rented in the Künsterhaus because of its storerooms would avail themselves of some of these amenities. But the building itself was also wrong from the start for such purposes. Only a minority of the studios for rent had the desirable light to the north; the building did not heat well because of its large central atrium (making working with models difficult).

Still, the project of art as part of civic education through broad participation, as represented in the building and the association that inhabited it, however, was never forsaken, no matter how much history was stacked against it by the end of the century.

Part of this dedication stemmed from the fact that Salzburg had the memory of being an independent political entity. Stefanie Habsburg-Halbgebauer notes that unification of Salzburg with Austria happened only in 1816: "The archbishopric Salzburg, earlier oriented toward art, mutated at its integration into Austria in 2826 into an insignificant province"[21]—a situation that even the 1844 founding of the Kunstverein could not help maintain. It lingered too long with historicism and genre painting, purportedly leaving Salzburg in the second ranks behind Berlin, Vienna, Prague, and Budapest, each of which had its own secession movements.

By the First World War, that situation had not improved. Salzburg had more or less missed the last wave of artistic innovation of the prewar period: Expressionism. The Munich Neue Künstlervereinigung spawned the Blauer Reiter, the group that has become the movement's benchmark identity. At the same time, Dresden's artists moved away from Impressionism to founded Die Brücke in 1905, which moved to Berlin in 1911. Vienna saw Schiele and friends founding the Neukunstgruppe ("New Art Group," 1909), as yet another reaction against the

---

21 Habsburg-Halbgebauer, "Aufbruch zu neuen Ufern," 425.

Academy, a group of fifteen artists who would prepare the way for Austrian "Farbexpressionismus,"[22] including most importantly not only Schiele, but also his brother-in-law Anton Peschka, Anton Kolig, and Albert Paris Gütersloh.[23] Just as importantly for the present purpose is that it included the Salzburg Painter Anton Faistauer. The Künstlerhaus managed to exhibit even during the war, but it had become limited in its outlook, sticking with the tried and true, landscapes and cityscapes, not least because they sold well, where experimental art did not. More crucially, many artistic eyes and voices were lost in the First World War and the Spanish flu of 1919. But for a moment, albeit briefly, history was again on Salzburg's side. If in the nineteenth century, the Salzburg art scene had self-identified in its resistance to Vienna's historicism, in the interwar era, it became a lifeboat for European art trends, a way-station for artists from both Munich and Vienna and other parts of the monarchy that was knocked to pieces in 1918—a place where what was beginning to shatter politically (Europe) was still held together artistically.

The Material Ground of the Arts between the Wars

As traced here, art in Salzburg after the First World War was still marked by duality: the Salzburg Museum and the Künstlerhaus again played roles in the reshaping of *Stadt und Land Salzburg*. But other factors play into the interwar arts scene there. Remember that Salzburg, while long associated with the Habsburgs, was not always part of their Empire after 1806. Yet in 1918, the world's politicians handled Salzburg as it did

---

22 Ibid., 425.
23 The story of the various artist groups in the germanophone world is complicated, with many multiple memberships across national lines. For the immediate context of such organizations around Wassermann, see Jesse, "'[…] schon wieder eine 'Gruppe' mehr […]" and Auer, "So denn. Kein Programm." Wilhelmi, *Künstlergruppen in Deutschland, Österreich und der Schweiz seit 1900* is the broadest reference book identifying memberships and dates of existence. Finally, much information is available in widely scattered sources. For verification of names and dates, the "Salzburg Wiki" (https://sn.at/wiki or https://salzburgwiki.at), sponsored by the *Salzburger Nachrichten*, is an excellent source for tracking down basic information on individuals who are difficult to reference online in other ways, including terminology unique to Salzburg's political and social organization. Similarly, the German-language Wikipedia has many entries on lesser-known figures, as well, usually with references to contemporaneous documents, which, in turn, are available online through the Austrian National Libraries ANNO project (fully searchable newspapers in pdf form, starting from their beginnings in Austrian territories).

the other of Austria-Hungary's Crown Lands (Kronländer): as a pawn in the transition to what would become the Second Republic, scarcely fifty years after it had finally separated from Linz.

Salzburg's art and cultural legacies were part of that political evolution. Most critical in this context was the transition for one-time imperial and state properties into new political hands: the *Hofärar*, state property that had been used and managed by the ruling dynasty (now deposed, but never abdicated). In one sense, transferring that property was straightforward, because the state as *fiscus* (the party responsible for the economy) was not contested: the Habsburgs had always kept strict records that differentiated between state property, property held in trust for the family (the *Familienfideikommiss, Familienfonds des Allerhöchsten Erzhauses*, or family trust/entail), and the private property of individuals in the family.

After November 12, 1918, when the Court ceased to exercise a function in the state, the state property was conveyed to a temporary political entity, *Deutschösterreich*, until the so-called *Habsburgergesetz* of April 3, 1919, gave control of the *Hofärar* and the *Fideikommiss* to the Republik Österreich. That law also essentially banned the Habsburgs from any official role in the country, which caused many family members to flee. (Note, too, that the Nazis expropriated the remaining Habsburg personal family holdings left in the country, and the Russians, as part of the 1955 Staatsvertag [State Treaty], insisted on prolonging this state of affairs.) That commonly held and personally held family property was included remains a matter of continued legal wrangling today.

This ruling impacted two properties associated with Salzburg's Art Museum: Schloß Klessheim, the Habsburg-controlled property in which resided the Archduke Ludwig Viktor (Franz Joseph's brother who had been banned from Vienna, because of inappropriate behavior toward males, and who died in January 1919), and the Salzburger Residenz, long the palace of the Prince-Archbishops, and, after 1803, of members of the Habsburg family. The Residenz had been in use for art exhibits, and nationalization of the property involved moving familiar artworks around.[24] Additionally, Ludwig Viktor was an art collector who did support the Salzburger Kunstverein and other cultural institutions. Thus it was crucial for Salzburg, after his death, that there was a stoploss in his testament: a provision that the works contained in this property not all go back to Vienna. Losing that cultural patrimony would have meant the loss of a Salzburg identity on the level of high art—a forced merger into an "Austrian" identity. Overall, then, "serious art" that had been available to Salzburg was threatened by institutional dislocations associated with the era's shift of ownership and patronage.

---

24 Juffinger, "Residenz," tracks where specific artworks went.

Nonetheless, geopolitics also opened up opportunities for new art to arrive. Nikolaus Shaffer, himself a recent ex-director of the Salzburger Museum, considered the postwar era in Salzburg under the rubric of a "Kurzer Höhenflug und langsames Stranden" (a brief soaring to the heights and slowing being left high and dry, his essay title). Shaffer tracks Salzburg's artworld of the 1920s as a contestation of local voices:

> For a while it looked like Salzburg could take over a leading role in the visual arts of the 20th century. This "heroic phase," to use the rather high-flown phrase, is indivisibly bound up together with the name of the artist group Der Wasserman.[25]

The Wassermann remains today in art historical memory as the most public eruption of "new art" in the region, yet one that is too often considered to be a late starter in the history of Expressionist art, almost half a generation behind other major cities.

Schaffer notes that Salzburg had indeed missed the 1900 wave that crested with Impressionism and broke into Expressionism, but the situation changed quickly after the war, as the *Zugereiste* (the immigrants, those who were newly arrived) came in and rebooted the city's art scene all at once, introducing the "missing" art movements from the prior twenty to forty years. The result was a local "birth of the modern" in one short period of time:

> These [interlopers] did not appear in homogenous form, but rather appeared on the map with high-handed claims to a comprehensive spiritual renewal, yes almost as saviors. In a time of social and political upheaval, nothing seemed more urgent to them than to take up the project of a cultural transformation.[26]

Many groupings sprang up to continue work disrupted by the war. What would become Der Wassermann (Aquarius), for instance, started out as the "New Union of Salzburg's Visual Artists" (Neue Vereinigung blidender Künstler Salzburgs).

Why it became Aquarius has various explanations, perhaps all true. Astrologically it's the sign for fluidity, for that which is not reified. Some claim Salzburg itself is under that sign. The astrologist/writer Oscar H. Schmitz (Kubin's brother-in-law) seems to have suggested the zodiac sign for the founding date.[27] Habsburg, in contrast, notes that one of the

---

25 Schaffer, "Kurzer Höhenflug und langsames Stranden," 114.
26 Ibid., 115.
27 See Dohle and Mitterecker, *Salzburg 1918–1919*, 429.

artists central to the group, Felix Albrecht Harta, had said it referred to a fountain that actually stood in the Schiller Park (now Furtwängler Park) near the Festspielhaus.[28] The uncertainty of naming did not mean a lack of clarity about the group's goal: the official founding of the artist group that would move in the direction set by the Künstlerhaus in exhibiting and collection. Its leadership would be principally in the hands of the aforenamed, Budapest-born Felix Albrecht Harta and the Salzburg painter Anton Faistauer.

Both explicitly tied the emergence of new art to the region's political situation. They hoped explicitly to make the city "a Venice to the north of the Alps," and to "use the fortunate location of the city to create a European forum for the living art of our epoch."[29] Faistauer, for example, described Austria as historically international, due to its geographic location. As he explained in 1923:

> Thus Habsburg Austria is, relatively speaking, the most international country on the continent. The Austrian type is more international than all other people. Its geographic location, in the center among 10 nations, makes it so, and also the atmosphere of the country raises them to be that way. Nature exerts its influence. Its capital houses all nations in percentage-wise greater numbers than any other world city. This situation of the Austrian people is also central to the development of its artists.[30]

Harta concurred that 1919 was a special moment in history, from which Salzburg profited:

> Salzburg had turned from a sleepy small town into a culture center. Out of the dislocation of the disintegration of the monarchy arose in all of us the common wish of creating a new Austria of the muses out of the left-over pieces, which was the birth of an artists' union.[31]

The transformation of politics thus had its objective correlative in art exhibitions.

---

28 Most scholars defer to Gustav Pichler's account, based on a conversation with Harta (1969): the naming was all about the fountain. Let me here thank Rupert Indinger at the Salzburg University Library for making the catalog of the 1969 exhibition that contains this essay available to me in mid-2020.
29 Kaut, "Nach fünfzig Jahren," n.p.
30 Cited in Habsburg, "Aufbruch zu neuen Ufern," 425.
31 Cited in Svoboda, "Zur Geschichte des Salzburger Kunstvereins," 39.

The Kunstverein had been active during the war, particularly with retrospective exhibits, especially of those artists who fell in the war. As far back as 1918, however, five modern painters had already been included in the KV's yearly show, over some local resistance: Felix Albrecht Harta, Anton Faistauer, Karl Reisenbichler, E. Tony Angerer, and Eduard Veith. One of them, Faistauer, who had already had exhibitions elsewhere before he was included in Salzburg, won the year's gold medal. Faistauer had started his painting career in the Secession style, following Klimt, but soon realized that his own gifts were in colors, not planes, and so he described the roots of his own artistic lineage in the French painting of the late nineteenth century—he became an early Austrian advocate for Cézanne.

This exhibit was the start of a new chapter in art exhibition in Salzburg. The city was still on the East–West travel corridor through Austria, and it became a place of refuge for many who fled the larger cities (especially Munich and Vienna) to avoid famine and postwar unrest. This included artists like Alfred Kubin, and authors like Hugo von Hofmannsthal, Hermann Bahr, and Stefan Zweig. Max Reinhardt would eventually make it his home, as part of the emergence of the Salzburg Festival. Hermann Bahr, ever the publicist, even called Salzburg the "Capital of Europe" (perhaps, as Kling argues earlier in this volume, as a satire) as he advocated for the Festival idea. The city also became one of the sources for Bahr's interest in the Baroque as defining Austria's cultural identity, and he was instrumental in making Hofmannsthal and Reinhardt's *Jedermann* possible. Support for the arts, however, remained a communal project in the era, a position much like that claimed by the visual arts in the nineteenth century—theater was not a luxury, it was part and parcel of the community. Literature and music stood next to the visual arts in this new world.

Before now-local talent banded together in the Festival, however, the artist's union Der Wassermann emerged as an earlier voice for the city's art renaissance. Founded on January 8, 1919 in Hotel Bristol, the group was designed to foster three branches of the arts. Harta was head of the section for Visual Arts, Stefan Zweig headed the literary group, and Bernhard Paumgartener (director of the Mozarteum, a musician and the jurist who wrote the organization's statures[32]) organized the music section. And the newspapers agreed that Salzburg was the place for this to happen—the war hadn't changed that fact:

Salzburg is the bridge between Austria and the rest of southern Germany. Salzburg is on the crossing of the railways that tie the

---

32 See Kaut, "Nach fünfzig Jahren," n.p.

Adriatic and the North Sea, the Atlantic Ocean with the Black Sea. Salzburg lies in the center of Europe. [...] *Aquarius* wants to use the city's location to enable discriminations between and unions among the various movements that the new spirit has let stream forth out of the heavens. It wants nothing more than to create a European forum for the living art of our epoch.[33]

Wassermann's founding statutes echoed those of the nineteenth-century Künstlerhaus: it focused on contemporary art and on help for practicing artists. Further goals were the exchange of ideas, holding exhibitions and lectures in common with other organizations, and to generally further the cause of art in Salzburg. Significant in another way is that the union board had three male painters, one female one (Elfriede Mayer), and one female sculptor and ceramics artist (Luise Spannring), which continued the impetus of the pre-war Künstlerhaus in its representation of female artists and applied arts.

Beyond Faistauer, the other leader of the group (and its actual instigator), Salzburger Felix Albrecht Harta, had studied in Vienna, Munich, and Paris in the era of art nouveau, and had ongoing interests in Greco, Goya, and Velázquez. Like Faistauer, Harta already had an established reputation in Europe. Both hoped to gain access to the Künstlerhaus for their exhibition of the moderns. The space had ended up in the hands of a pre-war surviving old guard, but the gap was managed (especially when an older critic died[34]), and, on August 3, 1919, the first Wassermann exhibit opened. The artists represented included Harta, Faistauer, Emma Schlangenhausen, Robin C. Andersen, Anton Kolig, Albert Paris Gütersloh, Egon Schiele, Franz Wiegele, and Max Unhold (see the Appendix at the end of this chapter for a complete list of artists for 1919 and 1921). Their focus was, like their pre-war peers, recovering genres that had gone fallow—in this case, religious art. Harta's oils *The Three Kings* and *Saint Martin* were displayed next to gothic sculptures, and the Künstlerhaus again became a center where new art confronted old.[35]

Wassermann's second exhibit was put together in 1920, in conjunction with the first *Jedermann* (*Everyman*) of the Salzburg Festival, after the artists had again taken up studios in the Künstlerhaus. This exhibition featured artists who would be in the European canon: Cézanne,

---

33 Habsburg-Halbgebauer, "Aufbruch," 429.
34 See Schaffer, "Weltkrieg und Künstlerfehden Salzburger Kunst und Erster Weltkrieg — eine nüchterne Bilanz." See the Appendix at the end of this chapter for the lists of artists in the 1919 and 1921 shows; in 1920, they showed only foreign artists.
35 Habsburg-Halbgebauer, "Aufbruch," 431–2, summarizes this exhibit.

Courbet, Gauguin, Manet, and Klimt, who had not been shown in Salzburg before the year's exhibits. The exhibit was again a success. The planners of these exhibits also paid attention to educating the art public. They sought the establishment of a larger permanent collection in the city, not only yearly exhibits. Their goal was to get Salzburg's art treasure together in their own gallery—which succeeded by 1923, when the Residenzgalerie was founded. Faistauer also lobbied for artwork to come out of storage and be displayed in the regional capitals' museums rather than be out of sight.[36] In 1920, the group also made another stab at establishing an art school, a Moderne Kunstakademie that was to be located at the Künstlerhaus and that was to train locals in ways that to this point had only been available in Vienna, including classes in art history, theory of color, and anatomy. Unfortunately, there were no funds available from public coffers; it took another thirty years before Oskar Kokoschka managed to found his "International Summer Academy for Visual Arts" in 1953 (also a Schule des Sehens), which to date has had about three hundred students each year from all over the world in its quarters at the Festung Hohensalzburg.

The Wassermann board did manage to get public support for another gallery for the city, dedicated to showing modern art, to keep public interest up. In 1921, the Künstlerhaus hosted what was to be the third and last Wassermann exhibit, an *Internationale Schwarz-Weiß-Ausstellung* (an "international black-white exhibit") organized by Harta and Faistauer. Its focus was on international graphic arts, from the nineteenth and twentieth centuries, with considerable space also devoted to Japanese art from the eighteenth century onwards.[37] The foreword to the 1921 catalog was written by Faistauer, stressing that their goal was to make visible the international character of art, and to rebuild bridges from one decade and county to another that had been broken by the war: "We can probably consider it successful: it gave the public insight into the sprit and experience of artists of many lands, in order that they might gain support and wisdom."[38]

That exhibit did indeed bring modern art to Salzburg. Yet *Der Wassermann* would not last long. Harta, who had both summoned the group into existence and held it together, eventually moved back to

---

36 Habsburg-Halbgebauer, "Aufbruch," lists: from France, great names like Daumier, Delacroix, Géricault, Manet, Picasso, Pissarro, Toulouse-Lautrec, and Rodin were represented. Barlach, Grosz, Heckel, Kollwitz, Liebermann, and Menzel, among others from Germany, were shown. Austria was represented, aside from Faistauer and Harta, by Klimt, Schiele and Kokoschka (432).
37 Cited in Habsburg-Halbgebauer, "Aufbruch," 432.
38 Cited in Habsburg, "Aufbruch," 433.

Vienna, and so Faistauer took over leadership for a brief time, but he had many other projects (one of many who became active in the Festival), and so Der Wassermann ceased to exist by 1922. One critic notes, however that "The activity of the art association Der Wassermann and the founding of the Salzburg Festival transformed the quiet provincial city of Salzburg after the First World War into a city of art and culture."[39]

Schaffer, however, also situates Faistauer's various projects into the context of the Second World War in more pragmatic contexts: in the wake of the First World War, the artist was one of many addressing and experiencing aftermaths of the war, expressed in art showing desperation and stress about the desperate art situation in Vienna, where he was familiar. He was one of several who were looking for a space between Munich's "Bolshevism" and Vienna's stagnation in decadence. In January 1919, he had reacted to Harta's initiative to found the Wassermann with some hesitation, but he nonetheless offered to help with organization, in no small part because of his earlier experience in exhibiting. As he wrote to Harta:

> I have my own reasons for assuming that we can execute a *coup d'état* in the case of art. […] I know the Salzburgers. They can be won over, which can be proved if we win easily. […] The press is easily bribed and cajoled. When my boy is healthy again, I'll come there for a few days.[40]

Another reason was his need to move beyond the war as subject material for art, and its stagnation in a kind of late Expressionism. In Faistauer's case, that move beyond the war included his return to religious art, as well.

Such an assessment of Salzburg as ripe for a modern art takeover because of the war, however, underplays the city's half-century support for the building up of an art public, and of accommodating art within its public sphere and spaces, an ethic that is generally associated with the Festival alone. Harta, the Budapest-born and Vienna-bred instigator of Der Wassermann, saw in Salzburg a place between the Vienna and Munich art scenes with which he was familiar. Faistauer, as a local born in *Land* Salzburg, would have experienced its general public reacting to new art, as well as the limits of its art scene (as Schaffer's account defines it), explaining his initial reticence to move back to Salzburg. No

---

39 Schaffer, "Weltkrieg," 562; this essay chronicles Faistauer's career arc.
40 See Schaffer, "Weltkrieg," 563–4, for the more positive assessment of what Salzburg offered artists.

one, in 1922, would have found it questionable if established arts would leave that too-small art scene relatively soon. Nonetheless, interwar Salzburg did indeed serve to reboot the directions of modern art that had almost died with the First World War, attempting to reestablish art as part of European culture rather than replaying Expressionism or the stagnation of decadent Impressionism. To be sure, the city never had a huge art market, but it lay halfway between the intensive politics of Munich and Vienna, among a wealth of small towns with comparatively easier access to food, if not to opportunity, and a place to regroup after the First World War. Critics overlook that the Spanish flu probably also played a role—Faistauer's child was ill, as his response indicates, and he lost his wife just as the exhibit opened.

Still, the Wasserman exhibits were successful in moving the Salzburg public out of the traditions of the Kunstverein and even past the Künstlervereinigung—and had a significant number of visitors. Despite their limitations, then, *Stadt und Land Salzburg* offered many artists a respite, a place to find food and a less competitive art market after the First World War—and a chance to experiment. What they produced never turned into a commercial juggernaut with an established brand—many of the artists had been members of more highly profiled art groups before and after the war, from Der blaue Reiter through any number of smaller groups that lasted into and even through the Second World War.

The art produced in Salzburg is often judged as lacking by art critics focusing on established art scenes and profiled brands like Expressionism.[41] What these critics and scholars mis-assess is precisely the need for post-First World War art and artists to regroup and find their ways forward into roles not constrained by a past and a traditional art market that no longer existed. As we shall see, Salzburg's particular commitment to internationalism, its location between Munich and Vienna, and its offering to the art of the present a space would be critical in allowing a new philosophy and practice of art to emerge, critical for individuals to survive into a next generation, yet without the stylistic unity that too many academic critics demand.

Der Wassermann managed, instead, to extend Salzburg's then-traditional emphasis on rebooting the old to serve the new.

---

41 "Die Gegenwartskunst ist eine Weltbürgerkunst, die sich an die gesamte Menschheit, nicht nur an ein einzelnes Volk wendet" (Mühlmann, in the foreword to *Ausstellungs-Katalog*), here 4.

Part II Der Wassermann in Self-Presentation

Exhibits from and for Salzburg

As already sketched, the actual exhibits of the Wassermann were carefully staged to establish context for the innovations they presented. The first of the three (1919) was held in the Künstlerhaus, thereby capitalizing on the traditional dynamics of the site (and probably on Faistauer's and Harta's reputations here); it was also careful to juxtapose great works from the past with what they hoped would be the next generation.

The 1919 exhibition catalog had a foreword by Dr. Josef Mühlmann, known art writer (to whom we shall return later). That foreword raised hackles in Salzburg, even as it introduced the basic principles underlying the public event. His Wassermann was pictured as embarking on its first coherent exhibition, he notes, with artworks from *Stadt und Land Salzburg*, Vienna, and the German *Reich*, yet with the intent of connecting them to artists from elsewhere: "The art of the present is a cosmopolitan art, that addresses not just a single people, but all of mankind."[42] Yet this cosmopolitan art is also adapted to each location where artists create to address the "sensibilities of the present" ("lebendig zu schaffen aus dem Empfinden der Gegenwart").[43] The artists of his day needed to reestablish ties that had been broken by the Great War, and the audiences needed to see that art. Mühlmann agreed that Salzburg was particularly suited to stage this re-connection, with a long tradition of art and as a "center for tourism and for Europe's connection to the world" (4).

The exhibition would also give that Salzburg a chance to come to know the newest art. Yet Mühlmann was not generous to this audience:

> Salzburgers will shake their heads. And that is their good inherited right. It won't matter that the artists' names are known well beyond Germany. Just that they should not be content with head-shaking but should make the effort of doing justice to the things, at least by looking at them for a longer period.
>
> (4)

Mühlmann thought that contemporaneous artworks were strong enough to have the effect of "true art." At the same time, however, the

---

42 Subsequent quotations by Mühlmann from this catalog are listed by page number in parentheses in the text.
43 Mühlmann, "Der Wassermann," 83. Subsequent quotations from this essay are in parentheses in the text.

modern artist must also learn to find a way to the audience ("especially in a place like Salzburg that has, in terms of its understanding, been left relatively far behind" [5])—to simply look down on the audience will not do, since the art is created for the public who will also judge it.

That should not be a problem, Mühlmann continued, because new representational art is more relatable than the old masters or individualistic experiments in style:

> Contemporary art has not originated in the willfulness of individuals, it is the necessary expression of its time, the unconscious wishing and wanting of its spiritual ideals; it has become as necessary as our present language, as our entire [habits of] thinking and feeling.
>
> (5)

Modern art, Mühlmann says, often does not seem challenging, because even artists can be weak in their old age, which leaves them without the strength to express their modernity, the place where they have moved beyond their younger peers. This may be the case for the Expressionists.

Mühlmann points out that the nineteenth century had already gone through "all phases" of naturalism/realism (5), telling stories through pictures. At the end of the century, he continues, Impressionism enriched the existing visual vocabulary (especially in presenting sunlight and free air), but lost much in its content, particularly because it leveled everything in nature to "the visible," be it animal or human being. At the same time, he asserts, Impressionist art can be very subjective, because it represents the point of view of an observer at a particular moment, presenting something from the visible conveyed to the eye of the spirit (*Auge des Geistes* [6]).

After that moment, Expressionism synthesized both impetuses, combining an urgency to express both outer and inner vision. This combination, Mühlmann notes, was revealed at the core of the 1919 exposition, an art that was specifically trying to counter the externality of Impressionism through interiority (*die Seele der Erscheinungswelt* [8]). The resulting form of Expressionism is a Gedankenkunst, an art of ideas based not only on abstracts, but also on sensations and feelings that reach beyond concepts—an art still seeking its ultimate form. Lay viewers, he notes for his readers, should try to pursue this art rather than to reject it, as audiences often do with new art, showing "pigheadedness without end, injustice screaming at the art of the most recent times" (8).

Most significantly for the present context: Mühlmann closes the essay with a slur against Salzburg:

Before the war, Salzburg had sought its fame in the production of good beer and brewpubs. The war ruined the beer, closed the pubs, sobered the heads. The intellectual youth of the city dreams of a European cultural site, of a spiritual meeting place. If such dreams should come true, post-war Salzburg would not be called the city of beer- and art-philistines. The exhibit shows the way.

(8)

Such comments were, of course, not well received: just as the exhibit itself was accused of being alien (*Landfremdheit*, an accusation made by Hans Seebach), the artists were called cultural bolshevists (*Kunstbolschewiken*), and their art "toothbrush art" (*Zahnbürstelmalerei*). Ludwig Praehauser (renowned founder of modern pedagogy through art) rose to Wasserman's defense by defaming Seebach.

These accusations were made in the tone of critics more concerned with the art than the public. Nonetheless, Mühlmann remained a visible voice for Wassermann. After the catalog introduction, he again reviewed the exhibition in 1919, stressing a return to religious art and to Expressionism as understandable reactions to the war. He also wrote a longer appreciation of the Wassermann for the 1920 issue of a Viennese journal called *Die graphischen Künste*. His mission in that essay was to introduce the graphic arts components of Der Wassermann as an attempt to "move artistic creativity from the large cities into the provinces" and as an attempt to heal art.[44] Such comments again clearly designate Salzburg as provincial.

This is not an overstatement, because Mühlmann continues that this move had the effect of "refreshing small town art" (*Auffrischung der Kleinstadtkunst* [83]). By that, Mühlmann clarifies, he means that in most small towns, art was stuck in the "dated academic style of the 19th century," with little reception of Impressionism or any subsequent evolutions, and that their yearly exhibits keep repeating old style art: "the eternal return of tradition motifs, pleasant nature studies, the usual landscapes, photographically faithful portraits" (84).

Such judgments simply did not reflect Salzburg's entire reality. Mühlmann, for example, did not acknowledge the fact that Faistauer had gone beyond that kind of work in his earlier medal-winning submission to the Künstlerverein show. Why Mühlmann makes this case reveals some of his argument strategy: publicity. Mühlmann (correctly) situates the origin of Wassermann in the efforts of Harta to bring modern art to Salzburg, where he was then joined by Faistauer (who had

---

44 For information on this organization, see http://www.malerkolonie.at/ and https://www.sn.at/wiki/Zinkenbacher_Malerkolonie.

returned there from Vienna). Against this background, the 1919 exhibit then emerged as a coup, "the first exhibition that was an artistic deed of the first rank for the city of Salzburg, and the cause of intense intellectual excitement for its inhabitants" (89). Nonetheless, Mühlmann then dials his enthusiasm back, noting that that exhibit cannot yet be judged to the fullest because the modern art it showed is still evolving and because it included both older and newer styles of graphic arts. He stands by only one claim: that the exhibit had decisively moved beyond Impressionism. Thereafter, he turns to discussing individual works in terms of the problems of artistic representation posed and resolved in how audiences were addressed in each.

Mühlmann's essays, I believe, must both be understood with a degree of caution, not just as documentation. He was a native of *Land* Salzburg (1886–1972) who lost his lower-middle-class father as a small child, and then, after being raised for years by his mother, was brought up by a stepfather of farmer descent. After completing a *Matura* at age twenty-two, he did a PhD with Max Dvořák in Vienna and then got an internship with the Zentralkommission für Denkmalpflege in Vienna, along with a stipend to write a monograph on Albert Maulbertsch (his dissertation topic). He joined Wassermann in 1919 on the basis of his work as an art historian, restorer (for the Residenzgalerie), and art journalist—probably the credentials that got him the assignment of writing the foreword. By the mid-1920s, he and his younger half-brother Kajetan (PhD Salzburg, 1926) were both involved in the planning for the Salzburg Festival, especially for its publicity.

Thereafter, the Mühlmann story gets darker, marked perhaps by opportunism: Kajetan Mühlmann became one of the chief perpetrators of Nazi art thefts in Poland, France, Belgium, and the Netherlands; he also provided certain works to high Nazis out of Salzburg's own collections. After becoming a friend of Arthur Seyß-Inquart around 1930, he had started to serve the party by 1934. After joining the party in 1938 (that is his dating, but he had earlier been involved in illegal Nazi activities), Kajetan was an SS-Oberführer by 1939, who was then detailed to Poland, where he oversaw the regime's mass art robbery. He inventoried the Polish national museum and opened up other offices in Paris, the Hague, and Brussels. In this era, Kajetan worked directly with Göring and was so successful that the art unit was named after him.

Josef was drawn into the project. He had organized an exhibition in Salzburg in 1938, then worked in Poland with his brother until 1940, when he was let go because he had given stolen art as gifts to a girlfriend. He then ran the Paris office for his brother. Both Mühlmanns were captured by the US Army at the end of the war and interned; Kajetan escaped, while Josef was being investigated by the courts in Linz, which were halted by 1952. Cleared of his Nazi involvement,

Josef continued his career in Salzburg, working for the Museum Carolino Augusteum (today's Salzburg Museum) and eventually receiving a pension.

While hindsight is always 20/20 and reading a person's action as "proto-Nazi" is a completely ahistorical assessment, reading from Mühlmann's essays on the Wassermann into this history seems to confirm certain resentments against Salzburg's art scene, or at least an unwillingness to accept an art scene focused on the audiences rather than on artists' innovation. On the one hand, his assessments of individual artists' work fall very much in line with his contemporaries', but he clearly also wants to present Salzburg as a backwater art scene rather than considering the overall problem of reestablishing art in the wake of the Great War. The seeming success of the Wassermann exhibits also seems to contradict his overall assessments of Salzburg's art community. Mühlmann's transition into National Socialism may have been opportunistic; his entrance into that forum may have been facilitated by his contact with the Zinkenbacher Malerkolonie, a group of painters which began to meet in 1927 under the leadership of Ferdinand Kitt. It was not overtly political in any single direction, although by 1932, it became more public and perhaps more polarized.[45] By 1938, the group threw out its Jewish members, but at least one of them ended up with their work on the Nazi list of *entartete Kunst*.

Mühlmann's participation in Wassermann, as well as his and Kajetan's work in the context of the Salzburg Festival, thus may be indices for the era's stresses that led individuals toward ever more extreme ideologies. Mühlmann began with scorn toward the Salzburg bourgeoisie that did not (want to) comprehend modern art—a bow to the ideology of genius inherited from German Romanticism and Nietzsche, expressed by an art historian from a non-privileged background who was at the peripheries of many of the day's art movements, in Vienna as well as Salzburg. Yet his preference for the artist as prophet lies profoundly distant from the art sought by Faistauer and the Wassermann group, an art that would engage with its moment and help give shape to their collective experience.

The Wassermann did not just foment revolution against modern art. Its first exhibition had more than three thousand visitors, and the 1920 exhibit was held in conjunction with the Festspiel and featured artists like Courbet, Cézanne, Gaugin, and Manet alongside Klimt and Kolig. The 1921 "Black-White" exhibition of graphic art enabled them to open up a "Neue Gallerie" on the Alter Markt. The 1920 exhibit did not have

---

45 *Katalog der internationalen Schwarz-Weiss Ausstellung*, 5. Subsequent citations from this catalog are listed by page number in parentheses in the text.

a catalog, but the 1921 follow-up catalog began to express more overtly what was to follow in Impressionism and Expressionism—what art Salzburg might have been able to incubate for the next generation.

The Artist's Voice in Wassermann

The introduction to the 1921 catalog, signed F (Faistauer), reflects overt pride in the international selection of works that were brought together (he calls them art with international reach, *Kunstwerke internationaler Spannung*[46]). He acknowledges that the assemblage was facilitated by material forces: the greater ease of finding and shipping graphics, even if he regrets that Munch and some French Impressionists were inadequately represented in an exhibit tracking international connections between artworks and artists.

His goal in the exhibit, his catalog essay asserts, was to foster comparisons of representations from across the globe. Thus the exhibit featured Japanese woodcuts, which came to the continent over England and influenced Austrian artists like Klimt, Schiele, and Orlik, as well as the early Kokoschka. Alfred Kubin's work reaches out to the world and so facilitates comparisons, because his work reflected and re-presented many different influences. Northern German art parallels England's:

> Liebermann, Slevogt, Corinth are unthinkable without the French Impressionists. Barlach, in the same sense, a marked Russian disposition, and Käthe Kollwitz, not without Steinlen, the younger Germans not without Daumier, Toulouse Lautrec, Cézanne, van Gogh, etc. The entire New German school is built in the Western spirit, partially still in a strong battle with its own. [...] Even Munch, in his early phase, was inspired by France, only late focusing totally on his own art.
>
> (6)

Faistauer's point in setting up these comparisons is to underscore how broad, geographically and temporally, artistic networks actually are, and to reveal the ground on which the artist actually flourished, how far around the earth and into the past they have reached for creative inspiration (7). Notably, he rejected the idea that an artist is "delimited nationally" or "must be oriented toward the homeland" (*national*

---

46 Note that his hostility may also be class-bound. He is describing a public who rejects art they may not like and that possibly also reacts to the costs of borrowing foreign art—remember that Faistauer's essay started with a comment on how cheap it was to assemble a credible graphic arts exhibition.

abgegrenzt, auf ihre Heimat gestellt [7]) to make a contribution to their own land. It is critical, he feels, for art to make such contacts and for the exhibit to reestablish the connections lost in the war:

> To the artist, though, for whom the exhibit is perhaps even more critical, it brings a number of examples of the deepest explorations, strength of self-offering, possibilities of the empowering *ingenium* that he needs to create new works or augmentations that are able to intervene in the spiritual mechanisms that drive the world forward.
>
> (7)

These goals were met, he feels, by the 1921 Wassermann exhibit.

The contrast between this 1921 introduction and Mühlmann's of 1919 could not be starker. Mühlmann and Faistauer agreed on their exhibitions' purposes of internationalism and setting a course into the new world of postwar art. Both agree that Impressionism has passed its prime and that Expressionism arose as a correction to Impressionism's lack of interiority, a response to the war and its dislocations.

Yet Faistauer trusts his audiences in a way that Mühlmann did not. Faistauer believes the exhibition's audience will learn from the connections that the displays suggest, not just reject the unfamiliar. Mühlmann's comment reflected a different aesthetic: the stereotype of the artist as the voice of their era, as German philosophers of aesthetics since Herder and Schiller would insist, and as his training under Max Dvořák, an art historian and *Geistesgeschichtler*, would have defined as the proper object of study. Accordingly, Mühlmann evaluated the Salzburg public as comprised of philistines.[47]

Another factor may come into play here in the difference between the two programmatic descriptions: Faistauer was trained as a painter, not an art historian, in Vienna, where huge arguments about how to think about art were emerging in the evolving discipline of art history, which was a highly contested topic at the time within what came to be known as the Vienna School of Art History—a broad debate beyond the scope of the present essay, but well documented if little understood.[48] Still, the connection is suggestive, since Faistauer's 1923 aesthetics essay echoes the most familiar of the names in that debate, Alois Riegl. Riegl's work

---

47 The now-standard account of the Vienna School is Cordileone, *Alois Riegl in Vienna 1875–1905*.
48 Faistauer rejects "all nonsensical phrases" that refer to art periods—there is "no cause" to call a world "gothic," and consider it an "explanation," for example. It will "be left to history" to name this era's art (Faistuer, *Neue Malerei*, 86). Subsequent references to this text are in parentheses in the text.

supports a tie between art and cultural communities that Faistauer adapts and makes his own in assessing what art is to be and do. More important is the fact that the Vienna School was interested in how styles of representation corresponded with the lived experiences shared by artists/artisans and their audiences, not to historical eras. Der Wassermann's three exhibits followed this strategy, insisting simply that the past and contemporaneous art that was shown was unified in speaking to times of transition like their own age in Europe. The art shown, the catalogs imply, arose in an age of transition that was seeking to represent experiences that had dislodged tradition in many ways and found its tools in Europe and in the relationships forged between Europe and the rest of the world. At the time, Faistauer's judgments about contemporary art were considered *spitzzüngig* (sharp-tongued) and the product of a relatively insignificant painter. Art history largely dismisses him as neo-baroque or as a religious painter or muralist (the latter on the basis of his work in the Festspielhaus). Yet in the Salzburg context native to Faistauer, and in the context of specifically Austrian views of art that his career and activities represented, the organization of the exhibits were grounded in a very specific aesthetic centered around the audience's relationship to the artwork, not to abstractions like periodization.[49]

This point is confirmed in Faistauer's 1923 *New Painting in Austria* (*Neue Malerei in Österreich*), with a foreword dated in 1921 (and with the volume actually coming out in November 1922). This slim volume of less than eighty text pages confirms his commitment to art being part of communal life rather than to individual genius, to art grounded in the present rather than the past or future. Such statements connect to the public art traditions of Salzburg's pre-war Künstlerverein, as well as to the Vienna School.

New Painting in Austria starts by noting that he is writing in a time of disruption and in support of the participation of a lay audience in an art world in a time of transition:

> The following book is dedicated to the search for the Authentic in the Babel of new artistic developments; it intends to contribute to the orientation of a serious collective [*Kamaradschaft*] and to communicate today's artistic goals [*Kunstwillen*] to lay readers.
>
> (1)

---

49 Faistauer's own reception within art history circles also seems to be influenced by Riegl's canonization as an expert in Baroque art and as an art historical of a formalist bent—a term with implication of "structure of experience" rather than the constitution of the work, as it would in German aesthetics since Classicism.

The important word here is *Kunstwillen*, a will to art, which echoes Alois Riegl's important term *Kunstwollen* (often also translated as *will to art*, but which might better be translated as *disposition toward art*), a commonality which may help to illuminate the century-old debate in art historical circles about what the latter term actually means.[50]

Riegl's *Kunstwollen* is generally understood as the direction or techniques of representation and media by means of which an era develops and practices its art—a cognitive patterning distinctive to a nation or era centered on a kind of (almost rhetorical) comprehensibility rather than an aesthetic philosophy or technology alone. An example would be an era focused on abstraction as its point of interest will innovate more strongly in the formal issues that abstraction implicates.

In *New Painting in Austria*, Faistauer uses the clear correlate *Kunstwillen* for a much more focused purpose: he attaches it to the "absolute objectivity" (1) that surrounds artists, meaning the totality of their material contexts and practices, their mental frameworks which leads them to make art. Thus, for example, one should read what artists write (he cites Delacroix, van Gogh, Gaugin, Rodin, Michelangelo, and other artists' letters—*Künstlerbriefe*, in the sense of Vasari—as evidence of what an era considered needful of experienced and representation). This recommendation, however, is more than traditional historicism or *Geistesgeschichte* that historicizes periods and styles of art.

Instead, Faistauer sketches a different hermeneutics of how to understand artworks, as he points to an era's structure of experience rather than to the work's aesthetic structure. His interest is in how individuals are habituated to interact or communicate with their surroundings and its cultural inheritance. *Style* is a word used by art historians to speak of a quality of artworks. Faistauer (and Riegl) instead consider it more as a disposition of optics connecting the painter, work, and audience—a structure of experience with material force behind it, underlying the artwork's strategies of representation and its audiences' interactions with it. Riegl used this heuristic to describe the change of "eras" in art as a change of structures of experience. Faistauer speaks of artists producing work out of and for its era.

This central tenet of the Viennese School of Art History is often misconstrued as a formalist corrective to materialist historiographies. Riegl, for instance, uses the term "primitive art" as a term, but one that does not refer to a single epoch, nor mark the sites where it applies as something to "progress beyond," as Hegelian histories would insist; he also

---

50 "Dafür fehlt aber auch die Einheitlichkeit des Strebens, wenigstens vorläufig. Eine einheitliche Weltanschauung hat noch nicht durchgegriffen. Alles steht in Reibung und Kampf" (6).

does not see "the primitive" as part of the healthy root of the nation. Instead, his "primitive art" results from communities' more direct engagement with the concrete facts of their existence—a set of ornaments and/or representations that result from a confrontation between mind and art, relatively unmediated by ideologies or institution of art practice. It is the art of a community with a public sphere structured a particular way; it is an art that is authentic to a moment, not to the genetic identity of a nation. "Primitive" art will potentially emerge in communities close to nature and the facts of their communities' life; its particular style, while always close to nature, will differ at each site of its emergence according to the habits and experiences of its community, on which it is grounded.

As a practicing artist, Faistauer agrees that styles do not "progress," but they can recur across time and space, meaning that artists of one era may find and borrow strategies of representation broadly across time and across borders, adapted to their presents. Yet he is more interested in how individual artists and art projects strategically engage with their eras: how artworks document psychic (*geistig*) engagement with their communities on the part of both artist and audience. Art from very different works may be engaged with parallel historical moments, each with its own style: Dürer's 1514 *Melancholia* represents the same *Wille* as Rodin's *Bürger von Calais*, as "dissimilar works born out of the same spirit" ("die ungleichen Werke […] aus dem gleichen Geiste geboren" [1]). The works are not parallel in artistic form nor in their genres or materials, but they aim at representing particular challenges of contemporaneous experience (in these cases, times of political disarray).

Faistauer's first chapter, "Das österreichische Problem" (The Austrian Problem), defines the artwork in these terms. He notes that people are born into their environments and are made by their inheritances, and artists take those facts as motivations for their works, such as is the case of low-born artists:

> [The artist] will transform the passions and longings inherent in low origins into motors for his creating, in service of art. He will transform the tribulations of the poor into creative drives. His heritage is also certainly not indifferent, neither is the landscape, not the climate in which the artist grows up. The landscape is important for the psychic development of the child, as it is for the adult, the climate helps form human character, as do upbringing, school, and society.
>
> (5)

Faistauer's Austrian artists will thus not represent a "national type" because they are Central European, a mix of many cultures—most differentiated and most extreme (*verschiedenst, extremsten*), a kind of disposition of spirit (*Gemütsart*) that is radically different and "does not immediately emerge in a clear form" (*und nicht sofort in klarer Form heraustreten läßt*). That disposition of spirit is grounded in Habsburg history, as a nation that lies in the midst of ten nations:

> The Habsburg Monarchy, which for many centuries held so many people unified in one state, held the way open for cultural assimilation of the east to the west, with its alliances bringing the north and the south together. In this way, the Austria of the Habsburgs was the relatively most international land on the continent. Most particularly, the Austrian is more international than all others. [...] Its capital shelters all nations in higher numbers, percentagewise, than any other world city. This situation of the Austrian human being is also very critical to the development of the artist.
>
> (5–6)

Nature—its various landscapes—as well as the organizations of culture all create the concrete, material influences that help create talent, but not necessarily a national identity.

Here, the essay's logic skews towards more modern ideals of nationalism—or maybe to a more accurate address to the contemporaneous audience's politics. Faistauer starts by noting that it lacks a clear identity because it is not "streng völkisch"/comprised strictly of a single ethnic group. In consequence, the Austrian nation is always at odds with itself: "For that reason, it also lacks the unity of its striving, at least for now. It has not yet formed a unified *Weltanschauung*. Everything is in a state of friction and struggle."[51] He includes Czechs from the north; from the east, Poles, Slovaks, Hungarians; Slovenes from the south; and from the west, the Germans, all striving in "toward the middle" (*nach der Mitte*).

But then the essay turns toward valuing such diversity rather than decrying it. Most critically, he notes, the Jewish peoples of the region have played a significant role in creating the experience for "Austrians" ("Ein außerordentlich schwerwiegendes Element sind die Juden" [6]).

---

51 "Seine Bilder sind gleich Zierteppichen an die Wand zu hängen, sie dienen wie Goebelins" (13). One might consider Friedensreich Hundertwasser (1928–2000) as the artist who made this leap more successfully, two generations later—combining both decorative and fine arts that bridged museums and public architecture.

And diversity is critical to the production of art: a multilingual and multicultural city like Vienna contributes much experience for individuals to "drink in" and which "opens their psyche" (*öffnen ihre Psyche* [6]), with its known contrasts between the traditional Austrian organization of the First District, and the "exotics" in other districts (*Exoten*). However, this First District in Faistauer's 1923 is clearly marked as a historical fossil:

> The Vienna of yore lives in the museums and on the walls of collectors who also, mostly, no longer possess the documentation of its Kultur by dint of inheritance.
>
> There is today almost no "Viennese tradition." It has been inundated by these influences. In-fluences in the literal sense. Where that tradition is still upheld, it appears be-wigged in its visual arts, sentimental and inauthentic.
>
> (6–7)

He then identifies that bygone "Viennese tradition" with the Biedermeier (he mentions explicitly Waldmüller and Rudolf Alt), and notes that Makart's subsequent experiments in the Baroque failed (7).

Instead, Faistauer's Austria produces art overlayered with many traditions of representation. Earlier in its history, Austria had been influenced by the south (implying the Baroque from Italy); then by the Germans, from the west. Yet those influences are largely in the past, except for impetuses from the north that are still influential in sculpture (he mentions Hanak). In contrast, Klimt's "decorative" art is "oriental," from the east. Aside from that, artists from the Alps (*aus älplerischer Abstammung*) have since assimilated experiences from the "Welsch" (the "French," but his example is a Swiss painter: "irgendwo ist es auch welsch begeistert, wie bei Hödler" [7]).

Despite what today's ears will experience as clear nationalist overtones, Faistaurer is not rejecting these "national" experiences as grounding art, just reducing their relevance by rejecting the kinds of emphasis on roots present in German historicism in favor of a model of cultural contact and transformation. In this aesthetic, art is seen in terms of a constellation of experience that is materially present, not as part of a national style of art originating in its "spirit," which is an abstraction, a scholarly fiction. Thus in his estimation, Rudolf von Alt (remembered today for his cityscapes from Old Vienna) was critical in establishing the Secession as an urban art movement, a critical move in Austrian arts. In contrast, the Secession movement of the turn of the century created a kind of experiential sectarianism by insisting it represented the spirit of the new age, which ultimately created a "dangerous vacuum" in its takeover of the Viennese art scene (*ein gefährliches Vakuum* [8]).

This is a distinct rejection of *elitist* art (not of skilled fine art, based on elite skills). When such sectarianism is present, he notes, fine art stagnates within what we today would call silos. The consequence for early twentieth-century Austria was that it was the applied arts that were transformative, as artists outside silos like Secessionism responded to newer influences from Russia, Slovakia, the Balkans, and Moravia. The fine arts had become divided in their ability to express experiences of the era:

> Personal preoccupations and sectarianism won the upper hand, until finally the applied arts, it seems, won the day. That result was facilitated by the moral constitution of the city and the material constitution of the state, the mercantile spirit itself. No artist arose who might have been capable of calculating the sum that was "Austria," summarizing its riches into something that would have been fruitful. The hope for a summation of Austrian human value would arise again only later.
>
> (8)

Unfortunately, Faistauer continues, such innovations happened mainly in German painting—today, we assume he is referring to the work of groups like the Wiener Werkstätte. In Vienna, fir exanokem Impressionism, as a school of painting, did not break through from its antecedents:

> In Berlin, the Secession had created space around Liebermann, in Munich, it had acclimated itself to the earth that supported a "Munich style." In Vienna, however, Impressionism did not have the power to break through to the point where it would have been a school with names that could have borne art forward.
>
> (8)

Instead, the visual arts of Vienna veered toward the decorative and ornamental, not infrequently in affiliation with architects—Olbrich, Wagner, Hoffmann, Loos—where it competed and was still competitive with the Germans. Within the silo of the traditional fine arts, Faistauer judges that the painter Klimt was the only force in Vienna who might have pushed through into a new set of confrontations with contemporary experience, because Kolo Moser (known today mostly as a designer) and Alfred Roller (remembered for his theater scene designs) would ultimately be counted among proponents of the decorative arts—they were pigeonholed in art history.

Such assertions start Faistauer's essay on a trek through different painters he deemed significant in the era, starting with Klimt. In his accounts, he looks for art that affected the public vision in significant ways. Here again, he starts by following traditional Weimar German aesthetics in assuming that art is revelatory, but he looks for that revelation in eliciting public discussion, not in the structure of the works themselves. Thus Klimt, he notes, had started with a school around him, but he found few artistic interlocutors among them: the members of that "school" were weaker and fell away (11), and so he developed his art in the realm of ornament and worked with architects. Klimt's new discussions, moreover, were not based on Austrian traditions, which also made them difficult to root within Austrian public discussions. Faistauer describes Klimt as first having been influenced by Belgian artists, especially the neo-impressionist Théo van Rysselberghe, who is remembered as an Orientalist and a co-founder of *Les XX*, a group which included Ensor, Pissarro, Claude Monet, Seurat, Gauguin, Cézanne, and Vincent van Gogh. Nonetheless, in what he ultimately produced, Klimt remains an "outsider among Europeans" (*unter den Europäern ein Außenseiter* [11]) who does not fit anywhere on the traditional European art map or its map of experience: "His whole spiritual constitution is an oriental one. Eros plays a dominant role, his taste in women is an almost Turkish one. His whole nature is inspired playfulness" (11). Faistauer also identifies a "Belgian" or Neoimpressionist vein in Klimt's work that found expression in his early landscapes (soon given up)—in their *Schule*, their predisposition in strategies of representation. In his subsequent work, Faistaurer continues, Klimt largely avoided engaging with dimension or space (*Raum*) and so does not paint in reference to western concepts of spatiality (*Kraft, Schwere, Tiefe* [120]). Thus, unlike his contemporaries, the body of work Klimt produced does not speak to western art (France or Germany), and he simply missed the Italian influences after 1500 on which those art projects were founded.

Extending this point of view, Faistauer calls Klimt "oriental," a figure from "Vienna, Budapest, or Constantinople" who did not speak to the contemporaneous European audience experience, but rather to a very specialized artistic project that was formidable and interesting to small groups, but not necessarily engaging for his era's broader public, given that his reference points were the late Cézanne and Moorish Spain. Klimt's art thus remained somehow related to the applied arts, but in a way alien to his own audiences: "His pictures are like decorative tapestries intended to hang on the walls, like Gobelins."[52] His approach to seeing the world was neither naturalistic nor liable to engage the contemporary: "Today's *Weltgeist* was alien to him. He saw the world as a primitive one, flat" (13). In consequence, he was drawn to architecture, which provided objectivity, where he achieved wonders with Moser and Hoffmann, and created works that brought Paris to Vienna.

According to Faistauer, Klimt had only one disciple in painting: the early Egon Schiele, for whom he, as a mentor, opened doors in difficult times, as he had done for Kokoschka. In this way, Klimt did enable a new generation of art to emerge, while not himself leading that art into the new age. In Faistauer's estimation, then, Klimt himself was more or less a dead end in the evolution of Austrian art, despite his great gifts and sensibilities: a unicorn in the Viennese setting who combined influences that no other painter had in Vienna, creating experiences that no one else had, yet which did not speak to a broader audience as transformative. Nonetheless, he was unmatched in facilitating the emergence of a new art community:

> I have never seen nor felt such warm sincerity, a friendlier will and understanding, than in the circle that Klimt headed with his expansive goodness. Klimt had a great group of adherents with deeply grateful hearts, even if he remained without a successor in the arts.
>
> (14)

Faistauer explains that Klimt's influence was felt primarily in his collaborations, not in his innovative art practice that spoke to a relatively small public at its point of origin, in its own small community. Instead,

---

52 Bettina Naber ("Bilder aus einer Epoche der Erneuerung: Das Ernst Barlach Haus zeigt 54 Werke der Malerei aus der Zwischenkriegszeit") still agrees that Expressionism represented an "Epoch of Renewal," albeit situated in the 1930s rather than the early 1920s (probably because she is speaking to a Hamburg exhibition audience). She also points to the insecurity of post-First World War Austrian circumstances, but finds in them innovation: "Expressionismus, die Neue Sachlichkeit bis hin zum Konstruktivismus und auch kubistische Ansätze waren im Österreich der Zwischenkriegszeit anzutreffen. Es dominierte aber der gemäßigte Expressionismus, in Österreich auch Farbexpressionismus genannt. In vieler Munde war in den dreißiger Jahren eine 'neue Innerlichkeit' und damit der Versuch, eine neue Geistigkeit in der Kunst einzuführen; Ziel war es, mehr zu zeigen als das Sichtbare, die innere Wahrheit der Motive darzustellen" (n.p.). She then cites Kokoschka as a precursor to her era of renewal, but none of the other early experiments cited in the present discussion.

it was Egon Schiele who initiated the innovations in Austrian art. He was the link figure to the innovations of the Wassermann (here unmentioned), even though he had died in 1919 of the Spanish flu, together with his wife and unborn child. Schiele had learned from Klimt, but then managed to break free from his influence to find his own project: a new perception of space and mass that became Schiele's own distinctive project, apart from Klimt's.

Faistauer's Klimt had painted for a specific public, as the "painter of high finance" ("Maler der Hochfinanz") who "drew the light, shallowly exuberant monied Jews from the inner city, and he became their painter" ("Klimt zog das leichte, seicht ausgelassene Geldjudentum der Inneren Stadt an und er wurde sein Maler" [18])—an uncomfortable phrase, seen historically, but one that pointed to Vienna's reputation as a city of patronage in the arts, rather than innovation. Faistauer's Schiele, in contrast, was the painter of the proletariat, breaking free from painting models in the studio culture and from the villa suburbs, taking his palette from proletarian life. Both painters, then, had avoided the normal bourgeois audience, but Schiele did so differently than Klimt, inaugurating a style that spoke to the problems of the day: "unbürgerlich, exzentrisch, pervers" (18). Faistauer compares Klimt's and Schiele's drawings, noting how Klimt draws lines close to the body, and how Schiele who breaks through to a new sense of how bodies exist in space, a new corporeality: "a quite unbelievable depth of representation. The problem of form and space [...] won an extraordinary breadth in his work and seemed to be the opening of truly great creative days of creation" (16).

This description of artistic representation helps to explain what Faistauer expands on in his subsequent chapter on the *Zeitgeist*: it emphasizes how forms of representation speak of, out of, and to particularly moments of experience, configured by society and history, that may recur. For instance, the near-revolutionary moment of 1830 France facilitated the emergence of Impressionism, because a shift in real political circumstances required a shift in the discussions that art needed to engage—a new consciousness brought about by "political or social foment" (*politische oder soziale Gärung*).

Such moments bring artists to seek and respond to influences from other countries, in Faistauer's Austria, from countries in the east (25). These included cubism and futurism, which he notes are not western in origin: his Matisse is Hungarian, and his French Impressionism is actually Slavic. The result was a completely unanticipated new form of art in Austria after the social revolutions brought by the Great War:

> Pre-war cubism may have been a weak embarrassment, futurism a fantastic wrong turn, expressionism is an act of desperation of destructive element, born out of a wrong turn and into confusion.

> [...] The genius of humanity stood benumbed, mute, and blinded from the trials and fog of [the war's' fearful machines]. The freedom of the world appeared to be annihilated, oppressed by hunger, death and offensive. There was no path that pointed ahead into the year 1913.
>
> (27)

At this point, Faistauer describes the experiential configuration of this new art, Expressionism, a turn toward inwardness, virtually a religious conversion, a "flight into the transcendental" ("Flucht in das Transzendentale") that had been ignored by the materialism of Impressionism:

> It may have been a natural reaction to realism and the impressionist painting of the last decade, this craving for inwardness, for a new expression.
>
> (31)

Impressionism had, in other words, lost its relevance to the era's spirit of creation, its *ingenium*. It had expanded the *material* of painting (31) and brought a new kind of technical proficiency, but using strategies that no longer were able to represent real experience to contemporary audiences.[53]

Faistauer finds that such transformations have recurred through history. For instance, the Gothic era stressed *namelessness* (*Namenslosigkeit* [33]) as its characteristic practice, producing an art of spirituality that pointed beyond the individual. In Expressionism, the artists turned to represent a brutality that existed to encompass everything, again reaching beyond individuals (he even calls Emil Nolde a *Neugotiker*, a "Neogoth"). This spiritual turn created its new form using influences inherited from North German art, which seems to include the history-painting so favored by Prussia:

> North Germans lack the playful ways of the applied arts, as is present among the Viennese. They are substantially more intellectual, more spiritual. They fill their surfaces in more expansive ways, but more barbarian ones. They are decorators in large format. That they are drawn to monumental painting is a specific German form of vanity, already present in prior decades. This was also the format adopted by the Expressionists.
>
> (33)

---

53 "Kunst ist Weltaneignung, ist da, die Schöpfung zu erfassen, sie der Menschheit zu schenken. Ein Ding derart zu ergreifen oder einen Afpel in seiner Wesenheit klar ins Bewußtsein des Beschauers zu bringen, ist Aufgabe genug" (53).

Faistauer also locates in Rodin echoes of Expressionism's brutal snapshots of random impressions from the era's chaos—attempts to render chaos into linear forms. True Expressionist work of the day, like Nolde's, also reflected other influences: Kandinsky's geometries (22), or even Cubism (a "run-down form of academy painting"/"ein ganz verstiegener Akademismus" [36] that stole styles from everyone, including indigenous artist of the colonies). These movements broke the spiritual logjam of representation and prepared the audience for understanding Munch, van Gogh, and Kokoschka (Faistauer's chapter "Beim Publikum" calls them "Durchpeitscher"/"whippers-in" or metaphorical steamrollers [36]).

These are the stimuli (new experiences) and the ground (strategies of representation that the audience has learned to understand) for the new art of the postwar era. Yet there is still the question of how these compulsions turn into art, which Faistauer addresses in a chapter called "Kunstwerden, Kunstwille" ("becoming art, the will to art"). Here, he describes how art by definition evolves expressions and representation strategies in response to world circumstances.

As Faistauer explains it, most pictures come out of tradition and "school discipline," the training considered appropriate to producing art (*Schuldisziplin*: "liebevoller Pflege der Tradition und wirkt in einer weiten Idee" [41]). Every age also has its own dominant ideas (e.g., truth, freedom, and others), and a will to express then. Each individual artwork "battles for its life" ("Ringen um das Leben des Werkes" [39]), recording how an individual artist grappled with a problem needing representation. How that problem is solved reflects its era's particular *Kunstwille* in a particular place: "Art served as a mirror, [as it] was an invitation and an aide" (41).

With this, Faistauer reaches the art of his contemporary scene: not a continuation of pre-war Expressionism, but an art that charts new ways of seeing, like the work of van Gogh, which has a specific rhythm in its strategy of creation (42). Van Gogh's work was not a product of personal vanity or calculation, but rather of how he had given himself over to "the world of things"—specifically to nature— and became the "instrument of the will to art" that his audiences needed (his "extreme submission to nature"/"äußerste Hingabe an die Natur" [42]):

> He gave himself over to things, and the world went through him, poured out of him, ran into his fingers, sprayed out of them, and collected itself into a picture. [... he was] an instrument of the will to art.
>
> (43)

No wonder, then, that van Gogh eschewed academy style and refused to specialize in any one genre. He represented new ways of seeing how the world was experienced.

In a chapter entitled "Tempo," Faistauer then turns toward the primary context in which people confront art: exhibitions in the metropolis. Such exhibitions, he claims, actually deform the life of art in the community rather than raising taste and perceptions. Too many works painted for exhibitions (like Expressionist art, he claims) try only to call attention to themselves in shameless ways ("Prahlhänsereien des Gehirns oder Schamlosigkeiten" [47]), and so they do not answer to the era or engage the audience's experiences ("Den Bildern mangelt schon die Besinnung nur des nächsten Tages" [47]). Expressionist art, for instance, has fallen into this kind of chasing sensationalism (*Sensationsjagd* [48]), even at the cost of an inauthenticity to the act of creating representation. In a similar vein, abstract painting is no better than Expressionism: "a mad fabrication, if not pure fraud" ("eine grobe Irrlehre, wenn nicht reiner Betrug" [48]).

In contrast to artists of Expressionism, Faistauer posits that other contemporaneous artists have tried more directly to engage the era's fundamental experience: the Great War. Franz Wiegele, of local origin (a veteran, and member of the *Nötscherkreis* and the *Hagenbund* along with Kolig), would do various views of objects to understand them as objects and recapture them to re-present them to his audiences.[54] An admirer of Manet, Cézanne, Veronese, Delacroix, and Ingres (56), he was grappling with the materiality of objects and bodies (as did Kokoschka), but less with a psychologized or pathologized representation of that (56). Similarly, Anton Kolig filled the era's need to represent feelings ("in Kolig 'ist' eine Gefühlsleitung lebendig" [63]). Following on early French Impressionism, Kolig problematized the interaction of subject and object, yet without devolving into "feeble objectivity"/"flauer Objecktivismus" (66) as it had in German Impressionism.

Faistauer's most important third example occupies its own chapter: Oskar Kokoschka, whom he considers the most prominent of his day's German-speaking painters because he was able to unsettle individual

---

54 "Er stellt uns das Monstrum Mensch auf den Tisch, löst das Geheimnis aus dem Winkel, schlägt in die Gefängnismauer, ins Irrenhaus ein kleines Fenster, zieht von einem Sterbenden die Hülle. Lauter Wirklichkeiten, nicht einmal übertrieben" (75).

viewers' points of view, their gaze or *Blick*, by forcing them to look and see in new ways that helped them to engage *their* worlds of experience:

> In Kokoschka's work there lies a demonic power, that dangerous, uncanny power that grabs without exception, that is also able to fascinate humanity. As a result, our society is in the process of learning proper terror. In Kokoschka they find the ghost, the inexplicable, that grabs them by the heart, that lingers a while between the eyes, that puts pressure on the mind.
> (71)

Kokoschka becomes the Dostoyevsky of painters, with a mixture of farmer and city instincts in the power of his direct observations. His work does not suffer weaknesses in materials or focus, but instead clearly targets the experiences to be represented. Kokoschka is "grandiose" (74) because he can portray humans in their multiples states of being, both good and bad, "the human monster."[55] Alfred Kubin falls into this category, as well, with his grotesques and "inner obseration" (*inneres Schauen*), as does Edvard Munch, one of the "most visionary painters" who can shape uncanny experiences into "physiognomies" (75).

Here, Faistauer finishes his *Painting* book, consciously avoiding more recent artists who can be too calculated or intellectual, and thus more idea than materiality. More critically, the current generation has forgotten that art is supposed to serve humanity, not only aesthetic principles. He is not optimistic:

> The inartistic, that wit without feeling, has attacked Central Europe on a broad Front and is eating out the heart of art, hollowing it out so that it must necessarily collapse, if there is not soon a turning, if artists don't pay attention to creation, to the world.
> (86)

Such judgments again reinforce Faistauer's reputation as an ill-tempered critic whose moment had passed. Yet there is a broader script at play here: his wife had died just before the first Wassermann exhibit, after which he supposedly reverted to old fashioned styles of art, standard accounts continue, moving to religious art in frescos, first in the little Church at Morzg (supposedly for food), and then as the 1926 murals

---

55 The catalog *Faistauer, Schiele, Harta & Co.* has an extensive timeline of Faistauer's life.

in Salzburg's Kleines Festspielhaus.[56] That mural style is often tagged as "Baroque," falling in line with Hermann Bahr's campaign of identifying Baroque art as native to Austria. But these assessments are the products of an art-history establishment that equates great art with personal style. Faistauer was looking rather for *relevant* art, an art that rendered palpable the issues of his age, not an art that solved problems of form or presented new ideas. His aesthetic favored art that formed conversations—not "academy" art, or other "fine arts," but an art that would help understand the world between the two world wars.

The Wassermann followed this notion in the ground plan of its exhibits; it even managed to open up its own small gallery after the 1921 graphic arts exhibit. But that was not to last. Harta left Salzburg after the Wassermann exhibits, and Faistauer left in the mid-1920s, to return to Vienna and his established connections.

Some Conclusions: Salzburg's *Age of Aquarius*

The Wassermann exhibits were conceived and executed in a very particular climate for art production and circulation: in a Salzburg that had "belonged" to Austria for less than seventy-five years and that had maintained a civic identity that included art for the people in all its forms. While the realities may have been much more class bound or otherwise limited than these theories, it is undeniable that art in many forms and people's access to it were part of civic planning in the region,

---

56 Art history seldom recognizes the role that Salzburg played in reconnecting pre- and post-First World War artists with their publics. Yet Western Austria had more than just Salzburg's tradition, which suggests the need for further tracking of many shorter- and longer-lived art institutions in the region. The Oberösterreichische Kunstverein had been founded in 1851 (with Adalbert Stifter as a co-founder), as second oldest in the region, behind Salzburg. A breakaway group from this group formed in 1913 in Linz under the name MAERZ. And in the 1920s, a number of small, local artists guilds formed, such as, in 1923, the Innviertler Künstlergilde in Braunau, one of many small associations that served the artists taking shelter in the area.

The Salzburg Wiki, in tandem with de.wikipedia.org, helps to draw a picture of how art networks grew, with noteworthy entries on the Hagenbund, the Neukunstgruppe, Sema (1911–1912 in Munich), the Sonderbund, and the Wassermann, as well as many of the details of Salzburg social and political life; see https://www.sn.at. Small museums and specialized sites also expand on the history of visual arts in *Stadt und Land Salzburg*; see for example the Anton Faistauer Forum (http://www.antonfaistauerforum.at/), the site of the Noetsch erkreis (https://noetscherkreis.at/), or the Zinkenbacher Malerkolonie that exists to this day (https://de.wikipedia.org/wiki/Zinkenbacher_Malerkolonie).

and that Der Wassermann allowed a certain group of artists a chance to exhibit and rethink their roles.

To be sure, the art exhibited in Der Wasserman's three exhibits was neither unknown nor unexhibited. Even the black-white organizing theme for the 1921 exhibit was also commonplace, at least since a 1912 exhibition of Der blaue Reiter. Any number of the artists involved were trained in Vienna, Munich, Berlin, or the other capitals of the Austro-Hungarian Empire and Europe. Yet the catalogs and particularly Faistauer's work on modern painting showed a commitment to an art that was not just for the elite purchaser.

In a real sense, their project was based on a redefinition of art debated heftily in Vienna and remembered today as central to the Vienna School of Art History. Alois Riegl has been mentioned above, as a modern founder of the discipline. Riegl shifted analyses of art away from questions of taste to questions of style (*Stilfragen*, the title of his 1894 work), a move introducing formalism to art analysis. This impetus was carried forward by Wilhelm Worringer and his most famous work, *Abstraction and Empathy* (*Abstraktion und Einfühlung*, 1907). Where Riegl defined art in terms of a historical *Kunstwollen* (a pattern of sensibility driving the art-making particular to a time and place), Worringer went further to define abstraction as central to his era's art, filling a psychological need, thereby legitimizing Expressionism's entry into the canon. On the other side of the debate stood Heinrich Wölfflin, who was noted for his 1888 text *Renaissance und Barock* and the subsequent 1915 *Kunstgeschichtliche Grundbegriffe*, which specified objective criteria for observing art and delineated the criteria that define historical art epochs.

Faistauer's work and the plans for the Wassermann exhibits, however, suggest a different reading of Riegl's later work, which focused on art as part of cultural history. Riegl's *Historische Grammatik der bildenden Künste*, unfinished at his 1905 death, worked more to tie art to cultural experience, as a record of the forms representing confrontations between humans and nature. Recall Faistauer's insistence on art arising within a group and giving form and expression to its experience, his *Kunstwillen*, the will to make art as a record of experience, not just the art works' inherent qualities, nor of any historical progression toward art that is somehow more advanced. Faistauer wants to move beyond Impressionism and Expressionism because they have become stale and reify past states of experience, pre-war and wartime. But the postwar era, he feels, needs different tools to represent the day's issues, and the artist must seek out forms of expression on the basis of their own experience plus the repertoire of references that are shared with the audience. Art again needs to function to raise experience to awareness and discussion—to a conversation that is more than the work itself—it has to reference more than inherited conventions of art (no matter *for* or *against*). If there is a formalism involved in understanding the work, it is not the formalism of the artifact and its style—whether, for example, it uses perspective or conventions for portraiture or handling the paint on the canvas. The formalism that Faistauer shares with the late Riegl is a formalism that is embodied in the experience and place of those intended to look at it, an understanding of culture embedded in its members—a concept of the group more familiar from the work of Wilhelm Dilthey.

The Wassermann exhibits thus embody a late resurgence of Salzburg's tradition of bringing new art to its publics in accessible ways, and to showing the relevance of art to contemporary life, not just to academy norms. They also deserve attention as documentation of the missing transitions between the First World War era art movements like Expressionism and the emergence of art that would become associated with the Nazi project, in a preference for art that would speak to common experience, rather than the art of abstraction which is the possession of the few. Yet the potential of this fleeting assemblage of voices also pointed in quite a different direction, far distant from the aesthetic ideals of the Romanticism and Weimar Classicism that provided Nazi artists with an ideology of cultural leadership that intended to renew society, by force if necessary.

Faistauer's essays confirm a commitment to an art of the present, not the future, and a fidelity to historical tradition as meaningful but never authoritative—a move that might profitably been seen as a parallel to Hofmannsthal's later attempts to reboot European drama forms for the new era. Salzburg's age of Aquarius offers thus a glimpse into an art community that wanted to both learn from and teach its audiences, to reaffirm the value of legible tradition without attributing normative authority to it, and to reclaim the power of the visual arts for communities. Too many voices were lost to war, the Spanish flu, poverty, and even opportunism for that promise to be fulfilled, but recovering it offers a new context for Austria's interwar arts communities (including literature and performing arts, not just visual arts). This age of Aquarius sought to move beyond elitist art and to model an elite art that contributed to the minds and hearts of the new art communities of the interwar period.[57]

---

57 ISBN: 978-3-900088-99-6 (279 pp). The book itself has no publisher data listed; it is available from the Salzburg Museum or Facultas Verlags- & Buchhandels AG (Stolberggasse 26, A-1050 Wien; www.facultas.at). See also https://www.salzburgmuseum.at/ausstellungen/rueckblick/ausstellungen-seit-2015/faistauer-schiele-harta-co-painting-connects-us/.

Bibliography

Exhibition Catalogs (listed chronologically)

Ausstellungs-Katalog des neuen Vereinigung bildender Künstler Salzburgs "Der Wassermann." Salzburg: R. Kiesel, 1919 (16 S., 12 Taf.)

Katalog der internationalen Schwarz-Weiss Ausstellung: veranstaltet von der Künstlervereinigung "Der Wassermann" in Salzburg im Verein mit Würthle & Sohn Nachf. (19. August bis 3. Oktober 1921 im Salzburger Künstlerhaus). Wien: "Verlag Neuer Graphik" der Rikola Verlag A.G, 1921 (edition of 700 copies).

125 Jahre Salzburger Kunstverein: Jubiläumsausstellung "Der Wassermann" (15.Juli–18. August 1969). Salzburg: Salzburger Kunstverein/Künstlerhaus, 1969.

150 Jahre Salzburger Kunstverein: Kunst und Öffentlichkeit. Salzburg: Salzburger Kunstverein, 1994.

Faistauer, Schiele, Harta & Co.: Malerei Verbindet—Das Belvedere zu Gast im Salzburg Museum (Kunsthalle der Neuen Rezidenz, July 12–October 1, 2019). Salzburg Museum: Ausstellungskatalog Bd. 51. Salzburg: Salzburg Museum, 2019.

Secondary Literature

Auer, Stephanie. "So denn. Kein Programm." In *Faistauer, Schiele, Harta & Co.* (exhibition catalog), 117–34.

Cordileone, Diana Reynolds. *Alois Riegl in Vienna 1875–1905: An Institutional Biography.* New York: Routledge, 2014.

Dohle, Oskar, and Thomas Mitterecker, eds. *Salzburg 1918–1919: Vom Kronland zum Bundesland.* Wien: Böhlau, 2018.

Faistauer, Anton. *Neue Malerei in Österreich: Betrachtungen eines Malers.* Zürich/Leipzig/Wien: Amalthea-Verlag, 1923 [actually, November 1922].

"Faustauer, Schiele, Harta – Biografien." In *Faistauer, Schiele, Harta & Co.* (exhibition catalog), 11–22.

Fraueneder, Hildegard. "Weiblichkeit und Kunst: 'Ein Kunstwerk ist solange gut, als man weiß, von wem es ist' – Künstlerinnen im Salzburger Kunstverein: 1868–1945." In Salzburger Kunstverein, ed., *150 Jahre Salzburger Kunstverein: Kunst und Öffentlichkeit*, 78–113. Salzburg: Salzburger Kunstverein, 1994.

Habsburg-Halbgebauer, Stefanie. "Aufbruch zu neuen Ufern: Umbruch von Tradition zur Moderne in der Kunst." In Oskar Dohle and Thomas Mitterecker, eds., *Salzburg 1918–1919: Vom Kronland zum Bundesland*, 425–40. Wien: Böhlau, 2018.

Höllbacher, Roman. "Das Künstlerhaus als Denkmal des Kunstvereins." In Salzburger Kunstverein, ed., *150 Jahre Salzburger Kunstverein: Kunst und Öffentlichkeit*, 47–77. Salzburg: Salzburger Kunstverein, 1994.

Jandl-Jörg, Eva. "Nachmittag Schieles bei uns […] – Im Umfeld von Faistauer, Schiele, Harta & Co." In *Faistauer, Schiele, Harta & Co.* (exhibition catalog), 25–60.

Jandl-Jörg, Eva. "'Der Wassermann': Ein europäisches Forum für die lebendige Kunst." In *Faistauer, Schiele, Harta & Co.* (exhibition catalog), 61–87.

Jesse, Kerstin. "'[…] schon wieder eine 'Gruppe' mehr […]' – Akademierevolution 1909: Gruppendynamik, Netzwerke und Künstlervereine rund um Egon Schiele." In *Faistauer, Schiele, Harta & Co.* (exhibition catalog), 89–116.

Juffinger, Roswitha. "Die Salzburger Residenz: Dokumentation zur Nutzung und Ausstattung 1918/1919." In Oskar Dohle and Thomas Mitterecker, eds., *Salzburg 1918–1919: Vom Kronland zum Bundesland*, 447–50. Wien: Böhlau, 2018.

Juffinger, Roswitha. "Schloß Klessheim: Zum Wendepunkt in der Geschichte des Schlosses nach dem Tod von Erzherzog Ludwig Viktor am 18. Jänner 1919." In Oskar Dohle and Thomas Mitterecker, eds., *Salzburg 1918–1919: Vom Kronland zum Bundesland*, 441–6. Wien: Böhlau, 2018.

Kaut, Josef. "Nach fünfzig Jahren: Wieder 'Wassermann'-Ausstellung." In Salzburger Kunstverein, ed., *125 Jahre Salzburger Kunstverein: Jubiläumsausstellung "Der Wassermann"* (15.Juli–18. August 1969), (n.p.—two pages). Salzburg: Salzburger Kunstverein/Künstlerhaus, 1969.

Mühlmann, Josef. "*Der Wassermann.*" *Die graphischen Künste*, Jg. XLIII, 1920, S. 83–93. Available online: https://doi.org/10.11588/diglit.4137#0099; https://digi.ub.uni-heidelberg.de/diglit/gk1920/0099 (accessed July 27, 2023).

Mühlmann, Josef. "Wassermannausstellung: Geistige Auffassung der Malerei." In *Salzburger Chronik für Stadt und Land*, Jg. 55, Nr. 192, August 24, 1919, S. 2–3. Available online: https://anno.onb.ac.at/cgi-content/anno?aid=sch (accessed July 27, 2023).

Naber, Bettina. "Bilder aus einer Epoche der Erneuerung: Das Ernst Barlach Haus zeigt 54 Werke der Malerei aus der Zwischenkriegszeit." *Hamburger Abendblatt*, May 5, 2007 (two pages). Available online: https://www.abendblatt.de/ratgeber/extra-journal/article108955707/Bilder-aus-einer-Epoche-der-Erneuerung.html (accessed July 27, 2023).

Pichler, Gustav. "Woher hat der 'Wassermann' seinen Namen?" In Salzburger Kunstverein, ed., *125 Jahre Salzburger Kunstverein: Jubiläumsausstellung "Der Wassermann"* (15. Juli-18. August 1969), n.p. (7?). Salzburg: Salzburger Kunstverein/Künstlerhaus, 1969.

Riegl, Alois. *Historische Grammatik der bildenden Künste*. Ed. Karl M. Swoboda and Otto Pächt. Köln/Graz: Böhlau, 1966.

Riegl, Alois. *Stilfragen: Grundlegungen zu einer Geschichte der Ornamentik*. Berlin: Georg Siemens, 1893.

Schaffer, Nikolaus. "Kurzer Höhenflug und langsames Stranden: Oppositionen innerhalb des Kunstvereins – 'Wassermann' und 'Sonderbund'." In Salzburger Kunstverein, ed., *150 Jahre Salzburger Kunstverein: Kunst und Öffentlichkeit*, 114–43. Salzburg: Salzburger Kunstverein, 2019.

Schaffer, Nikolaus. "Schiele und Faistauer, die 'ungleichen Brüder': Anton Faistauer und seine Sammler – Die 'reninghaus' Konkurrenz." In *Faistauer, Schiele, Harta & Co.* (exhibition catalog), 155–87.

Schaffer, Nikolaus. "Weltkrieg und Künstlerfehden Salzburger Kunst und Erster Weltkrieg — eine nüchterne Bilanz." *Mitt(h)eilungen der Gesellschaft für Salzburger Landeskunde*, 154–5 (2014/15), 541–69.

Smola, Franz. "Partnerinnen und Künstlerinnen im Umkreis von Anton Faistauer, Egon Schiele und Felix Albrecht Harta." In *Faistauer, Schiele, Harta & Co.* (exhibition catalog), 135–54.

Svoboda, Christa. "Zur Geschichte des Salzburger Kunstvereins." In Salzburger Kunstverei, ed., *150 Jahre Salzburger Kunstverein: Kunst und Öffentlichkeit*, 9–46. Salzburg: Salzburger Kunstverein, 1994.

Wilhelmi, Christoph. *Künstlergruppen in Deutschland, Österreich und der Schweiz seit 1900 – Ein Handbuch*. Stuttgart: Hauswedell, 1996

Wölfflin, Heinrich. *Kunstgeschichtliche Grundbegriffe: Das Problem der Stilentwicklung in der neueren Kunst*. München: Bruckmann, 1915.

Wölfflin, Heinrich. *Renaissance und Barock: Eine Untersuchung über Wesen und Entstehung des Barockstils in Italien*. München: Theodor Ackermann, 1888.

Worringer, Wilhelm. *Abstraktion und Einfühlung*. München: Piper, 1908.

Appendix

List of Artists

1919 Exhibition

Andersen Robin C. (Wien)
Caspar Karl (München)
Caspar-Filser Marie (München)
Eckert Robert (München)
Exner Hilde (Salzburg)
Faistauer Anton (Wien, Dzt. Zell am See)
Fischer Johannes V. (Wien)
Funke Rigobert (Salzburg)
Gütersloh Paris (Wien)
Haack Traute (München)
Harta Felix Albrecht (Salzburg)
Kars Georg (Prag)
Kolig Anton (Wien)
Koller Broncia (Wien)
Koro-Otei-Lipka Wilh. (Wien)
Krakauer L. (Wien)
Kubin Alfred (Wernstein, O-Ö)
Masareel Frans (Zürich)
Mayer Elfriede (Salzburg)
Peschka Anton (Wien)
Reichel Karl Anton (Kirchdorf, O-Ö)
Reiner Fritz (München)
Schiele Egon (Wien)
Schlangenhausen Emma (Morzg)
Scholein Julius Wolfgang (München)
Schroder Heinrich (München)
Spannring Louise (Salzburg)
Trubel Otto (Wien)
Unold Max (München)
Vonwiller Oskar (Salzburg)
Wagner Dr. Ernst (Wien)
Wiegele Franz (Zürich)
Wimmer Paula (Dachau)
Zimpel Julius (Wien)

1921 Exhibition

Amerika
Donald Shaw
Mac Laughlan
Joseph Pennel
Sion L. Wenban

Deutschland
Ernst Barlach
René Béeh
Lovis Corinth
H. M. Davringhausen
Josef Eberz
August Gebhard
Willi Geiger
Robert Genin
Rudolf Grossmann
George Grosz
Erich Heckel
Bernhard Hoetger
Ludwig von Hofmann
Paul Klee
Max Klinger
Käthe Kollwitz
Wilhelm Lehmbruck
Max Liebermann
Max Mayrshofer
Hans Meid
Adolph von Menzel
Walter Ophey
Max Oppenheimer
Paul Paeschke
Max Pechstein
Edwin Scharff
Adolf Schinnerer
Georg Schrimpf
Richard Seewald
Max Slevogt
Karl Stauffer-Bern
O. Th. W. Stein
Hans Thoma

Max Unold
Karl Walser

England
Alfred Bentley
Muirhead Bone
Frank Brangwyn
David Yeames Cameron
E. W. Charlton
Alfred East
Hedley Fitton
Seymour Haden
Oliver Hall
Charles Holroyd
Albany F. Howarth
Frank Laing
Sidney Lee
Ernest Lumbsdon
William Strang
Francis Sidney Unwin
Henry Winslow

Frankreich
Eugène Béjot
Auguste Besnard
George Braque
A. Brouet
Eugène Carrière <Nach>
Edgar Chahine
Cham <Amédée De Noé>
Puvis de Chavanne
Honoré Daumier
Eugène Delacroix
Henri Fantin-Latour
Jean Louis Forain
Paul Gavarni
Theod. Géricault
Norbert Goeneutte
Marie Laurencin
Charles Léandre
Louis Legrand
Alphonse Legros
Auguste Lepère
Maximilien Luce
Edouard Manet
Le Meilleur
Charles Méryon
Pablo Picasso
Camille Pissaro
Jean Francois Raffaëlli
Auguste Renoir
Henri Le Riche
Auguste Rodin
Paul Signac
Alex. Theoph. Steinlen
Henri Toulouse-Lautrec
Louis Valtat

Italien
Giovanni Segantini

Niederlande
Kees van Dongen
Ludwig Ten Hompel
Jozef Israels
Frans Masereel
Félicien Rops
Vlaminck
Otto van Wätjen
Willem Witsen

Nordische Staaten
Carl Larsson
Edvard Munch
Anders Zorn

Oesterreich
Georg Ehrlich
Anton Faistauer
Felix Albrecht Harta
Ludwig Heinrich Jungnickel
Gustav Klimt
Oskar Kokoschka
Alfred Kubin
Erwin Lang
Oskar Laske
Willi Nowak
Jan Oeltjeni
Emil Orlik
Alphons Purtscher
Karl Rossing
Egon Schiele
Emma Schlangenhausen
Franz Schrempf
Lilly Steiner
Jan Stursa
Viktor Tischler
Ernst Wagner
Robert Wittek
Julius Zimpel

Ostasien
Chinesischer Künstler
Hiroshige
Japanische Künstler
Kunimune
Kunisada
Morikuni
Shunsho
Sukenobu
Suketada
Toyokuni I
Toyokuni Ii
Utamaro
Yeizan

Schweiz
Cuno Amiet
Felix Vallotton
Albert Welti

Plastik
Franz Barwig
Alexander Jaray
Jan Stursa

Four Notes on Salzburg and Cinema 1911–1938

Robert Dassanowsky

The city of Salzburg, in the province of the same name, made its post-imperial cultural debut as the proposed site of a high art drama, literature, and music festival. The proposed event was soon dubbed the Salzburger Festspiele (Salzburg Festival), although, as it was announced, it consisted of nothing more than solid commitments for its space among the baroque edifices and the monumental steps leading into the Salzburg Cathedral. Nonetheless, its founders had hoped this might become a national and then international pilgrimage site for art and culture in a unique environment, which would help to turn the city and the nation away from the catastrophes Austria had suffered since the end of the war.

Setting such a festival in Salzburg could show the world that Salzburg represented the survival of aspects of national culture beyond Vienna. In the new Austrian Republic, there were certainly larger and more developed secondary cities outside Vienna, with better articulated infrastructures and designed for business and economic growth, yet in the new geometry of national planning, Salzburg would need to be another cultural hub of Austria and bring attention to the western provincial part of the newly reduced state. It would stimulate national and international interest and recall Austria's larger pre-war artistic reputation.

Reconnecting Austria with Europe and the world through Salzburg would also revive the idea of Austria continuing the legacies of former imperial territories, linked to the former crownlands and their polyglot Central European culture. Despite its reduction into a small republic, this almost mystical concept of a shared intellectual mission of high culture by and beyond Vienna would move beyond Vienna's visibility as a rebuilt central hub of the fractured *Mitteleuropa*. The possibility of a world-class festival in Salzburg made the new nation a *Kulturstaat* (cultural state) that transcended the geographical outlines of the new state and the political tensions of the region, still connected with its old crownlands, now sovereign nations.

This was no doubt about the goal of those who dreamed and encouraged the re-creation of this Salzburg in a festival in "the Heart of Europe" in 1920. Through the festival, Hugo von Hofmannsthal, Max Reinhardt, Richard Strauss, Alfred Roller, and Franz Schalk wanted to bring Austria back into Europe's cultural center again, out of a geographical location more central to that Europe than Vienna. In creating the Salzburger Festspiele, they managed to tie European culture to the rising of a phoenix in Austria: a festival open to the world that would celebrate Salzburg and its music. Just as importantly, this attempt to realign postimperial Austria would allow it to recover from its great geopolitical losses, at least in its imagination, and Salzburg's cultural landmark success would ideally also displace the elitist German pilgrimage to Bayreuth and the spells of Wagner. By the 1930s, the Festival had indeed become a well-defined and internationally valued cultural counterpoint to the racist and political "Blood and Soil" art spectacles of Nazi Germany.

Nevertheless, the First Republic gave way to the new Austrian clerico-authoritarian regime in 1933, which ultimately offered its own nationalist demonstrations poised against Nazism, Marxism, and capitalism following a brief but bloody Civil War beginning in 1934. The result was that the Festival became much the spectacle of a large outdoor public Catholic mass. No matter, the Salzburger Festspiele remained definitive in their mission as a model for the growth of sophisticated cosmopolitan musical and dramatic art that opened a new chapter for Europe's traditions of high art.

The early years of the Festspiele were also defining moments for cinema in Austria. And Salzburg, not surprisingly, not only moved towards being Austria's second cultural city in the interwar years, but also would seize an opportunity to be Austria's second film capital, grown out of the interdisciplinary artistic base of the city and its proximity to Munich, as will be traced in the present essay.

This proposition was no pipedream. Whatever political hostilities remained between Vienna, Budapest, and Prague after the First World War (including fears of revanchist plots, the possible return of the Habsburgs, and the growing influence of Mussolini's Rome since the 1920s), these film capitals still functioned more or less transnationally, as they had before the war. Moreover, the golden triangle, as it was known, that mapped the locations of the major film studios of Vienna, Prague, and Budapest became its own replacement "empire" in cinema. At the start of the era, that filmmaking empire was poised to invest and work with the studios of Berlin ... but then, beginning in 1933, it tried, ultimately unsuccessfully, to set itself against German production under Nazi control, which was espousing antisemitism and virulent racism at odds with Austria's tradition of a more cosmopolitan film culture. And although Austria was successfully willing to co-produce with Rome, the Rome-Berlin Pact of 1936 dissolved whatever protective ideals Mussolini had had for sheltering Austria—and northern Italy—from a possible German invasion.

Salzburg's film studio production thus always remained sparse, although the use of Salzburg itself for "on location" Austrian, German, and other international productions that featured the city or the province was popular and became even more so in the decades following the Second World War. Overall, the use of the Festspiele and Salzburg's culture as a venue to relaunch a prestige cinema alongside other forms of high culture had not blossomed, although it remained an encouraging, even necessary, possibility for incubating a new generation of films.

That hope for a new Austrian cinema came to naught, just as had the unfulfilled promise of the salvation of a Hollywood-Vienna co-production pact in 1936/37 that would have freed Austria's filmmakers from Nazi German political and economic manipulations and racist demands to control the sovereign state.

Figure 4.1 The famous theater director Prof. Max Reinhardt (*right*) signing his first US sound-film contract, together with the German-American film producer, director, and press representative Curt (Curtis) Melnitz. Photo by Georg Pahl (May 1930).

Figure 4.2 Max Reinhardt, actor and director, with Lady Diana Manners (actress, later Lady Diana Cooper) in the Park of Schloss Leopoldskon, Salzburg, 1905. Photo by ullstein bild Dtl.via Getty Images.

First Perceptions: Incubating Film in Salzburg

The plans for Salzburg's future in film productions were in fact never fabulations, but rather based on solid historical assessments. First and foremost, the city had contributed significantly to the earliest pre-technology of film.

For example, the first stroboscopic disk, an early technology for making pictures move, is called the Stampfer disk after its inventor, the Salzburg-born Simon Stampfer (1792–1864), who later co-founded the Technical University in Vienna. The disk was the first device to show "simply drawn moving images [...] the basis for the development of the film camera and projector."[1] The system was advanced by Stampfer's pupil, physicist Christian Doppler (1792–1864).

August Arnold (1898–1983), from Werfen in Pongau, co-founded the ARRI company in 1917 in Salzburg, which eventually became one

---

1 Strasser, *Location Salzburg*, 12.

of the two largest producers of motion picture equipment worldwide. Arnold is credited with creating the first reflex motion picture camera and is today considered a pioneer in film technology. His Arriflex 35 camera from 1937 remained the most popular camera in international film production for several decades. He was ultimately awarded twelve technical Oscars for his technical achievements in cinema.

Rudolf Oppelt (1893–1971) was born in Vienna but lived and worked primarily in Salzburg. As a technician, scriptwriter, and director, he was one of the recognized silent-film pioneers in both cities. In addition to his artistic work as writer and director, and his inventions in the field of lighting design, Oppelt directed Salzburg's own film studio and production firm, the Salzburger-Kunstfilm-Industrie A.G. (Salzburg-Art Film-Industry, Ltd.).

But while several studios emerged in larger and more commercial cities such as Graz, which already hosted Alpin-Film, Opern-Film and Miropa-Musikfilm, among other early production companies, and Innsbruck, with its Tiroler-*Heimatfilm* (between 1919 and 1921), Salzburg's sudden cinematic birth originally seemed an unexpected one, from today's point of view.

Following the birth of film internationally in 1895, Vienna had begun its industry at early production houses and screenings by traveling cinemas across the empire between 1908 and 1910. Yet Salzburg began its own minor productions in 1909 and was subsequently registered as a representative of the early postimperial Bundesländer-Filmfirmen, an entity that tracked and reorganized the status of the former empire's provincial studios. Neither a developed commercial urban site, nor a city with a significant active artistic presence, Salzburg was often unfairly dismissed in such reorganizations as an unimportant border city, overshadowed by Munich. That situation, however, was primed to change, stimulated by the potential of the city's historical and aesthetic qualities, and most of all, by the promise of a permanent music festival which would showcase talent in an "expansion" of the new Austria beyond Vienna.

The earliest surviving film from the Salzburg region is the 95-meter-long *Zell am See/Zell on the Sea* (Austria-Hungary 1911), a successful culture short by Vienna-based film pioneers Louise and Anton Kolm, cameraman Jakob Fleck, and their new Wiener-Kunstfilm company. The film functioned as a powerful source of escapism for urban viewers, featuring a steamboat ride across Lake Zell and a glance into the picturesque town of Zell in the Salzburg Salzkammergut lake region. Salzburg had also appeared in other short films that marked the start of the film industry in Austria, yielding images that placed it firmly in the public mind, along with Vienna, Melk, Zagreb, Trieste, and other historically or culturally important venues of the empire, and as part of an emerging wave of tourism from Austro-Hungarians and other film audiences. Yet these early offerings were only followed up on after the end of the Great War.

Nonetheless, even during the war, Salzburg prepared itself to assume a new role in the postwar film industry. Salzburg's own film studio was opened in 1917, built on the Maxglan estate of Heinrich Kiener, owner of Austria's Stiegl Brewery, and would briefly be touted as "Das größte und modernste Studio Deutschösterreichs,"[2] until an even more cutting-edge studio was built in Vienna in 1923 by Louise Kolm and Jakob Fleck. Along with rival Sascha Kolowrat, they were the most productive Austrian silent feature film and documentary filmmakers during the war. The Vienna studio was first utilized by Vita-Film, and then expanded as the Tobis-Sascha sound film complex until 1938.

Kiener's Maxglan-Salzburg studio boasted spaces for two hundred artisans and its film editing and production laboratory was partially adapted from a large farm building belonging to the Stiegl brewery. It had initially suffered from the problem widely shared by the postimperial Austrian state: how to rebrand itself as a cultural center for a "German Austria" (as opposed to the other former multi-ethnic and polyglot "Austrian" territories of the Habsburg Empire), when that name was forbidden by treaty so as to forestall any hint of a possible annexation of the new Austrian Republic to the newly truncated Germany called the Weimar Republic.

What worked on the side of this new film production facility was the fact that the studio's financial footing was solidly integrated with the new Salzburg arts culture. The company board was represented by leading business figures from Salzburg, many of whom were involved with the original Festival concept, as well, such as Dr. Friedrich Gehmacher, an insurance company director who supported the Mozarteum Music Academy and the construction of the Festival Theater (Festspielhaus) on the premises of the former court riding stables. He was supported by financiers from Vienna, such as the director of the Pax-Film company, Gustav Mayer, who invested the capital from his entire company in stocks in the new studio, in the amount of three million Krone in shares and 1.8 million in currency, and film producer Max Biehl who also invested the entire capital of his film atelier.

Still, it was the music and theatrical festival concepts offered by Austrian playwright and author Hugo von Hofmannsthal and the future Austro-Hollywood stage director/impresario Max Reinhardt that solidified the concept of Salzburg as another possible "tentpole" for world-class Austrian culture, originating beyond Vienna and the

---

2   *Salzburger Chronik*, November 7, 1921, 4.

new republic's political establishments—a promise that arguably had already taken form in the Kiener Studio as well as in the planning for the Festspiele.

As a very visible author, Hofmannsthal was central to directing the interest of the music world away from the former eastern realms of the lost empire, now the capitals of new Central European republics, and towards the topography of provincial Austria, now to be given a new value as a rebranded national consciousness that highlighted the western Alpine region of Salzburg and its environs. On August 22, 1920, that new cultural era indeed began with the performance of Hofmannsthal's famous moralist drama, *Jedermann* (Everyman), directed by Max Reinhardt in the permanent makeshift "theater" of the monumental space in front of Salzburg Cathedral. The Festival's publicity, which had capitalized on renewed interest in Mozart and the baroque in the latter half of the nineteenth century, helped to eventually shine the spotlight on the city's architectural environment and natural beauty, as well as its growing concert presentations, which had also been represented in even the earliest examples of early cinema in Salzburg.

After the publicity for that new kind of *Gesamtkunstwerk* event in a "new" but old cultural center, the moment was ripe for the Kiener film complex to emerge onto this now popular arts landscape. The first film in the new Salzburg's art of motion pictures actually came from the Vienna company founded by film pioneer, producer/director Louise Kolm, her husband, Anton Kolm, and their cameraman Jakob Fleck, under the banner of the Österreichische-Ungarische Kinoindustrie GmbH (Austrian-Hungarian Film Company), which had produced short culture films and the first Austrian feature films before the war (along with their rival the wealthy industrialist, Sascha Kolowrat-Krakowsky and his Sacha-Film Company). Culture films (including mountain and landscape films) had become popular in the last days of the monarchy. By 1912, culture film with Salzburg as a setting and a theme had arrived in Vienna and across the screens of the early cinemas and traveling tent theaters: *Schuhplattler zu Aufführung/ Schuhplattler in Performance* (Austria-Hungary 1912), circulated along with the now lost short documentary *Im Auto durch die Österreichischen Alpen*, made by Kolowrat's Sascha studio.

Yet it was the Festspiele themselves that made the case that the once provincial towns now carried much of the active weight of culture, art, and the limitations of and relationships to the new postimperial Austria geography—a burden that the Salzburg film studios were ready to assume. The "official" birth of the entertainment film industry in Salzburg thus fell after the war, alongside the Festspiel planning, in 1919, after the empire had ceased to exist, and when the provinces and cities that remained part of the new Republic were reassessed as valuable to not only industry, economy, and geopolitics, but to the very definition of what this Austria represented or was represented by.

The pre-war culture films now had its successors, a distant eight years later and a world away from the vanished monarchy, with three advanced, plot-driven cinematic films set against Salzburg's alpine beauty. These first films produced in Salzburg as a postwar federal state of what was now briefly known as the German-Austrian Republic (Deutschösterreich) were created by independent Salzburg-based talent, which introduced itself to Vienna and other regionally established film venues with films featuring the Salzburg region.

Alpentragödie/Alpine Tragedy (Austria 1919) was shot in the town of Krimml and on the Grossvenediger Mountain within the Hohe Tauern range, on the border of the state of Tyrol with the state of Salzburg; and *Der weisse Tod/The White Death* (Austria 1919), shot on the mountain sides of the majestic Grossglockner, which had become Austria's highest mountain after the 1919 Treaty of Saint-Germain ceded South Tyrol and its Alpine range to Italy. The film already anticipates the narrative adventure genre known as the *Bergfilm* (mountain film) that emerged in Austria and particularly Germany in the 1920s and 1930s.

After that "official" birth, the Salzburg film establishment found its feet in 1921, the year after the initial performance of *Jedermann*, which became a particularly important year for film and its production in Salzburg in many ways. It was the year in which Salzburg Festival author and supporter Hofmannsthal wrote what is considered one of the first attempts at film theory. It was the year in which Salzburg celebrated the 165th birthday of its musical genius, Wolfgang Amadeus Mozart; and it was the year that a new film company by the name of Salzburger Kunstfilm-Industrie-A.G. was established at an office in Maxglan, a district in the city of Salzburg, 400 km in distance from Bavaria and the Münchner-Kunstfilm in the new federated German national state known as the Weimar Republic. That proximity of Maxglan to Bavaria became useful in the future of the Salzburg studio and also problematic, given the political influences moving across the Austrian-German frontier after 1933.

Max Neufeld, Richard Oswald, Otto Kreisler, Carl Lamac: The New Salzburg Film Industry

Although entertainment, documentary, war reportage, and propaganda films had been steadily produced before and during the war by Austro-Hungarian companies, along with polyglot films from the crownlands and provinces, the new Austrian state produced around seven hundred films between 1918 and 1930, mostly in Vienna. These included a few culture films and other short films that featured footage of Salzburg.

As noted, the first "industry" film studio in Salzburg had been created by the Stiegl Brewery; it was renamed the Salzburger Kunstfilm studio in 1917. It was, however, director Max Neufeld's 1919 feature-length film that showed the potential for a film industry outside Vienna: *Lasset die Kleinen zu mir kommen/Let the Little Children Come Unto Me* (Austria 1919, premiering in Vienna in February 1920), a religious melodrama about a village pastor and the love of his youth under the banner of Christ's blessing of the children. Neufeld was to become one of the most popular and significant Austrian directors of the interwar period, and aspects of his famous later work, *Singende Jugend* aka *Mit Musik durchs Leben/An Orphan Boy from Vienna* (Austria/Netherlands 1936) are already apparent in this film, which again also suggests the early *Bergfilm*, in its setting of the Grossglockner mountain and its focus on Salzburg's Zell im See and the Kaprunertal.

While the success of Neufeld's Salzburg setting and story resulted in two other important films: Emil Leyde's Bergfilm *Alpentragödie/Alpine Tragedy* (Austria 1920) shot near the Grossvenediger Alpine peak (on the border between Salzburg and East Tyrol) and Cornelius Hinter's *Der Weisse Tod/The White Death* (Austria 1921), shot in the Grossglockner region, and produced by and starring Carmen Cartellieri—another Austrian female silent film pioneer who ran her own production company and who already could be classified as having the career of an early cinema star.

Salzburg-based film companies also attempted to demonstrate the cultural and artistic contributions they could offer outside Vienna, which took shape as the Festival culture did. The new *Salzburger-Kunstfilm* company presented its first documentary film, *Die Festspiele 1921/The Festival 1921* (Austria 1921), featuring excerpts from the *Jedermann* production, and ballet performances in the Mirabell palace gardens. 1921 was also the year that *Helios-Film* produced a sprawling silent film attempting to re-enact Mozart's life: Otto Kreisler's *Mozarts Leben, Lieben und Leiden/Mozart's Life, Loves and Sorrows* aka *Ein Künstlerleben/ An Artist's Life* (Austria 1921). Long considered lost, it has more recently been partially restored from fragments discovered in Amsterdam by the Film Archive Vienna. Despite the incomplete state of the work, the power of the original filmmaking in its technical experimentation, narrative vision, and photography of the cinematic Salzburg castle, Mirabell Garden, and Hellbrunn city are all stunningly progressive. This five-act epic was also shot on location in Vienna, Munich, London, and Rome. Kreisler would continue to direct significant historical and biographical films, such as *Theodor Herzl* (Austria 1921) and *Ludwig II* (Austria 1922).

The following year, Salzburger-Kunstfilm emerged with its own contribution to regional film sophistication with the premiere of a full-length (1,800-meter, five-act) silent film production), *Die Tragödie des Carlo Pinetti/The Tragedy of Carlo Pinetti* (Austria 1924). The film's rumination on fate focuses on the character of Carlo, a talented and honest young singer, who is caught up in criminal activity initiated by his scheming wife and a corrupt American jeweler, both attempting to have Carlo committed to an asylum. He escapes their grasp in a dangerous chase over the roofs of Salzburg and wins back his freedom, while the plotters are subsequently killed in a mountain accident. The film reflects some of the Manichean struggle and the moralism of Hugo von Hofmansthal's *Jedermann* and might have fit well as one of the first films (following the Mozart biography) to screen at the nascent Festival. However, its thriller and entertainment qualities were successful with general audiences, and its Salzburg debut was followed by one in Vienna the following year.

It is worth noting that some of the directors working in silent film in Salzburg, were already displaying the aesthetics and themes that would make Austrian (Vienna) cinema unique a few years later in early sound film. There is no question that filmmakers responsible for popular and critical development of Austrian film nurtured in Vienna during the late silent era used Salzburg as a testing ground for the art in early and even progressive productions in Salzburg.

A parallel successful move by German filmmakers and the Munich film industry used the natural setting of Salzburg just across its border to film a romantic comedy written by Oscar Blumenthal and Gustav Kadelburg and adapted for the screen by Alfred Halm: *Im weissen Rössl/In the White Horse Inn* (Germany 1926), which would become an internationally known and adapted stage operetta and musical film. It began as a sprightly silent comic play about visitors to a Salzburg hotel, on which the very famous operetta film set on the Wolfgangsee (Lake Wolfgang) would later be based. The cinematic rebirth of this play into a film that then ultimately launched an operetta made it a success in Germany and Austria and as far as the stages of New York's Broadway, and then back to film into the 1950s and further stage adaptations that always were set at that self-same "White Horse Inn" on the beloved Wolfgangsee or in neighboring sites in the picturesque Salzkammergut lake region.

Among the first flood of 1930s sound films in the German-speaking film industries was a major UFA Berlin production of *Liebling der Götter/Darling of the Gods* (Germany 1930), a musical directed by Hanns Schwarz. It was created for the star actor Emil Jannings, who had just completed one of the gems of Weimar German cinema and his own career, *Der blaue Engel/The Blue Angel* (Germany 1930), based on the novel by Heinrich Mann, with Marlene Dietrich and Austrian/Hollywood director Josef von Sternberg. The somewhat satirical *Götter* film exploited the massive fame of Jannings, Austrian comedy star Hans Moser, leading lady Olga Tschechowa, and, above all, the Wolfgangsee location to create another audience-pleaser in which a famous opera singer's (Jannings) vocal ailment is healed by the air of the Wolfgangsee.

It was clear that the subgenre of Wolfgangsee films, related in parody or satire to the original play and operetta, were certainly successes that called for imitation: the on-location filming of these adaptations served to give the audiences an irresistible "cinematic holiday" in Salzburg at the Wolfgangsee, where the stresses of economic depression, runaway inflation, poverty, unemployment, political instability, and the continuing crisis of the Austrian nation's identity might be forgotten in operetta and stage comedy. The Wolfgangsee films solidified Salzburg as a unique film venue in Austria rather than simply as a site that utilized studios based on traditional production practices. It became clear, even prior to sound, that creating a film in Salzburg was costly, and that there was little reason to do so there if it were not specifically to exploit Salzburg (city and province), its historical connections or new cinematic legends—which by now included all sorts of adventures at the Wolfgangsee and the now world-famous fictional hotel.

Yet from the first, these Wolfgangsee films were implicated in both economics and politics. Blumenthal and Kadelburg's *Im weissen Rössl* gained its most impressive adaptation in 1930, as a *Singspiel* (a play with musical inserts, closer to the American musical than the traditional Viennese operetta) by a trio of postimperial (or "Silver Age") Viennese operetta composers, Robert Stolz, Ralph Benatzky, and Bruno Granichstaedten. It was followed by another film, *Hochzeit am Wolfgangsee/Wedding at Lake Wolfgang* (Germany 1933), directed by Hans Behrend in Berlin and at St. Wolfgang on the Wolfgangsee. This director attempted to frame the theme and music in a traditional *Heimatfilm* context and setting (shot in Berlin and at the Wolfgangsee) with provincial wisdom and lessons of virtue. Despite the German director's roster of historicist epics on Prussia and on classic German literature, however, the film was deemed unwelcome by the new National Socialist government due to the director's Jewish extraction. Behrend fled to Austria, which had become a corporatist and clerical authoritarian or Catholic political state in 1933. He continued to work there in the *Emigrantenfilm* (emigrant film) which produced films of various and classic genres that were forbidden to import to Nazi Germany but that had an international following and were of interest to Hollywood studios for its talent, remake interest, and possible co-production.

Remember, too, that after 1933, Austria essentially had two film industries—a mainstream one led by the major studios and their

"Aryan" talent which was allowed to export its films to Austria's most important trade partner, Germany; and the *Emigrantenfilm* which accepted anti-Nazi and Jewish talent from Austria and Germany. These productions were forbidden in Germany. The *Emigrantenfilm* roster of talent and progressive style of filmmaking interested Hollywood studios, leading to plans (made between 1936 and 1937) for a possible co-production pact which might have allowed the Austrian film industry to break with Nazi Germany's racist industry demands and economic manipulations and become a significant partner with Hollywood studios. That initiative failed due to German economic destabilization and diplomatic subversion.

Other versions of the *Im weissen Rössl* material followed, including a lavish operetta film co-produced by Austria's Ondra-Lamac-Film and Germany's Bavaria-Film (1935) and starring the Austrians Christl Mardayn and Hermann Thimig, alongside Germany's famed lanky comic actor, Theo Lingen. As a "mainstream" Austrian film in co-production with Germany, that production stood under the demand that Austrian talent follow Nazi racial laws even prior to the annexation in 1938. This thus became the only "aryanized" version of *Im weissen Rössl* produced for film. Nevertheless, the previous *Heimatfilm*-style Benatzky Singspiel/musical of 1930 was also immediately banned at the Nazi assumption of power in Germany in 1933 for its Jewish co-creators and the "degenerate" manner with which it purportedly dealt with folkloric artistic concepts—especially its jazzy score, which includes a satire on a Berlin tourist of questionable taste ("Was kann der Sigismund dafür, dass er so schön ist").

The replacement for such a popular work was not long in coming from the competing German film industry itself. That film employed the Reich's most popular and "system conforming" operetta composer, Fred Raymond, whose essential revision of the Benatzky musical, *Saison in Salzburg* (A Season in Salzburg) premiered in Kiel in December 1938. It removed the "degenerate" jazz elements, reversed the tourism satire of the Benatzky musical to encourage tourism, moved the focus of the narrative from Wolfgangsee to Salzburg city proper, and created its own very popular song, "Salzburger Nockerln" (Salzburg Dumplings), and with it, the operetta's new (and political) emphatic declaration: "Salzburg als die schönste Stadt Deutschlands" (Salzburg as the most beautiful city *in Germany*). This "celebration" of the annexation of Austria in March of that year as part of the operetta also insisted on increased Reich tourism to the new Ostmark.[3]

---

3   Schmidl, "*Saison in Salzburg* (1938): 'Die schönste Stadt Deutschlands' in Fred Raymonds Operetta."

Hofmannsthal, Salzburg, and Film

While such popular films enhanced Salzburg's brand for tourists, the city's more serious artistic side was also represented in its film industry. Austrian author, playwright, and Salzburg Festival conceptualist Hugo von Hofmannsthal had long sought a medium to reach beyond what he considered the flatness of dialogue on the stage and the lyric word on paper.[4] That search had led him first to opera, beginning with the libretto for Richard Strauss's *Elektra* in 1908. His scenario for the 1911 ballet pantomime *Amor und Psyche* and its companion piece *Das fremde Mädchen*, however, points toward far more than a wordless tableaux for the ballet, or an aesthetic that the author had desired in "eine Sprache, in welcher die stummen Dinge zuweilen zu mir sprechen."[5] With his libretto for Strauss's 1911 opera *Der Rosenkavalier*, Hofmannsthal stepped up his demands, hoping that words and music might fuse into a "Fluidium,"[6] which would open out the panorama of lost times and be held together by "die imaginäre Sprache der Zeit"—a presentation at once authentic and artificial, and representing character, social status, time, and place.[7] At the same time the author returned to the power of the word in this opera and with the drama *Jedermann* (1911), he also became aware of cinema as a medium which promised to fulfill his concept of a consciousness-altering art that would reach out to the masses in wordless, dreamlike quality. He urged that his pantomime ballets be filmed, and in 1913, *Das fremde Mädchen* flashed onto the screen with Viennese modern dance diva Grete Wiesenthal.

Still, despite working on several scenarios (and likely because of the war), Hofmannsthal did not move into the cinematic realm again until the mid-1920s, when he considered that film might be an integral part of the Salzburger Festspiele, after his libretto for Richard Strauss's opera *Der Rosenkavalier* became one of the final grand-scale Austrian films of the silent era. Directed in 1925 by Robert Wiene, who had found international fame for his 1919 expressionist film *Das Cabinet des Dr. Caligari*, that Austrian-French co-production utilized an international cast and approximately ten thousand extras. Hofmannsthal's vision for the film had, however, been undermined by Wiene, who had abandoned Hofmannsthal's original scenario. That original expanded fantasia on the opera and Baroque Vienna was deemed unfilmable by the director.

---

4 This section is a heavily revised version of materials from an earlier discussion: Dassanowsky, "Post-*Chandos*, Post-Imperial and Pre-Sound."
5 Hofmannsthal, "Ein Brief," 472.
6 Hofmannsthal, "Ungeschriebenes Nachwort zum *Rosenkavalier*," 147.
7 Hofmannsthal, "*Der Rosenkavalier*: Zum Geleit," 150.

The author responded by labeling the director's lavish mounting of the original opera libretto, which found popular success but divided critical evaluation, an "extremely amateurish and clumsy film."[8]

But it was not only this willful misappropriation of his great libretto that drove Hofmannsthal to engage with film. Prior to his ultimate involvement with silent film, the author's mourning for the imperial world, represented in his 1921 play *Der Schwierige/The Difficult Gentleman* had already collided with his fascination for the film medium to produce his foray into film criticism. The result, his essay "Ersatz für Träume," published in the same year as the play, must count among the first German-language attempts at cogent film theory. It posits the ability of the medium to satisfy the psychological need for a vicarious or substitute life, a dreamlike escape for the masses from the tedium of daily existence in a world that had become disconnected from its myths. For the author, film could subconsciously influence society in a way that "surface" and "indirect" language inherited from a now-vanished past could not. "Es ist zu viel von der Algebra in dieser Sprache,"[9] Hofmannsthal concludes, for any such words to reconnect post-First World War society with the lost myths and values of the past. Film would thus be the perfect medium to amplify the goals he sought to bring about through the visual/emotional effects of musical drama and dance: a reconnection of experience to a new narrative about the past. The possibilities of capturing, extending, and mythologizing performance through film provided Hofmannsthal with his post-verbal paradigm.[10]

Unfortunately for this vision, the sociopolitical conditions Hofmannsthal believed were necessary for Austrian-German culture and for a healthy European future disintegrated in the wake of the catastrophic war and its aftermath, which led the author to stress the need for a "counter-experience."[11] By 1925 Hofmannsthal even refers to "eine schöpferische Restauration"[12] (a creative restoration). Quite clearly, silent cinema and the new Salzburg Festspiel culture provided Hofmannsthal with a vision of re-animating the lost old order (even to create a new narrative of the past) and establishing a new platform, beyond the traditional theater, to showcase Vienna's high-art cultural tradition and transcend the verbal crisis that ballet and opera had only partially succeeded in doing. For Hofmannsthal, the veiled propagandist, film imagery would (re)create a sense of socio-cultural continuity

---

8 Dassanowsky, *Austrian Cinema: A History*, 35.
9 *Ersatz*, 143.
10 Brandstetter, "Der Traum vom anderen Tanz," 57.
11 Gottfried, "Hugo von Hofmannsthal and the Interwar European Right," 6.
12 The point of Kern, *Zur Gedankenwelt des späten Hofmannsthal*.

with Old Austria, his "conservative revolution," and even the European Idea[13] on a subconscious level. Rhetoric had failed the author in this quest and, despite his facility with and affection for the "schöne Sprache" (beautiful speech) of traditional art forms, he understood that it had been responsible for the subversion of traditional values and the confusion of social and political identity in the postwar era—taking up old words in the new contexts without such reconsiderations would simply render them irrelevant.

The play *Der Schwierige/The Difficult Gentleman* (1921) suggests that the author also considered a cinematic approach to theater as a method for greater social critique, particularly in a text that may have at one point envisioned an alternate outcome of the 1914–1918 war and which conveys so much of its ideals through moments of silence and choreographed movement, rather than through the small talk of the salon comedy that the play's text satirizes. The verbosity of *Der Schwierige* is both augmented and subverted by the cinematic simulacrum built into its staging, which suggests its nearness to the early medium of silent film. Hofmannsthal's medial translation of silent cinema to the stage in *Der Schwierige* can straightforwardly be recovered in assessing its use of physical communication (detailed directions for facial expressions and body language), tableaux and theatrical translations of the montage, and its attention to cinematographic conventions, such as the close-up, editing shifts, and dissolves. Moreover, such a reading also suggests the author's view about the paratextual relationship between the cinema performer and the spectator.

Beyond the hope that film would surpass theater, dance, or opera and somehow unify aspects of all these arts in a transcendent *Gesamtkunstwerk* as part of the new multidisciplinary venue of the Salzburg Festival stage, Hofmannsthal considered film a propaganda vehicle through which mass audiences might reconnect to the mythic and the lost totality of a pre-war world. Oksiloff even posits that Hofmannsthal's desire to use the new medium to provide the concepts of the reconstructive and the spiritual/eternal to be at the root of the author's "archaic modernism." Hofmannsthal's cinema activism was certainly tied to class and to his hope for reconstituting the lost Austria and its values disintegrated by the Great War. He clearly considers film as the medium by which he could enforce the auratic quality of his specific *Weltanschauung*, winning back the alienated working class from empty modernist (Marxist?) ideologies, while the upper classes retained their more sophisticated cultural understanding through the immutable

---

13 See Hofmannsthal, "Das Schrifttum als Geistiger Raum der Nation," 24–41. See also Gottfried, "Hugo von Hofmannsthal and the Interwar European Right."

schöne Sprache that was leaving the day's mass audiences behind.[14] Both these aspects are at work in *Der Schwierige*. The stage-bound mimicry of cinematic processes (rather than the silent film image itself) is clearly intended to reframe this *Sprache*, now the property of high society, for a broader theater audience. The socio-political strife of the early First Republic would require such a new *gesellige Sprache*, apparently being no less in need of a benevolent recollection of an elite imperial Austria.[15]

Even as a wordy salon tragicomedy, then, *Der Schwierige* fits well into the silent film projects Hofmannsthal planned. All of them anchored the visual pleasure of dream and hallucination in reactionary or idealistic socio-political concepts with the optical metaphysics of his 1903 "Die Bühne als Traumbild,"[16] transferred to what became for Hofmannsthal a medium with more restorative powers, cinema. The filmed dance pantomime *Das fremde Mädchen* gives to idealistic beauty that almost messianic relevance, while pessimistically suggesting that the commonness of the masses would overpower the ideal. That project of new media continued to occupy Hofmannsthal.

Lucidor, written for the actress Elisabeth Bergner between 1922 and 1926, and which ultimately became the libretto for Richard Strauss's opera *Arabella*, is once again set in the aristocratic Viennese world. The plot of this unmade film relates significantly to Austrian national identity: a widow of limited means decides that only one of her two daughters, Arabella, can be properly cultivated and introduced to society as a noblewoman, the other, named Zdenka in the opera, must be dressed as a boy. The fact that masking and gender-role reassignment does not change her essential identity as a good and loving woman, can be understood as allegory regarding the seemingly different postimperial Austria, which Hofmannsthal rejects here as mere costume, as pose. Its essentialism cannot be lost through reduced or even significantly altered circumstances—it's not the clothes that launch a girl into society and give her a future, it's the person's qualities.

The final unproduced Hofmannsthal film scenario, a *Heimkehrerstück* (a scenario about those returning from the war) from 1928, was planned to involve American silent screen star Lillian Gish and Salzburg's famed

---

14   Oksiloff, "Archaic Modernism," 145.
15   Hofmannsthal noted in 1926: "Im *Schwierigen* Andeutung des Verhältnisses zwischen Phantasiegestalten und der Realität. Das Soziale – perspektivisch behandelt," qtd. in Stern, "Zeugnisse," 528. Also, "Haltung: soziale – österreichische (der "feine kluge Wiener"). Anschluß an eine Tradition. Absichtlich Mittelbarkeit. (Haltung des "Schwierigen" in einer nuancenlosen Welt)," cited in Stern, "Zeugnisse," 529. The term "gesellig" was used in "Zum Wert und Ehre deutscher Sprache."
16   Hofmannsthal, "Die Bühne als Traumbild," 490–3.

impresario and director Max Reinhardt—another clear indication of the author's desire to cinematically rewrite history for his present day. The untitled script is set in November 1918, as thousands of Austrian soldiers were returning to a starving land. The character constellation of Hofmannsthal's messianic allegory includes the nature-bound forester and his daughter Resi, representing law and order; a returning soldier Hans and his mother, symbolizing the rupture of the traditional family structure; and Kasper, a Bolshevik who has a hunchbacked son, Euseb. Hans attempts to hunt for food to feed his starving mother and accidentally shoots the forester, but it is another's bullet that kills him. He nevertheless takes the blame and attempts to support Resi and her younger siblings in what is a re-formation of the family unit. Subsequently, a mob from the town accuses the couple of the murder of Resi's father and imprisons them with the Bolsheviks. An almost biblical flood destroys the prison and kills Kasper, whose son Euseb confesses to the parish priest that Hans and Resi are indeed innocent. The remaining Bolsheviks are freed from their captivity by the flood and take control of the town. They witness Resi's hands bleeding with stigmata as she forgives Euseb. All are transformed by this moving event, and Resi is embraced as a saintly figure announcing spiritual transcendence and a new world order—a perfect Lilian Gish role.

A *Heimatfilm* with aspects of the socio-critical melodrama popular in Austrian cinema during the 1920s, the Gish project offered a mystical resolution that signals redemption and a national rebirth foreshadowing the 1933–1938 anti-Nazi and anti-Socialist political Catholicism of Engelbert Dollfuss and the clerico-authoritarianism and corporate state (*Ständestaat*) often called Austrofascism. It can be read as the author's attempt to defend Austria's virtuousness in the war and in its aftermath, providing a miraculous religious exit from the trauma of the loss of the empire and the dislocation of the new remnant state. What *Der Schwierige* attempted to do as an experiment in film theory, through the timeless extension of and critical sympathy for the lost aristocratic world, the Gish project intended to realize on a proletarian cinematic level that transformed national suffering by looking beyond loss to a new era. Both scripts also rely on the promise of the silent visual and the transmitted or enacted.

While the Gish scenario seems melodramatic (in a mode that was Gish's trademark), it also shows Hofmannsthal's awareness of the audience. The music and theater festivals in Vienna, like the Salzburg and Mariazell Festivals, and others that sprouted across Austria during this era, were often anchored in Catholic mysticism. Rudolf Henz, who designed many of these events and theorized them, found that the very renewal of Austrian arts under Dollfuss and the more bourgeois Schuschnigg regimes emerged from an appeal to mass audiences through open devotion to the liturgy, which sparked a positive creativity based on Central Europe's Christian heritage. Remember, too, that in Germany, upon Hitler's rise to power in 1933, National Socialism modeled elements of its self-presentation and ritualization not only after abstracted elements of the Catholic Mass of Hitler's own experiences (the ceremonious touching of the "Blood Flag" used in the failed 1923 Putsch as shown in *Triumph des Willens*, for example), but after Christian liturgy as well—mainly from Protestant traditions.[17]

Hofmannsthal's instincts were, however, also affirmed by the political opposition that would eventually sweep memories of Austrian legacies away. The mysticism in such National Socialist events began to insist on the deification of Hitler and, by association, suggested the superiority of German culture through the purity of the blood and race, which is also emphasized in *Triumph des Willens* by Riefenstahl's cutting repeatedly between the singular figure of the leader and the jubilant masses. Austrofascist mass presentations ranging from art and cultural celebrations to specific political holidays and actual religious festivals represented a force beyond the leader—divine and embodied in the group of believers. Such presentations issued the call to a divine power, to the mass acceptance of the liturgical power and spiritual re-conversion, and, most importantly, to their subsequent *Weihung* or consecration to that power which dominated every event. In essence, then, there was no such thing as a secular festival or celebration under Austrofascism because of its address to the cultural Catholicism inherent in Austrian history. Following Dollfuss's assassination in 1934 by banned Austrian Nazis, a cult even arose around his consecration as Heldenkanzler (Heroic Chancellor) and Märtyrerkanzler (Martyr Chancellor), and his sacrifice for Austria was equated with Christ's sacrifice for humanity. Celebrating Dollfuss brought out other religious connotations, as well, including memorialization of him as a prayer-worthy saint-like figure across Austria, which validated the continuation of his political direction.[18]

Also significant is the fact that such events were often designed specifically to be cinematic productions, as was the case for propaganda films like *Triumph des Willens*. The filming of these mass events remained loyal to three aesthetic/philosophic concepts that Hofmannsthal had underscored in his own contexts: a commitment to realistic representation that stemmed from early social critical/proletarian Austrian film; the capturing of a diversity that was respectful of the polyglot nature of the regional past now estranged from the Austrian nation; and the

---

17 Vondung, *Magie und Manipulation*, 6.
18 Janke, *Politische Massenfestspiele in Österreich*, 333.

emphasis on a multicultural (and a seemingly fresh multiregional) nature of the present. Such films thus paralleled the Hofmannsthalian archaic modernism which encouraged an elite individualism and the recasting of the past to frame an evolutionary rather than revolutionary present.[19]

As Germany's National Socialist newsreels exhorted the nation-altering drama and might of the New Order and cloaked it in a history that it infiltrated and co-opted with Wagnerian music and old German script, Austrian newsreels recorded what appeared to be non-uniform even in a uniformed official gathering—the local, not just the divine calling of a blessed leader. An essential aspect of Austrofascist propaganda in the newsreel-related culture films was the rediscovery and emphasis on the western and Alpine regions of Austria. This territory had been of minor importance in the sprawl of the monarchy, but the Republic had shifted the geocultural identity of the small nation to the rural Alpine and propaganda film attempted to ameliorate the differential between cosmopolitan Vienna and the rural majority of the new country. Max Reinhardt and Hugo von Hofmannsthal had desired just that in creating the Salzburg Festival. This focus on rural culture in documentary film coincided with the rare *Heimatfilm*, which in the Austrian version of the genre, emphasized Catholic values in the rural world, to distance it from the *völkisch*/racist ideas of National Socialism.

This working through of the iconography and representational forms of Austrian history, however, cannot be seen in isolation, but as part of the reception of Austria as a haven for Jews and German emigres in the creative sector—a perhaps more cynical gesture. The opportunity to work relatively freely in the arts, particularly in the divided film industry, was a momentary respite for most Jewish arts professionals, many of whom were involved with films using such explicitly Christian iconography. Many had already decided on Paris, Prague, London, or Hollywood as their ultimate goals, while others hoped that Vienna's industry would not be significantly infiltrated by racism and Nazi subversion and that its filmmaking would continue to spark international interest. It would perhaps have been more obvious to the creators of fiction or alternative reality that a state that sought to re-Catholicize itself in the manner of Germany's enforced *Gleichschaltung* (total switching over) to National Socialism could have no real desire to support a Jewish population, other than for the sake of proving it was not Nazi Germany. The temporary reassurance that Austria was somehow different came

---

19 For an in-depth discussion of this concept in the author's literature, see Oksiloff, "Archaic Modernism."

with the fact that Austrofascism had always defined itself more by what it was not than by what it could offer.

Nonetheless, the program shared by Hofmannsthal and the mass-event creators evolved within Austria until the *Anschluss*: music, literature, architecture, and the visual arts did not have to forgo artistic freedom for the sake of an antimodern, racist artistic ideology, as it had to in Germany. But with growing antisemitism fueled by both the repressed Austrian Nazis and German infiltration, Jews that assimilated into and even contributed to the Catholic culture of the First Republic became less "inside" than they might well have been or yet become.[20] Lisa Silverman's 2015 example of the functional Jewish involvement in the Catholic-baroque ideology of the Salzburg Festival exemplifies how these hopes were implemented in practice: the interest in and affinity of Catholic culture by Austrian artists is what enabled Jewish filmmakers' careers in film under Austrofascist political Catholicism, regardless of their personal loyalties to Judaism (as in the case of Franz Werfel, who would in continue that trend with his 1941 novel *Song of Bernadette*, which would become a Hollywood film in 1943). Directors such as Max Neufeld, Richard Oswald, Fritz Schulz, Hermann Kosterlitz, and other Jewish, "non-Aryan" (or Jewish-associated/anti-Nazi professionals, as in the case of Austria's film pioneer Louise Kolm-Fleck) film talents were able to prove, for a short time and in contradistinction to the mainstream directors such as Willi Forst, Geza von Bolvary, Werner Hochbaum, and others, how "mainstream" and even pro-Catholic their work was or could be.

Had such significant filmmakers been allowed to contribute to the mainstream film industry, it would have possibly replicated the humanist political Catholic cinematic quality that Michael Steinberg considers was the original goal for the Catholic-Jewish mix at the Salzburg Festival: "a theater of Catholic pageantry imbued with a more progressive, enlightened nationalism of inclusion," a "nationalist cosmopolitanism." One can certainly perceive the elements that try to "reconstitute and represent the present [...] in the image of a golden past"[21] in the Viennese film, the music film, and the costume melodrama created by mostly Austrian filmmakers in the mainstream industry, as we also witness the progressive and cosmopolitan qualities in "visiting" directors as Paul Fejos, Werner Hochbaum, Erich Engel, and, of course, across established and nascent genres (including early screwball comedy and

---

20 Caroline Kita's *Jewish Difference and the Arts in Vienna* (2019) demonstrates convincingly that Jewish composers were in the late nineteenth century and pre-war eras already using biblical scenarios from the Old Testament to combat the German nationalism of Richard Wagner's Bayreuth.
21 Steinberg, *Austria as Theater and Ideology*, 170; and Silverman, *Becoming Austrian*, 160.

proto-*film noir*) of the truly cosmopolitan/transcultural independent *Emigrantenfilm*. The potential was there (although lost) to create a popular European iconography for such films that would have reconstituted the "mittlere Sprache" that Hofmannsthal had feared lost.

Salzburg in Film and Cinematic Coding

Remarkably, only a handful of feature films from the more than 120 sound films produced during the clerico-authoritarian regime from 1933 to March of 1938 in Austria was shot in Salzburg or its environs. These can also be considered mild Catholic "propaganda" by dint of their setting in baroque Salzburg rather than in a political/republican (or even socialist) Vienna.

The first hardly fulfilled its mission. *Unsterbliches Lied/Silent Night* (Austria/Switzerland 1934), an Alpine co-production recounting the 1818 creation of the famous Christmas song "Stille Nacht" (Silent Night), was directed by Hans Marr, a German actor active in Austrian film. It is often noted for its on-location production in Salzburg and in the village of Oberndorf, and for actor Franz Xaver Gruber Jr., who portrays his own grandfather, schoolmaster Franz Gruber, who set the song's lyrics written by the local priest, Father Joseph Mohr, to music. However, the film manipulates its Napoleonic setting into an anti-French pseudo-historical allegory that is also clearly aimed to stress contemporary German nationalist sentiments.

Singende Jugend/An Orphan Boy of Vienna (Austria/Netherlands 1936), an Austrian-Dutch independent *Emigrantenfilm* co-production, was constructed as a vehicle for the Vienna Boys' Choir by director Max Neufeld and writer Hermann Heinz Ortner. Shot mostly on location in Vienna and the Tyrol by Hans Theyer, it begins as a naturalistic/pre-neorealistic Austrian melodrama about an orphaned boy, Toni (Martin Lojda), who lives in poverty with his street-musician friend (Hans Olden). Toni dreams of joining the Boys' Choir, and his friend convinces the priest-rector of the choir's school (Ferdinand Maierhofer) and a nun, Sister Maria (Julia Janssen), to accept the boy for training. During a summer trip to the Tyrol with the choir, Toni risks his life to defend Sister Maria, who has become a mother figure to him, from suspicion of theft. After nearly drowning in a river, and the subsequent resolution of the melodrama, Toni is finally welcomed into a new home and identity.

Singende Jugend may well have influenced the troubled-but-good-orphan-boy theme in later Hollywood films, such as Norman Taurog's *Boys Town* (USA 1938) and Austro-Hungarian expatriate Michael Curtiz's *Angels with Dirty Faces* (USA 1938). The film found success internationally with audiences beyond Austria, in France, England, and Czechoslovakia.[22] A close reading of *Singende Jugend* reveals the qualities that make it the quintessential propagandistic entertainment film under Austrofascism, especially in establishing the cinematic vocabulary that supported the regime's ideology. The son of a Jewish father and a gentile mother, director Max Neufeld's sensitivity to political Catholicism, to the point of generating its imagined "national front" imagery, is revealed in the ambivalence that characterized the relationship between the specific politically conservative aspects of the Austrian Jewish population and the Austrofascist regime. It documents how, although unable to participate in the religious basis of that value system, many Austrian Jews identified with the Austrofascist regime's anti-Nazism, anti-Socialism, Viennese imperial cosmopolitanism, and even monarchist tendencies—and the cultural Catholicism of the festival cultures of the era. Noteworthy as part of the rewriting of Austrian history in the era is the fact that, despite (or because of?) strong Jewish involvement with the independent or *Emigrantenfilm*, the productions did not feature Jewish characters. Much as in Hollywood at the time, Jewish actors played gentiles or suggested Jewish ethnic clichés in only very light doses.[23]

The viewer is bound in sympathy to *Singende Jugend*'s central character, the orphan boy Toni, from the first shot. He is blond, attractive, and, except for his use of proletarian Viennese dialect, might be interchangeable with any of the young male actors who were portraying Hitler Youth in contemporary German films. Bearing a name that is a de-Germanized version of Anton, Toni lives with an unkempt and bitter cobbler who exploits and abuses him, punishing the boy for every wrong move. The cobbler's overwhelming interests are the money he fails to make and the wine he sends the boy to buy. While not quite an indictment of the capitalist system, the negative characterization of the cobbler underscores the destructive materialism and spiritual poverty of a working class that might well be associated with the Left and is fallow ground for Nazism.

It is music, particularly that of composers Mozart and Johann Strauss Jr., which bridges the romantic divide between urban corruption and

---

22 Czechoslovakia voted it the Best Foreign Film of 1936, and it received a New York film festival award the same year. In addition to a top Category I rating by the unofficial but influential Catholic film publication *Der gute Film* (The Good Film). *Singende Jugend* received an additional official attribute, "für Schülervorstellungen geeignet" (appropriate for school or student screenings) from the Ministry of Education (*Der gute Film* 172(73) (1936), 6–7).
23 See Dassanowsky, *Austrian Cinema*, ch. 2.

nature's purity. As an ironic and disturbing allusion to Austria's past cultural greatness, Toni, dressed in his tattered clothing, plays Strauss's *On the Beautiful Blue Danube* waltz on his harmonica as he wanders through the forlorn and dusty tenement passageways of an unrecognizable Vienna. Our introduction to the clean and natural beauty of the choir's school is also accompanied by the students' vocalizing which again serves as a corrective to Toni's dark world. A later performance by the choir in period costume against the beauty of the Tyrolean landscape attempts to fulfill the longing the film wishes to create in the audience for a "suitable" set piece that would transcend the urban squalor and unite music and location into a nostalgic/kitsch romanticism framed by a benevolent and omnipresent Catholicism. This contrast between rural cleanliness and beauty and the disorderly world of the tenements also figures prominently in German Hitler Youth propaganda films, particularly *Hitlerjunge Quex: Ein Film vom Opfergeist der deutschen Jugend/Our Flags Lead Us Forward* (Germany 1933). But in the Austrian film, Toni provides an allegory for the image of postimperial Austria as a humane community, not a plea to join an ideological training camp. As an abused and dejected orphan, he wanders through the claustrophobic streets of squalid working-class Vienna, unable to connect with anyone or anything.

The connection with an Austrian past is also highlighted in *Singende Jugend* in one of the very few sympathetic Viennese characters in the film. Never directly associated with Catholicism, Blüml appears to be the surviving cultural icon figure of the *Natursänger* (an untrained but impressively effective street or *Heurigen* singer). He sings about singing, disregarding his lack of money, and thus underscores the value of the spiritualized *Kulturstaat* (in the form of Austrian music) over materialism. His name is important not only for its association with nature and beauty, but also, given that it is the diminutive form of the word for flower (and unmistakably a reference to Jewish names from Central Europe), it also prefigures the edelweiss that Toni will later pick for his new mother figure, Sister Maria. Blüml is thus destined to be united symbolically with her in a spiritual reconstruction of the family and in metaphor of a traditionalized Austrian nation for the sake of their "adopted" child, Toni. The Catholic Church has provided mother and father for this orphan, not simply a cadre of age-mates. Blüml invites the boy in, sings with him, feeds him, and is taken aback as Toni thinks he will be beaten when Blüml reaches out to stroke his head in sympathy. He also enforces cleanliness and a wry twist on the Nazi slogan *Kraft durch Freude* (Strength through Joy) with the more genteel and aesthetically pleasing formula: *Immer sauber; durch Schönheit zur Kraft* (Cleanliness always; with beauty to strength). Like the Nazi propaganda that posited the Weimar Republic as "dirty," so too did Austrofascism define the First Republic and its "Red Vienna"[24] as unclean. It also, however, considered National Socialism as part of the same socialist corruption, hence the suturing of the *"immer sauber"* motto that would suggest a blatant corrective of the Nazi's slogan of empowerment. In comparison with the dirty and ill-mannered cobbler, Blüml keeps an impossibly neat hovel under a bridge, manages to have one good suit, and displays an endearingly clumsy attempt at being a gentleman. The absurdity of the postman who cannot locate Blüml's nonexistent address but who automatically exchanges greetings with the homeless man using the imperial-era deferential formula, *"Habe die Ehre"* (I have the honor) indicates the attempted embourgeoisement of the proletariat that these films address and that was a hallmark of Viennese pre-war class-bound manners.

The regime claimed that its corporatism could transcend class conflict, as could Catholicism and idealized notions of a national front. In this regard, it is telling that, in escaping the police, Blüml and Toni find refuge in a church where the Vienna Boys' Choir is performing. The close shot of Toni's face indicates an epiphany: his sudden self-realization through identification with the other boys' voices and a suggestion of spiritual relief from squalor and abuse through the *Gesamtkunstwerk* (total work of art) of the church's aesthetic environment, ritual, and music. As the sequence ends, both characters instinctively cross themselves to clearly convey to the audience that even the lost, poor, and immoral (like the nation as a whole) will find a home in and can become "good" again through a reconnection with Catholicism.

For a few moments on the screen, the film enforces an intellectual and spiritual identity as the compass symbol of the clerico-authoritarian and corporatist regime as a way forward into the future. The film uses an image of the monumental Grossglockner-Hochalpenstrasse (Grossglockner High Alpine Road), an engineering marvel completed in 1935 to encourage motorized tourism during the continuing economic depression as the highest surfaced mountain pass road in Austria. It connects Bruck in the state of Salzburg with Heiligenblut in the state of Carinthia. Its completion proved to be one of the most successful major building projects of the regime. In the film, the image of the road as seen by the characters and the audience imprints a unity or "front" among the "spectators" on screen and in the theater. It is a world-class construction that connects Vienna and the memory of the lost east with the distant but now accessible Austria (to Austrians and international travelers) of

---

24 The extensive social reforms undertaken by the Social Democratic Party in Vienna during the First Republic, which included the construction of pioneering and influential worker's housing, gained the city the moniker of "Red Vienna."

the present and future. Beyond this, the centrality of Salzburg to this road as a city and state with a strong historical representation of Catholicism, Baroque culture, and a tangible icon of the "new" Austria. One of the most interesting *Emigrantenfilm* and Catholic features that also integrates Salzburg is *Der Pfarrer von Kirchfeld/The Pastor of Kirchfeld* (Austria 1937), produced and directed by Louise Kolm-Fleck and her husband Jakob Fleck as their third (and first sound) treatment and production of Ludwig Anzengruber's 1870 naturalist drama of the same name, in an adaptation by Austrian author Friedrich Torberg and starring Hans Jaray, Hansi Stork, Ludwig Stoessel, and the Vienna Boys' Choir. The narrative, set in the province of Salzburg, and played against the backdrop of Austria's alpine scenery, revolves around the reputation of a priest who has taken an orphaned girl as his housekeeper. The man responsible for the hateful gossip that turns the parish against the priest is ultimately transformed through personal tragedy. With the housekeeper finally wed to her beloved, the town learns from the experience, and the priest can move on to do God's work elsewhere ... namely, the city of Salzburg.

The film's on-location production mode, the theme, and the limited budget of this *Emigrantenfilm* made it a late example for the regime's aspiration to establish a stronger independent cinema in Austria and to resist the racist, manipulative, and highly censored Nazi German market, with or without the hoped-for co-production pact with Hollywood studios. The Catholic press, however, distanced itself from what it felt was the film's pro-Catholic reframing of what was originally an unambiguous critique of clericalism.[25]

Along with *Singende Jugend*, the film solidifies the elements that would become the basis for the Austrian *Heimatfilm* following the war into the late 1950s—provincial setting, presence of the church, music, and a story about failed morality that is corrected by traditional values. The mixing of the *Bergfilm* (mountain film) genre and the subgenre of

---

25 The film was considered a model of cost-cutting independent production by using a text in the public domain, establishing a short photography schedule with limited studio use, and including actual local festivals instead of costly mass scenes. Distribution agreements were concluded with several countries during the filming, a procedure that has become the standard for contemporary European and American film production (see *Der Wiener Film* 37 (1937), 3). Antisemitic protests (aimed at co-director Jakob Fleck and some of the cast and crew) greeted the film's screenings in Austria. These protests hindered its full commercial possibilities, but the film managed impressive box-office returns in Vienna. See *Österreichische Film-Zeitung* 2 (1938), 1. Regarding Louise Kolm-Fleck as female film pioneer and her Austrian patriotism, see Dassanowsky, "Louise Kolm-Fleck, Senses of Cinema Great Directors."

the sport/skiing film, which became part of the Austrian and German *Heimatfilm* of the postwar era, had originated in Weimar German cinema and continued in Germany after 1933, although, as I have already suggested, it was already present in Austrian provincial film before the Anschluss. Far from Vienna or even Salzburg, its snow-bound settings erased national borders and identities for a vaguer Alpine regional setting, while unfortunately also suggesting that Austria was part of Germany, or that national borders and identities no longer mattered, and often for market demands.

Der Pfarrer von Kirchfeld opens with a local provincial festival march through the town. It immediately recalls the Nazi German films that either emulate in period costume or actually recreate National Socialist parades seen in the propaganda documentaries and newsreels. Like *Singende Jugend*, this film also challenges (or even deconstructs) Nazi cinematic martial imagery. Even the film's establishing shots, particularly the angles from above the town, recall Riefenstahl's *Triumph des Willens* and clearly connect with Nazi spectacle, until the narrative subverts the visual and gives the film its true ideological quality. In that first shot, the Riefenstahlian shot from below and against the sky, is here actually a point of view shot that represents what an impoverished and isolated man standing on a cliff sees, and the march of the traditionally garbed population of the town is not a political one, but rather part of the village's festivities for a Catholic wedding. However, the very choreographed quality of the parade suggests far more than an impromptu wedding celebration. Its visual similarity to provincial parades of the regime's Fatherland Front is not accidental.[26] Further, the cuts between the parade and the lone man parody the editing between the masses and Hitler in Riefenstahl's work, but the man's torn clothes and disturbed demeanor suggests a troubled outsider when cut against the happy, well-dressed, and celebratory folk. This sequence thus flips Riefenstahl's pattern of cutting between the sole superiority of the leader and the worshipful masses, by making the members of the attractive Austrian provincial/traditional parade the attractive bearers of normalcy, whereas the lone man, Sepp (Karl Paryla), gazing down onto the celebration, suggests neither power nor superiority, but rather alienation and pathos.

We soon discover the reasons for his anger and pain, when we hear the men below ridicule Sepp (in heavy regional Austrian dialect) and his hatred of weddings because he "lost his girl." The film cuts again,

---

26 See Kriechbaumer, *Ein Vaterländisches Bilderbuch*, regarding the Austrofascist style of public spectacle as a crossover between Catholic ritual and traditional provincial festivals.

this time to the interior of the hut Sepp shares with his old mother Josefa (Frida Richard). We see an old picture of a young woman, which is decorated by little blossoms, as a shrine. When his mother comments on the wedding, Sepp bends over her mother in tears. She asks him why he cannot try to forget the past after such a long time. As she returns to her rosary, Sepp comments that he also once knew how to pray that way but has forgotten how because "it does not help." Later, when Sepp appears in the village, the townsfolk attempt to include him in the ongoing celebration. They hand him a stein of beer. Despite Sepp's anger and sadness, he obviously desires to be with the community and so follows the crowd into the inn, where there is more drinking and dancing.

This opening sequence is the most adventurous of the film's pseudo-documentary cinematography. It also appears to have been a distinct choice by the directing couple, since Louise Kolm-Fleck's other works in silent film and early sound, such as the independent screwball comedy *Csardas/Her Wildest Night* (Austria/Czechoslovakia 1935), are much more visually creative. However, the "Austrian ideology" of the film—meaning its traditional provincial and church-based settings and moralistic messages—are in fact best served by such simple highlighting of nature, architecture, and the cool, almost anthropological gaze on the film's characters and the society as a whole. Like *Singende Jugend*, which also sutures the comedic/melodramatic acting to documentary photography of the fictionalized home life of the Vienna Boys' Choir and the natural beauty of Alpine landscapes, Louise Kolm-Fleck's film is clearly intended as an antidote to Nazi German propaganda films (the party documentaries and fictional narratives) as well as to the early sound proletarian films of the Left.

The production touted the fact that its budgetary constraints dictated that the film would have a very short production schedule of fourteen days (only seven of those in a studio setting) and that actual on-location venues would be used as much as possible. This proto-neorealist approach included cinematographer Ernst Mühlrad's incorporation of a Salzburg church festival in St. Gilgen and a *Trachtenfest* (traditional costume festival) in St. Wolfgang as the mass scenes that give the film production values without adding to the budget.[27] Given the Flecks' abilities, the film does not look inconsistent in quality or cheaply made,

---

27 Loacker and Prucha, "Die unabhängigen Filme," 180. The budget, however, did increase from the proudly announced 150,000 Schillings to 200,000 Schillings. Although not the most inexpensive film made in Austria during the era, as newspaper articles originally touted, its budget was still on the lesser end of independent film production costs.

as does for example, Richard Oswald's *Abenteuer am Lido/Adventure on the Lido* (Austria 1933), one of the earliest independent sound films, in which limited studio space, ineffectual art direction, and visual continuity breaks undercut the potentially attractive realism of the on-location scenes. In contrast, the Flecks' choices successfully impart a quality of cinematic "honesty" and cultural realism, when compared to the generically "German" (and often lavish) mainstream Austrian studio film or those co-produced with Germany (with their few Austrian character actors to impart locale beyond the usual introductory stock footage of Vienna) in the year before the Anschluss. The best of these imitations of Viennese film made in Berlin or Munich studios were by actor Paul Hörbiger's and director E. W. Emo's Algefa company, which used Austrian actors and exterior shots done in Vienna. These films were considered flattering impersonations by the Austrian press and the public, but disliked by independent filmmakers and the government, which correctly understood them as a way of manipulating content, production, and export levels of "Austrian" film (and they were marketed abroad as such) directly from Berlin, undercutting the productions made in Austria.

In the Flecks' pro-Catholic adaptation of the Anzengruber drama, the character of Sepp represents those lost to the faith; he is the instigator of the main conflict of the film, a rumor of sexual desire that would ruin two "pure" Catholic lives—that of the self-doubting but endeavoring young priest, Father Hell (the name in translation means "light"), and the good and virginal Annerl. Sepp (whose name is a village nickname for Joseph) first shows an interest in her while sharing a bench with the villager Michael, who speaks not only of his attraction to her but also of his shyness in making himself known. Sepp then offers to carry Annerl's bags as she walks from the town to the neighboring village of Kirchfeld. He even offers to buy her a drink in the tavern on the way. Upon learning that the priest at Kirchfeld has taken on Annerl as a housekeeper, he throws her bags down and abruptly abandons her. We learn that Sepp has targeted the Church as the source of all his troubles when the tavern owner informs him he should visit church more often than her tavern. The tavern owner's willingness to forgo the money she could make from Sepp's drinking habit is a surprising anti-capitalist twist on the cliché cinematic figure of the provincial tavern owner who is usually willing to take financial advantage of all who enter the inn.

Continuing her walk to Kirchfeld, Annerl is linked to the calm nature that surrounds her pathway. In wide-angle shots, she seems to emerge from the beautiful landscape that frames her. The linking of the female to nature (and the male to technology) is a significant part of the narrative structure of one of the forerunners of what would become the Austrian and German *Heimatfilm*, the silent German mountain films of the 1920s. In that genre, the changing emotional and erotic quality of the female is mirrored by the often-violent changes in weather that confound and confuse the male. Here, however, the female is linked to an inordinately calm nature that seems to be informed by the concept of Catholic grace (the image or suggestion of the Virgin Mary that reappears throughout the film) and a balanced, godly order. It is the godless Sepp, whose abusive desire to find a scapegoat for his pain and anger that covers the narrative with darkness like the onset of a heavy cloud.

The following extended sequence also makes traditional stereotypes more complex as it relativizes the meaning of darkness and light originally set up in the earlier part of the film as a simplistic binary. In these set of scenes, "natural" light and darkness ultimately lose their meaning in the face of the greater idea of "spiritual light." When the older priest returns to his parish, he informs Hell that he had been in the "city" visiting the Cardinal who wants Hell to leave Kirchfeld for Salzburg. But Hell believes that this is a ploy to remove him as a cause of gossip. The older priest *enlightens* him by suggesting that injustice is not being done to him, but that a priest must always keep injustice from happening to others, so he must be ready to sacrifice. Hell comprehends that he must abandon his closeness to Annerl, even if it is innocent. This understanding of sacrifice and goodness now occurs in the relative darkness of the old church. There is a sudden shift to daylight at the cliffs, where tragedy occurs. We see Sepp attempting to reach his mother, who once again tries to fly and falls to her death. Hell hears this while on a walk and rushes to the scene. As he prays over the dead woman, townspeople gather to comfort Sepp and tell him that God will help him. Rejecting such consolation, Sepp rushes away in tears.

The film cuts to a darkened interior, where Hell reads a letter which contains the cross necklace returned to him. He crumples the paper and then signs the official documents that transfer him to Salzburg. The darkness is increased as we see Sepp digging a grave in the night. We then see him approach Hell's house, which has light pouring from a single window. Hell brings him inside, and Sepp pleads for his mother's Catholic burial despite her suicide. He does not want her buried outside the cemetery "wie ein Hund" (like a dog). A non-Catholic or non-Christian existence is underscored as a cruel state not only in life (Sepp), but also in death. Father Hell thanks Sepp for finally coming to see him. He tells Sepp he will speak for his mother, and all will surely say "Amen." Sepp is so moved that he collapses in tears in Hell's arms. He blesses Hell and tells him that today he finally found what he had so long been looking for. The final shot of this scene is Sepp looking at the crucifix on the wall. The audience is thus moved to "experience" religious transformation by fathoming and empathizing with accessible grief for the death of a parent.

In the epilogue to *Der Pfarrer von Kirchfeld*, all the characters have been transformed by this transcendence into faith. Michael has apparently gained courage and is seen sitting on a bench with Annerl, telling her he never believed in any of the gossip. Annerl responds in her usual cryptic manner that equalizes gender by telling him she thinks he is a "good boy," and he then asks her for her hand in marriage. She accepts, as Michael's friend silently cheers him on from afar. The wedding becomes Father Hell's final duty, and the townsfolk, dressed in traditional costume as in the first scene, follow the couple to the church in a festive parade. An interior shot shows it completely filled. Count von Finsterberg arrives last, but he now seems to have understood something the audience is not privy to and can only guess at (his name means "dark mountain"). He is nonetheless at peace and genuflects as he enters the church.

The wedding ceremony is shot from the audience point of view to literally include the spectator in the church ceremony, just as was the style in the cinematography of the Catholic Mass in *Singende Jugend*. It shifts between close-up shots of the couple, Father Hell, the choirboys, and the immediate guests. We see Sepp arrive late. He is well groomed, wearing his traditional costume, and smiling. Following the ceremony, the Count shakes Father Hell's hand and informs him that he has heard of his move to Salzburg. "Schade" (a pity), he adds, as this nominal rapprochement between the political and the religious (and two classes) suggests the re-Catholicization that Dollfuss had hoped for, as a synthesis of Austrian Catholic identity and sociopolitical basis.

While Anzengruber's original play was critical of Catholicism, the new film adaptation, like *Singende Jugend*, provided entertainment that was supportive of the regime by enforcing the Catholic Church as a moral-ethical arbiter and as center of the national culture. *Der Pfarrer von Kirchfeld* premiered in Vienna in November 1937, and *Der gute Film* surprisingly dismissed the film with a second to lowest rating (Category IV). Rather than praise the work as ideologically appropriate, it again highlighted the differences between Austrian and German films in the era of Austrofascism by focusing on the film's clear attempts to subvert and correct what it deemed a *"Tendenzstück"* (propaganda work) of the *Kulturkampf* [28] inauthentic and sensationalistic.[29] Nevertheless, the film was considered a success by the dwindling independent *Emigrantenfilm* industry and with impressively sizable audiences that

---

28 *Kulturkampf* was an anti-Catholic secularization program of the German Empire promoted by Chancellor Bismarck between 1871 and 1877. It sought to strengthen the power of the state and Protestantism and to Germanize the empire's Polish-speaking territories.
29 *Der gute Film* 227 (1937), 13–14.

sought it out for its blend of melodrama, visual pleasure, and "Austrian values," perhaps even for its fable-like protest against cryptic secularism, capitalism, and even Nazism.

Salzburg's film history and Salzburg in films has one further historical twist. The "music film," *Opernring/Thank You, Madame* (Austria/Italy 1936), starring Polish singer and matinee idol Jan Kiepura, received the first double world film premiere in Austrian film history to that point—*in both Vienna and Salzburg*—signifying that Vienna was indeed not the only center of world-class popular arts in the country. That event gave the divided Austrian film industry hope, even in competition with German and Hollywood imports. The Kiepura film was one directed by an Italian, Carmine Gallone, in the heady years in which Mussolini maintained protection of Austria from a possible German invasion following the assassination of Austrian leader Engelbert Dollfuss. What emerged was an Italian-Austrian co-production scheme in which the Italian film industry hoped to emulate and reinvent particularly the internationally popular "Wiener Film" (Viennese Film genre) and the Austrian internationalist style of comedy and historical melodramas patterns in building its own wide cinema recognition.

The first co-production of that scheme, *Casta Diva* of 1934 (the title recalls a famous aria from Bellini's *Norma*), was based on a script by Walter Reisch, directed by Carmine Gallone and featuring Marta Eggerth, Kiepura's Hungarian operetta star wife. The film was produced by the new Roman film showcase, the Alleanza Cinematographica Italiana, or ACI, which was followed by the building of the new Cinecittà studio complex in Rome to demonstrate the positive aspects of the Italian/Austrian cooperation in film and the other arts. Italy continued to turn its back on German racist demands regarding Austria until the Rome-Berlin Pact of 1936 collapsed the Austrian-Italian co-production phase and nullified the Rome Protocols. During this end-phase with Rome, Vienna had been working to establish a similar shared production and dubbing program with Hollywood. There was far more than just a momentary hope, unfortunately scuttled by intrigue between German and Austrian Nazi infiltration in the Vienna film industry and in Hollywood. Nevertheless, by 1937, Jewish/German/Austrian talent that had participated in Vienna's early sound film industry had already left the country for fear of eventual Nazi annexation.

Vienna/Hollywood/Salzburg: A Last Hope

The final chapter in the evolution of Salzburg's film industry was anchored in international economics and a last attempt by industry professionals to maintain their independence from the increasingly controlled (Nazi) German film network.

The Vienna-Hollywood initiative of 1936, aiming at studio co-production between the two nations that would support Austrian film through international distribution, began with New York negotiations between the Austrian Ministry of Trade Councilor responsible for the film industry, Dr. Eugene Lanske, and the Hays Organization, which nominally represented all Hollywood studios through the self-censoring Production Code. This move was also an attempt to reconnect with the strong expatriate Austrian and Austro-Hungarian influence in Hollywood. Its plausibility would rest on the fact that Austria had a leading international cinema since the silent era, which seeded other cinemas, and that Austria stood ready to regain this status if it could free itself from Nazi infiltration and market control. Moreover, its expatriate cinematic talents were in fact already established Austrian "colonizers" in the most powerful cinema in the world, Hollywood. Austrian film was already, in this sense, to be united with American film. A thorough reconnection would strengthen an Austrian identity and provide an even more natural political ally or "big brother" (the United States) than Italy had been before Mussolini abandoned Austria to its alliance with Hitler.

At the start of the Vienna-Hollywood campaign, Lanske did not waste his time considering possibilities but instead promptly sailed to New York in April 1936 to meet with Dormer and the Hays Organization and its head censor Joseph Breen. He would make stops in Chicago, San Francisco, and finally Hollywood, where the Hays Organization would introduce him to studio representatives.[30] Hardly a secret trip, Lanske's journey on the French Line to meet with Hollywood was trumpeted for all its publicity effect in the Austrian papers and was picked up by the Hollywood trades, *Variety* and *The Hollywood Reporter* and its London editions. *Der Wiener Film* responded with lengthy discussions about Hollywood remakes of Austrian film and the necessity of dubbing Austrian films for export. It criticized the fact that German-speaking film was limited in that "[er] wendet sich in USA, ausschließlich an den Teil der Bevölkerung, welcher deutsch versteht" (it is aimed exclusively in the USA at the segment of the population that understands German). This could be remedied by a solid new dubbing industry, and it called for American cinema theaters to be as open to such European films (in dubbed versions) in the same way Europe has always been open to distributing American film.[31]

The Lanske trip had reenergized the idea of a strong independent Austrian cinema that would not be ideologically controlled by

---

30 Letter from Lanske to Dormer, April 17, 1936 (ÖSTA 97946 WPA/36 re: "Filmverhandlungen mit USA").
31 *Der Wiener Film* 4 (1936), 4.

German financial investment and exhibition interests. It would nullify the German-Austrian film agreements, including the aforementioned restriction of Austrian international dealings without German notification insisted upon in the stalled March meetings regarding frozen assets in Germany. The Austrian trade papers suggested that Austrian films might also base production on willing Dutch investment, a suggestion that was to materialize briefly with one of Austria's most popular mid-1930s productions, *Singende Jugend/An Orphan Boy of Vienna*. The sudden promise of an actual relationship with Hollywood also pushed the discouraging reportage from Berlin aside with positive news that appeared to be stimulated by Lanske's trip. Salzburg seemingly became an option in negotiations not just for production but in premiere "Festival" distribution. Notices appeared indicating that Jack Warner, head of Warner Brothers, was traveling personally to a Salzburg meeting with Max Reinhardt at his Schloss Leopoldskron to negotiate the production plans for Vienna and Paris location filming of "Danton,"[32] or that exiled German star in Hollywood Conrad Veidt was being lured back to German language film in a British production that would involve the Vienna industry.[33]

This was a real threat to Nazi Germany's control of the culture market. Such hints about the possibilities of an Austrian film production that would find less need for German investment and import in the opening of Hollywood and even London to Vienna were immediately countered by propaganda about Berlin's new willingness to import German-speaking or German-dubbed films from Hungary and Czechoslovakia. The open battle for Central European film dominance had begun. These were Austria's second most important export markets, which functioned as co-production venues for the independent Austrian *Emigrantenfilm*. It suggested Germany's apparently shrinking interest in "unreliable" Austrian imports because only certain directors, performers, and companies were racially acceptable to Berlin, whereas these regulations were not imposed on films from Czechoslovakia and Hungary. What made this even more a form of brinkmanship was the fact that the German-Austrian agreements on new import quotas, investment, and the frozen Austrian earnings in Germany were on the table for negotiations to start at the end of 1936.

The Vienna-Hollywood agreement process played out quite openly in trade publications. *The London Reporter* greeted this news with a front-page announcement on May 27, 1936 that Dr. Eugen Lanske, Head of the Austrian State Film Department, had secured agreements

---

32 *Der Wiener Film* 16 (1936), 2
33 *Der Wiener Film* 21 (1936), 1.

with MGM and Twentieth Century-Fox to make two pictures each in Austria in 1937. That paper openly declared, "This is all part of a move to counteract the present Nazi domination of Austrian film production, and is expected to give sufficient support to Austrian film production to prevent the collapse at present threatened because of the Nazi control."[34] The *Reporter* would offer a relatively large amount of news from Vienna in the following months, documenting the serious support Hollywood was willing to give. There were announcements regarding the Austrian arrangement for more releases of major British films from United Artists;[35] a note that MGM's *Top Hat* and *Broadway Melody*, both running in undubbed English, were grossing majorly in the Austrian market;[36] and plans indicating that Warner Brothers' purchase of Benatzky's famous "Salzburg" operetta, *Im Weissen Rössl/The White Horse Inn*, would first run on Broadway and then be filmed by the studio, possibly in Austria.[37] There was also an apparent race to score a contract with independent film leading man, Hans Jaray: "Statements that Hal Wallis negotiated with Hans Jaray for Warners are followed by reports that the author-player has received a cable from Louis B. Mayer, claiming him for MGM."[38]

Eminent actor Fritz Kortner was already preparing to portray the life of Theodor Herzl in a film scripted by Austrian writers and to be directed by Max Reinhardt, who first intended to produce it as a play in New York and then film it as a Vienna-Hollywood co-production in Austria. The publication indicates that "the tale opens with the Dreyfus Trial in Paris, [and] includes the first Zionist Congress in Basle, subsequently covering the more private aspects of Dr. Herzl's life."[39] The nervous excitement brought about by such Viennese ambition and Hollywood's seemingly sudden cold shoulder to Germany was heightened when ten to fifteen Austrian films were purchased for the Swedish market.[40] It was also reported that expat Austrian producer at MGM, Gregor Rabinovitsch, who was set to head the studio's unit in London, was possibly looking to do more pictures than the two musicals ostensibly arranged by Lanske for 1937.[41]

Several other voices emerged in this discussion as well. The director of Tobis-Sascha Studio in Vienna, Oskar Pilzer, underscores additionally

---

34 "MGM and 20th-Fox to Make in Austria," *The London Reporter*, May 27, 1936, 1.
35 "Vienna Firm Deal for U.A. Product," *The London Reporter*, June 8, 1936, 5.
36 "Top Hat is Tops in Austrian Market," *The London Reporter*, June 8, 1936, 5.
37 "Warners to Produce 'White Horse Inn,'" *The London Reporter*, June 9, 1936, 7.
38 "Hollywood Majors battling for Jaray," *The London Reporter*, June 9, 1936, 7.
39 "Fritz Kortner to do Dr. Herzl Biography," *The London Reporter*, June 16, 1936, 7.
40 "Swedish Film Chief Buying in Vienna," *The London Reporter*, June 23, 1936, 6.
41 "Rabinovitch to Shoot in Austria?" *The London Reporter*, June 25, 1936, 3.

interesting possibilities that would have helped the Vienna-Hollywood co-production initiative, ones that did not make the sensationalist trade press surrounding the Austrian initiative. In a letter, he relates that Walter Reisch, who was well known internationally, would be willing to script and direct a Hollywood film that would provide the crossover prototype with Viennese film and would serve as a showcase for an Austrian actor, in this case "Paula Wessely who has already given her agreement in principle." Moreover, Pilzer informed Waller that Marlene Dietrich was preparing a project with Alexander Korda in London, and that Dietrich's studio Paramount might well be persuaded to also produce a Dietrich film in Vienna and Salzburg, which Reisch also would write and direct. Pilzer encouraged Waller to take up contact with producer Gregor Rabinovitsch, who not only understands the film business relationships in Europe, but could supply a great deal of information.[42] Rabinovitsch was briefly considered as MGM's man for co-production in Vienna, and Reisch would indeed script Hollywood films (receiving an Oscar for *Titanic* in 1954) following his impoverished exit from Vienna in 1936 to work with Alexander Korda in London before receiving an offer from MGM's Louis B. Mayer.

Joseph Breen, the powerful director of head of the Production Code and Hollywood's leading censor, also appears to have had significant impact on Hollywood's relationship with Nazi Germany beyond the studio heads—he was influential in both the encouragement and the ultimate abandonment of the Vienna-Hollywood co-production deal. His message to Lanske during his stay in New York was that as a Catholic he has great sympathy for Austria in its struggle against Nazism and that he declares himself ready to promote Austria's wishes in the Hollywood film industry.[43] That dispatch quite literally gave the Austrian initiative its semi-official Hollywood support, but his abandonment of this planned action also signaled back-room deals with Germany for the sake of the Hollywood market.[44]

The last act of this Austro-American drama fell in August of 1936, when Max Reinhardt presented Salzburg with a plan to create a major Filmfestspiel which would expand the image of Salzburg and compliment the high art of the established music and drama Festspiele. Very

---

42 Letter from Director Oskar Pilzer of Tobis-Sascha to Consul General Waller, August 8, 1936 (ÖSTA 94.181 WPA/36). (Document is unattached copy from original with no Zl. code number assigned.)
43 Memoranda from Lanske to the Minister of Trade, 16 July 1936 (ÖSTA 94.181 WPA/36).
44 For detailed examination of the Vienna-Hollywood co-production plans and international involvement, see Dassanowsky, *Screening Transcendence*, 341–88.

large open-air screenings would take place in Schloss Mirabell Park, reminiscent of the very beginnings of film presentation in wandering tents. Smaller screenings would be projected in the salons and halls of the palace. "The Carabiniere-Hall in the Archbishop's residence would also serve these needs well." Reinhardt also suggested a festival film award presented by an international jury. "I am convinced that the 'Filmfestspiele' in Salzburg would find great interest across the world."[45]

This, of course, never happened. In 1938, Max Reinhardt fled Austria for Britain and then the USA to direct stage and film. Although Austria has several prominent film festivals and awards today, and Salzburg has become a well-known Austrian, American, and international site for filmmaking, attempts at postwar construction of a cinema at the Salzburg Festspielhaus have never been successful.

Bibliography

Archival Sources

Archiv der Wiener Handelskammer:
Akten der Kammer für Handel, Gewerbe, und Verkehr.
Sektion Film, Vienna. Files, memoranda and correspondence regarding the Vienna municipal government relationship with the Vienna-based Austrian film industry 1920–1938. (WHK)
Österreichisches Staatsarchiv:
Akten des Bundesministeriums für Handel und Verkehr (Federal Ministry of Trade and Transport), Vienna.
Files regarding the Ministry of Education (BMU).
Film proceedings with Hollywood 1936–1937.
Ministerial files, memoranda and correspondence pertaining to film and newsreel production.
Proceedings of RFK Berlin and Austrian Film Conference negotiations 1936 (ÖSTA).

Periodicals

Der gute Film (Vienna).
Das kleine Blatt (Vienna).
Der Wiener Film (Vienna).
Neue Freie Presse (Vienna).
Österreichische Film-Zeitung (Vienna).
Salzburger Chronik.

---

45 *Wiener Film*, August 11, 1936, 1. Translation by author.

Published Sources

Brandstetter, Gabriele. "Der Traum vom anderem Tanz: Hofmannstahls Ästhetik des Schöpferischen im Dialog Furcht." In Elsbeth Dangel-Pelloquin (ed.), *Hugo von Hofmannsthal: Neue Wege der Forschung*, 41–61. Darmstadt: Wissenschaftliche Buchgesellschaft, 2007.

Dassanowsky, Robert. *Austrian Cinema: A History*. Jefferson, NC, and London: McFarland, 2005.

Dassanowsky, Robert. "Louise Kolm-Fleck. *Senses of Cinema* Great Directors." (2004). Available online: https://www.sensesofcinema.com/2004/great-directors/kolm_fleck/ (accessed August 10, 2023).

Dassanowsky, Robert. "Post-*Chandos*, Post-Imperial and Pre-Sound: The Cinematic Influence on *Der Schwierige*." In Christophe Fricker, Martin Liebscher, and Robert Dassanowsky, eds., *Hugo von Hofmannsthal's Der Schwierige: A Classic Revisited*, 176–93. IGRS Series, University of London. Munich: Iudicium Verlag, 2011.

Dassanowsky, Robert. *Screening Transcendence: Film under Austrofascism and the Hollywood Hope, 1933–1938*. Bloomington: Illinois UP, 2018.

Gottfried, Paul. "Hugo von Hofmannsthal and the Interwar European Right." *Modern Age* 49(4) (Fall 2007), 508–19.

Hofmannsthal, Hugo von. "Ein Brief." In Bernd Schoeller, ed., *Erzählungen, Erfundene Gespräche und Briefe, Reisen. Gesammelte Werke in zehn Einzelbände*, 461–72. Frankfurt am Main: S. Fischer, 1979.

Hofmannsthal, Hugo von. "Die Bühne als Traumbild." In Bernd Schoeller, ed., *Reden und Aufsätze I 1891–1913. Gesammelte Werke in zehn Einzelbände*, 490–3. Frankfurt am Main: S. Fischer, 1979.

Hofmannsthal, Hugo von. "*Der Rosenkavalier*: Zum Geleit." In Bernd Schoeller, ed., *Dramen V: Operndichtungen. Gesammelte Werke in zehn Einzelbände*, 148–51. Frankfurt am Main: S. Fischer, 1979.

Hofmannsthal, Hugo von. "Das Schriftum als Geistiger Raum der Nation." In Bernd Schoeller, ed., *Reden und Aufsätze III 1925–1929. Gesammelte Werke in zehn Einzelbände*, 24–41. Frankfurt am Main: S. Fischer, 1979.

Hofmannsthal, Hugo von. "Ersatz für Träume." In Bernd Schoeller, ed., *Reden und Aufsätze II 1914–1924. Gesammelte Werke in zehn Einzelbände*, 141–5. Frankfurt am Main: S. Fischer, 1979.

Hofmannsthal, Hugo von. "Ungeschriebenes Nachwort zum Rosenkavalier." In Bernd Schoeller, ed., *Dramen V: Operndichtungen. Gesammelte Werke in zehn Einzelbände*, 146–7. Frankfurt am Main: S. Fischer, 1979.

Janke, Pia. *Politischemassenfestspielen in Österreich zwischen 1918 und 1938*. Vienna: Böhlau, 2010.

Kern, Peter Christoph. *Zur Gedankenwelt des späten Hofmannsthal. Die Idee einer schöpferischen Restauration*. Heidelberg: Carl Winter Universitätsverlag, 1969.

Kita, Caroline. *Jewish Difference and the Arts in Vienna: Composing Compassion in Music and Biblical Theater*. Bloomington: Indiana UP, 2019.

Kreichbaumer, Robert. *Ein Vaterländisches Bilderbuch: Propaganda, Selbstinszinierung, und Aesthetik der Vaterländischen Front 1933–1938*. Vienna: Böhlau, 2002.

Krenn, Günther, ed. *Mozart im Kino: Betrachtungen zur kinematographischen Karriere des Johannes Chrysostomus Wolfgangus Theophilus Mozart*. Vienna: Filmarchiv Austria, 2005.

Oksiloff, Assenka. "Archaic Modernism: Hofmannsthal's Cinematic Aesthetics." *The Germanic Review* 73(1) (2001), 70–85.

Vondung, Klaus. *Magie und Manipulation: Ideologischer Kult und politischer Religion des Nationalsozialismus*. Gottingen: Vanderhoeck & Ruprecht, 1971.

Schmidl, Stefan. "*Saison in Salzburg* (1938): 'Die schönste Stadt Deutschlands' in Fred Raymonds Operetta." Operetta 1938 Conference: "Angeschlossen und missbraucht." Vienna: Austrian Academy of Sciences, June 2013.

Silverman, Lisa. *Becoming Austrian: Jews and Culture Between the World Wars*. Oxford: Oxford UP, 2015.

Steinberg, Michael P. *Austria as Theater and Ideology: The Meaning of the Salzburg Festival*. Ithica NY: Cornell UP, 1990.

Stern, Martin. "Zeugnisse." In Hugo von Hofmannsthal, *Der Schwierig: Lustspiel in drei Akten. Sämtliche Werke*, Bd, XII: Dramen 10, 528–9. Ed. Martin Stern. Frankfurt am Main: S. Fischer, 1993.

Strasser, Christian. *The Sound of Klein-Hollywood: Filmproduktion in Salzburg – Salzburg im Film*. Vienna and St. Johann/Pongau: Österreichischer Kunst- und Kulturverlag, 1993.

Strasser, Christian. *Location Salzburg: Die schönsten Schauplätze in TV und Kino*. Salzburg: Verlag Anton Pustet, 2013.

Part II

Choosing Salzburg: Cosmopolitan Refuge and the Search for a Third Way

Five   The "World of Doomed Enchantment": Carl Zuckmayer and the "Henndorf Circle"

Christopher Dietz, translated by Vincent Kling

Introduction: Small and Large Worlds

"Large nations, when they mean to plan a test/Choose Austria, though smaller than the rest," says Friedrich Hebbel in his *Prologue to February 26, 1862*.[1] His observation has often been quoted since then, whenever the topic is Austria's role—for better or for worse—as a laboratory of historical development of similar processes. What Hebbel, a German writer who resided in Vienna, stated about Austria at large could pertain equally, if in reduced measure, to the village of Henndorf in the Salzburg area and its role in the period between the two world wars, the era mainly under discussion here. Quite a fair amount of the culturally intense multiplicity and the political contradictions prevailing in Austria before the *Anschluss* as well as during the time of National Socialism is reflected in the history of this small vacation spot and its permanent residents and guests—opportunists, "illegals"[2] and silent observers on the one hand, unselfish helpers, cosmopolites, and opponents of the regime on the other, with just about every shade in between.

And in the midst of it all another German writer resident in Austria: Carl Zuckmayer, born in Nackenheim (Rhine-Hesse) on December 27, 1896 and occupant since 1926 of an estate called the "Wiesmühl" on the outskirts of Henndorf, his personal "paradise."[3] Thomas Bernhard,

---

1   Hebbel lived in Vienna from 1845 to his death in 1863.
2   That was the name given in Austria to adherents of the National Socialist Party after it was prohibited in Austria on June 19, 1933.
3   "A Moment in Paradise" is the title of the first chapter of Zuckmayer's autobiography *Als wär's ein Stück von mir* (1969).

himself a guest there as a child, remembers that "absolutely every kind of artist and scholar came and went in the so-called Wiesmühl" during the twelve and a half years Zuckmayer lived there with his family.[4] That genius of the theater Max Reinhardt was among them, the highly successful author Stefan Zweig, the Oscar winner Emil Jannings (see below), and numerous others, who couldn't (or didn't want to) resist the sometimes rather exuberant personality of the owner in his role as host.

"And if at home good balance is attained/Then peace in larger nations is regained," Hebbel goes on to say, and here too the analogy can be further extended, although in reverse. Hand in hand with the precarious balance prevailing in Zuckmayer's Henndorf paradise for several years went the darkness of the *Anschluss*, the annexation of Austria by its German neighbor that culminated in Zuckmayer's exile. In his autobiography titled *Als wär's ein Stück von mir (A Part of Myself)*, which appeared in 1966—thus four decades after he had settled in his "paradise" and twenty-eight years after being driven out of it—Zuckmayer referred to those days of March 1938 as an "expulsion."[5] Most of the information about Zuckmayer's Henndorf years is taken from these memoirs.[6] Here too, however, as always when it comes to (auto)biographical testimony, a cautious approach is in order; not everything can always be taken as historically accurate information.[7]

Christian Strasser's definitive book from 1996 is very valuable regarding this era. Strasser devotes himself to the "Henndorf Circle,"[8] and, in the process of examining its members, draws on numerous hitherto unpublished materials from literary estates and archives. As a

---

4 Bernhard, *Ein Kind*, 467. For more on Bernhard and his grandfather Johannes Freumbichler, see later in this chapter.
5 Zuckmayer, *A Part of Myself*, 51. "It was a witches' sabbath of the mob. All that makes for human dignity was buried," writes Zuckmayer in his memoirs about the *Anschluss*, the annexation of Austria by Germany—the term "expulsion" fits into this semantic field, notwithstanding that it was Zuckmayer who was expelled by the Nazis, and not the other way around.
6 What gets passed over in the book are the hostilities directed against the Zuckmayers by local National Socialists (windows smashed, dogs poisoned, and so on); see Strasser, *Carl Zuckmayer*, 190.
7 See Nickel, *Carl Zuckmayer's Autobiographie*, 13: "[…] thus there results in Zuckmayer's work a variance from factuality because of his attempt to tell his story in a pointed, entertaining, and efficient way, thereby sacrificing precise factuality to narrative compression and dramatic effect."
8 See Strasser, "Carl Zuckmayer," 91f. Zuckmayer himself spoke of the "Wiesmühl Circle" (Zuckmayer, *Aufruf zum Leben: Porträts und Zeugnisse aus bewegten Zeiten*, 99).

result, the small area of Henndorf and the surrounding region around Salzburg emerge with particular vividness.

The word "circle" is deceptive, however—anyone expecting a self-enclosed coterie untied by similar views will be disappointed. The "Henndorf Circle" achieved cohesion above all through its central star, whose members revolved around it like satellites. The personality of Carl Zuckmayer, with his great talent for friendship,[9] was what in those years cemented a group of people who could hardly have been more disparate:

> Fellow writers banned from Germany, destitute Austrian authors, well-heeled and well-liked proponents of the National Socialist regime, collaborators and professed resistance fighters, shining stars of literature and hopeful beginners, prohibited authors and party-line authors, Jews and antisemites.[10]

The star around which this group orbited was binary, however. Alice Herdan-Zuckmayer, the writer's Austrian wife, played a significant part in this "circle," though she is not listed by Strasser or other commentators[11] as an actual member.

An Adoptive Austrian in the Salzburg Area

After more or less successful years in Kiel and Berlin, Zuckmayer experienced his great literary (and financial) breakthrough with his play *Der fröhliche Weinberg* (*The Merry Vineyard*), set in his native region of Rhine-Hesse, while at the same time earning severe criticism from German-national and antisemitic groups, which saw their convictions being subjected to judgment on by this "half-Jew";[12] that term was by then put into service as a defamation.[13]

In the same year Zuckmayer married Alice Frank, née (von) Herdan, a Viennese. After a failed marriage with his childhood sweetheart Annemarie Graz and his separation from the actor Annemarie "Mirl" Seidel, Alice Herdan became the writer's lifelong companion (see the

---

9 Strasser estimates that in the course of his life Zuckmayer was "friends or acquaintances with upwards of a thousand artists," Strasser, *Carl Zuckmayer*, 168.
10 See Strasser, *Carl Zuckmayer*, 91.
11 See, for example, *Henndorfer Kreis*, https://de.wikipedia.org/wiki/Henndorfer_Kreis.
12 Zuckmayer's mother Amalie, née Goldschmidt, came from a Jewish family.
13 This folk play, rather crude at times, was slandered as a "swinery," though it had earned Zuckmayer the Kleist Prize; see, for example, Albrecht, *Carl Zuckmayer im Exil*, 174f.

section "At the Center of the Circle: Alice Herdan-Zuckmayer" below). His wife's birthplace, but even more the way in which comments in the public media of the German Reich kept turning more and more against him, finally induced Zuckmayer to relocate his life's focus to neighboring Austria.[14] This proximity to the Salzburg Festival, which had existed since 1920 with Max Reinhardt as a cofounder, was likewise not exactly a drawback for a playwright.

The story of Richard Billinger's alcohol-drenched portrayal of the Wiesmühl, located in Henndorf near Salzburg, and of its ensuing purchase by Zuckmayer has often been told.[15] The royalties from *The Merry Vineyard*[16] made this acquisition possible, and from 1926 on—on a permanent basis beginning in 1933 and ending only with the *Anschluss* in 1938—the Zuckmayers, along with their two daughters Winnetou and Michaela,[17] spent their time predominantly in Henndorf.[18] "You don't know me if you don't know me in Henndorf,"[19] Zuckmayer wrote in 1930 to Hans Schiebelhuth, a close friend since their youth.

It is anything but random chance that led Zuckmayer to design his memoirs with this episode at the outset instead of chronologically. Emulating creation history, at least concerning his own emergence to full humanity, *A Part of Myself* begins with and in Henndorf, which Zuckmayer felt to be "my chosen home, the one I had made my own."[20]

---

14 Ironically, Zuckmayer did not receive Austrian citizenship during his years in Henndorf, even though he was of the opinion that it had been conferred on him (see Zuckmayer, *A Part of Myself*, 47). He had applied for an Austrian passport shortly before the *Anschluss* but had never received it (see Strasser, *Carl Zuckmayer*, 205). Only in 1958 was he in fact granted Austrian citizenship.
15 Zuckmayer's memoirs open with this anecdote. See Zuckmayer, *A Part of Myself*, 3–4. At the opposite end of the German-speaking world, as it were, on the island of Hiddensee in the Baltic Sea, his friend and fellow writer Richard Billinger, who came from the Innviertel district not far from Salzburg and who would likewise become a member of the "Henndorf Circle," had raved about this property, and Zuckmayer bought it without delay.
16 For the sum of 123,692 Reichsmark, today approximately 480,000 euro (https://de.wikipedia.org/wiki/Reichsmark). This was also a fortune large enough to accommodate the purchase of a nine-room apartment in Berlin (Zuckmayer and Joseph, *Briefwechsel 1922–1972*, 687 [afterword by Gunther Nickel]).
17 Alice Herdan's daughter from her first marriage with Karl Frank.
18 In addition, the couple maintained an apartment in Vienna. For their changing addresses in Vienna, see Strasser, *Carl Zuckmayer*, 91, n. 177.
19 Zuckmayer to Hans Schiebelhuth (1930), qtd. in Bengesser, *Literaturlandschaft Flachgau*, 87.
20 Zuckmayer, *A Part of Myself*, 3. Zuckmayer largely excluded from his memoirs how the area around Lake Waller was notable for strong antisemitism and how so many vacation resorts boasted of being *"judenrein"* or free of Jews, just as he did not mention that he himself was the target of attacks by National Socialists in Henndorf (windows smashed, dogs poisoned)—see Strasser, *Carl Zuckmayer*, 190.

Carl Zuckmayer and the "Henndorf Circle" 143

The power to make free decisions and choices apparently played a major role for this son of a manufacturer who produced corks for wine bottles, this artist who had had earned neither success nor income for long years (and had discontinued his studies in several fields[21]) but nonetheless preferred a writer's existence to the comfortable life of an industrialist's son. A strong emphasis on autonomy and a need for independence, including in material matters, are constants in Zuckmayer's biography, up to and including his existence—forced to begin with, but then consciously adopted—as literally a self-sufficient rustic in his destitute exile in Vermont.

It's arguable that the imprint of Catholicism on Rhine-Hesse-reared Zuckmayer played a part in predisposing him to the culturally kindred southern area of the German-speaking world.[22] Zuckmayer, the author of a play that unmasked Prussian militaristic authority—*Der Hauptmann von Köpenick* (*The Captain of Köpenick*)—claimed that "Austrians were a far more balanced people [than Germans]. Centuries of political education in holding together a community of nationalities had given them a certain distaste […] for militarism and strict organization"[23]— meaning Prussian-Teutonic ways.

Salzburg and Its Festival as the "Cultural Hub of Central Europe"

One of the considerations guiding Max Reinhardt and Hugo von Hofmannsthal[24] in conceiving the Salzburg Festival some years before had been the hope for a moderating influence on young, Protestant Prussia by the older Catholic-Austrian culture, with its power to connect various nationalities. It's not a far leap from the "Austrian idea" propagated mainly by Hofmannsthal to the "Habsburg myth."[25] The very fact that this quasi-religious myth of an ideal empire, uniting nationalities and serving a higher vision is more closely redolent of a culturally shaped, apolitical utopia than to any description of actual political and historical

---

21 Law, political economy, literature, and art history as well as biology and zoology in Heidelberg and Frankfurt am Main (see Carl Zuckmayer Gesellschaft, *Carl Zuckmayer Biografie*).
22 Musulin, "Zuckmayer, der Österreicher," 83, among others, speaks of an "existential affinity […] between Rhinelanders and Austrians."
23 Zuckmayer, *A Part of Myself*, 16.
24 Both were guests of Zuckmayer at the "Wiesmühl."
25 This concept was formulated in 1963 by Claudio Magris in a book entitled *Der habsburgische Mythos in der österreichischen Literatur/Il mito absburgico nella letteratura austriaca moderna*, which in turn, to be sure, had warned against the co-opting of this myth or the idea of Central Europe by "a conservative stance toward politics and culture" (Magris, *Der habsburgische Mythos*, 13).

realities, is what constitutes its great attraction, which partly includes that of the Salzburg Festival as well.

Why Salzburg, though, the comparatively provincial cathedral town at the opposite end of the young republic? The small nation in the center of Europe to which the Habsburg monarchy had shrunk after the dissolution of the empire meant, especially for the former imperial capital of Vienna, an enormous loss of significance, from which the periphery, and in our context Salzburg above all, was able to profit; Hermann Bahr, one of the spiritual founding fathers of the Festival, had as early as 1900 marked out Salzburg and its surrounding area as the "capital city of Europe."[26] In addition, Germany was (and is) not very distant, in contrast to Vienna.

Moreover, after the historic turning point of the First World War many culturally productive persons (and their audiences along with them) turned their backs on the large cities; in their need for some respite, and not seldom impelled by visions of an alleged (pre-war) Golden Age, they sought authenticity and a return to their roots in the countryside while electing to leave the "filthy metropolis"—often governed by Social Democrats, for that matter—in the hands of the proletariat and its leisure pursuits, often judged to be profane.[27] "In the country" people could keep up the tradition of the invigorating summer vacation, enjoy becoming acquainted with the surrounding locations and landscapes during their stay, and take pleasure in what they considered the picturesque folkways and customs of "the locals" (to whom they sometimes assimilated on a grand scale by wearing the traditional country attire or *Tracht*).[28]

---

26 "The Capital City of Europe: A Fantasy in Salzburg," Bahr, *Kritische Schriften*, Bd. 7, 87–92. One of the speakers of this "fantasy" has this to say about the prospective audience: "These men and women with great yearning but scattered throughout the world are feeling the same things, hoping for the same things, anxious about the same things we are; they are our true native country."

27 The split between "Red Vienna" and rest of the federal states, which are mainly conservative, has lasted to the present; according to a recent comment by Matthias Dusini (Pesl and Dusini, *Gott, Kaiser und Hakenkreuz*), it originated at this time: "Vienna, imperial residence without an empire, was transformed into a testing ground for Socialist public policies. Architects and urban planners revolutionized housing, just as pedagogues did with education and feminists with sexuality. […] Christian-Socialist Salzburg placed itself in opposition to the 'Jewish government' in the metropolis as the 'true Austria' as against 'unAustrian Vienna.'"

28 Marginal comment: the *Dirndl*, an outfit used mostly by city dwellers and tourists in Austria to display their advocacy of tradition, began its triumphal progress through the world at just this time, reaching its high point at the very latest through the Hollywood film *The Sound of Music* (1965, the musical dating from 1959) and its protagonists, the members of the Trapp family, all outfitted in *Tracht* (the generic term for folkdress).

Carl Zuckmayer and the "Henndorf Circle" 145

Alongside the classic spas like Bad Ischl and Bad Aussee, smaller localities like St. Wolfgang or, for that matter, Henndorf,[29] gained favor with the public—the closer to the festival city of Salzburg the better. A bus ran between Salzburg and Henndorf, for instance; in addition, more and more people owned their own automobile.

In positioning itself deliberately at the opposite pole to the exclusive Bayreuth Festival,[30] the Salzburg Festival, founded in 1920, hoped to attract an audience equally conservative, to be sure, but relatively cosmopolitan and international—preferably aristocratic too—and that endeavor met with success, thanks to political and ecclesiastical support.[31]

Michael P. Steinberg provides a very impressive analysis of the strangely ambivalent nature of the "Salzburg Festival ideology." The founding fathers of the Festival were concerned with nothing more nor less than a reorientation of reality by way of representation,[32] specifically via Baroque-nationalistic perspectives on one hand and cosmopolitan-liberal ones on the other. With aptness and only seeming paradox, Steinberg dubs the fundamental attitude "nationalistic cosmopolitanism," a cast of mind which could accommodate Pan-German nationalism.[33] Europe, having lost its orientation after the war, could "recover through the German-Austrian character," as it were, and Salzburg would become the "cultural hub of Europe," a mediator between east and west, north and south.[34]

Much as this all meant a gratifying increase in revenue for (Festival) tourism, many nonetheless felt upset at the hordes of (often) foreign or cosmopolitan-urban guests. More than a few considered the crowds to be an invasion by "foreign elements," and the antisemitic press in particular interpreted the confluence of these different constituencies as a clash between "German by heritage" and "rootless" Jewish culture.

Ever since 1933, when the National Socialists had attained power in Germany, Austria—set up as a so-called "corporate state," likewise

---

29 "Toward the end of the last century [the 19th, note by C.D]," however, well before Zuckmayer's move there, that is, Henndorf had already been "a Parnassus inside our borders" (see Zuckmayer, *Henndorfer Pastorale*, 41).
30 A composer, a genre, a place.
31 Out of a combination of interest in its economic advantages and antipathy to Vienna, the Christian-Socialist governor of Salzburg, Franz Rehrl, was very receptive to the festival project, which was also supported by Archbishop Ignaz Rieder (see Steinberg, *Ursprung und Ideologie der Salzburger Festspiele*, 77).
32 See Steinberg, *Ursprung*, 9.
33 Steinberg, *Ursprung*, 11.
34 See Steinberg, *Ursprung*, 65, where extracts from advertisements provided by the "Festival House Community" (founded in 1918, with offices in Vienna and Salzburg) are reproduced.

authoritarian and fascist, to be sure, but ruled more moderately in comparison—had emerged as an attractive place of exile for those German intellectuals not tolerated by the Nazi regime, especially the areas of the country close to the German border, among them the Salzburg region:

> To intellectuals, and especially to refugees from Hitler Germany, "independent Austria" seemed distinctly the lesser evil [...] The agitators and climbers who counted on making careers and exercising power under Nazism had to go about their business with conspiratorial secrecy—in contrast to Germany, where under the shield of the freest kind of democracy they had been able to rage and incite against that democracy for years.[35]

The "Henndorf Circle" and Its Members[36]

This was how the situation was judged by Zuckmayer, for whose family of four the Wiesmühl, purchased earlier, served as permanent residence as of 1933. The atmosphere in Germany had grown more and more adverse; the National Socialists slandered him as a "half-Jew" and Socialist, and his works were among those burned on May 10, 1933 in the course of the Nazi campaign titled "Against the Un-German Spirit." Financially as well as politically, remaining in Germany was shaping up to be more and more difficult. Under pressure from the regime, Zuckmayer's publisher Ullstein cancelled its contract with him, and Gottfried Bermann Fischer, himself exiled in Vienna, became Zuckmayer's new publisher, but of course with a significantly smaller sales radius.

In 1933 and again in 1934, Zuckmayer applied for membership in the *Reichsverband Deutscher Schriftsteller* (RDS),[37] the Reich Federation of German Authors, to which any writer had to belong if they wanted to publish in Germany. His application was first marked "questionable" but finally approved the second time around, possibly because the applicant had named Heinz Hilpert and Paul Fechter as guarantors on the second attempt, along with Werner Krauß.[38] His membership was

---

35 Zuckmayer, *A Part of Myself*, 15–16.
36 See also Strasser, "Ein Haus der Emigration." Strasser differentiates between "camp-followers" and "local residents." As a third category Strasser refers to the "migratory birds," by which he means guests stopping through, such as Hans Albers, Thomas Mann, and numerous others.
37 Integrated into the *Reichschrifttumskammer* (RSK) or Reich Bureau of Authorship at the end of 1933.
38 See Strasser, *Carl Zuckmayer*, 186.

cancelled as early as 1935, however, for the good bureaucratic reason that there was no provision authorizing membership to authors who lived abroad.[39]

It seems all commentators agree that the years in Salzburg spared Zuckmayer the necessity of directly confronting the new political realities in his German homeland, at least for a time. An author who felt to the depths of his soul that he was German simply did not want to admit to himself that he was no longer welcome in the country in which he had finally celebrated such enormous triumphs. Even in 1938, for that matter, when he finally had to leave Austria and his Henndorf paradise, it happened in the most urgent rush, and then only because Alice was able to persuade him how senseless it would be to hang on heroically. The "[...] tension between lived political reality and fairy-tale-like description"[40] that marked Zuckmayer's portrayal of this period could finally no longer be sustained.

"Local Residents"

Zuckmayer was successful in his renewed efforts to establish a network in nearby Salzburg and in Vienna; his friendly attitude and his open hospitality aided his efforts. It also proved very advantageous that numerous literary and theater people were already resident in the area: Alexander Lernet-Holenia lived in a villa in St. Wolfgang, and Emil Jannings had an extensive estate on the edge of Lake Wolfgang just across from Lernet's residence. Friends with one another, they were classified by Strasser as "local residents"[41] of the "Henndorf Circle," along with the actor Werner Krauß, who lived in Scharfling on Lake Mond. They all visited back and forth, "Alexander Lernet-Holenia traveling by bicycle, [...] Emil Jannings chauffeured in his car, Werner Krauß on foot over the wooded mountains of Lake Mond or by the venerable old Ischl railroad line [...]."[42] In addition, there were the residents of Salzburg itself, around 20 kilometers away; these "neighbors" were Max Reinhardt and Stefan Zweig.

Stefan Zweig

As early as 1919, in search of a quieter location to work, the highly acclaimed writer Stefan Zweig (1881–1942) had moved to Salzburg and found just the right place in the "Paschinger Chateau" on Capuchin

---

39 See Albrecht, *Carl Zuckmayer im Exil*, 182f.
40 Haslinger, *Zuckmayer und seine Dichterkollegen in Salzburg*, 202.
41 Strasser, "Ein Haus der Emigration," 1996.
42 Zuckmayer, *Henndorfer Pastorale*, 38ff.

Mountain. The Zuckmayers were indebted to Zweig to no slight extent; this renowned author, fifteen years older and one of the most striking examples of forthcoming generosity in all of literary history—think only of his support for Joseph Roth—introduced the couple, whom he had befriended, into the notoriously conservative society of Salzburg, to which Zuckmayer, decried as a "socialist,"[43] would quite probably never have gained entrance on his own. Zweig, who had given the Zuckmayers a rustic tiled stove as a moving-in present and later on presented them with two dogs, would regularly check in on his friends' bucolic idyll. "Stefan Zweig would show up at regular intervals and allow me to drag him to the point of exhaustion along nearly impassible trails and through bodies of water with no bridges [...]."[44] The two writers worked together, including on a farce about the Salzburg Festival, and Zweig's wife Friderike ("Fritzi") was close friends with the Zuckmayers as well.

Both of them, however, Zweig and Zuckmayer alike, were confronted with increasing hostility throughout the 1930s by the antisemitic propaganda mouthpieces in Salzburg. Zweig had left the country in 1934 and settled in England; it was during a visit by Zuckmayer in London that he warned his guest not to return to Austria: "You're walking into a trap." Yet Zuckmayer stayed in Henndorf for four more years, "four good, fulfilled years [...], and perhaps those years stored up within us the spiritual reserves of strength that made us able to endure the frightful things that came afterwards."[45]

In 1930, Zweig had referred to the Nazi electoral victory that year as a "revolt of youth against exalted politics"[46]—which was putting it mildly—but by 1937 he had sold his "villa in Europe"[47] and begun trudging the road of exile, which ended with his suicide in Petropolis, Brazil, in 1942. Zuckmayer, meantime himself now exiled in Vermont, was deeply shaken and in response wrote his *Aufruf zum Leben* (A Call to Live), addressed to his remaining friends and fellow exiles; he requested of them, as it were, that they should not emulate Zweig: "As long as a single person goes on living, even under the direst persecution,

---

43 As a young man, in the form of publications in the expressionist-socialist journal *Die Aktion*, among others, Zuckmayer had flirted with socialism. Hans Mayer, *Zur deutschen Literatur der Zeit*, speaks of "Zuckmayer's ethical socialism."
44 Zuckmayer, *Henndorfer Pastorale*, 38.
45 Zuckmayer, *A Part of Myself*, 39.
46 Quoted from Bolbecher and Kaiser, *Lexikon der österreichischen Exilliteratur*, 730.
47 Romain Rolland had given Zweig's small chateau this name, because during the years of Zweig's residence it had come to be a meeting point for all of European intellectual life.

someone who thinks, feels, believes and desires in a way different from the persecutor, then Hitler has not conquered."[48]

Max Reinhardt

Zuckmayer gained a great deal from Max Reinhardt's rootedness in the cultural life of Salzburg (Reinhardt lived from 1873 to 1943). He was a frequent guest at Reinhardt's sumptuous parties at Castle Leopoldskron. In return, Reinhardt graced the "Wiesmühl" with his own presence, "to say nothing of his entourage of artists and celebrities, among which were enchanting English ladies and American film divas—or millionairesses," to quote Zuckmayer's recollection of these luxuries.[49]

Zuckmayer exaggerated somewhat in his autobiography when he portrayed his relations with Reinhardt as a close friendship; after all, who would not have wanted to bask in the light of this "theater wizard" during those years? After the First World War (and with diminishing professional success in Berlin), Reinhardt had come to identify Baroque Salzburg as the place where he felt he could best realize his "mission of purification through theater,"[50] that is treating theater not as trite "summer stock" meant for mere entertainment but rather as a serious, indeed a solemn event.

No collaboration ever came about between Reinhardt and Zuckmayer at the Salzburg Festival, however.[51] The renowned director never staged a piece by Zuckmayer in spite of holding his talent as a playwright in high esteem.[52] On the other hand, the author gave courses and workshops in dramaturgy and theater history from 1935 to 1938 at the renowned "Reinhardt Seminar," the school Max Reinhardt had founded in Vienna in 1929.

Throughout all of Austria, but especially in Salzburg, antisemitic propaganda intensified in the 1930s, frequently turning into open violence. Stefan Zweig's house had been ransacked by the police in 1934; Max Reinhardt was similarly the victim of antisemitic aggressions, above all when Nazi saboteurs blasted his property, Castle

---

48 Zuckmayer, *Aufruf zum Leben*, 13.
49 Zuckmayer, *Henndorfer Pastorale*, 39.
50 Steinberg, *Ursprung*, 56.
51 For that matter, no play by Zuckmayer was ever performed at the Salzburg Festival. Though the author was working on a play for the Salzburg Festival in 1974, it was never finished. His last stage work, *Der Rattenfänger* (The Rat Catcher), received its premiere at the *Schauspielhaus Zurich* in 1975 (see Bernhard and Unseld, *Der Briefwechsel*, 381).
52 See Strasser, *Carl Zuckmayer*, 138ff.

Leopoldskron, with high-caliber fireworks and heavily damaged it in part. It is alleged that Werner Krauß, an alumnus of the Reinhardt Seminar, offered to have him officially designated an "honorary Aryan" as a means of protection but that Reinhardt declined.[53]

In 1937, in the same year Stefan Zweig left, Reinhardt likewise fled Europe for the United States. The official National Socialist newspaper, the *Völkischer Beobachter*, fulminated as follows after the departure of this founding member of the Salzburg Festival:

> [...] With support from a system alien to our people [...] Reinhardt-Goldmann attempted to deal a fatal blow to a genuinely German art. Thanks to his influence, the Festival had been made totally Jewish; the much-lauded "international" audience consisted mostly of nouveau riche Eastern Jews, which meant that any visit to the Festival city was spoiled for all decent people.[54]

In Hollywood and later in New York City, where he lived with his wife Helene Thimig until his death in 1943, Reinhardt never succeeded—as did so many other emigrants—in establishing himself.

Alexander Lernet-Holenia

Zuckmayer and his fellow writer Alexander Lernet-Holenia (1897–1976) were bound by an especially close friendship, documented in the form of a correspondence lasting over decades.[55] On his sixtieth birthday, adoptive Austrian Zuckmayer wrote admiringly to his friend, who was a scant year younger:

> Strange – in the early years of our acquaintance and friendship I always felt as if you were the older or more mature one, even though I slipped into the year 1896 just under the wire: the reason is most likely an air of prudent restraint I always admired about you [...]. A wisdom about measure and proportion in Goethe's sense, about the Golden Ratio, which constitutes the essence of a true artwork and also that of a significant human life. For my part, I had to have this feeling for due proportion instilled into me—not without being bruised and battered (though not too

---

53 See Strasser, *Carl Zuckmayer*, 124.
54 *Völkischer Beobachter* (November 25, 1938), qtd. in Strasser, *Carl Zuckmayer*, 263.
55 Zuckmayer and Lernet-Holenia, *Briefwechsel und andere Beiträge zur Zuckmayer-Forschung*.

drastically bruised and battered), and then only later in life at that. You always had it, though, whether from early discipline, from stylish indolence, or from your Austrian heritage, all of which lie close together.[56]

Given the background of this characterization, it is not surprising that Lernet-Holenia had a positive attitude toward the Salzburg Festival; his understanding of Hofmannsthal's concept for the Festival[57] was readily compatible with his own idea about the writer as the intellectual leader of the nation.[58] Later on, however, Lernet-Holenia would take a critical stance toward the precedence the Festival granted to economic and political interests.

"Alexander" and "Zuck," die *"Dischder"*[59] friends (as they called themselves in their exchange of letters) shared the same viewpoint about world affairs as well as the non-political character—by and large—of their common pursuit.

The two were also of one mind in regard to the power holders, though Lernet-Holenia compromised himself even less than Zuckmayer, who had after all once voiced himself as emphatically against Goebbels. After taking part in the Polish Campaign, as it was called, where he was able to transfer to the rear area quite early on, in fact after only a few days, because of a minor injury, Lernet-Holenia spent the rest of the Second World War commuting between the "Heeresfilmstelle" (the Military Film Department) in Berlin—where he reviewed,

---

56 Zuckmayer to Lernet-Holenia, October 17, 1957, Zuckmayer and Lernet Holenia (2006), *Briefwechsel*, 59. Lernet in turn acknowledged the deep affinity between him and Zuckmayer with the statement "Zuck is part of us" (qtd. in Musulin, "Zuckmayer, der Österreicher," 85).
57 "Music and dance, and a stage upon the stage, a complete epoch as backdrop, Molière's France and the Greek gods, and the people and the marketplace and the churches and we ourselves. And lo, when he saw the people, he called them to mind and realized that there was something of yet deeper concern to them: the nation. What had been preparing itself in him—as yet unconsciously, expanding broadly—was clear to him all of a sudden, and what emerged to view was that the most authentic calling of a writer is: to lead" (Lernet-Holenia, "Hofmannsthals Werk," 2).
58 "It is not up to the artist to take part is what the nation is doing; instead, the nation is obliged to take part in what the artist is doing […] Writers are the aristocrats of the nation, not its mere affiliates" (Alexander Lernet-Holenia, Letter to Gottfried Benn, May 27, 1933, Deutsches Literaturarchiv Marbach am Neckar, qtd. here from Hübet and Müller, eds., *Alexander Lernet-Holenia*, 57ff.). In 1947 Lernet-Holenia's play *Die Frau des Potiphar* (Potiphar's Wife), with stage music by Gottfried von Einem, had its premiere at the Salzburg Festival.
59 Hessian dialect for standard German *"Dichter"* ("writer").

reworked, and at times also wrote screenplays[60]—Vienna, and St. Wolfgang.[61] Lernet-Holenia, a genius at "networking," had an outstanding gift for using appropriate contacts in the military and the Nazi cultural apparatus to his own advantage without making common cause ideologically with National Socialism.[62] After the war he was able to point to not only a brief and comparatively harmless military involvement but also to the novel he had composed immediately after taking part in the attack on Poland, *Mars im Widder* (*Mars in Aries*), which many interpreters consider the sole "novel of resistance" produced during the Nazi era.[63]

Lernet-Holenia was able not only to keep on after 1945 with the great successes he had enjoyed in the time between the wars; he occupied so eminent a status in Austria's postwar literary life that it led Hans Weigel to coin a much-quoted *bon mot* in 1948: there are currently only two authors in Austria, Lernet and Holenia—whose attitude it was, however, to affect a bored lack of interest in literature and in the literary scene, including his own work, which he purported to be writing mostly for the money.[64] His lyric poetry, which for today's ears sounds opulently classical, was the one achievement he considered lasting.

In any event, the friendship between Zuckmayer and Lernet-Holenia was marked by open admiration (especially Zuckmayer's for Lernet[65])

---

60 Among them was the National Socialist fight-to-the-end production *Die große Liebe* (The Great Love), still remembered through the songs of Zarah Leander (*Davon geht die Welt nicht unter* and *Ich weiß, es wird einmal ein Wunder gescheh'n*) (*That won't be the end of the world* and *I know some day a miracle will come*).
61 See among others Dietz, *Alexander Lernet-Holenia und Lotte Sweceny: Briefe*, and Roček, *Die neun Leben des Alexander Lernet-Holenia. Eine Biographie*. *Mars im Widder* first appeared only in installments in the fashion magazine *Die Dame*; the book version was confiscated by Goebbels himself, literally on the day of its distribution (and did not appear until 1947 in Stockholm).
62 Details about Lernet-Holenia's persistent and eventually successful efforts to be exempted from the military because of indispensable service elsewhere are found in Dietz, *Alexander Lernet-Holenia und Lotte Sweceny*.
63 See Dassanowsky, *Phantom Empires*, among others. Critical assessment in Menasse, *Überbau und Untergrund*, 67, among others.
64 See his letter to Zuckmayer dated March 3, 1949: "[...] I'm not writing anything, and it's only when not doing any work that a person can think; but anyone who puts his mental powers in a bad way; here in a few words you have the entire cause of the absurd state we're in. [...] I have contempt for work, which I say flat out. The one excuse for working is that a person has to make a living, because the morons have done us out of our means" (Zuckmayer and Lernet-Holenia, *Briefwechsel*, 45).
65 "Zuckmayer followed Lernet's literary development more attentively than that of almost any other of his fellow writers" (Zuckmayer and Lernet-Holenia, *Briefwechsel*, 21 [Foreword]).

and a self-mocking courtliness that not seldom affects third parties, ones from later generations above all, as comical:[66]

> With and through and partly in spirt of all his foibles, Alexander, is by far the most exceptional and substantial person in our whole circle of friends and acquaintances./Sometimes it can be good to enjoy his company more through letters for a while; then you appreciate him twice as much. But by all means he's an eternal part of our inventory and our holdings […][67]

Thus Zuckmayer in a letter to their mutual friend Albrecht Joseph, who for his part was one of the "house guests" (see the section on "House Guests" later in this chapter). It may have been easier, of course, too, for Zuckmayer to hold all the higher in his esteem a writer who fished in different waters than he did: Lernet's days as a successful playwright were already a thing of the past by the late 1930s.

Werner Krauß

Zuckmayer's friendships with his actor friends Werner Krauß and Emil Jannings, who likewise lived in the vicinity, took a more complicated form.

Zuckmayer had been friends with Werner Krauß (1884–1959) since the 1920s. As early as 1913, Krauß had come to Max Reinhardt's Deutsches Theater in Berlin and was rapidly assessed as one of the greats of his craft; Zuckmayer was hired as a dramaturg (along with Bertolt Brecht, incidentally) at the same theater in 1924. After the Nazi "takeover," Krauß advanced very rapidly to become one of the most avidly courted actors of the new regime, attested by invitations from Dollfuss, Mussolini, and Hitler, his appointment as "Official State Actor" (by Hermann Göring) and as deputy president of the *Reichstheaterkammer*, the National Socialist Theater Organization, culminating in his elevation to the "Exceptionally Gifted List."[68]

Considered an extraordinary talent, Krauß played the title role in Zuckmayer's *The Captain of Köpenick* at the *Deutsches Theater Berlin* in 1931. In 1920, Krauß had played both Death and the Devil (!) in Hofmannthal's *Jedermann* (*Everyman*) in the first season of the Salzburg Festival.

---

66 Impressively documented in Zuckmayer and Lernet-Holenia, *Briefwechsel*, where it is performed very openly at times, especially in criticizing fellow men and women writers.
67 Letter from February 2, 1936 (Zuckmayer and Joseph, *Briefwechsel*, 156).
68 A list of over a thousand persons considered by the regime as irreplaceable (as a result of which they enjoyed numerous privileges, including exemption from duty at the front); the list was compiled in 1943 by Hitler and Goebbels.

Zuckmayer more than once[69] provided memorable examples of Krauß's uncanny (in both senses) acting talent: outfitted with a rigid, grimacing mask whose expression he was unable to change, he could portray any emotion, any role compellingly, to the delight but also the discomfiture of his audience.

A low point of Krauß's career—from the standpoint of his critics but of course the opposite from the standpoint of the regime[70]—was reached through his collaboration with director Veit Harlan in the infamous antisemitic propaganda film *Jud Süß* (*Jew Süss*) (1940), in which Krauß used his extraordinary changeability to play no fewer than four Jewish characters.

Paradoxically it was just this lack of a fixed point, this changeability (inner as well) of the acting profession in general that Zuckmayer would later—despite the unmistakable cooling off of their friendship during the Third Reich[71]—adduce in Krauß's favor. In the character sketch he provided in his *Geheimreport* (*Confidential Report*), a book-length dossier on fellow artists and public figures he prepared for the American Office of Strategic Services, Zuckmayer classified Krauß (as well as Jannings) under "Group 3: Special Cases, partly positive, partly negative."[72]

What is common to Zuckmayer's depictions of both luminaries of the theater world—they were originally "as close in brotherhood as the Dioscuri" but then vied for the favor of the National Socialist cultural apparatus—is the author's more or less transparent effort to exculpate them from their involvements by determining that the personality structures inherent to the acting profession were what made them susceptible: "Actors are entirely in-between beings psychologically."[73]

> The German stage must never lose this actor [Werner Krauß] as long as he lives. How an actor like him might have conducted himself in any given instance during the Nazi period is perhaps of not much importance [...]/God only knows what takes

---

69 In his autobiography as well as in his portrait of Krauß in his book *Geheimreport* (*Confidential Report*).
70 Goebbels: "An antisemitic film such as we could only dream of. I'm happy with it" (diary entry of September 18, 1940).
71 At its most intense phase, this friendship between the two men (though it's tempting to say between two overgrown schoolboys), these two admirers of Karl May played "cowboys and Indians" in the wood around Henndorf, as Zuckmayer reports in *A Part of Myself*.
72 Zuckmayer sets up a total of four categories: "Group 1: Positive (untouched by Nazi influence, opposed, reliable) [...] Group 2: Negative (Nazis, toadies, pocket-liners, lapdogs) [...] Group 3: Special Cases, partly positive, partly negative [...] Group 4: apathetic, opaque, vague, problematic" (Zuckmayer, *Geheimreport*, 15).
73 Zuckmayer, *Geheimreport*, 10.

place in a fantasy-laden but not intellectually strong mind like Werner Krauss's. [...] On the other hand—anyone familiar with the journalistic methods of the Third Reich knows that what's printed in a newspaper never provides reliable grounds for saying that someone really did voice the given opinion or consent to whatever [...] Was Werner Krauss [...] an antisemite? If so, then not in a political sense, but at most in a more nebulous and unclear, instinctive way.[74]

A "'causa turpis,' at heart a morally repugnant matter,"[75] was how Erwin Rotermund referred to Zuckmayer's advocacy of his actor friends. The "perspective of a vitalistic ethics"[76] misled him into minimizing Krauß's and Jannings's close involvement with the National Socialist regime. It's a matter of fact that Zuckmayer testified in Krauß's favor at the actor's denazification hearing in 1947;[77] Krauß was then classed as *"minderbelastet"* or incriminated to only a lesser degree and remained active as a celebrated star in the ensemble of Vienna Burgtheater, among others, until his death in 1959.

Emil Jannings

In the case of Emil Jannings (actually Theodor Emil Janenz, 1884–1950), the first Oscar winner in history, Zuckmayer openly declares himself a "champion": "I just love the old bastard."[78] In contrast to Krauß, who was "more primal, more complicated, gloomier, more filled with genius, less worldly wise, less amusing"[79] than his colleague, Jannings was for Zuckmayer the veritable embodiment of the outstanding, larger-than-life individual.

The two had been friends since working together on *Der blaue Engel/The Blue Angel* (1930), to which Zuckmayer had contributed the

---

74 Zuckmayer, *Geheimreport*, 149ff.
75 Rotermund, "'Charaktere' und 'Verräter': Carl Zuckmayers 'Geheimreport' von 1943/44," 367.
76 Rotermund, "'Charaktere' und 'Verräter'," 370.
77 And was at no loss to justify himself later on, in 1947, for instance, replying to an open letter in the newspaper *Münchener Mittag*, which accused him of judging actors differently from "ordinary mortals": "Nonetheless I make every effort, perhaps related to my profession as a playwright, to understand people essentially from the standpoint of their individual natures and predispositions. [...] What we most need to guard against, and today more than ever, is generalization as an organizing principle, oversimplifying on theory. Doing so means we will never emerge from the moral and spiritual catastrophe of our time (not just Germany's, either)" (qtd. in Zuckmayer, *Geheimreport*, 352 [commentary]).
78 Zuckmayer, *Geheimreport*, 136.
79 Zuckmayer, *Geheimreport*, 146.

screenplay (based on Heinrich Mann's novel *Professor Unrat*). Under the direction of Josef von Sternberg, Jannings had played the role of Professor Immanuel Rath, who falls hopelessly in love with the cabaret singer Lola (Marlene Dietrich in her first major role).

Jannings lived with his wife, the actress Gussy Holl, and Ruth, a daughter from his first marriage, on a large estate in Strobl, on a peninsula opposite St. Wolfgang.[80] The place was a rendezvous for everyone who was anyone on the National Socialist cultural scene, once even visited by Joseph Goebbels, the propaganda minister, on the occasion of his attending the Salzburg Festival.

People in Zuckmayer's circle of friends were not of one mind about "the Janningses": whereas Zuckmayer's character sketch basically consists of a great declaration of love—one just as readable as it is conflicted, for reasons already named—his friend Albrecht Joseph (and even his daughter Winnetou) considered both husband and wife cruel, arrogant, and pretentious.[81] Emil Jannings was "coldly calculating and ruthlessly egotistical," in Klaus Mann's judgment.[82] Jannings's egotism and opportunism did not escape Zuckmayer's notice, either—these traits of character, along with a "lifelong, never-ending rivalry with his old friend and colleague Werner Krauss," a fascination for the "'showmanship' of the Nazis" and an almost pathological hunger for power,[83] were the reasons for Jannings's cooperation with the National Socialist regime.

Another reason for Zuckmayer's solidarity with Jannings was no doubt that the discredited author was hoping to have a powerful advocate in Berlin in the person of this influential "Reich cultural senator"[84]—a deceptive hope, in that it was Jannings, after all, who advised Zuckmayer after the *Anschluss* not to flee—"a pathetic Jewish refugee."[85]

Zuckmayer summed up as follows after the war:

> Emil is widely hated; at few others is the intolerance of the righteous directed so fanatically and with such humorless severity. It's understandable, though, that many emigrants—earlier friends who now see him as a traitor—and especially Jewish people—

---

80 In acquiring this real estate, Jannings profited from a forced sale by owners persecuted for racial reasons.
81 See Strasser, *Carl Zuckmayer*, 128.
82 Qtd. from Klee, *Das Kulturlexikon zum Dritten Reich*, 280.
83 See Zuckmayer, *Geheimreport*, 143.
84 During the Second World War, Jannings was helpful in keeping Lernet-Holenia away from the front. "Emil did a great deal during the war to rescue me from the claws of that jackass Hitler" (Lernet-Holenia to Zuckmayer, March 9, 1946; Lernet-Holenia and Zuckmayer, *Briefwechsel*, 32).
85 As reported by Albrecht Joseph, qtd. in Strasser, *Carl Zuckmayer*, 218.

have bad feelings toward him. But if he were being pursued, I would hide him if it were in any way possible. This is part and parcel of his makeup.[86]

Jannings set great value on Zuckmayer's loyalty: "Zuckmayer, who through it all remained the same decent lad he always was, came to my defense not only in words but in deeds as well."[87] Not with the same success, however, as with Jannings's eternal rival Werner Krauß (see above): the Allies imposed on the "Hitler favorite"[88] a lifelong prohibition against performing—imposed on one who, during the silent-film era at least—had been considered the best actor in the world.

"House Guests"

Many of the Zuckmayers's friends were far from being in the privileged position of owning property in the area around Henndorf, neither as their main residence nor as their second home. Not a few of them nonetheless enjoyed the couple's hospitality as guests for weeks or months at a time at the Wiesmühl, whether just to work or to reside totally.

Albrecht Joseph

One frequent visitor who stayed for long periods, for example, was Albrecht Joseph (1901– 1991), nicknamed "Jowes." His friendship with Zuckmayer reached back to the 1920s, to the time they spent together at the Vereinigtes Städtisches Theater (United Municipal Theater) in Kiel, where Zuckmayer worked as a dramaturg and Joseph as a director—and from which they were both fired in 1923 because of youthfully provocative productions (and financial incompetence).

Even as they were first formed, relations between the two were tilted toward recognition and success on Zuckmayer's part, but not without some participation by Joseph, who was involved, for instance, in his friend's great stage (and later film) success[89] *The Captain of Köpenick* as well as consulting with him on dramaturgical and other literary matters.

---

86 Zuckmayer, *Geheimreport*, 136.
87 Jannings to Arnolt Bronnen, March 5, 1947 (DLA, Bronnen papers, qtd. in Zuckmayer, *Geheimreport*, 343).
88 Zuckmayer, *Geheimreport*, 142.
89 In the first nine months alone, the play earned Zuckmayer 160,000 Reichmark (c. 640,000 euro today; see note 16 above). Carl Zuckmayer did succeed, however, in having Albrecht Joseph listed as co-author of the film script directed by Richard Oswald (Zuckmayer and Joseph, *Briefwechsel*, 689 [afterword]).

From 1933 on, Joseph was virtually a permanent guest of the Zuckmayers in Henndorf:

> The house was an old mill, the "Wiesmühl," and on the property, about fifty meters away, was a log cabin [...]. I lived there for many months at a stretch during the next five years. It was a lovely time for me, though I knew even then and know even more clearly today that I must have been a rather tiresome guest at times.[90]

So wrote Joseph, somewhat peevishly, in his memoirs titled *Ein Tisch bei Romanoff's: Vom expressionistischen Theater zur Westernserie* (1991) (*A Table at Romanoff's: From Expressionistic Theater to Western Series*). These memoirs as well as letters to third parties, especially to his brother Rudolf, paint a picture of a man for whom life had in store nothing beyond a "supporting role."[91]

Later on, though probably even during the 1930s, Joseph chafed under his dependence on Zuckmayer and what he thought of as the man's second-rate[92]—at best—literary talent. At the same time, it was Joseph's view that Zuckmayer deliberately minimized him, a man who at the beginning of their friendship had been the more successful one; notwithstanding all his support, Zuckmayer never offered him a financial share of what Joseph considered their joint successes.

What is being voiced here, in a letter by Joseph to his brother Rudolf (dated January 8, 1937), is an unstable relationship of dependency, almost like that between parents and a child struggling to become self-supporting:

> I made clear to him and Liccie [Alice Herdan-Zuckmayer, C.D.] that I can't be his shadow all my life, not financially either [...]. But Z. [Carl Zuckmayer, C.D.] and Liccie, though they hope to see me financially secure and self-supporting on the one hand, hate with a passion any move toward independence in my life on the other, whether concerning a woman to whom they feel I'm too strongly attached or my own work, especially as a writer, which Z doesn't want to see and considers an outright intrusion into his realm.[93]

---

90 Joseph, *Ein Tisch bei Romanoff's*, 167.
91 See Zuckmayer and Joseph, *Briefwechsel*, 682 (afterword).
92 "He [Carl Zuckmayer] is forever purporting to be a major literary figure, but he was never on that level. I did my tactful best to anchor him to practical solid ground theatrically, but it never worked out" (A. Joseph to Rudolf Joseph, February 4, 1967, qtd. in Zuckmayer and Joseph, *Briefwechsel*, 697 (Letters to Rudolf Joseph in the German Exile Archive (*Deutsches Exilarchiv*, papers of R.J.).
93 Qtd. in Zuckmayer and Joseph, *Briefwechsel*, 693ff.

During and after the period of emigration the ill-matched friends grew ever farther apart: Albrecht Joseph worked on an (unsuccessful) new film version of *The Captain of Köpenick* without letting Carl Zuckmayer know. There then arose differing opinions about the quality of Zuckmayer's play *Des Teufels General*[94] (*The Devil's General*, trans. Ingrid Komar); finally, Joseph was disappointed at being mentioned so seldom in Zuckmayer's autobiography *A Part of Myself*.

It seems in retrospect that Albrecht Joseph was not very comfortable with Zuckmayer's "vitalism."[95] Even in the early days in Kiel, Zuckmayer had played the role of "front-line soldier"[96] and acted superior to colleagues with no experience of war—an appraisal surely not altogether unjustified.

Joseph's final, unforgiving judgment on his friend only a few days after Zuckmayer's death: "inconsiderate, unreliable, opportunistic, and immensely egotistical."[97]

Franz Horch

Franz Horch was another active advisor to Zuckmayer, especially in dramaturgical matters, but he was apparently paid for his work by Zuckmayer, who made no secret of it, thus incurring Albrecht Joseph's resentment in yet another way: "Horch gets paid for accomplishing less than I offer to do [...], and very well at that, while I never got anything." (There is no record, however, that Horch was provided with room and board at the "Wiesmühl" as extensively as Joseph.)

Franz Horch (1901–1951) came from an upper-middle-class Viennese family and had pursued a career in theater; it took him from Friedrich Rosenthal's "Österreichische Wanderbühne" (Austrian Traveling Theater) and the Wiener Kammerspiele (Vienna Chamber Theater) to the Theater in der Josefstadt, where he was a dramaturg under Max Reinhardt from 1926 to 1932 and editor of the *Blätter des Theaters in der Josefstadt* (Bulletin of the Theater in der Josefstadt). He was also employed as dramaturg at the Deutsches Theater in Berlin in 1929 and 1930, in addition to which he worked for the Deutsches

---

94 A. Joseph to Rudolf Joseph, October 27, 1962: "insufferable ideological blather" (qtd. in Zuckmayer and Joseph, *Briefwechsel*, 709).
95 A. Joseph to Rudolf Joseph, December 4, 1966 (qtd. in Zuckmayer and Joseph, *Briefwechsel*, 697).
96 Joseph, *Ein Tisch bei Romanoff's*, 73. A frequent pattern, one communicated—among other instances—by Elias Canetti about an encounter he had with Heimito von Doderer. When Canetti replied with an outraged negative to Doderer's question as to whether Canetti had ever killed a man, Doderer retorted that in that case Canetti was still a "virgin."
97 A. Joseph to Rudolf Joseph, February 3, 1977 (qtd. in Zuckmayer and Joseph, *Briefwechsel*, 699).

Lichtspielsyndikat (Syndicate for German Cinema). Like so many others, he left Berlin in 1933 and returned to the supposedly greater safety of Vienna, where he worked in the theater distribution department at Zsolnay Publishers.[98]

Horch was also part of the group of friends that met on March 11, 1938, the day of the Anschluss, Austria's annexation to the German Reich, to take counsel as to what they should do. Zuckmayer detailed this poignant scene in his autobiography,[99] though depicting Horch in not very flattering terms: "Horch was a man of nervous temperament anyway, and today his whole body was shaking and he was constantly repressing tears."[100] Among the other friends, "shipwreck victims on a sinking vessel,"[101] were some who were part of the "Henndorf Circle": Ödön von Horváth, Franz Theodor Csokor, Albrecht Joseph, and Alexander Lernet-Holenia; in addition, according to Strasser, Horváth's brother Lajos.[102] Except for Lernet-Holenia, who, despite a body of work "not to be tolerated by National Socialist audiences,"[103] managed to remain in the country (Austria and Germany alike) but away from the front lines, all of them had to leave Austria sooner or later.

Franz Horch emigrated that same year to New York City via Zurich, where he was active as a literary agent—among others for Franz Werfel, Thomas Mann, and Upton Sinclair[104]—until his early death in 1951. When the Zuckmayers followed later, Horch helped wherever he could and greeting them on their arrival, "wildly waving."[105]

Franz Theodor Csokor

"*Amicus amicorum*"—this was the superlative with which Zuckmayer characterized his friend Franz Theodor Csokor (1885–1969) at an after-dinner speech to honor the older writer's eightieth birthday in 1965. Like Zuckmayer, Csokor had infuriated the National Socialists early on by protesting—especially against the book burnings they organized—at

---

98 See "Horch, Franz."
99 Zuckmayer, *A Part of Myself*, 50.
100 Zuckmayer, *A Part of Myself*, 62.
101 Zuckmayer, *A Part of Myself*, 62.
102 Strasser, *Carl Zuckmayer*, 102.
103 NS-Kulturgemeinde, Kulturpolitisches Archiv: Schreiben an die Filmkontingentstelle (Bundesarchiv, NS 15, Aktenband 138b, fol. 3). Berlin, February 12, 1935 (qtd. by Sommer, "*Er dient um die Erlaubnis*" 181). Relevant details in Dietz, *Alexander Lernet-Holenia und Lotte Sweceny*).
104 Strobel, "Schöne Gedichte – 'Mäßige Schriftstellerei': Thomas Mann und Carl Zuckmayer," 254.
105 Zuckmayer, *A Part of Myself*, 396. Always ready to help, Horch had already secured US visas for the Zuckmayers, although they did not want to make use of them at that time (see Strasser, *Carl Zuckmayer*, 117).

the congress of the International P.E.N. Club in Dubrovnik in 1933. He would go on in later years to become the vice-president of P.E.N. Csokor, who favored the concept of an international Salzburg Festival, is the author of many informative first-hand accounts about the atmosphere that prevailed during the Festival summers in the 1930s.[106]

His earliest plays had appeared during the First World War, earning him a reputation as one of the most significant expressionistic authors in Austria. He wrote one of his most best-known works as a guest of the Zuckmayers in 1936, "[...] in the log cabin we had had built on our property for guests, [...] his most successful play, *November 3, 1918*, which earned him the [highly prestigious—translator's note] Ring of the Burgtheater." Zuckmayer's esteem for Csokor was more as a friend than as a dramatist, as emerges in a letter to Albrecht Joseph from January 19, 1965: "[...] he is the grand elder statesman of Vienna [...] [He] keeps on writing plays that are not performed but get printed by subsidized publishing houses."[107] Csokor's odyssey in his flight from the Nazis took him through Poland, Romania, Yugoslavia, and Italy, and had taken on the quality of legend—a legend equal to his "once, in earlier days, having written good plays," in Zuckmayer's somewhat catty words, "which can really only be said to some extent about *November 3, 1918*, written in the log cabin in Henndorf [...]."[108]

It's likely that Zuckmayer considered his "best of all friends" as a rival, in reference not only to his work as a playwright[109] but also to the favored status enjoyed by their younger mutual friend Ödön von Horváth, whom Csokor had come to know in 1933 through Zuckmayer.[110]

After that flight through half of Europe, Csokor attached himself to the British army in the liberated area of southern Italy, worked for the BBC, and ended up returning to Vienna in 1946. In December of that year, he attended the premiere of *The Devil's General* in a United States military uniform, as Zuckmayer recalls.[111] From 1947 on he was active in the Austrian P.E.N. Club, among other functions as president. He died in Vienna in 1969.

Ödön von Horváth

Zuckmayer (and not only he) considered the third member of this "triumvirate of writers,"[112] Zuckmayer-Csokor-Horváth, Ödön von

---

106 As documented in Klauhs, *Franz Theodor Csokor: Leben und Werk bis 1938 im Überblick*.
107 Zuckmayer & Joseph, *Briefwechsel*, 426f.
108 Zuckmayer & Joseph, *Briefwechsel*, 427.
109 See Strasser, "Ein Haus der Emigration."
110 Strasser, "Carl Zuckmayer," 103.
111 Zuckmayer, *A Part of Myself*, 399.
112 See Strasser, "Ein Haus der Emigration."

Horváth (1901–1938), to be "the strongest dramatic talent of our time [...] after Brecht."[113] Horváth visited Henndorf for the first time in 1933,[114] where he became a welcome guest, in fact—along with "his dearest and most faithful pal Franz Theodor Csokor"—the most frequent visitor among the "Wiesmühl Circle."[115] Zuckmayer had made the acquaintance of Horváth, around five years younger, at the Berliner Volksbühne (Berlin Popular Theater) in 1929. They quickly became friends, and Zuckmayer, always adept at combining personal and professional matters, placed his colleague with his own publisher, Ullstein, who took Horváth under contract for twelve months.[116]

After the National Socialists had expelled Horváth from Germany in 1936, he repeatedly spent periods of several months in Henndorf, usually staying at the time-honored but rather creepy "Caspar Moser Inn,"[117] where he preferred to write in the taproom. It was during this time that he wrote *Figaro lässt sich scheiden* (*Figaro Gets Divorced*, trans. Christopher Hampton), *Don Juan kommt aus dem Krieg* (*Don Juan Comes Back from the War*, trans. Christopher Hampton), and *Jugend ohne Gott* (*Youth without God*, trans. Thomas R. Willis). Horváth spent the fall and winter months of 1937 as well as the first weeks of 1938 in Henndorf, up till the *Anschluss* forced him to flee to Budapest.

Horváth's death in 1938 is among the most bizarre in literary history; he was fatally wounded by a falling tree branch in Paris. The mishap gains an even more poignant aspect through the fact that Horváth was in essence on his way to visit the Zuckmayers, who had meanwhile fled to Chardonne in Switzerland. And it was Zuckmayer who held the funeral oration at his friend's grave.[118] "We were together on the night

---

113 Zuckmayer, *A Part of Myself*, 86. In 1931, on Zuckmayer's recommendation, Horváth had been awarded the Kleist Prize, the most prestigious literary prize of the Weimar Republic. Altogether, numerous winners of the Kleist Prize were part of the Henndorf Circle: Alexander Lernet-Holenia (1926), Horváth, already mentioned (1931), Richard Billinger (1932), to whom Zuckmayer preferred Horváth, and not least—before all the rest, too—Zuckmayer himself (1925). Not until long after his death was Horváth performed in Salzburg, however, with *Figaro Gets Divorced* in 1970, directed by Oscar Fritz Schuh as the first production (Salzburger Festspiel Archiv, n.d.).
114 In his book *Aufruf zum Leben*, Zuckmayer himself dates this visit to 1935, but erroneously, as Strasser has documented (*Carl Zuckmayer*, 99).
115 Zuckmayer, *Aufruf zum Leben*, 99.
116 See Lernet-Holenia and Zuckmayer, *Briefwechsel*, 163 (commentary).
117 What the games of "cowboys and Indians" were to Zuckmayer's friendship with Werner Krauß was in Horváth's case a belief in ghosts: Horváth believed and took delight in the ghost stories that circulated in the old tavern in Henndorf. See Strasser, *Carl Zuckmayer*, 100.
118 At the St. Ouen cemetery in Paris. In 1988, Horváth's remains were transferred to a grave of honor at the Heiligenstadt Cemetery in Vienna.

Austria was obliterated," he said, "and we shook hands that night for the last time, before the winds blew us apart."[119]

Alfred Ibach

Unlike Horváth, Alfred Ibach (1902–1948) is largely forgotten today. Like Albrecht Joseph and Franz Horch, other members of the "Wiesmühl Circle" who were roughly the same age, Ibach was a man of the theater; the *Österreichisches Biographisches Lexikon* (Austrian Biographical Dictionary) lists him as "theater expert," dramaturge, and publisher.[120] In addition, Ibach, born in Saarland, was active as a writer, producing short stories, poems, a (worshipful) biography of prominent actor Paula Wessely (*Wessely*, 1943), and (among other works) the screenplay for the film *Das andere Leben* (The Other Life; director Rudolf Steinböck), based on the novella *Der 20. Juli* (July 20) by Alexander Lernet-Holenia (see above).

Ibach is mentioned only sparingly in Zuckmayer's memoirs and letters—with one (conspicuous) exception: in *Geheimreport* Zuckmayer characterizes his friend as a man "of unusually discriminating intelligence and finely attuned responsiveness" and recommends him emphatically to head "a new German Cultural Ministry":

> He is what could be called a "man of understanding," himself not creative and without artistic imagination or shaping power of his own, but endowed with an ever-alert and lively understanding of all matters artistic and at all times prepared [...] to help and stand by the side of productive individuals.[121]

An "intransigent anti-Nazi" in heart and head, Ibach is remarkable for "integrity of character as well as delicacy and utter devotedness in friendship, loyalty to those he is close to or who seem estimable to him."[122] It was Ibach who went with Zuckmayer to his train in Vienna when the latter departed from Vienna at the last moment, "prepared to stay by my side, in case he was needed."[123]

---

119 Zuckmayer, *Aufruf zum Leben*, 105.
120 See the entry "Ibach, Alfred (1902–1948), Dramaturg und Verleger, 1961." Ibach was "one of the best theater people in Vienna and Germany and might well be one of the most astute and perceptive dramaturgs who have ever worked at the Theater in der Josefstadt," it goes on to say. Regarding Ibach's activity as a publisher—he was involved with E. P. Tal & Co., of which he became the head in March 1938 as part of an "'internal Aryanization'" and later changed into Alfred Ibach Publishers—see Hall, *Österreichische Verlagsgeschichte*, 409ff.
121 Zuckmayer, *Geheimreport*, 28f.
122 Zuckmayer, *Geheimreport*, 30.
123 Zuckmayer, *A Part of Myself*, 57.

The fragile health Zuckmayer also mentions in his report might well have been a factor contributing to Ibach's death in Vienna as early as 1948.

Hans Schiebelhuth

A similarly short life was likewise granted to Hans Schiebelhuth, Zuckmayer's friend from their younger days. This poet and translator, born in Darmstadt in 1895, worked so intently during the 1930s—at times as a guest at the Wiesmühl—on translations from American English (Thomas Wolfe and William Faulkner) that his heart ailment[124] grew worse, so that on his physician's advice he settled in the Hamptons, where the climate was favorable and where he died, in East Hampton, New York, in 1944.

"From first glance on there was so much love between us," writes Zuckmayer about the first encounter between him and "Scheeby" after the First World War,

> that he spent the night on a wicker chair in my attic room, and stayed on for some time afterwards. Our affection for each other—for it was more than friendship—never stopped; he became a third son to my parents, a playmate to our daughters, a virtual member of the household in Henndorf, and a comfort in exile, where he was almost the only person with whom I could talk about Germany and know that my feelings would be understood.[125]

At the beginning of the "Expulsion" chapter of his memoirs, Zuckmayer related what his friend had to say about the enduring inner pictures in our memories.[126]

Schiebelhuth is one of the friends of Zuckmayer—and their number is not small—who died during the time of his exile; others were Max Reinhardt (d. 1943), Carlo Mierendorff (d. 1943), and Stefan Zweig (d. 1942). Schiebelhuth's death affected Zuckmayer like none other: "In the period of eclipse [during the Nazi regime and in exile, C.D.] [...] nothing had so strengthened and encouraged me as his existence, nothing so depressed me and so nearly undermined what self-command I had as the loss of him at the beginning of that somber year, 1944."[127]

---

124 Zuckmayer, *A Part of Myself*, 338.
125 Zuckmayer, *A Part of Myself*, 205.
126 "The image within is everlasting" (Zuckmayer, *A Part of Myself*, 30).
127 Zuckmayer, *A Part of Myself*, 339.

Additional Members

Three more writers should be mentioned as members of the "Henndorf Circle,"[128] notwithstanding that Zuckmayer did not include them in the rather loose grouping of friends and acquaintances he himself referred to as the "Wiesmühl Circle." They were part of neither the local residents nor the regular "house guests."

Richard Billinger

It was Richard Billinger (1890–1965) who had told Zuckmayer in 1926 about the "Wiesmühl" and its availability. Zuckmayer was one of Billinger's numerous benefactors. Son of a salesman, he came from St. Marienkirchen near Schärding and developed into a respected lyric poet under the patronage of major figures like Hugo von Hofmannsthal; starting in the mid-1920s he presented himself more as a playwright. His play *Perchtenspiel* had its premiere at the Salzburg Festival in 1928.

Billinger allowed himself to be coopted by the National Socialists after 1933. In him they saw—at least in the beginning[129]—a "blood and soil" poet altogether to their taste, an assessment Billinger not only did not dispute but pointedly underscored through "dedicatory verses" to Adolf Hitler in 1938. Along with Karl Heinrich Waggerl, Josef Weinheber, and others, Billinger permitted his name to appear on the list titled *Dichter bekennen sich zur Heimkehr ins Reich* (*Poets Endorse Austria's Return to the German Reich*) compiled by the former Viennese *Gauleiter* or district superior Alfred Frauenfeld.[130]

Billinger did not meet with approval among some of the members of the Wiesmühl Circle, and as his friend became increasingly loyal to the regime, Zuckmayer himself grew ever more distant, finally writing a pointedly negative appraisal in his *Geheimreport*, which was powerless, however, to diminish Billinger's career after the Second World War,[131] because in the end too little evidence concerning Billinger's active participation with Nazism could be found.

---

128 In Strasser, *Carl Zuckmayer*, and in the German-language Wikipedia article, which seems to be mainly indebted to Strasser's book.
129 Billinger's homosexuality was a thorn in the side of the new holders of power, however; Billinger had even spent time in jail in 1935 for "unnatural sexual practices."
130 Klee, "Politisch gut ausgerichtet."
131 In 1954, award by the Upper Austrian parliament of a monthly stipend for life; in 1961 named a member of the Bavarian Academy of Fine Arts; in 1963 the Grillparzer Prize (Klee, *Das Kulturlexikon zum Dritten Reich: Wer war was vor und nach 1945*, 52).

Among other reasons, Zuckmayer explained Billinger's faulty judgment by his originating "[...] from the same area of Austria as Hitler, the Innviertel [...]," "[...] a breeding ground for clairvoyants, inscrutable orators, daydreamers, moonstruck people and for everything involving sorcery, demonology, and the all-around delusional."[132] Yet more severe:

> Billinger is a degenerate farmer, a perfumed bumpkin, a village decadent, meaning he's exactly the type the Nazis would consider the very embodiment of the "blood and soil" poet. [...] He is conceited, vengeful, totally unreliable, incredibly cowardly and always ready to betray anyone, especially those he hates because he's beholden to them or those who have seen through his mask of "primitive earthiness."[133]

Later mellowed by age, Zuckmayer, writing in his *Henndorfer Pastorale* (1970), expressed himself more leniently toward Billinger, once promoted, now estranged and resting for five years in a grave of honor provided by the state of Upper Austria.

Johannes Freumbichler

Another writer encouraged by Zuckmayer was Johannes Freumbichler (1881–1949), born in Henndorf; today the Henndorf Literature House is located in his former home. Freumbicher's renown is at second hand today: the grandfather of the writer Thomas Bernhard, he appears in various places in his grandson's work; his influence on his famous grandson (who grew up without a father) was considerable.

There is testimony from several quarters that Freumbichler was indebted to the Zuckmayers for his (none too brilliant) career.[134] Above all, Alice Herdan-Zuckmayer advocated for Freumbichler, who lived between 1935 and 1938 in Seekirchen, a few kilometers from Henndorf, and who frequently came to the "Wiesmühl" in 1936 on working visits. "Four or five times a week" they would revise Freumbichler's extensive novel *Philomena Ellenhub* in a group:[135]

> The more time I spent reading this manuscript, the greater grew my respect for this man—I might almost say my awe. The most daunting times of my life were sitting with this man at the large

---

132 Zuckmayer, *Geheimreport*, 69.
133 Zuckmayer, *Geheimreport*, 70.
134 Strasser, *Carl Zuckmayer*, 161.
135 "[...] a book Zuckmayer would himself like to have written [...]" (Strasser, *Carl Zuckmayer*, 164).

wooden table in our mill room and having a hand in this glory of literature.[136]

Carl Zuckmayer brought both author and manuscript to the attention of the Zsolnay Press in Vienna, where the novel appeared at the end of 1936. "This is the life's work of a mature man of peasant stock but called to be a writer and dedicating his entire existence to this calling without ever having enjoyed access to the public, to reaction, or to success," wrote Zuckmayer in his "Essay on *Philomena Ellenhub.*"[137] This novel earned Freumbichler the Great Austrian State Prize for Literature (Emerging Artist), the one official recognition he would ever earn for his work during his lifetime.

Jakob Haringer

Mention should be made in closing of the writer Jakob Haringer (1898–1948), born in Dresden, raised in Munich and Salzburg. His itinerant life took him for several years in the 1930s to Salzburg, where he drifted into the circle around the Zuckmayers. When Haringer was about to be expelled from Salzburg in 1935, Zuckmayer intervened on his behalf successfully.[138] There followed in 1938 his flight via Prague

---

136 Alice Herdan-Zuckmayer, Afterword to *Philomena Ellenhub*, qtd. in Bengesser, *Literaturlandschaft Flachgau*, 76. Freumbicher at times brought his grandson Thomas Bernhard along on his visits. The younger man recalls: "During these months he [Freumbichler, C.D.] was invited fairly often to visit the famous writer, who had helped him achieve his first and only success and at whose home people at least as famous as he came and went every day. The famous writer had two daughters, with whom I was allowed to play; they were somewhat older than I and had a small log cabin to themselves, located on the grounds of the famous writer's house, which had once been a mill. [...] The world of fame was a sensation for me. When famous people arrived, got out of their cars and went through the garden, we children looked through the skylight in the attic of the log cabin and admired them" (Bernhard, *Ein Kind*, 67f.). Whether Thomas Bernhard was thinking of Zuckmayer's father when he created the figure of the "wine-bottle cork manufacturer" in his novel *Die Auslöschung (Extinction)* must remain speculation; Zuckmayer's father had earned his living by producing corks for wine bottles.
137 Qtd. in Bengesser, *Literaturlandschaft Flachgau*, 77. Zuckmayer's commitment extended as well to Freumbichler's grandson Thomas Bernhard, whose works Zuckmayer emphatically praised again and again (see the relevant passages in Bernhard and Unseld, *Der Briefwechsel*). Zuckmayer's review of Bernhard's first novel *Frost* was instrumental in its success ("one of the most provocative and striking prose works" ("Ein Sinnbild," *Die Zeit*, 25 [June 21, 1963]). Thomas Bernhard at a memorial in the *Schauspielhaus Zürich* on January 31, 1977, to mark Zuckmayer's passing: "As far as my work is concerned, [Zuckmayer] had a sensitivity like none other (Bernhard and Unseld, *Der Briefwechsel*, 514).
138 Details in Strasser, *Carl Zuckmayer*, 156ff.

and Strassburg to Switzerland, where he was interned in a work camp in 1940 and then involuntarily confined to psychiatric institutions on several occasions. Haringer died in Zurich in 1948.[139] Except for the interventions documented in Zuckmayer's letters, Haringer is not mentioned in the works germane to our present study—not in Zuckmayer's memoirs, not in his correspondence with Albrecht Joseph, and not in the *Geheimreport*.

At the Center of the Circle: Alice Herdan-Zuckmayer

As tentative or even uncertain as the affiliation of this or that person to the "Henndorf Circle" might occasionally be, one person is undeniably linked with it for all time to come: Alice Henriette Alberta Herdan-Harris von Valbonne und Belmont (1901–1991), or, in brief, Alice von Herdan, and simply Alice Herdan after 1918, when the "von" of aristocratic titles was abolished in Austria. There is certainly reason enough for the indissoluble linkage—not only was "Liccie" or "Jobs," as her friends called her, the actual owner (entered in the registry of deeds, the *Grundbuch*) of the "Wiesmühl,"[140] but her ability to create harmony among the common group of friends was powerful, not to say integral.

Alice was born in Vienna in 1901, the daughter of Maurice Herdan, an attorney, and of Claire Liesenberg, an actor. She attended a girls' school held in high favor by the liberal middle class in Vienna, the *Gymnasium* run by Eugenie Schwarzwald (who developed friendly relations with the Zuckmayers in later years). Adolf Loos and Oskar Kokoschka taught there, among others. She took acting and dancing lessons and in 1918–1919 worked as a governess at Harthof in the Semmering region.[141] She married Communist youth leader and journalist Karl Frank in 1919 but divorced soon after. Her daughter Michaela was a product of this union.

She met Carl Zuckmayer in Berlin, where she had moved with Hans Frank. Zuckmayer hired her to do secretarial work; they married in 1925, and in 1926 their daughter Winnetou was born. Until they moved to the "Wiesmühl" for good (1933), the couple lived in Berlin, where Alice had finished her *Abitur*, her certificate of graduation, and begun studying medicine (which she was unable to continue because of her emigration to Austria).[142]

---

139 Bolbecher and Kaiser, *Lexikon der österreichischen Exilliteratur*, 283f.
140 See Strasser, *Carl Zuckmayer*, 29.
141 See Bolbecher and Kaiser, *Lexikon der österreichischen Exilliteratur*, 299–301.
142 See Rühe-Freist (n.d.), *Alice Herdan-Zuckmayer*.

In his memoirs, Zuckmayer makes no secret of how deeply he was indebted to his wife, not least for his being able to flee Austria for Switzerland in the very nick of time. Confronted with the imminent *Anschluss*, Alice Herdan-Zuckmayer displayed a far greater sense of reality and political insight than her husband, who was seriously contemplating a hero's death under armed defense. In order to throw a smokescreen over her husband's flight—he went alone—Alice Herdan traveled to Berlin with her daughter Winnetou.

After the breakup of his first, youthful marriage to Annemarie Ganz (he shared with his second wife the experience of divorce from the first spouse), Zuckmayer found his true life partner in Alice Herdan. This alliance of a native Rhinelander with an Austrian might well have been by more than pure coincidence (see the section above on "An Adoptive Austrian in the Salzburg Area"); at any rate, this marriage created a convenient entrée into the "better" social circles of Vienna and Salzburg, or, as Janko Musulin discreetly expresses it:

> The reader will have noticed that Zuckmayer's wife, Alice Herdan-Zuckmayer, came from Austria; it is not without significance that he had a sensitive exponent constantly standing by his side during the years of his growing familiar and learning to feel at home; she was an intelligent, discreet, extremely tactful intermediary who had prepared him well to understand many a verbal nuance and shade of meaning.[143]

It is Zuckmayer's own assessment that Alice was actually the human "midpoint" during the time in Henndorf: "So in those least years before the final 'expulsion' (through Hitler's invasion), we lived in a kind of symbiosis with my wife as the central point."[144] This observation refers specifically to the friendship of both Zuckmayers with Ödön von Horváth but can be extended without strain to many of their other friendships, such as with Albrecht Joseph, who owed his rather lengthy stay at the "Wiesmühl" to Alice's intervention with "Zuck"[145]—or with Alexander Lernet-Holenia[146] and to Friderike and Stefan Zweig.

Alice Herdan's advocacy of Johannes Freumbichler's novel *Philomena Ellenhub* has already been touched on (see above), but especially

---

143 Musulin, "Zuckmayer, der Österreicher," 84.
144 Zuckmayer, *Aufruf zum Leben*, 100.
145 See Joseph, *Ein Tisch bei Romanoff's*, 166.
146 He would sometimes sign his letters to Alice with "Your Alexander, rapid-fire copulator," an inside joke with Carl, Alice, and himself.

close, and likewise already mentioned, was the connection to Ödön von Horváth:

> His first visit immediately created an aura of complete intimacy and trust; he at once formed a brotherly closeness to my wife in particular, and there prevailed altogether among the three of us a kind of understanding one seldom has even with blood relatives. We loved Ödön, and he was [...] at home with us.[147]

Alice Herdan depicted the exile years in her own literary work, which she took up during their exile in Vermont (*Die Farm in den grünen Bergen*, 1949—*The Farm in the Green Mountains*, trans. Ida H. Washington and Carole E. Washington; *Das Scheusal*, 1972). She died in Visp (Switzerland) in 1991, not far from Sass-Fee, where the couple had had its last residence since 1957.

Epilogue

When the "Wiesmühl" was restored to the Zuckmayers in 1948, they did not move back to the property they had so loved but instead sold it two years later. Carl Zuckmayer paid one more visit to Henndorf, in an official capacity in 1970, when presented with the community's Ring of Honor, as can be read in his story *Henndorfer Pastorale*, replete with memories and somewhat sentimental. In it he passes the interwar years in review. In his autobiography, Zuckmayer also described the unusual mood that must have prevailed during those years in Salzburg and the surrounding area:

> [...] in this world of doomed enchantment politics were underplayed—perhaps because everyone knew that in the long run he would not be able to escape their iron grip. It was somewhat like Versailles in the days of the Bastille, only more alert, more aware, intellectually more lucid, as is only proper for an elite devoted to the Muses. For it was just such an elite that had set the tone in Salzburg and that gave those days and nights their unique glory.[148]

The "Henndorf Circle" (or "Wiesmühl Circle," to use Zuckmayer's own term) responded in a similar manner: the attractions of friendship

---

147 Zuckmayer, *Aufruf zum Leben*, 97. Both Zuckmayers had to live through attending their beloved friend's interment in St. Ouen.
148 Zuckmayer, *A Part of Myself*, 41.

played their part, as did shared tendencies and misgivings as well as a more or less diffuse awareness that these times were drawing toward an end. No one was inclined to be genuinely political at that time; at least shared political convictions played no significant part in this "circle."[149] The emphasis on the personal was also what made it possible for socially and politically critical artists like Horváth or Csokor to be as securely at home as Nazi collaborators and opportunists like Krauß and Jannings. In the end, all were united by their friendship with Carl and Alice Zuckmayer, in whose small world of Henndorf the larger one planned "its test" for twelve and a half years.

Bibliography

Albrecht, Richard. "Carl Zuckmayer im Exil, 1933–1946: Ein dokumentarischer Essay." *Internationales Archiv für Sozialgeschichte der deutschen Literatur (IASL)*, 14 (1989), 165–202. Available online: https://doi.org/10.1515/iasl.1989.14.1.165 (accessed 4 August 2023).
Bahr, Hermann. *Kritische Schriften, Bd. 7: Bildung, Essays*. Weimar: VDG, 2010.
Bengesser, Silvia-Scharinger. *Literaturlandschaft Flachgau: Salzburger Literaturführer*. Salzburg: Ed. Eizenbergerhof, 2017.
Bernhard, Thomas. Ein Kind. Werke, Bd. 10: *Die Autobiographie*. Eds. Martin Huber and Manfred Mittermayer. Frankfurt am Main: Suhrkamp, 2004.
Bernhard, Thomas, and Siegfried Unseld. *Der Briefwechsel*. Eds. Raimund Fellinger, Martin Huber, and Julia Ketterer. Frankfurt am Main: Suhrkamp, 2009.
Bolbecher, Sieglinde, and Konstantin Kaiser. *Lexikon der österreichischen Exilliteratur*. Wien–München: Deuticke, 2000.
Carl Zuckmayer Gesellschaft. *Carl Zuckmayer Biografie*. Available online: https://www.carl-zuckmayer.com/carlzuckmayer (accessed June 25, 2020).
Dassanowsky, Robert. *Phantom Empires: The Novels of Alexander Lernet-Holenia and the Question of Postimperial Austrian Identity*. Riverside: Ariadne Press, 1996.
Dietz, Christopher. *Alexander Lernet-Holenia und Lotte Sweceny: Briefe 1938–1945*. Wien–Köln–Weimar: Böhlau, 2013.
Hall, Murray J. *Österreichische Verlagsgeschichte 1918–1938*. Bd. 1: Geschichte des österreichischen Verlagswesens. Wien–Köln–Graz: Böhlau, 1985.
Haslinger, Adolf. "Zuckmayer und seine Dichterkollegen in Salzburg." *Zuckmayer-Jahrbuch*, Bd. 1. Eds. Gunther Nickel, Erwin Rotermund, and Hans Wagener, 197–213. St. Ingbert: Röhrig Universitätsverlag, (1998).
Henndorfer Kreis. Available online: https://de.wikipedia.org/wiki/Henndorfer_Kreis (accessed May 2, 2020).

---

149 That said, members of the subsequent "Kreisau Circle" met for the first time at the "Wiesmühl," including Hellmuth von Moltke, Theodor Haubach, and Carlo Mierendorff. See Strasser, *Carl Zuckmayer*, 178f. Zuckmayer dedicated his play dated from 1945 to "Theodor Haubach, Wilhelm Leuschner, and Hellmuth Count von Moltke, friends hanged by Germany's executioners."

"Horch, Franz." In Rudolf Vierhaus, ed., *Deutsche Biographische Enzyklopädie*. 2nd ed. München: K. G. Saur, 2006. Bd. 5: 136.

"Ibach, Alfred (1902–1948), Dramaturg und Verleger." *Österreichisches Biographisches Lexikon*. Wien: Verlag der Österreichischen Akademie der Wissenschaften, 1961. Bd. 3, Lfg. 11: 25.

Joseph, Albrecht. *Ein Tisch bei Romanoff's: Vom expressionistischen Theater zur Westernserie. Erinnerungen*. Möchengladbach: Juni Verlag, 1991.

Klauhs, Harald. *Franz Theodor Csokor: Leben und Werk bis 1938 im Überblick*. Stuttgart: Heinz, 1988.

Klee, Ernst. *Das Kulturlexikon zum Dritten Reich: Wer war was vor und nach 1945*. Frankfurt am Main: S. Fischer, 2007a.

Klee, Ernst. "Politisch gut ausgerichtet." *Die Zeit*, 11 (March 8, 2007b). Available online: https://www.zeit.de/2007/11/OE-3_Reich/komplettansicht (accessed November 24, 2021).

Lernet-Holenia, Alexander. *Die Lust an der Ungleichzeitigkeit*. Eds. Thomas Hübel and Manfred Müller. Wien: Zsolnay, 1997.

Lernet-Holenia, Alexander. "Hofmannsthals Werk." *Neue Freie Presse* (March 23, 1924), 32–3.

Magris, Claudio. *Der habsburgische Mythos in der österreichischen Literatur*. Wien–München: Zsolnay, 2000. [= *Il mito absburgico nella letteratura austriaca moderna*, 1963]

Mayer, Hans. *Zur deutschen Literatur der Zeit*. Reinbek bei Hamburg: Rowohlt, 2017.

Menasse, Robert. *Überbau und Untergrund. Die sozialpartnerschaftliche Ästhetik. Essays zum österreichischen Geist*. Frankfurt am Main: Suhrkamp, 1997.

Musulin, Janko. "Zuckmayer, der Österreicher." *Festschrift für Carl Zuckmayer zu seinem 80. Geburtstag am 27. Dezember 1976*. In Barbara Glauert-Hesse (for the Landeshaupstadt Mainz und der Carl-zuckmayer-gesellschaft E. V), 83–9. Mainz: Verlag Dr. Hanns Krach, 1976.

Nickel, Gunther. "Carl Zuckmayers Autobiographie *Als wär's ein Stück von mir* – eine Erkundung." In Gunther Nickel and Erwin Rotermund, eds., *Carl Zuckmayers Autobiographie: Eine Erkundung und andere Beiträge zur Zuckmayer-Forschung. Zuckmayer-Jahrbuch*, Bd. 12, 9–24. Göttingen: Wallstein, 2013–2014.

Nickel, Gunther, and Erwin Rotermund, eds. *Carl Zuckmayers Autobiographie: Eine Erkundung; und andere Beiträge zur Zuckmayer-Forschung*. Reihe: *Zuckmayer-Jahrbuch*, Bd. 12. Göttingen: Wallstein, 2014.

Pesl, Martin, and Matthias Dusini. "Gott, Kaiser und Hakenkreuz." *Falter*, 30 (July 22, 2020), 24–6. Available online: https://www.falter.at/zeitung/20200721/gott-kaiser-und-hakenkreuz (accessed June 15, 2023).

Roček, Ranom. *Die neun Leben des Alexander Lernet-Holenia: Eine Biographie*. Wien–Köln–Weimar: Böhlau, 1997.

Rotermund, Erwin. "'Charaktere' und 'Verräter': Carl Zuckmayers *Geheimreport* von 1943/44: Beurteilungskriterien und Beurteilungspraxis." In Carl Zuckmeyer and Alexander Lernet Holenia, *Briefwechsel und andere Beiträge zur Zuckmayer-Forschung. Zuckmayer-Jahrbuch*, Bd. 8, 2005/06, 357–76. Göttingen: Wallstein, 2006.

Rühe-Freist, Birgit-E. "Alice Herdan-Zuckmayer." *Fembio. Frauen Biographieforschung*, n.d. Available online: https://www.fembio.org/biographie.php/frau/biographie/alice-herdan-zuckmayer/ (accessed December 21, 2020).

Salzburger Festspiel Archiv. Available online: https://archive.salzburgerfestspiele.at/ (accessed November 27, 2020).

Sommer, Gerald. "'Er dient um die Erlaubnis, eine öffentliche Heimsuchung sein zu dürfen': Anmerkungen zu Willkür und Wohlwollen fiskalischer Organe, ausgehend von Alexander Lernet-Holenias Roman *Das Finanzamt*." In *Alexander Lernet-Holenia: Resignation und Rebellion (Bin ich denn wirklich, was ihr einst wart?)* – Beiträge des Wiener Symposions zum 100. Geburtstag des Dichters, Eds. Thomas Hübel, Manfred Müller, and Gerald Sommer, 171–87. Riverside, CA: Ariadne Press, 2005.

Steinberg, Michael P. *Ursprung und Ideologie der Salzburger Festspiele 1890–1938*. Trans. Marion Kagerer. Salzburg: Anton Pustet, 2000.

Strasser, Christian. *Carl Zuckmayer: Deutsche Künstler im Salzburger Exil 1933–1938*. Wien: Böhlau, 1996a.

Strasser, Christian. "Ein Haus der Emigration." *Salzburger Nachrichten* (June 20, 1996) II (Leben heute), 85.

Strobel, Jochen. "'Schöne Gedichte' – 'Mäßige Schriftstellerei': Thomas Mann und Carl Zuckmayer." In Carl Zuckmayer and Alexander Lernet-Holenia, *Briefwechsel und andere Beiträge zur Zuckmayer-Forschung. Zuckmayer Jahrbuch* 8 (2005/06), 189–254. Göttingen: Wallstein, 2006.

Zuckmayer, Carl. *Als wär's ein Stück von mir. Horen der Freundschaft*. Frankfurt am Main: Fischer Taschenbuch Verlag, 1969.

Zuckmayer, Carl. *Aufruf zum Leben: Porträts und Zeugnisse aus bewegten Zeiten*. Frankfurt am Main: Fischer Taschenbuch Verlag, 1982.

Zuckmayer, Carl. *Geheimreport*. Eds. Gunther Nickel and Johanna Schrön. Göttingen: Wallstein, 2002.

Zuckmayer, Carl. *Henndorfer Pastorale*. St. Pölten–Salzburg: Residenz, 2004.

Zuckmayer, Carl. *A Part of Myself*. Trans. Richard Winston and Clara Winston. New York: Harcourt Brace Jovanovich, 1970.

Zuckmayer, Carl. "Ein Sinnbild der großen Kälte"(review of Bernhard's *Frost*). *Die Zeit*, 25 (June 21, 1963).

Zuckmayer, Carl, and Albrecht Joseph. *Briefwechsel 1922–1972*. Ed. Gunther Nickel. Göttingen: Wallstein, 2007.

Zuckmayer, Carl, and Alexander Lernet Holenia. *Briefwechsel und andere Beiträge zur Zuckmayer-Forschung. Zuckmayer-Jahrbuch*, Bd. 8, 2005/06. Göttingen: Wallstein, 2006.

Part III

Being Salzburg: Cultures Found and Lost

Six Sport Cultures in Salzburg Between State and Dictatorship

Andreas Praher

Sport Beyond the Metropolis

In the interwar period, Austria's sport culture was deeply influenced by the main political forces in the First Republic. Its hallmark in the 1920s and 1930s was a rivalry in Austrian society between a right-wing civic faction and a left-wing socialist faction, polarized across clear ideological boundaries.[1] Sports activities had at the same time become more accessible to the masses. For example, since the 1920s, football and skiing in Europe and Austria alike had begun to attract an increasing number of ordinary people, not just the rich.[2]

In the era leading up to the ascendence of the Austrofascist regime in 1933, an increasing number of clubs were founded in both urban and rural areas of the First Republic, from east to west. Communities and cities financed sport events, and the media discovered the sport world.[3] For the first time in history, the Austrian state even tried to promote sport as an instrument of education and health policy.[4] When Austrofascism took over the state in 1933, the regime began to take more conscious control over institutions for sport and physical fitness as part of its new identity. After 1934, for instance, workers' sport clubs were forbidden, and the Austrofascist government tried to control illegal National Socialist activity that took place in sport clubs and

---

1 Rudolf Müllner, *Perspektiven*, 67.
2 Matthias Marschik, *Bewegte Körper*, 41.
3 Matthias Marschik, *Sportdiktatur Bewegungskulturen*, 31.
4 Müllner, *Perspektiven*, 67.

societies,[5] which created an imbalance between public desires and political policy.

Yet there were strong regional differences in what sports activities were actually present and what they represented in the Austrian socio-cultural landscape. From the 1920s on into the 1930s, certain sport organizations were in a virtually continuous project of radicalization, such as the German *Turnvereine* (gymnastics societies) or alpine clubs.[6] Not surprisingly, antisemitism was clearly practiced on and off the pitch, on the playing fields, and in the gymnasiums. This was particularly the case in Vienna, where Jewish engagement in sports was large and well-established;[7] Salzburg saw less activity, since sports engagement was more marginal and limited—the city was more of a no-man's-land for organized sports.

Antisemitism was nonetheless evident in how sport clubs practiced politics of exclusion. In the era, football infrastructure in Austria was largely underdeveloped, the sport's financial input into the economy marginal, and its degree of professionalization limited.[8] Yet football had the advantage of being a manageable sports scene. Outside of Vienna, its leagues were highly concentrated and dominated by a few clubs, giving the sport a local or provincial character—unlike skiing, which would develop a long-term international profile in the western provinces of Austria.[9]

This essay focuses on some major key developments which strongly shaped the field of sport in the city and province of Salzburg, and which show how sports was implicated with the era's shifting politics. I will first characterize the sport cultures in Salzburg of the interwar period, focusing on the emergence and development of popular sports such as football or skiing in times of political and economic crises between the two world wars. That will allow me to elucidate the socio-political meaning of certain sport movements in the interwar society of Salzburg.

---

5   For the history of sport in the Austrofascist Era, see Matthias Marschik, "Turnen und Sport im Austrofaschismus (1934–1938)."
6   For an exemplary account in English of how sports were radicalized, see Tait Keller, *Apostles of the Alps*.
7   Susanne Helene Betz, Monika Löscher and Pia Schölnberger, "Die Hakoah lebt!," 11; Michael John, "'Körperlich ebenbürtig … ': Juden im österreichischen Fußballsport," 232–4.
8   This anthology treats this topic in several articles: Siegfried Göllner Albert Lichtblau, Christian Muckenhumer, Andreas Praher, and Robert Schwarzbauer, eds., *Zwischen Provinz und Metropole: Fußball in Österreich*.
9   For the history of the internationalization of skiing in the interwar period, see Andreas Praher, *Österreichs Skisport im Nationalsozialismus*, 51–61.

Dominance of Bourgeois Football

Compared to the capital Vienna or other federal states, football in Salzburg in the 1920s and 1930s remained very provincial, with most of the clubs focused on the city of Salzburg and its surroundings. In contrast to Upper Austria or Styria, the province of Salzburg had only a few major industrial towns or commercial centers which hosted football teams. One of them was the city of Hallein south of Salzburg; another one was the small town Oberndorf next to the German border in the north. These towns had notable football clubs: in Hallein, the Halleiner SK (1922), and in Oberndorf, with the 1st Oberndorfer Sportklub (1920). Outside of the central area in the alpine region, smaller industrial towns like Lend or Tenneck and a town at the important railway junction, Bischofshofen, were places where workers could establish local football clubs.[10] Such an alignment of club football with working-class players and spectators persists in many parts of Germany (and the UK) today.

Yet also like today's sports markets, money talked on the interwar football landscape. In the provincial capital itself, it was the bourgeois Salzburger Athlethiksportklub 1914 (SAK 1914) which dominated the championships in a different kind of club sport network. The concentration of football in the regional center of Salzburg after the First World War can straightforwardly be traced back to Austria's geography and its social and economic conditions. The poorly connected and structurally weak mountain areas did not provide sufficient support for strong club foundations, which, in turn, made league operation almost impossible. It was the city of Salzburg and the central region that formed the primary economic driver for the sport, with the largest population density, and thus able to sustain an organized football league.[11]

It was also characteristic for the social structure of Salzburg that the first football club that was founded shortly before outbreak of the First World War was not a workers' club. Instead, the SAK 1914 had its origin in an upper-class and academic milieu. After the end of the First World War, the SAK 1914 was reestablished and soon became an important player on the local and regional football scene. The club had promoters from bourgeois circles and enjoyed the prestige of support from high-ranking politicians.[12]

---

10 Toni Wallinger, *50 Jahre Salzburger Fußballverband*, 16, 65, 69, 71; Robert Schwarzbauer, "Ein 'Zeugnis vom Wirken einer Schar sportbegeisterter Jugend,'" 177–80.
11 Christian Dirninger, "Konjunkturelle Dynamik und struktureller Wandel in der wirtschaftlichen Entwicklung des Landes Salzburg im 20. Jahrhundert," 2747.
12 Andreas Praher, "Politische Radikalisierung im Salzburger Fußballsport in der Zwischenkriegszeit," in Göllner et al., eds., *Zwischen Provinz und Metropole*, 106.

At the same time, since the early 1920s, the political orientation of the club was German-national and antisemitic. At the general assembly in 1922, a majority in the SAK 1914 decided to introduce an Aryan Paragraph into the club's statutes. The assembly took place in the well-known Café Corso at the Salzach River on January 12, 1922.[13] According to a manuscript written by the club historian Walter Riebl, the introduction of the Aryan Paragraph led to the "exclusion of Mr. Morawetz and Comrades."[14] Ferdinand Morawetz, a Catholic businessman with Jewish roots who came from the small Hungarian town Diószeg (today Sládkovičovo in Slovakia),[15] had been club president since April 1921.[16] Because of his Jewish mother, Morawetz was seen as half Jew and therefore attacked in the antisemitic newspaper *Der Eiserne Besen* (The Iron Broom).[17] Subsequently, Morawetz and other Jewish sportsmen became target of antisemitic agitation, to which I will return later.

Let us for now return to the SAK 1914 and its dominant role in football as a hallmark for the position of sports in Salzburg's public culture. The city's general political climate in the interwar years which was characterized by a cross-class German nationalism,[18] which helped the SAK 1914 to get ideological and financial support and led to its long-lasting success. Despite the fact that the football club was infiltrated by National Socialists in the 1930s, Christian-Social representatives showed no fear of contact, probably because of a shared nationalist bias. Because the city of Salzburg lacked a strong worker's movement and the later 1934 ban of socialist organizations and clubs, the SAK 1914 could thus preserve its supremacy through these other ideological appeals.

The results of this link between ideology and club organization were clear in terms of SAK 1914's infrastructure and personnel: the club always had the better players and dominated the regional championship until the outbreak of the Second World War. The SAK 1914 was champion fifteen times in series in the province of Salzburg and played in the finals of the Austrian amateur championship three times.[19] Only with the establishment of the football club Austria Salzburg in 1933 did a strong opponent appear. But it took until the postwar period to reverse the imbalance of power that had favored the more bourgeois club.

---

13 *Salzburger Volksblatt*, January 13, 1922, 5.
14 Walter Riebl, Entstehung und Gründung des Salzburger Athletik-Sportklub 1914, unpublished manuscript.
15 Salzburger Landesarchiv (SLA), Meldekartei Ferdinand Morawetz.
16 *Salzburger Chronik*, April 10, 1921, 6.
17 *Der Eiserne Besen*, January 8, 1926, 5.
18 Helga Embacher, "The Jewish Community of Salzburg from its Reestablishment during Liberalism to the Present," 46–7.
19 Andreas Praher, "Spielball des Nationalsozialismus oder loyaler Erfüllungsgehilfe?," 133.

Olympic Intermezzo: A Brief Moment of Football Glory

Probably the biggest success on the international level was, surprisingly, due in no small part to Salzburg's football establishment: four SAK-players participated in the 1936 Olympic Games in Berlin. In 1935 The Austrian Football Association (ÖFB) decided to send an amateur team to the games in Berlin and started planning. Their new coaching staff was headed by the Englishman Jimmy Hogan (1882–1974), who had been engaged by Hugo Meisl, the national coach and "father" of what eventually was the so-called *Wunderteam*.[20] Hogan had been born in the northwest of England, in Lancashire, into an Irish Catholic family. Shortly before his eighteenth birthday, he signed a semi-professional contract with his hometown club, Nelson FC, but left after only one year to play for Burnley and later for Fulham and Bolton. At the age of twenty-eight, he left England to become the youngest British coach in Europe at that time.[21] Like other English football players in the first half of the twentieth century, Hogan found his way through labor migration to Vienna first and then later on to the Austrian provinces.[22] In 1912, Meisl, already a leading figure in European football (1904 board member of the First Vienna Football Club and 1911–1912 board member of the Wiener Amateur-SV, later Austria Wien), convinced Hogan to prepare the Austrian national squad for the Stockholm Olympics.[23] This was the beginning of Hogan's real international career as a coach and simultaneously his link to the 1936 Olympics with the Austrian amateur team.

In his search for talented players for Austria's Olympic team, Hogan toured the provinces to scout teams for the best players. After recruiting players from several clubs all over Austria, the potential team held its final training camp in Salzburg.[24] Hogan nominated four players from Salzburg for the national Olympic team. Not surprisingly, all four played for SAK 1914. Two of them, Ernst Bacher and Adolf Laudon, originally came from Vienna. The two others, Edi and Karl Kainberger, were born in Salzburg.

The team was not particularly a public favorite, especially in Vienna, because the players were relatively unknown—it was called the "team

---

20 Andreas Praher, "Salzburg und Olympia 1936 – Sichtweisen und Reflexionen," 98–9.
21 Keith Baker, *Fathers of Football*, 110–15.
22 British football pioneers brought the sport at the beginning of the twentieth century to the second and third largest cities of Austria Graz and Linz.
23 Baker, *Fathers*, 117.
24 Praher, "Salzburg und Olympia," 99; *Sport-Tagblatt*, July 9, 1936, 3.

of the no-names." The ÖFB itself had contributed to this image because it had been unwilling to open membership to teams from the provinces in the 1930s.[25] But even in Salzburg, public expectations were low.[26] All the more surprising, then, was their second-place finish in the Olympic tournament from Berlin and their silver medal. "My father never talked much about it. It was not his style to specify. He just played well," Ernst Bacher's son Peter Bacher later remembered.[27] Ernst Bacher was famous for his free kicks and penalties; he had played for the *Rapid* amateur team before he moved to Salzburg in 1932, where he met Adolf Laudon, who had moved from the Viennese suburban football club Admira to the SAK 1914. Together with Eduard (Edi) and Karl Kainberger, these two players strongly influenced the football game in Salzburg. Their August 1936 Olympic silver medal (placing second to Italy's gold) was the highlight of their careers.

What is critical to note, however, is that, in Salzburg, these players remained amateur athletes. In contrast to football players in Vienna, they did not have professional contracts and had to struggle with unemployment in time of crises, despite their moment of glory.[28] Bacher could not find a job and sought assistance from the state government.[29] Later, he found employment with the state police. Karl Kainberger also had been on the dole and was looking for a job after the Olympic Games in 1936.[30] Only Edi Kainberger, who was the first keeper in all four matches and captain of the Austrian squad, benefited from his performance. Two years later, immediately after the Anschluss, he got an offer to play for the football team of TSV 1860 München.[31] That club was quite successful in the 1930s and 1940s and was supported by the Nazi party.[32]

Despite the success of the Austrian national *Wunderteam*, then, the achievement of the amateur footballers in Berlin did not find its way into Austrian collective consciousness: the team existed for too short a period of time, and its players were too unknown and "provincial," coming as they did from Salzburg.

---

25 Matthias Marschik, "Metropolen statt Provinz," 91.
26 *Salzburger Volksblatt*, November 22, 1935, 9.
27 Interview with Peter Bacher, June, 2013.
28 Praher, "Salzburg und Olympia," 102.
29 SLA, Rehrl-Brief 1933/0055.
30 SLA, Rehrl-Brief 1936/3218.
31 In April 1938, Edi Kainberger played on the team of TSV 1860 München against a representative Salzburg team in Salzburg. The game was a propaganda event for the Nazi referendum (*Salzburger Volksblatt*, April 2, 1938, 25).
32 Anton Löffelmeier, *Die "Löwen" unterm Hakenkreuz*.

Sport Cultures in Salzburg Between State and Dictatorship 183

Workers' Sport: Class Struggle on the Pitch

Even on the level of amateur football, the Salzburg scene was different to that in Vienna. The workers' sport movement was very powerful in so-called "Red Vienna" and in some more industrialized parts of Austria. In 1932, that organization had about 240,000 members in the capital of Austria alone.[33] We have no statistical numbers about members in workers' sport clubs in the provinces, only in Salzburg, but that does not necessarily mean that there had not been a workers' sport movement. As noted above, some regions in the province of Salzburg offered conditions where football could take root alongside the evolving labor situation. In Hallein, for instance, the Halleiner SK was strongly connected to the cellulose factory nearby. In Bischofshofen, railway workers who were organized in the Social Democratic or Communist party founded the club SK Bischofshofen in 1935. Even earlier, there had already been the local workers' Turnverein (ATSV) which tried to establish a football section.[34] In the city of Salzburg, as already noted, the SSK 1919 (Salzburg Sport Club) emerged at the end of the First World War as a newly established Salzburg-Austria sports club and vital opponent to the SAK 1914. Its vice-chairman Eduard Beck was an ardent Social Democrat.[35] Beck's story is a parable for workers' sport in the Salzburg region. Beck was managing director of and candidate for the Social Democratic Party in the Salzburg election of the local council in March 1919.[36] Although he was an influential employee and trade unionist, he was turned down as a candidate for vice-president of the Salzburg Football Federation (SFV) in August 1921 because of his political affiliation.[37] The bourgeois opposition was too strong.

Nevertheless, the SSK 1919 itself was evidence of a vital working-class football movement in Salzburg. Its founder was the former Vienna-player Hans Dobesch; Ferdinand Morawetz, later briefly president of the SAK 1914, also belonged among its founding members.[38] Still, the SSK 1919's main problem was infrastructure. The club did not have its own playing field or pitch, instead sharing a former military parade ground south of the city center with other clubs. In contrast, the SAK 1914 had its own pitch next to the old town, with sport facilities from 1921 onward. For a new working-class club in Grödig, just a

---

33 Müllner, *Perspektiven*, 67.
34 Schwarzbauer, "Zeugnis," 180.
35 Robert Schwarzbauer, "Der VAFÖ in Oberösterreich und Salzburg," 232.
36 *Salzburger Wacht*, March 22, 1919, 1.
37 *Salzburger Volksblatt*, August 27, 1921, 6.
38 Wallinger, *50 Jahre*, 6–7.

few miles south of Salzburg, the situation started out much worse and would not improve, as will be addressed below.[39]

The organizational structures of Austrian football on the national level in the 1920s did not help deescalate what was overtly a class struggle. Militarization and the latent danger of a civil war were noticeable on the pitch, a situation which was exacerbated starting in 1926.[40] The issue that brought class struggle to a head was the question of professionalism, which was discussed among both working class and bourgeois representatives in Austrian football. In June 1926, a workers' associations formed a committee and charged it with separating the National Football Association (the ÖFV) into two associations. Finally, on July 1, 1926, the Association of Amateur Football Clubs in Austria (Verband der Amateurfußballvereine Österreichs, VAFÖ) was established as a counterpart to the middle-class professional football. The professional football association (ÖFB) was founded on August 22, 1926.[41]

This "resolution" led to further internal conflicts. Until 1934, there had been member clubs in the association on the bourgeois side, aside from also taking part in the umbrella organization of the Workers' Sports Clubs (VAFÖ), which competed against each other on a highly political level. At the constituent assembly of the VAFÖ on November 27, 1926, the representatives of workers' sport were welcomed by representatives of the Social Democratic Party and the labor unions.[42] At the beginning of the 1930s, however, the workers' sports movement was predicting the speedy end of professional sport. Their political pronouncement was that the world economic crisis would not allow for the existence of professional sport.[43]

This struggle also reached the province of Salzburg in the mid-1920s. Just as in Vienna the workers' clubs in Salzburg established their own association on September 5, 1926 (VAFÖ), and played their own championship. The impact of this social separation on the football scene was not limited to the pitch. Newspaper reporting on both sides at the time was characterized by a constant criticism of political opponents. In the following years, the two daily newspapers, *Salzburger Wacht* and *Salzburger Chronik*, waged a verbal battle about football that echoed this class warfare. The Social Democratic newspaper *Salzburger Wacht* accused the bourgeois footballers of profiteering when they poached players from

---

39 Praher, "Politische Radikalisierung," 106–7.
40 *Salzburger Chronik*, September 6, 1926, 6; *Salzburger Volksblatt*, September 8, 1926, 8; *Salzburger Wacht*, September 6, 1926, 8.
41 Matthias Marschik, *Wir spielen nicht zum Vergnügen*, 86–8.
42 Marschik, *Wir spielen nicht zum Vergnügen*, 89–90.
43 Marschik, *Wir spielen nicht zum Vergnügen*, 105.

working class clubs for cash.⁴⁴ On the other side, the *Salzburger Chronik* claimed that the so-called non-political, bourgeois association ASFV (Allgemeiner Salzburger Fußballverband) "will only do and write what is good for sport and keep a watchful eye on politicians,"⁴⁵ an assertion that was seen as direct attack against the working class. The conflict culminated with the transfer of a club of working-class footballers from Rapid Salzburg to the bourgeois association in 1931.⁴⁶ The switch had, of course, ample economic justification in times of mass employment, but it was cast in the press as a betrayal of the working class.⁴⁷ As another result, players who changed from one association to another were no longer suspended, which only heightened the conflict.⁴⁸

Shortly after the separation in Salzburg, on September 26, 1926, a new football club was founded in Grödig, called ATSV Grödig-Fürstenbrunn.⁴⁹ This working-class team played its first away game on October 3, 1926 against SV Horekan Salzburg,⁵⁰ another working-class team which would win the local championship in 1927. Yet SV Horekan Salzburg was named after employees of several hotels, restaurants, and coffee shops in Salzburg, and so these were actually not equivalent "working-class" teams.⁵¹ ATSV Grödig-Fürstenbrunn lost the match 2:10. On material grounds this was not surprising. The team's home playing field was next to a station on the tram line and the Russian cemetery from the First World War.⁵² The pitch was in poor condition; the footballers used the local workers' center as a clubhouse. But not only was the team's infrastructure modest, its sporting performance was as well. The working-class footballers of Grödig lost their first home game on October 17, 1926 and their first championship game on May 15, 1927.⁵³ Due to a lack of players, the club had to quit playing after a few months.

That loss presaged an even worse situation to come. During that short time of Grödig's activity, there had been a vital exchange on a personal level with other working-class clubs in the city of Salzburg—teams such as ATSV Maxglan. As one example: Albin Schmalzhofer, who was

---

44 *Salzburger Wacht*, September 18, 1926, 8; *Salzburger Wacht*, September 10, 1926, 8.
45 "[W]ir werden nur das tun und schreiben, was dem Sport frommt und den Politischen auf die Finger schauen," *Salzburger Chronik*, September 25, 1926, 9.
46 Praher, "Politische Radikalisierung," 109.
47 *Salzburger Wacht*, July 8, 1931, 8.
48 Robert Schwarzbauer, "Der VAFÖ," 243.
49 *Salzburger Wacht*, September 25, 1926, 8.
50 *Salzburger Wacht*, October 2, 1926, 8; *Salzburger Wacht*, October 4, 1926, 8.
51 SV Horekan stands for Sportvereinigung der Hotel-, Restaurant- und Kaffeehausangestellten.
52 The Russian cemetery was part of the former prisoner-of-war-camp, situated in Grödig.
53 *Salzburger Wacht*, October 18, 1926, 8; *Salzburger Wacht*, May 17, 1927, 7.

born on December 15, 1906, and acted as an organizer in the workers union, had been a founding and board member of the ATSV Maxglan.[54] Besides that, he played football for the ATSV Grödig-Fürstenbrunn, was sport manager for the club, and also got involved into the local workers' cycling club in Grödig.[55] Schmalzhofer's example shows the strong ties between different sectors of the workers' sport movement, not only in the capital Vienna, but also in the province of Salzburg. Yet, with the Austrofascist regime, that kind of workers' solidarity was persecuted as subversive acts. In March 1936, Schmalzhofer had to face trial because he wrote for the social democratic publication *Der Gewerkschafter* (The Trade Unionist) which was classified as illegal by the Austro-Fascist government.[56] Such acts were simply the final death knells for the workers' sport movement throughout Austria.

The last big sport event in Vienna associated with the movement was organized by the workers' sport association (ASKÖ) and held in October 1933. On February 13, 1934, the ASKÖ was forbidden, and its associated clubs were closed by state officials.[57] By the end of February 1934, the workers' sport movement in Austria no longer officially existed. Yet there was still a sport and resistance culture in the underground. The strategies to survive such suppression differed. The players from SK Hallein, for instance, simply moved to the local bourgeois club (Athletic Club [AC] Hallein). And players from the working-class club Vorwärts Maxglan switched to the newly established club Austria Salzburg and founded their own section called SV Austria Maxglan.[58]

The depredations of Austrofascism directed against workers' sports were thus specially targeted, as other examples from the time argue. Catholic footballers, for instance, were able to establish their own playing fields in the heart of the city—an achievement comprehensible only within the context of the Catholic Church's power and influence in Salzburg. The area which had long been used for matches was in the neighborhood of the SAK 1914 and owned by the convent Stift Nonnberg. The passionate football player Georg Giglmayr arranged the deal for an upgrade as diocesan director of the Catholic Journeymen Association. Taking ten months to construct, a small football stadium was opened to the public in summer 1933, housing the teams of FC Altstadt and FC Hertha. Both clubs were relatively successful. Hertha

---

54 *Salzburger Amtsblatt*, December 15, 1985, 26; *Salzburger Wacht*, October 18, 1926, 8.
55 *Salzburger Wacht*, September 3, 1923, 4; *Salzburger Wacht*, June 12, 1926, 6.
56 *Salzburger Volksblatt*, March 18, 1936, 8; *Salzburger Volksblatt*, March 20, 1936, 10.
57 Reinhard Krammer, *Arbeitersport in Österreich*, 234–5.
58 Schwarzbauer, "Der VAFÖ," 251–2.

was four-time vice-champion behind the SAK. But their success story did not last for long. On September 13, 1933, FC Hertha was, together with FC Rapid Salzburg, merged into Austria Salzburg, and, due to the lack of players, the team of FC Altstadt was dissolved in October 1937.[59] The sport fields for these clubs were later occupied and used by the SS as a training facility and for competitions.[60]

Jewish Football and Antisemitism

The case of Jewish sportsmen and -women deserves special note in this context. The Jewish community in the province of Salzburg before 1938 never exceeded three hundred people. In this context, the population was hardly large enough to organize into clubs. Nevertheless, a few personalities had major impacts on the development of sport in the 1920s and 1930s in Salzburg, especially in football.[61]

At an early stage in the politicization of football along class lines, antisemitic hostility was not only noticeable but also clearly visible. The only Jewish member in the Salzburger Turnverein Albert Süß, for example, was thrown off his team, an exclusion that cannot be seen as an isolated case. Especially the antisemitic weekly newspaper *Der Eiserne Besen* propagated the kind of antisemitic policy that offended popular Jewish business- and sportsmen, among them the aforementioned Ferdinand Morawetz. As noted above, Morawatz was born on January 26, 1880 in Diószeg (Hungary/Slovakia) and moved to Vienna and then to Salzburg before the First World War. In Vienna, he had come into contact with the Jewish sport club Hakoah and with the English game of football. Shortly after his arrival in Salzburg, Morawetz established his own football club, named SK Olympia.[62] After the First World War, he reactivated the SK Olympia—now called SSK 1919, the club discussed above. Furthermore, he later became president of the SAK 1914 and invested his money into new sport facilities.[63]

The history of Morawetz's involvement with Salzburg sports was especially tragic as an early sign of antisemitism's growing influence. Morawetz had a newspaper business in the Salzburg's old city and was

---

59 Robert Schwarzbauer, "Der katholische Fußball in Oberösterreich und Salzburg in der Zwischenkriegszeit," here 122.
60 For the history of the Catholic Football in the City of Salzburg in the interwar period and in the Nazi Era, also see Andreas Praher, "Sportstadt Nonntal. Historische Perspektiven, Brüche und Kontinuitäten," here 328–30.
61 For more details, see Andreas Praher and Robert Schwarzbauer, "Der jüdische Sport im Salzburg der Zwischenkriegszeit."
62 *Salzburger Volksblatt*, July 19, 1914, 9; *Salzburger Chronik*, July 19, 1914, 5.
63 Praher and Schwarzbauer, "Der jüdische Sport," 60.

owner of a nationwide postcard publishing house. Despite his involvement in the community as a civic business leader, and because of his Jewish heritage, he was attacked in the *Eiserner Besen*. When Morawetz invited the Hakoah to Salzburg, for instance, the newspaper called him a "Semitic sport busybody."[64] Although he was Catholic, he was nonetheless seen as half-Jewish and so excluded from the SAK in 1922. In November 1938, exactly on Kristallnacht, the night of the November pogrom, he was "admitted" to the psychiatric clinic (Landesnervenklinik) in Linz, where he died on December 2, 1938, of apoplexy. When he was delivered to the hospital, Morawetz had been classified as mentally confused and as a danger to himself.[65]

Other Jewish citizens of Salzburg played important roles in the local sport scene of Salzburg. One was Johann (Isak) Dachinger, one of the founding members of *Austria Salzburg* in September 1933. Dachinger was born in 1899 in Graz and moved to the city of Salzburg in the 1920s. The tradesman was owner of a textile business. Before he co-founded Austria Salzburg, he had already played for the working-class club 1. Arbeiter-Sportklub Salzburg together with other Jewish footballers and was member of the club's board.[66] Dachinger, after the slander in *Der Eiserne Besen*,[67] managed to escape together with his wife Bert(h)a and his two sons Kurt and Manfred from Vienna via Genoa to New York in November 1938.[68] There had also been some other Jewish football players in different clubs, like Erwin Bonyhadi or the two brothers Alfred und Friedrich Pirak, although there had never been an independent Jewish sport club in the whole province of Salzburg. All three would also escape to the United States.[69] And there had been a football team sponsored by the Jewish department store Schwarz. The team had been founded as independent section of SK Admira and was called SK Kaufhaus Schwarz. It is worth noting that, although the family Schwarz was a prominent and wealthy Jewish family, the football section was not entirely Jewish. Alfred and Friedrich Pirak were in fact the only Jews playing on this team. The SK Kaufhaus Schwarz played about twenty friendly games against other company teams in the amateur workers' football association (VAFÖ) but was forbidden in 1934, like all other workers' clubs.[70]

---

64 *Der Eiserne Besen*, May 8, 1925, 3.
65 Praher and Schwarzbauer, "Der jüdische Sport," 63.
66 *Salzburger Sportblatt*, April 10, 1926, 3–4; *Salzburger Sportblatt*, April 17, 1926, 1; *Salzburger Sportblatt*, May 15, 1926, 5.
67 *Der Eiserne Besen*, January 8, 1926, 5.
68 New York, Passenger Lists, 1820–1957, Johann Dachinger. Available online: www.ancestry.com (accessed December 3, 2021).
69 Praher and Schwarzbauer, "Der jüdische Sport," 65–7.
70 Praher and Schwarzbauer, "Der jüdische Sport," 67.

Sport Cultures in Salzburg Between State and Dictatorship   189

Beyond Football: Other Sports and Their Politics in Salzburg

Other historic legacies tie Salzburg's culture into sports in other ways. One must remember, for instance, that sports and *Turnen* were still separated in the interwar period. Since the early nineteenth century, there had been the German tradition of organized gymnastics associated with Friedrich Ludwig "Turnvater" Jahn, along with its nationalist variants, such as the Sokol Movement, started in 1862 in Prague to improve the physical, moral, and intellectual training for all classes and genders in the Czech nation.[71] The German gymnastic movement had originated in the Napoleonic era. Military exercises and radicalization along ideological boundaries were part of the game from the first, as well and especially in the mid-nineteenth century, as part of university fraternity practice.[72] By the 1920s, training in gymnastic associations, regardless of their political or religious affiliation, was also strongly influenced by the front experience of the First World War.[73] Both Christian-German gymnastic clubs and German national gymnastic clubs had long promoted paramilitary training and were in some ways antisemitic. Nevertheless, there had been major differences that set the Austrian variants off from German ones. The Christian-German *Turner* in Austria understood themselves as national, Austrian, and strictly Catholic.[74] They were driven by a religious antisemitism and not by the more strictly ethnic one associated with *großdeutsch* political imperialism of the Prussian nineteenth century. Not surprisingly, German gymnastics or the so-called *Deutsches Turnen* gained not only adherents but also new political power in the interwar period.[75]

In Salzburg proper, representative events at the Festival Hall demonstrated the influence of the *Turner* and connected them beyond the city. One early political difference emerged in terms of gender representation. Although the German *Turner* movement also had female members, its management was entirely masculine. Male board members dominated the political agenda and built up its power networks. In the 1930s, then, many members collaborated with the illegal National Socialist Party and their new political ideologies in Germany.

---

71 On the history of the Czech Sokol movement, see Diethelm Blecking, "Gelehrige Körper der Nation und des Sozialismus," 242–3.
72 On the development, history, and ideology of the German gymnastics movement, see Lorenz Peiffer, *Die deutsche Turnerschaft*; Michael Krüger, *Einführung in die Geschichte der Leibeserziehung und des Sports. Teil 2: Leibeserziehung im 19. Jahrhundert: Turnen fürs Vaterland*.
73 Andreas Praher, "Sport und Körperkultur," 274–5.
74 Ernst Hanisch, "Politik und Sport in der Ersten Republik," 25–6.
75 Hanisch, "Politik und Sport," 18.

For example, the German *Turner* did not accept the parliamentary system and were driven by an increasingly radical antisemitism.[76] Yet the antisemitism of the *Turner* by no means originated solely in Germany. As early as 1887, the Salzburg *Turnverein* banned its only Jewish member, Albert Süß, from his ranks. On March 3, 1892 the Salzburg gymnastics club had refused the participation of three Jewish girls in gymnastics, purportedly due to its statutes.[77] Thirty years later, in 1928, the Salzburg *Turnverein* declared "ethnic renewal" (*völkische Erneuerung*) as one of its most important goals in youth work.[78] The youth officer in charge at this time was Adolf Michel, responsible for a thousand children, who will figure prominently in subsequent *Turner* politics.

The German *Turner* were placed under state administration in 1934, and illegal Nazi activities were supervised and supposedly controlled by the Austrofascist government. Yet there was no real ban, and the German *Turner* kept on as they had earlier.[79] Only in January 1938 was the youth section of the *Salzburger Turnverein* finally forbidden by the state.[80] In many ways, the *Salzburger Turnverein*, like other German-nationalist *Turnvereine* in Austria, played a key role in building (illegal) National Socialist communities and networks before the Anschluss. Immediately thereafter, they officially took over sport political functions.[81] Even short biographical examples show how deeply involved the German *Turnverein* had been in Nazi activities before March 1938.

Adolf Michel, mentioned earlier, here plays a typical role. Born on July 28, 1897, in Vienna, he came from a middle-class family whose father had been a bank official in Bohemia. Michel graduated from the Academy of Commerce and then served in the First World War. Two years after the war, he joined the German national *Turnverein*, an act marked by his war experiences, as would be the case for many of his generation. Like his father, he worked in a bank and moved from Vienna to Salzburg in May 1926.[82] By 1937, Michel was in the leadership for the *Turnerbund* youth organization throughout Austria, where he

---

76 Müllner, *Perspektiven*, 67.
77 *Salzburger Zeitung*, November 22, 1943, 4; Embacher, "The Jewish Commmunity," 45.
78 Die Salzburger Turnerjugend im Jahre 1928: Ein Rückblick in Worten, Bildern und Zahlen, unserer Jugend zur Erinnerung an schöne Stunden zum Julfest 1928, gewidmet von Adolf Michel, 7 and 28.
79 Andreas Praher, "Sport und Körperkultur," 279.
80 *Salzburger Chronik*, January 20, 1938, 6; *Salzburger Volksblatt*, January 19, 1938, 10.
81 Marschik, *Sportdiktatur*, 30; Praher, "Sport und Körperkultur," 286–7; Andreas Praher, "SportlerInnen für den Krieg – KriegerInnen für den Sport," in Dimitriou et al., eds., *Salzburgs Sport in der NS-Zeit*, 255–90, 256–7.
82 Bundesarchiv Berlin (BArch) R/1501/209067; for the biography of Adolf Michel, see Praher, "SportlerInnen," 257–9.

was therefore responsible for content alignment of the organization's principles. At this time, he was already a party member of the (illegal) NSDAP. Already in 1928, he had described German *Turnen* as "one of the few hopes of the German people."[83] Since the early 1930s, Michel had organized paramilitary youth camps in the southern part of Carinthia, together with his brother in spirit Karl Springenschmid.[84] There, he met the later *Gauleiter* of Nazi-era Salzburg, Friedrich Rainer.

The sportsman Rainer was also quite naturally a member of the German *Turnverein*, in no small part because he likely wanted to take political advantage from his affiliation with the *Turner* movement. Rainer had been a party member from 1930 onward and supported the NSDAP with help of the *Turnverein*.[85] He joined the SS in January 1934 and became one of the leading figures in the National Socialist movement in Austria.

Turnen was not the only sport doubly implicated in both military ideologies and national identity. Mechanization and the emergence of military skiing in the First World War had a significant impact on the development of ski sport in the interwar period. "[N]ationalism and imperialism of the nineteenth century, which culminated in the First World War, provided the most important impulse for the establishment of skiing as a collective culture in Austria,"[86] says historian Rudolf Müllner. Moving beyond its early roles in the military and as a bourgeois sport, skiing became a mass activity and attraction in the interwar period. The Arlberg-technique developed by Hannes Schneider (in Austria) not only revolutionized alpine skiing by offering a pattern for systematic training in skiing (one that persists until today, starting with the snowplow move), but also made the Arlberg and skiing in Austria world-famous. The ski films of Arnold Fanck also helped to make alpine skiing and its actors worldwide export hits.

In some mountain areas of Salzburg, skiing (the "other" Olympic sport) was even more popular and widespread than football. Mountain regions in Vorarlberg, Tyrol, or Salzburg had been granted a new significance on the world stage (or screens).[87] In 1923 the first public ski school in the province of Salzburg was established in Mühlbach at the *Hochkönig*, 70 kilometres south of Salzburg.[88] Others followed. The

---

83 Adolf Michel, *Die Salzburger Turnerjugend im Jahre 1928* (Salzburg: n.p., 1928), 7.
84 Karl Springenschmid was later head of the National Socialist Teachers Federation (*NS-Lehrerbund*) and organized the book burning in the city of Salzburg in 1938.
85 Andreas Praher, "Sportführer Friedrich Rainer und seine sportpolitischen Ambitionen," 153–4.
86 Rudolf Müllner, "The Importance of Skiing in Austria," 661.
87 John Hughes, "Austria and the Alps: Introduction," 4.
88 Praher, "SportlerInnen," 266; Praher, *Österreichs Skisport*, 69.

192   Interwar Salzburg

Skiclub Salzburg (SCS), located in the provincial capital, became an important talent factory. Young skiers like Josef Bradl, Hans Hauser, and Käthe Lettner were trained there by former ski troopers. Bradl, who grew up in Mühlbach and later moved to the city of Salzburg, was the first one who jumped over 100 meters with skis in 1936. Hauser, who was three-time Austrian ski champion, was engaged at the ski school in Sun Valley (Idaho) in the same year, and Lettner, the daughter of steel edge inventor Rudolf Lettner, was part of the Olympic team in 1936.[89] The province of Salzburg, along with the town of Zell am See or Bad Gastein, were transformed into centers of winter sports in the Alps. The city of Salzburg benefited from this winter tourism and international events, as well.

From the mid-1920s on, social factors also contributed to the boom. Social origin was no longer decisive for the practice of sport, since equipment had become more widely available and accessible. Moreover, new working environments and the leisure factor increased the perceived value of individual and collective physical training. Skiing and sports in general thus became a part of everyday and popular culture after the First World War. In the interwar period, alpine skiing became part of the population's leisure culture. Skiing had been introduced not only to the public and on movie screens, but, under the leadership of Karl Gaulhofer, the Ministry of Education introduced ski courses in the Austrian school system.[90] The number of members in the Austrian Ski Association (ÖSV) rose in 1923 for the first time to over ten thousand, where, before the First World War, there had only been about six thousand members.[91]

The ski sport scene of the 1930s can no longer be seen as a purely urban phenomenon, nor as a strictly upper-class one. Proof can be found in documentation of all sorts. The Ski Club Zell am See had two hundred members in 1934, out of a population in town of 3,800 people.[92] In addition to Tyrol, the province of Salzburg developed into a center of alpine winter sports in the 1930s, building out infrastructure. Important venues for ski races and ski championships were the Valley of Gastein or the town of Zell am See. And mechanization played its part. In 1927, the first cable car was built on the *Schmittenhöhe* in Zell am See.[93] Ten years later, in 1937, the international academic winter sport games were held in that small town of Zell am See.

---

89   For Josef Bradl, Hans Hauser, and Käthe Lettner, see Praher, *Österreichs Skisport*, 87–8, 97–9, and 269–76.
90   Müllner, "The Importance of Skiing in Austria," 663–4.
91   Anneliese Gidl, "Von elitären Versuchen zum Massensport," 129.
92   Salzburger Landes-Skiverband, *Jahresbericht* 1933/34, 6.
93   Ski-Klub Zell am See, *Festschrift zum 75-Jahr-Jubiläum*, Zell am See 1981, 30.

In the interwar years, then, the city of Salzburg not only hosted the newly established Salzburg Festival. The provincial capital also became a popular winter sports destination during the 1920s and 1930s. As noted, the Skiclub Salzburg (SCS) contributed to the alpine boom in the city. The club had over six hundred members in 1933, some of whom were quite prominent.[94] Already in 1923, more than two thousand spectators came to the opening competition of an international winter sports competition on the Zistel. Siegfried Amanshauser jumped a respectable 34.5 meters. In addition to the brothers Siegfried and Hermann Amanshauser, the Salzburg Skiclub also always promoted new talents, including the internationally known Hans Hauser and Josef Bradl. The Gaisberg became the most important winter sports destination for the urban population, next to the city of Salzburg itself. In January 1929 and 1935 the Salzburg State Championships were held there.[95]

Politics soon came to the fore in this development, as well. After the Anschluss, the National-Socialist leader of the *Turner* Friedrich Rainer also knew how to use this ski-enthusiasm for propaganda. He founded and organized the so-called *Volksskitage* (people's Ski Days) at the Gaisberg which became a model for similar events throughout the German Reich, organized in urban and rural areas in the Alps.[96] But that's another story.

The so-called local heroes in the interwar years were also impacted by these political winds, as well. Hans Hauser and his brother Max, who grew up at the Gaisberg, were both members of the Skiclub Salzburg, as was Bradl, who was one of the greatest hopes in ski-jumping. The half-orphan, whose father was killed in a mountain trip, found his sponsor in Peter Radacher senior, who operated the ski school at the Hochkönig. Radacher supported Bradl's talent with great success.

In the winter of 1932/33 Bradl jumped over 50 meters for the first time. In 1935, he qualified for the Winter Olympic Games in Garmisch-Partenkirchen.[97] But his biggest success was his record jump over 100 meters in Planica in 1936. Setting a tradition continuing to this day, Bradl got a job in a sports shop, the famous Sporthaus Lanz, and joined the local ski club (for him, the Skiclub Salzburg). His further career went steeply uphill but was at the same time marked by political disturbances. In 1937 he was imprisoned because of illegal actions for the SA. Bradl was released after a few months to start again for

---

94 Salzburger Landes-Skiverband, *Jahresbericht* 1933/34, 6.
95 75 Jahre Skiclub Salzburg 1910–1985 (Salzburg 1985), 21–2; 100 Jahre Skiclub Salzburg 1910–2010 (Salzburg 2010), 21–2.
96 Praher, *Österreichs Skisport*, 195.
97 Praher, "Salzburg und Olympia," 93.

the Austrian ski-team. From March 1938 onward, he was counted as one of the best ski-jumpers of the Reich.[98] In 1939, Bradl won the world championship in ski jumping in Polish Zakopane, and after his military service as a mountain trooper in occupied Greece, he coached the Hitler Youth[99]—another athlete who moved from his sporting and ideological home base in a Salzburg club into deeper political waters.

To be sure, skiing in Austria had always been highly political. Since the foundation of the ÖSV in 1905, German nationalist ideas were part of sportive discussions and debates. After the First World War, these ideas became concrete in the form of an Aryan Paragraph in sports, which was introduced in October 1923 and strongly promoted by leading members of the Skiclub Salzburg. But also in other regions, ski clubs came to represent German-national ideologies and policies.[100] On November 14, 1934, the Skiclub Zell am See recorded in its minutes that the club "was always unpolitical in the sense of the statutes of the association and its own views and that it adhered to this strict position at all its meetings and events."[101] However, the political affiliations of the club's leading members show a different picture.

Fritz Vogl, born in 1899, acted as the club's youth guard. He joined the NSDAP in November 1931 and later visited several training camps of the illegal National Socialist Teachers Federation (NS-Lehrerbund). After high school, Vogl attended the college of mining and then worked as a secondary school teacher. From 1934 onwards, he was not only a youth guard appointed in the ski club, but from 1935 on, also a youth guard leader (*Jungmannenwart*) in the Alpine Club. From May 1938 onwards, he made his career in the *Gauschulungsamt* (regional school administration), where he was responsible for "German History and Racial Policy."[102]

Salzburg's Sports on the International Stage

Despite these radical ideas and practices that helped the National Socialist regime to take root in regional and national Austrian cultures, Austrian sports as a culture rooted in Salzburg had another, more international face.

---

98 Praher, "SportlerInnen," 268.
99 For the NS involvement of Josef Bradl, see Praher, *Österreichs Sksipsort*, 269–76; Andreas Praher, "Austrian Skiing and National Socialism," 329.
100 On the German national course and antisemitic exclusion policy of the ÖSV and its member associations see Praher, *Österreichs Skisport*, 111–33.
101 Vereinsarchiv des Skiklub Zell am See, Protocol Skiclub Zell am See, unpublished manuscript, copy in possession of the author.
102 Andreas Praher, "'Skifahren ist für uns Deutsche in den Alpenländern mehr als nur ein Sport'," here 215.

For example, Austrian skiers had been very popular in the 1930s world of sport. Like other ski instructors from Austria, the Hauser brothers migrated seasonally to the United States. In 1936, most notably, they helped to build up the ski school at Sun Valley. Max returned to Austria and later became member of the SS, whereas Hans Hauser, who was more successful in skiing, remained in America and was later married to Virginia Hill.[103] Hans, born in 1911, was the first skier from Salzburg to win a medal at a World Cup event. In 1932 he won the vice world champion title in the combination events of Cortina d'Ampezzo.[104] Only a year later, he won the Austrian championship for the first time, and in the same year, he passed the state exam to certify as a ski instructor.[105] In 1936, however, he was not allowed to participate at the Olympic Games in Garmisch-Partenkirchen because of his professional status. Nevertheless, Hauser's success and know-how in skiing was already internationally known, and so finally he took the opportunity to migrate.

Here again, personal and financial hardships played roles in disseminating Austrian (ski-)culture. Hauser was the son of an innkeeper whose father had died in the First World War, leaving his mother to care for him and his brother alone. He was in his mid-twenties when he left Austria for the first time and went onboard a steamship from Bremerhaven to New York. During the world economic crises, crossing the Atlantic and traveling to the west must have been an impressive experience.

Otto Lang, who migrated from Salzburg in 1935 for the first time to the United States and founded a ski school there, described his own arrival in New York as follows: "The skyline of Manhattan appeared, overwhelming and unreal, a *fata morgana*, a city rising out of the sea."[106] Lang was born in Zenica, which belonged to Austria-Hungary (today Bosnia), and emigrated to Vienna and Salzburg after the First World War. From 1935 on, he directed a ski school at Mount Rainier, which soon became the center of alpine skiing in the Rockies. It was the first Hans Schneider branch ski school in the United States.[107] Lang had been a colleague of Hauser in Austria and later worked with him in Sun Valley.

---

103 Annie Gilbert Coleman, *Ski Style*, 52; Praher, "Salzburg und Olympia," 96; for the worldwide emigration of Austrian ski instructors, see Praher, *Österreichs Skisport*, 92–110. For Austrians in Sun Valley, see Günter Bischof, "American Bucks and Austrian Buccaneers." Note that she was mobster Bugsy Siegel's girlfriend; he was assassinated at her house in 1947; she married Hauser in 1950.
104 Salzburger Volksblatt, February 9, 1932, 4; 100 Jahre Skiclub Salzburg, 49.
105 *Salzburger Volksblatt*, February 13, 1933, 10.
106 Otto Lang, *A Bird of Passage*, 95.
107 Salzburger Landes-Skiverband, *Jahresbericht* 1933/34, 6.

This was another significant international connection. In December 1936, Sun Valley was opened as a development by Averell Harriman, then president of the Union Pacific Railway and later prominent in US politics. He had hired another Austrian, Felix Schaffgotsch from Upper Austria, to find the right place to start his resort.[108] "In 1936 Averell Harriman's resort complex at Sun Valley, Idaho, was called the St. Moritz of America even as it was being built,"[109] John Allen writes. Sun Valley soon became an attraction for Hollywood stars. With an outdoor heated swimming pool, a ballroom, and a ranch for horse riding, the ski resort had much more to offer than skiing. Hauser stayed there several seasons and managed the ski school.[110]

The Austrian was beloved by the media. Several newspapers published series about his teaching in Sun Valley.[111] Nonetheless, in 1942, Hauser was arrested as "enemy alien" and released only in 1945.[112] After the Second World War he started his career again. His marriage with the former girlfriend of mafia boss Benjamin (Bugsy) Siegl captured the attention of the media and US politics.[113] Facing deportation, Hauser returned with his family to Europe. While Virginia Hauser committed suicide in 1966 in Austria, his son Peter died in a car accident. Hauser himself died on July 27, 1974.

The Austrian ski legacy fared much better than its football one did on the world stage. With Austrian ski instructors such as Hauser, not only was the Arlberg technique introduced into American ski society but, along with it, a middle-European skiing culture which is still visible nowadays—a more egalitarian legacy than that of Switzerland's St. Moritz.[114] However, the migration was not limited to male ski instructors. Women also sought their luck in emigration to the United States as Salzburg descended into the National Socialist era. Elfriede Pembauer from Salzburg, who was part of the Austrian Olympic team in 1936, emigrated in November 1936 to teach skiing in Lake Placid.[115] The Frederick Loeser department store in Brooklyn, New York, hired her

---

108 John B. Allen, *The Culture and Sport of Skiing*, 231; John B. Allen, *From Skisport to Skiing*, 143.
109 John B. Allen, *From Skisport to Skiing*, 139.
110 Franz Martin, Julius Gallhuber, and Franz Mauler, *Skileben in Österreich* 1935, 91.
111 *The Pittsburgh Press*, January 8, 1939, 60.
112 *The Daily Item*, January 8, 1942, 16.
113 *The Los Angeles Times*, March 10, 1950, 7; *Star Tribune*, March 26, 1950, 61; *Daily News*, March 26, 1950, 91.
114 Coleman, *Ski Style*, 51.
115 New York, Passenger and Crew Lists, 1820–1957, Elfriede Pembauer. Available online: http://www.ancestry.com (accessed April 8, 2019); *The Brooklyn Daily Eagle*, November 22, 1936, 11.

for courses in ski gymnastics. After a short stay in New York, she got a contract as ski instructor in Quebec and moved to Canada.[116] In March 1937 Elfriede Pembauer, known as Mickey, would win the Dominion women's downhill and slalom ski titles.[117]

Despite a permanent economic and political crisis, a lively sports scene was able to establish itself in interwar Salzburg. Social change led to the participation of broad sectors of society and set into motion a wave of founding new sport clubs. In these sport clubs, men and women alike could participate on national and international levels. Salzburg's cultural legacies thus persist on an international stage—and for more than music and art.

Bibliography

Archival Sources

Salzburger Landesarchiv, Handbibliothek HB C 02253 1933/34, Salzburger Landes-Skiverband, *Jahresbericht* 1933/34.
Salzburger Landesarchiv, Meldekartei Ferdinand Morawetz.
Salzburger Landesarchiv, Rehrl-Brief 1933/0055.
Salzburger Landesarchiv, Rehrl-Brief 1936/3218.
Interview with Peter Bacher, June 2013.
[Adolf Michel Information]. Bundesarchiv Berlin (BArch) R/1501/209067.
Vereinsarchiv Skiklub Zell am See, Protocol Skiclub Zell am See, November 14, 1934, unpublished manuscript, copy in possession of the author.
Archiv des SAK 1914, Walter Riebl, *Entstehung und Gründung des Salzburger Athletik-Sportklub* 1914, unpublished manuscript, copy in possession of the author.

Newspapers

Salzburg:
Der Eiserne Besen
Salzburger Amtsblatt
Salzburger Chronik
Salzburger Sportblatt
Salzburger Volksblatt
Salzburger Wacht
Sport-Tagblatt

North America
The Pittsburgh Press
The Daily Item (Sunbury, PA)
The Los Angeles Times
Star Tribune (Minneapolis, MN)
Daily News (New York)
The Brooklyn Daily Eagle
The News Chronicle (Shippensburg, PA)
The Gazette (Montreal, Quebec, Canada)

---

116 *The Brooklyn Daily Eagle*, December 6, 1936, 86; *The News Chronicle*, February 1, 1938, 5.
117 *The Gazette*, March 15, 1937, 20.

Other Published Sources

75 Jahre Skiclub Salzburg 1910–1985. Salzburg: Skiclub Salzburg, 1985.
100 Jahre Skiclub Salzburg 1910–2010. Salzburg: Skiclub Salzburg, 2010.
Allen, John B. *The Culture and Sport of Skiing: From Antiquity to World War II.* Amherst: University of Massachusetts Press, 2007.
Allen, John B. *From Skisport to Skiing: One Hundred Years of an American Sport, 1840–1940.* Amherst: University of Massachusetts Press, 1993.
Baker, Keith. *Fathers of Football: Great Britons Who Took the Game to the World.* Durrington: Pitch Publishing, 2015. 110–15.
Betz, Susanne Helene, Monika Löscher, and Pia Schölnberger. "Die Hakoah lebt!" In Susanne Helene Betz, Monika Löscher, and Pia Schölnberger, eds., "*... mehr als ein Sportverein*": *100 Jahre Hakoah Wien 1909–2009*, 10–20. Innsbruck, Wien: Studienverlag, 2009.
Bischof, Günter. "American Bucks and Austrian Buccaneers: Sun Valley – The Making of America's First Winter Resort." In Philipp Strobl and Aneta Podkalicka, eds., *Leisure Cultures and the Making of Modern Ski Resorts*, 143–60. Cham: Palgrave, 2019.
Blecking, Diethelm. "Gelehrige Körper der Nation und des Sozialismus: Die Inszenierung von Körpern in der tschechischen Sokolbewegung und bei den tschechischen Spartakiaden." In Michael Krüger, ed., *Der deutsche Sport auf dem Weg in die Moderne: Carl Diem und seine Zeit*, 239–55. Berlin: Studien zur Geschichte des Sports, LIT, 2009.
Coleman, Annie Gilbert. *Ski Style: Sport and Culture in the Rockies.* Lawrence, KS: University Press of Kansas, 2004.
Dirninger, Christian. "Konjunkturelle Dynamik und struktureller Wandel in der wirtschaftlichen Entwicklung des Landes Salzburg im 20. Jahrhundert." In Heinz Dopsch and Hans Spatzenegger, eds., *Geschichte Salzburgs: Stadt und Land*, vol. II, 2743–812. Salzburg: Universitätsverlag Anton Pustet, 1991.
Embacher, Helga. "The Jewish Community of Salzburg from its Reestablishment during Liberalism to the Present." In Helga Embacher, ed., *Jews in Salzburg: History, Cultures, Fates*, 38–66. Salzburg: Pustet, 2002.
Gidl, Anneliese. "Von elitären Versuchen zum Massensport." In Wintersportmuseum Mürzzuschlag, ed., *3rd FIS Ski History Conference*, 121–9. Graz: Mürzzuschlag, 2004.
Göllner, Siegfried, Albert Lichtblau, Christian Muckenhumer, Andreas Praher, and Robert Schwarzbauer, eds. *Zwischen Provinz und Metropole: Fußball in Österreich – Beiträge zur 1. Salzburger Fußballtagung.* Göttingen: Verlag Die Werkstatt, 2014.
Hanisch, Ernst. "Politik und Sport in der Ersten Republik." In Minas Dimitriou, Oskar Dohle, Walter Pfaller, and Andreas Praher, eds., *Salzburgs Sport in der NS-Zeit: Zwischen Staat und Diktatur*, 15–30. Salzburg: Schriftenreihe des Salzburger Landesarchivs, 2018.
Hughes, John. "Austria and the Alps: Introduction." *Austrian Studies* 18 (January 2010), 4.
John, Michael. "'Körperlich ebenbürtig ... ': Juden im österreichischen Fußballsport." In Dietrich Schulze-Marmeling, ed., *Davidstern und Lederball: Die Geschichte der Juden im deutschen und internationalen Fußball*, 231–62. Göttingen: Die Werkstatt, 2003.
Keller, Tait. *Apostles of the Alps: Mountaineering and Nation Building in Germany and Austria, 1860–1939.* Chapel Hill: U of North Carolina P, 2016.

Krammer, Reinhard. *Arbeitersport in Österreich: Ein Beitrag zur Geschichte der Arbeiterkultur in Österreich bis 1938*, 234–5. Wien: Europaverlag, 1981.

Krüger, Michael. *Einführung in die Geschichte der Leibeserziehung und des Sports. Teil 2: Leibeserziehung im 19. Jahrhundert: Turnen fürs Vaterland*. Schorndorf: Hofmann, 2020.

Lang, Otto. *A Bird of Passage: The Story of My Life*. Missoula, MT: Pictorial Histories Publishing, 1996.

Löffelmeier, Anton. *Die "Löwen" unterm Hakenkreuz: Der TSV von 1860 München im Nationalsozialismus*. Göttingen: Verlag Die Werkstatt, 2009.

Marschik, Matthias. *Bewegte Körper: Historische Populärkulturen des Sports in Österreich*. Wien: LIT Verlag, 2020.

Marschik, Matthias. "Metropolen statt Provinz: Mitropa-Idee vs. Verösterreicherung des Fußballs in der Zwischenkriegszeit." In Göllner et al., eds., *Zwischen Provinz und Metropole*, 88–96.

Marschik, Matthias. *Sportdiktatur Bewegungskulturen im nationalsozialistischen Österreich*. Wien: Turia + Kant, 2008.

Marschik, Matthias. "Turnen und Sport im Austrofaschismus (1934–1938)." In Emmerich Tálos and Wolfgang Neugebauer, eds., *Austrofaschismus. Politik – Ökonomie – Kultur. 1933–1938*, 372–89. Wien, Berlin: LIT Verlag, 2014.

Marschik, Matthias. *Wir spielen nicht zum Vergnügen: Amateurfußball in der Ersten Republik*. Wien: Verlag für Gesellschaftskritik, 1994.

Martin, Franz, Julius Gallhuber, and Franz Mauler. *Skileben in Österreich 1935*. Jahrbuch des Österreichischen Ski-Verbandes. Wien: Adolf Holzhausens Nachfolger, 1935.

Michel, Adolf. *Die Salzburger Turnerjugend im Jahre 1928: Ein Rückblick in Worten, Bildern und Zahlen, unserer Jugend zur Erinnerung an schöne Stunden zum Julfest 1928*. Salzburg: n.p., 1928.

Müllner, Rudolf. "The Importance of Skiing in Austria." *The International Journal of the History of Sport* 30(6) (March 2013), 661.

Müllner, Rudolf. *Perspektiven der historischen Sport- und Bewegungskulturforschung*. Wien, Berlin: LIT Verlag, 2011.

Peiffer, Lorenz. *Die deutsche Turnerschaft: Ihre politische Stellung in der Zeit der Weimarer Republik und des Nationalsozialismus*. Ahrensburg: Czwalina, 1976.

Praher, Andreas. "Austrian Skiing and National Socialism: Participation Patterns and Fields of Action." *Stadion* 45(2) (2021), 329.

Praher, Andreas. *Österreichs Skisport im Nationalsozialismus: Anpassung – Verfolgung – Kollaboration*. Berlin, Boston: De Gruyter, 2021b. 51–61.

Praher, Andreas. "Politische Radikalisierung im Salzburger Fußballsport in der Zwischenkriegszeit." In Göllner et al., eds., *Zwischen Provinz und Metropole*, 105–15.

Praher, Andreas. "Salzburg und Olympia 1936 – Sichtweisen und Reflexionen." In Minas Dimitriou, Oskar Dohle, Walter Pfaller, and Andreas Praher, eds., *Salzburgs Sport in der NS-Zeit: Zwischen Staat und Diktatur*, 87–107. Salzburg: Schriftenreihe des Salzburger Landesarchivs, 2018.

Praher, Andreas. "'Skifahren ist für uns Deutsche in den Alpenländern mehr als nur ein Sport': Der österreichische Skisport als politische Kampfzone der 1930er-Jahre." In Marschik et al., eds., *Images des Sports in Österreich*, 201–17.

Praher, Andreas. "Spielball des Nationalsozialismus oder loyaler Erfüllungsgehilfe?: Der Salzburger Fußballsport 1938–1945." In Göllner et al., eds., *Zwischen Provinz und Metropole*, 133–44.

Praher, Andreas. "Sport und Körperkultur: 'Ohne Widerstand bis zum Endsieg.'" In Sabine Veits-Falk and Ernst Hanisch, eds., *Herrschaft und Kultur: Instrumentalisierung – Anpassung – Resistenz*, 268–317. Salzburg: Schriftenreihe des Archivs der Stadt Salzburg, 2013a.

Praher, Andreas. "Sportführer Friedrich Rainer und seine sportpolitischen Ambitionen." In Dimitriou et al., eds., *Salzburgs Sport in der NS-Zeit*, 153–70.

Praher, Andreas. "SportlerInnen für den Krieg – KriegerInnen für den Sport." In Dimitriou et al., eds., *Salzburgs Sport in der NS-Zeit*, 255–90.

Praher, Andreas. "Sportstadt Nonntal: Historische Perspektiven, Brüche und Kontinuitäten." In Peter F. Kramml, ed., *Quartiere im Welterbe Salzburg: Kaiviertel und Nonntal im Dialog – Geschichte, Entwicklung und Perspektiven*, 315–65. Salzburg: Schriftenreihe des Archivs der Stadt Salzburg, 2013b.

Praher, Andreas, and Robert Schwarzbauer. "Der jüdische Sport im Salzburg der Zwischenkriegszeit." *Aschkenas: Zeitschrift für Geschichte und Kultur der Juden* 27(1) (June 2017), 57–70.

Schwarzbauer, Robert. "Der katholische Fußball in Oberösterreich und Salzburg in der Zwischenkriegszeit." In Göllner et al., eds., *Zwischen Provinz und Metropole*, 116–24.

Schwarzbauer, Robert. "Der VAFÖ in Oberösterreich und Salzburg." In Johannes Gießauf, Walter M. Iber, and Harald Knoll, eds., *Fußball, Macht und Diktatur: Streiflichter auf den Stand der historischen Forschung*, 231–52. Innsbruck: Studienverlag, 2014.

Schwarzbauer, Robert. "Ein 'Zeugnis vom Wirken einer Schar sportbegeisterter Jugend': Die Chronik des Bischofshofener Sportklub 1935." In Matthias Marschik, Agnes Meisinger, Rudolf Müllner, Johann Skocek, and Georg Spitaler, eds., *Images des Sports in Österreich: Innensichten und Außenwahrnehmungen*, 175–86. Göttingen: V&R unipress GmbH, 2018.

Ski-Klub Zell am See. *Festschrift zum 75-Jahr-Jubiläum*. Zell am See: 1981.

Wallinger, Toni. *50 Jahre Salzburger Fußballverband: Die Geschichte des Fußballsportes im Land Salzburg*. Salzburg: Salzburger Fußballverband, 1971.

"[W]ir werden nur das tun und schreiben, was dem Sport frommt und den Politischen auf die Finger schauen." *Salzburger Chronik* (September 25, 1926), 9.

Seven Everyman and the New Man: Festival Culture in Interwar Austria

Alys X. George

"Feste der Festlosen" (celebrations for those devoid of celebration): this shared title of two articles from *Kunst und Volk* (Art and the People), the official periodical of the Social Democratic *Kunststelle* (Arts Bureau), marked festival culture as a cornerstone of cultural programming in "Red Vienna" while also identifying its target audience.[1] Important functionaries of the *Sozialdemokratische Arbeiterpartei Osterreichs* (Austrian Social Democratic Workers' Party, SDAPÖ), such as the articles' authors, David Josef Bach and Josef Luitpold Stern, held the dearth of pleasure in the lives of the working classes to be in desperate need of redress. "Das Recht auf Heiterkeit" (the right to gaiety) was seen as a fundamental human right, and collective cultural experiences—whether shared in stadiums, concert halls, theaters, or public spaces—could supply it.[2] The *Kunststelle* was founded in Vienna following the First World War, also the period during which the Salzburger Festspiele (Salzburg Festival) was created in Austria's second city. Salzburg, the festival's co-founder Max Reinhardt wrote, was to become a "Wallfahrtsort [...] für die zahllosen Menschen, die sich aus den blutigen Greuel dieser Zeit nach den Erlösungen der Kunst sehnen" (pilgrimage site for the countless people who long for the redemptions of art after the bloody

---

1 Josef Luitpold Stern, "Feste der Festlosen," *Kunst und Volk*, 3(1) (September 1928), 22; David Josef Bach, "Feste der Festlosen," *Kunst und Volk* 4(3) (November 1929), 74–5.
2 David Josef Bach, "Das Recht auf Heiterkeit," *Kunst und Volk* 1(10) (November 1926), 13.

horror of these times).³ Hugo von Hofmannsthal, his artistic partner in the initiative, concurred: now, more than ever, all people "[verlangen] nach geistigen Freuden" (are yearning for spiritual joys).⁴ Much separates the overtly political aims of the *Kunststelle* functionaries from the ostensible apoliticism of the Salzburg Festival masterminds, yet both fashioned rich interwar celebratory cultures in answer to a historical moment of utmost uncertainty for the new republic.

In its most general sense, the term *Festspiel* can refer to recurring cultural events, such as the Salzburger Festspiele, which comprise numerous individual productions. However, it also denotes large-scale performances, often called *Massenfestspiele* (perhaps best translated as "mass festival plays").⁵ Among the most impressive such displays was the opening ceremony of the Second International Workers' Socialist Olympiad held in Vienna on July 19–26, 1931. Coordinated by the *Kunststelle*, this *Massenfestspiel* was a choreographed historical revue, consisting of a series of fifty-seven staged scenes and over four thousand performers. It was designed to narrate the history of the working classes over half a millennium, from the Middle Ages to the present, in just under an hour. On first glance, the Olympic *Massenfestspiel* could hardly seem more diametrically opposed to the other, more familiar Salzburger Festspiele.⁶ The annual month-long, Catholic-conservative Salzburg Festival—which Stefan Zweig referred to as "die neuzeitlichen olympischen Spiele der Kunst" (the modern Olympic Games of art)⁷—had its inaugural season in 1920. Despite the difference in ideological inflection, both festivals were conceived in a very measurable sense as "Festakte im Dienst einer Idee" (celebratory acts in the service of an idea).⁸

---

3   Max Reinhardt, letter to Ferdinand Künzelmann, July 21, 1918; qtd. from Oskar Holl, "Dokumente zur Entstehung der Salzburger Festspiele," 175.
4   Hugo von Hofmannsthal, "Die Salzburger Festspiele," in Hofmannsthal, *Gesammelte Werke*, IX: 261.
5   See Pia Janke, *Politische Massenfestspiele in Österreich*.
6   Alfred Pfoser was the first to consider the Salzburg Festival systematically alongside Social Democratic festival culture in the wider context of mass aesthetics in Austria; see Alfred Pfoser, "Massenästhetik, Massenromantik, Massenspiel." Wendelin Schmidt-Dengler insisted that the SDAPÖ's festival culture could serve as a "foil" to the Salzburg Festival, while also yielding "many surprising parallels" (see "The Ideology of the Salzburg Festival," 174). See also Michael Burri's comparative analysis, "Austrian Festival Missions after 1918."
7   Stefan Zweig, *Die Welt van Gestern*, 394.
8   A comment on the Olympic *Massenfestspiel* by K. D., in Ingeborg Weber-Kellermann, *Saure Wochen*, 701.

This essay explores the founding ideas that underlay the two festivals, as well as their respective content, performative aesthetics, target audiences and reception. Although organizers from both camps largely disavowed the festivals' congruence, they mobilized to differing ends surprisingly similar strategies to achieve maximum impact and reach.[9]

I

The First Austrian Republic's festival culture built on and modified a robust regional celebratory tradition derived from the opulence of both Catholic liturgy and imperial ceremonial.[10] In Habsburg Austria, annual Corpus Christi processions and imperial jubilees gave frequent occasion for pomp and pageantry.[11] Such celebrations were at once laboratories for generating potent, captivating iconography and proving grounds for the symbolic assertion of that iconography. Festival culture is thus one example of what Eric Hobsbawm has called "invented traditions," the repeated ritual and symbolic practices by which societies instill norms and values by reference to history—even when that past, or the present connection to it, is (partly) imagined.[12] Like earlier imperial and liturgical celebrations, the interwar festivals considered here were designed to encapsulate narratives of enduring cultural and political heritage: the retrograde concept of "Austrian-ness" at the heart of the Salzburg Festival's program, and the SDAPÖ's staging of the history of the working classes. Such grand narratives of uninterrupted tradition are legitimizing models of continuity, serving as counterweights to the contingency and vicissitudes of history. Yet shared narratives, "invented traditions," are more than mere propaganda; they are the crucibles in which the *teloi* of collective identities and ideologies are forged vis-à-vis the past.[13] And festival cultures are the ceremonial arenas in which these varying conceptions of past, present, and future are staged. They thus serve as *Ordnungsutopien* (ordering utopias)—as Norbert Christian Wolf has called the Salzburg Festival—which satisfy a need for coherent historical narratives in times of epochal change.[14]

---

9   Janke, *Politische Massenfestspiele*, 9.
10 Pfoser, "Massenästhetik," 65–7.
11 See Daniel L. Unowsky, *The Pomp and Politics of Patriotism*.
12 Eric Hobsbawm, "Introduction: Inventing Tradition," in *The Invention of Tradition*, 1–2. Michael Steinberg employs Hobsbawm's terminology to analyze Hofmannsthal's Salzburg Festival programming (*Austria as Theater and Ideology*, 2–3).
13 See Janke, *Politische Massenfestspiele*, 9 and 24; Oliver Rathkolb, "In Salzburg eine Triumphpforte österreichischer Kunst errichten," 588.
14 Norbert Christian Wolf, "Ordnungsutopie oder Weltheaterschwindel?" See also Wendelin Schmidt-Dengler, "Bedürfnis nach Geschichte."

In Salzburg, the Festival was nothing less than a reformulation of what it meant to be "Austrian" after the age of empire. But this notion of "Austrian-ness" was regressive, Michael Steinberg has shown, consisting of a stylized artistic vision of a harmonious Christian world order and a recursive deployment of Baroque theater.[15] Hofmannsthal's *Jedermann: Das Spiel vom Sterben des reichen Mannes* (Everyman), the adapted morality play that was (and remains) the centerpiece of the Festival, is the paradigmatic manifestation of this vision. Hofmannsthal viewed it as the writer's responsibility to promote postwar coherence and healing by counterposing the "unsäglich gebrochenen Zustände" (unspeakably broken states of affairs) with "ein ungebrochenes Weltverhältnis" (unbroken world relations) in cultural production.[16] The Social Democratic party likewise saw the necessity of presenting a reasoned, intelligible narrative of its own raison d'être in a historicized fashion. One Social Democratic definition of the Festspiel as a genre demonstrates that the party line conceived of festival culture as encapsulating "die sozialen Konflikte, den Sinn der Revolution und die Würde des Arbeiters, sowie die Macht seiner Position" (the social conflicts, the reason for revolution and the dignity of the worker, as well as the power of his position).[17] The party was clear that the Festspiel genre offered "ungeahnte Möglichkeiten neuartiger *politischer Massenbeeinflussung*" (undreamt-of new possibilities for politically influencing the masses),[18] which was to result in a politically engaged "Neuer Mensch" (new [hu]man).

Beyond the specific narratives of what it meant to be "Austrian" or "socialist" in the interwar years, both *Jedermann* and the SDAPÖ's *Massenfestspiel* also staged humankind's fate in broader terms as a struggle between damnation and redemption.[19] This theme provides a clue to one of the sources of inspiration for the festivals: despite their differences, the Salzburg Festival and Social Democratic *Massenfestspiel* looked to the codified aesthetic ritualism of the Catholic Church with its ability to forge a sense of community and collective emotional fellowship.[20] The SDAPÖ drew on the church's stark symbolism, alternately playing up its theatricality and neutralizing its religious content in the service of identitarian party politics. Whereas the Social Democrats were at pains to conceal the clerical nature of their aesthetic inspiration, the organizers of the Salzburg Festival made no secret of its religious reference

---

15 Steinberg, *Austria as Theater and Ideology*, especially 1–36.
16 Hofmannsthal, "Das Spiel vor der Menge," GW III, 106.
17 Ernst Wagner, "Gesicht des Proletariats," 10.
18 Felix Kanitz, "Festspielepilog," 6. Emphasis in original.
19 Janke, *Politische Massenfestspiele*, 201.
20 Bela Rasky, *Arbeiterfesttage*; Janke, *Politische Massenfestspiele*, 50–1, 69–70; William J. McGrath, *Dionysian Art and Populist Politics in Austria*, 224.

Everyman and the New Man: Festival Culture in Interwar Austria 205

point, right down to the performance of *Jedermann* on the cathedral square in Salzburg. More generally, both camps adapted the ecclesiastical ritual calendar to their own ends, the SDAPÖ by supplanting it with secular celebratory programming, and the Salzburg Festival's creators by harmonizing their festival repertoire with it.[21]

The Social Democratic *Massenfestspiel* and the Salzburg Festival promoted performance as a participatory aesthetic experience by seamlessly melding backward-looking imperial-liturgical pageantry with experimental theatrical techniques. Max Reinhardt's embrace of Wagnerian total theater was a clarion call in both contexts.[22] The Wagnerian *Gesamtkunstwerk* and an appeal to a Nietzschean harnessing of Dionysian energies were also mutual touchstones, even while the Salzburg Festival was explicitly envisaged as a spectacular Austrian rival to Bayreuth, and the SDAPÖ found additional templates in Soviet and German agitprop theater.[23] Reinhardt, of course, directed the 1920 Salzburg *Jedermann*, but his influence was present in the Vienna stadium too, as Stephan (Stefan) Hock, a dramaturge and Reinhardt's deputy director at the *Theater in der Josefstadt* during the mid-1920s, choreographed the Olympic *Massenfestpiele*. The choreography and staging of the festivals sought to blur the lines between stage and reality, art and life; spectators should be elevated and transported as a collective from the routines of their daily lives to redirect their energies towards a specific cause. Festival culture was thus a powerful instrument for both the aestheticization of politics and the politicization of aesthetics in interwar Austria.

Ernst Bloch once remarked that public festivals inspire a potentially transformative hopefulness, one premised on the celebration in the present of a joy only later to be actualized.[24] They are in a general sense, then, "Feste der Festlosen"—in Bach's and Stern's terms—for they require the suspension of disbelief in the here-and-now, exchanged for the anticipation of a better future through redemption. Interwar festival cultures filled a postimperial cultural, political, and spiritual void with the promise of performative actualization and immersion. In the case of the Salzburg Festival that meant symbolically staging a hoped-for conservative reconstruction of Austria, while the SDAPÖ's *Massenfestspiel* enacted the desired historical inevitability of a socialist revolution.

---

21 Wolfgang Maderthaner, "Austro-Marxism: Mass Culture and Anticipatory Socialism," 24; Rasky, *Arbeiterfesttage*, 34–6; "Der weiße und der rote Umgang," 5; Hofmannsthal, "Die Salzburger Festspiele," GW IX: 258.
22 Pfoser, "Massenästhetik," 62–3, 68–9. For more on Reinhardt's concept of a *Massentheater* (theater of the masses), see Erika Fischer-Lichte, *Eine kurze Geschichte des deutschen Theaters*, 278.
23 Pfoser, "Massenästhetik," 67–8; Maderthaner, "Austro-Marxism," 24–5.
24 Ernst Bloch, *Das Prinzip Hoffnung*, II, 1068.

Festivals are thus fundamentally utopian undertakings, even if their calculated visions of unity, coherence and inclusivity are merely palliative—or contrived.

II

The Salzburg Festival, co-conceived by Hugo von Hofmannsthal, Max Reinhardt, Richard Strauss, and others, celebrated its inaugural season in the summer of 1920. The festival was designed to help Austrians rediscover their "eigentliche[s] geistige[s] Element" (essential spiritual element) in the wake of a war that had geopolitically rent not only the Austro-Hungarian Empire, but all of Europe, and many other parts of the world.[25] Salzburg was to be a centralized, fixed venue for the celebration of pan-European cultural harmony at the Catholic heart of the continent.[26] Hofmannsthal and Reinhardt agreed on the necessity of making "uralt Lebendiges aufs neue lebendig" (ancient living traditions live anew).[27] As Reinhardt phrased it in 1918: "Das Festliche, Feiertagliche, Einmalige, das alle Kunst hat und das auch das Theater zur Zeit der Antike hatte und auch zur Zeit, da es noch in der Wiege der katholischen Kirche lag, das muß dem Theater wiedergegeben werden" (The festive, holiday-like uniqueness that all art has and that theater, too, used to have in Ancient Greece and when it was still in the cradle of the Catholic Church—that must be re-instilled in the theater).[28] In other words, the Salzburg Festival was to revive a popular theater tradition, and the first production to be staged was Hofmannsthal's adaptation of *Jedermann*, the fifteenth-century English morality play.[29] The work had been premiered in a Berlin circus in 1911 under Max Reinhardt's direction; the setting this time was even more dramatic.

On August 22, 1920 in Salzburg, crowds assembled on the square before the cathedral to watch the inaugural performance. In Hofmannsthal's updated lyric drama, the wealthy character Everyman finds his comfortable life threatened by the figure of Death, who has come to take him to meet his maker. Bereft of family, friends, and, ultimately,

---

25 Hofmannsthal, "Festspiele in Salzburg," GW IX: 264.
26 Hofmannsthal, "Festspiele in Salzburg," GW IX: 264.
27 Hofmannsthal, "Festspiele in Salzburg," GW IX: 264.
28 Reinhardt, letter to Künzelmann, July 21, 1918, qtd. from Holl, "Dokumente," 177.
29 *Jedermann* was initially an interim solution, as the Festival's intended centerpiece, *Das Salzburger Große Welttheater* (The Great Salzburg World Theater), was not finished as planned. See Norbert Christian Wolf, *Eine Triumphpforte österreichischer Kunst*, 119–20, and Judith Beniston, *Welttheater*, 146–56.

his riches, Everyman's only companions are his Deeds and his Faith, as personified dramatic figures. The co-presence of Action and Conviction impels Everyman finally to repent of his sinful ways and convert to Christianity in order to perish a penitent believer, with Faith accompanying him into the grave. The staging, against the open-air backdrop of the seventeenth-century Salzburg cathedral, made explicit the link to an Austrian Baroque Catholic past. However, Hofmannsthal wedded the themes of money and death with an allegory of timeless morality. He described *Jedermann* as "[e]in menschliches Märchen [...] in christlichem Gewand" (a human fairy tale in Christian attire),[30] "allen Zeiten gehörig und allgemein gültig" (belonging to all ages and universally relevant),[31] stressing how the story's moral-theological basis had been re-contextualized to impart a broadly applicable humanistic message.

By reframing the themes of money and the exchange value of all things and beings, Hofmannsthal engaged directly with one of the most pressing issues of the day. A topic central to the play—a world of faulty economic relations embodied in the figure of Mammon (Wealth)—reads as if from the socialist playbook. Commenting on the broken order of things in an essay published at the play's premiere in 1911, Hofmannsthal wrote, "was wir besitzen sollten, das besitzt uns, und was das Mittel aller Mittel ist, das Geld, wird uns in dämonischer Verkehrtheit zum Zweck der Zwecke" (that which we should possess possesses us, and the means of all means—money—becomes for us in a demonic reversal the end of all ends).[32] The playwright thus revealed himself—despite the criticisms that would soon be levied at the Salzburg Festival—as an astute observer of the fiscal duress of the age.

This provides a common thematic bond with the Social Democratic *Massenfestspiel*, which pilloried capitalism. Hofmannsthal's *Everyman* adaptation likely was linked to his contemporaneous readings of the sociologist Georg Simmel's *Philosophie des Geldes* (Philosophy of Money, 1900) in the 1910s.[33] Yet Hofmannsthal was little interested in demonizing capitalism as such; it was the humanist message against greed and materialism that concerned him foremost. The irony of the play's denunciation of money cannot be lost on us, though, since it points to a paradox of the Salzburg Festival as a whole, with *Jedermann* as its

---

30 Hofmannsthal, "Das Spiel vor der Menge," GW III, 106.
31 Hofmannsthal, "Das alte Spiel von Jedermann," GW III, 89.
32 Hofmannsthal, "Das alte Spiel von Jedermann," GW III, 89.
33 For Hofmannsthal's thematization of finance see Wolf, *Eine Triumphpforte*, 120–61, also Karlheinz Rossbacher, "'Verse auf einer Banknote geschrieben': *Jedermann* und das Geld." For Hofmannsthal's readings of Simmel see Ursula Renner, "Hofmannsthals *Jedermann*," 435–48.

very emblem. That contradiction—the question of target audience and accessibility considered comparatively in this article's final section—is as hotly debated now as then.[34]

In 1921, Ernst Fischer reviewed the second annual performance of *Jedermann* in *Arbeiterwille*, the Graz-based, leading socialist daily for Styria and Carinthia. Given the publication venue, readers might have expected damning criticism, and Fischer does not initially disappoint. He argues that *Jedermann* might appear at first glance to be merely "katholisch[e] Propaganda" (Catholic propaganda) and, worse yet, even "[ein] gefährliche[r] Verjüngungsversuch" (a dangerous rejuvenation attempt) by Catholic conservatives to cloak art and religion in modern theatrical garb.[35] Fischer, however, is less troubled by the performance's overtly religious message and keeps the larger picture in the forefront. Anyone who witnesses the wedding of religion and spectacle on such a scale, he argues—and before a paying public, no less—"wird begreifen, daß die Jedermannspiele nichts mit einer katholischen Renaissance zu tun haben. Eine Religion, die sich dieser Mittel bedient, eine Religion, die zum *Kunstabenteuer* wird, ist dem Tode verfallen" (will grasp that *Jedermann* has nothing to do with a Catholic renaissance. A religion that avails itself of such methods, a religion that becomes an *art adventure*, is in its death throes).[36] It is precisely those methods—the performative aesthetics of *Jedermann*—that fascinate Fischer most, even while he upbraids the Church, and, implicitly, the Salzburg Festival, as nothing more than decadent *l'art pour l'art*. A later review in the *Arbeiter-Zeitung* was more pointed, branding the Salzburg Festival's offerings as mere "Treibhausgewächse der Kunst" (greenhouse art flowers), "gekünstelter und verschnörkelter Katholizismus" (aestheticized and ornate Catholicism).[37]

Fischer was nevertheless awestruck by the overall impression, and his review describes the performance in rapturous tones, calling it "eine berauschende Sensation" (an intoxicating sensation), a "Divina comedia [sic]" (divine comedy).[38] He marvels especially at the spectacular erasure of the boundary between the performance and the surrounding environment. From the eminence and skill of the actors Alexander Moissi and Werner Krauß to the lighting and sound, from the actors' emergence amidst the audience to the startled pigeons taking flight, from the stone-faced saints on the torch-lit cathedral façade to the impressive resonance of the tolling church-bells: "alles war da, [...] alles, alles spielte

---

34 Most famously by Karl Kraus, "Vom großen Welttheaterschwindell" (1922).
35 Ernst Fischer, "Jedermann in Salzburg," *Arbeiterwille*, August 25, 1921, 1.
36 Ernst Fischer, "Jedermann in Salzburg," 1. Emphasis in original.
37 "Schauspiel der Masse im Stadion," *Arbeiter-Zeitung*, July 19, 1931, 8.
38 Fischer, "Jedermann in Salzburg," 1.

mit" (everything was there, everything, everything played a part).[39] The effect was in keeping with Hofmannsthal's and Reinhardt's vision. They regarded the location as an indispensable dramatic character: in Salzburg "[spielt] der Ortsgeist selber mit" (the *genius loci* is itself part of the performance), Hofmannsthal wrote.[40] Elsewhere, he stated that at targeted moments in the performance the viewers were to be unclear whether the dramatic action was imagined or real.[41] On the cathedral square in Salzburg, this effect was realized by strategically deploying sound, pantomime and choreography in addition to using the surrounding architectonic space beyond the forward stage to create an immersive experience that undermined the line between stage and audience.

Although the Salzburg Festival's *Jedermann* was clearly conceived to make an impressive aesthetic statement, Hofmannsthal was not blind to the political relevance of staging universal themes.[42] In an essay that followed the Berlin premiere of *Jedermann* in 1911, he makes explicit the political intent of *all* theatrical engagement: "Gibt man sich mit dem Theater ab, es bleibt immer ein Politikum. Man handelt, indem man vor eine Menge tritt, denn man will auf sie wirken" (Involvement in theater is always a political matter. One acts by appearing before a crowd, for one wishes to make an impression on them).[43] The effect of that action is further strengthened, Hofmannsthal argues, if an unusual setting is chosen or if one performs before a diverse and unusually numerous audience. Fischer, for his part, succumbs to the aesthetic appeal of the performance, even while acknowledging that he has just witnessed propaganda. Yet he is generous in his interpretation that it serves not a Catholic, but a universalist ideology, calling *Jedermann* "eine Propaganda für das Göttliche in uns, für die menschliche Phantasie" (propaganda for the divine in us, for the human imagination).[44] He singles out Reinhardt for special praise in this context; the director is a beacon, revealing to Social Democrats aesthetic strategies they must harness for their own purposes. Fischer's *feuilleton* ends with an impatient call to action: "Wann werden wir Sozialisten den Menschen das erste Festspiel bereiten?" (When will we socialists offer the people their first *Festspiel*?).[45]

---

39 Fischer, "Jedermann in Salzburg," 2.
40 Hofmannsthal, "Zum Programm der Salzburger Festspiele 1928," GW X, 188.
41 Hofmannsthal, "Das alte Spiel von Jedermann," GW III, 97.
42 Oliver Rathkolb has pointed up Hofmannsthal's and Reinhardt's opportunistic approach to festival planning, which shifted according to context ("In Salzburg eine Triumphpforte," 589).
43 Hofmannsthal, "Das Spiel vor der Menge," GW III, 104.
44 Fischer, "Jedermann in Salzburg," 2.
45 Fischer, "Jedermann in Salzburg," 2.

III

SDAPÖ party faithful would have to wait a full decade after Fischer's review, not for the first socialist *Festspiel*, but for its most impressive realization: the *Massenfestspiel* that was the opening ceremony of the 1931 International Workers' Socialist Olympiad in Vienna. Although the SDAPÖ had long been aware of the necessity of fashioning its own iconography, the party struggled to articulate a unified and widely compelling line on matters of culture and education in the 1920s.[46] Workers' festival culture played an increasingly vital role in these efforts. Robert Ehrenzweig, editor of the journal *Die politische Bühne* (The Political Stage) and the mastermind behind the Olympic *Massenfestspiel*, noted the potency of such stagings. He called *Massenspiele* "eine der wirksamsten Waffen im Klassenkampf" (one of the most effective weapons in the class struggle) and predicted that one day they would be counted "zu den höchsten Gütern einer neuen Kultur" (among the greatest assets of a new culture).[47] In fact, festival culture was so important that the SDAPÖ centralized *Festspiele* under the purview of the *Kunststelle* in 1930.[48] While socialist festival culture of the early 1920s operated on a largely educational premise, the focus had shifted by the late 1920s to increasing ritualization and theatricalization. In its privileging of form over content, this second phase served foremost to sustain class consciousness and emotional identification with the party as continuing sources of collective identity.[49] The Olympic *Massenfestspiel* can thus be viewed as the apotheosis of the SDAPÖ's turn towards the aestheticization of politics.

Taken as a whole, the Second International Workers' Socialist Olympiad formed a monumental *Gesamtkunstwerk* that delivered an impressive symbolic display of power for a party, republic, and world in crisis.[50] The games drew close to eighty thousand athletes from all over the globe (almost half of them Austrian) and nearly a quarter of a million spectators attended the *Massenfestspiel* alone.[51] The Olympiad

---

46 Gruber, *Red Vienna*, 81–2, 111–12. See also Robert Pyrah, "The 'Enemy Within'?"
47 Robert Ehrenzweig, "Das Theater der Massen," *Die politische Bühne* (June 1932), n.p.
48 Gruber, *Red Vienna*, 108. Gruber notes that the SDAPÖ's attempt to gain control over grass-roots celebrations was largely unsuccessful in the long run, as entertainment value continued to eclipse educational substance. Rásky emphasizes the increasing politicization of festival culture in the early 1930s (*Arbeiterfesttage*, 143–5).
49 Rásky, *Arbeiterfesttage*, 3–4.
50 Janke, *Politische Massenfestspiele*, 122.
51 See Gruber, *Red Vienna*, 107, and Kanitz, "Festspielepilog." The Socialist Olympiad far exceeded the scope of the "regular" Olympic summer games held in 1932 in Los Angeles.

Everyman and the New Man: Festival Culture in Interwar Austria 211

thus served as a prime opportunity to stage both the party line and the "Neuer Mensch" the left sought to foster, in part through physical culture. Sports, Ernst Bloch reminds us, are never apolitical,[52] and the remarks of Julius Tandler, the renowned anatomist and Viennese Stadtrat für Wohlfahrts- und Gesundheitswesen (Municipal Councilor for Welfare and Healthcare), call to mind that assertion. Tandler declared it the "vornehmste Pflicht" (foremost duty) of both city and party "aus Weltkrieg, Zusammenbruch, Inflation und Weltwirtschaftskrise unsere Jugend zu retten, ihr durch die Freiheit des Körpers die Freiheit des Geistes zu geben" (to save our youth from world war, collapse, inflation and global economic crisis, to give them freedom of spirit through freedom of body).[53] One manifestation of this goal was the municipal government's Prater stadium, which had begun construction in 1928 as the centerpiece for the Olympiad.[54] But athletic events were not the only channels for messages about the physical strength, resilience and preparedness of workers in the fight against fascism and capitalist hegemony. The determination of the SDAPÖ and the Sozialistische Arbeitersport-Internationale (Socialist Workers' Sport International, SASI) to shape a new, transnational world order was equally conveyed by the Olympiad's cultural programming.[55] The *Massenfestspiel*, in particular, and the "Neue Menschen" who acted it out, embodied the overarching new culture the Social Democrats imagined.

The sixty thousand spectators present in the Vienna stadium on July 25, 1931 witnessed five thousand performers realizing the hourlong *Massenfestspiel*'s dramatic action.[56] On the playing field below, a three-storey wooden tower hung with blue drapes reached high into the evening sky.[57] The performance's fifty-seven scenes were divided

---

52 Bloch, *Das Prinzip Hoffnung*, I, 524.
53 *Festführer Sonderausgabe Arbeiterolympiade Wien 19–26. Juli 1931*, ed. Alfred Finkler, 3. See also Julius Deutsch, "Die Bedeutung der Welt-Olympiade des Arbeitersports," *Die politische Bühne*, June 1932, 4–5, and "Die Olympiade," *Arbeiter-Zeitung*, July 19, 1931, 4.
54 See Bernhard Hachleitner, "Das Wiener Praterstadion/Ernst-Happel-Stadion."
55 Other cultural events included an art contest in the Variété Licht, a choir concert at the Musikverein, and a staged matinee in the Apollo-Kino, Vienna's largest cinema.
56 Kanitz, "Festspielepilog." Many performers were members of the Wiener Arbeiterturner (Viennese Workers' Gymnastics Club), the Sozialistische Arbeiterjugend (Socialist Youth Workers), the Gewerkschaftsjugend (Youth Union), and the socialist youth leisure organization Rote Falken (Red Falcons).
57 My description synthesizes several reports, including "Schauspiel der Masse im Stadion"; K. D., "Bericht über das Festspiel anläßlich der zweiten Arbeiterolympiade in Wien," as cited in Ingeborg Weber-Kellermann, *Saure Wochen, frohe Feste: Fest und Alltag in der Sprache der Bräuche*; and F[elix] K[anitz], "Das Festspiel der Viertausend im Stadion," *Arbeiter-Zeitung*, June 28, 1931, 10.

into four thematic sections: "das Idyll vor der Maschine und dem Kapital" (the idyll before the machine and capital); "die Herrschaft der Maschine und des Kapitals" (the rule of the machine and capital); "der Krieg" (war); and "nach dem Krieg" (after the war). The opening harkened back to a prelapsarian pastoral symbolizing the unity of humans and nature. Joyously dancing actors portrayed medieval craftsmen and craftswomen, whose culture and labor were one. The utopia was overrun, however, by clanking and rattling machines heralding the dawn of the Industrial Age—and with it the triumph of capitalism. Columns of proletarian workers took the field, their tired bodies and somber faces portraying the effects of the fetters of their soulless labor. Clad in drab blues and greys, they painted a stark contrast to the vibrant color and animated dancing of the guilds in the prior scene. The tower, too, was transformed, as a four-by-four metre "goldene Fratze des Kapitalismus" (grotesque golden face of capitalism), topped with a cross, ascended from its upper tier. Surrounding it were signs bearing the keywords "Börse" (stock market), "Kapitalist" (capitalist), "Bilanz" (balance sheet), "Haben" (credit-balance). An audio montage conflating the rhetoric of religion with finance sounded out from the tower: "Von Bethlehem kam das Licht ..." (from Bethlehem there shone a light), "Bethlehemstahl steigt ..." (Bethlehem steel is on the rise).

Soon, though, the faint strains of "The Marseillaise" and a solitary red flag rising from amidst a workers' group marked the first, tentative proletarian revolt. Its few proponents were savagely put down, and a world war ensued. A violent battle played out on the field but halted suddenly when the exhortation "Du sollst nicht töten!" (Thou shalt not kill!) marked the end of the conflict. After the smoke cleared, the workers again took up their labor, and a second revolution was sparked. This time, all the workers united to storm the Tower of Capitalism, and the golden capitalist head was lowered into the tower, disappearing along with the cross. It was replaced by a gigantic red banner, and red standards were unfurled to swathe the tower. At this point, the distinction between actors and audience was dissolved: the spectators were encouraged to wave their own red flags and light torches to mirror the procession which had taken the field. "In diesem Augenblick wird die Wirklichkeit stärker als das Schauspiel" (at this moment reality becomes stronger than performance), remarked the *Arbeiter-Zeitung*.[58] The audience was to be infected not only with enthusiasm for the spectacular display, but also with participatory solidarity and a sense of collective identity and belonging. This effect was underscored by the

---

58 "Schauspiel der Masse im Stadion."

implementation of a *Sprechchor* (chorus of voices) at the ceremony's climax.⁵⁹ A voice from the tower harnessed the power of the crowd in a call-and-response socialist profession of faith that praised peace, justice, and freedom for the working classes. Finally, the *Internationale* rang out once more, and the movement's banners were carried ceremoniously into the stadium, as socialism triumphed.

The success of the *Massenfestspiel* far outstripped its organizers' expectations. Originally, two performances had been planned, but with the stadium already at capacity for the open rehearsal and legions of disappointed hopefuls turned away, two further performances were hastily arranged to meet the unexpected demand. In sum, the stadium was filled four times.⁶⁰ Ehrenzweig, co-founder of and writer for the *Politisches Kabarett*, composed the spectacle's content. As already noted, Reinhardt's colleague Stephan Hock was responsible for staging and choreography.⁶¹ The connection of Ehrenzweig and Hock to avant-garde theater is evident in their bold conception for the *Massenfestspiel*: by dissolving the boundaries between performance and reality, actors and audience, they sought nothing less than to explode "die Maße des Gegenwartstheaters" (the dimensions of contemporary theater).⁶²

Writing about the concept of the proletarian "Theater der Masse" (theater of the masses), Ehrenzweig proclaimed emotional identification as the key goal of festival performances—an idea which corresponded to the shift away from the reason-centered, pedagogical premise of Social Democratic cultural initiatives in the early 1920s. The spectators must be convinced, beyond a shadow of a doubt, that "[e]s ist dein Geschick, das hier dargestellt wird, es sind deine Gedanken, deine Sorgen, es ist dein Fühlen, deine Sehnsucht, dein Wille, der diesem Schauspiel Gestalt verliehen hat!" (It is your fate, your thoughts, your troubles, your emotions, your desires, your will, which have been given concrete shape in this performance).⁶³ According to Ehrenzweig, simple scenes juxtaposing historical and contemporary events should appeal to viewers' emotions and enable a direct comparison between past and present hardships.⁶⁴ The Olympic *Massenfestspiel* gave form to his ideas

---

59 For the role of the *Sprechchor* in Social Democrat cultural politics see Fritz Rosenfeld, "Gedanken zum Sprechchor," *Der Kampf* 19.2 (February 1926), 85–6, and Wolfgang Schumann, "Die Sprechchorbewegung," *Kunst und Volk* 2.6 (September 1927), 9–11.
60 "Heute kommen Dreißigtausend!" *Arbeiter-Zeitung*, July 22, 1931, 5; Kanitz, "Festspielepilog."
61 Pfoser, "Massenästhetik," 72.
62 "Schauspiel der Masse im Stadion."
63 Ehrenzweig, "Das Theater der Massen."
64 Ehrenzweig, "Das Theater der Massen."

by telling a version of world history through the lens of historical materialism, a story that ended with capitalism's collapse and humanity's redemption through socialism. It aimed to mobilize the masses through a curious combination of gymnastics, historical determinism and performance, laying at the audience's feet a participatory illusion in which history was no longer merely the purview of Great Men and uncontrollable forces, but called for action by all. Through an interactive union of form and content, the creators strove to create a "sozialistisches Erlebnis" (socialist experience), an "elementares Massenereignis" (elemental mass event), which would speak both to viewers' "Sinne" (senses) and their "Gesinnung" (convictions).[65] Remarking on the overall effect of the *Massenfestspiel*, an anonymous reviewer for the *Arbeiter-Zeitung* could barely contain his enthusiasm, summing up the overall impression as an unequivocal success: "ein Schauspiel nur? [...] Nein, das ist keine Dichtung [...]—das ist weltgeschichtliche Wirklichkeit" (a mere play? No, that is not poetry—that is world-historical reality).[66]

The political opposition was predictably critical but also nonplussed. The conservative *Reichspost*, for example, had anticipated that the *Massenfestspiel* would amount to nothing more than "parteipolitischer Unfug" (party-political nonsense).[67] Bernhard Birk opens a subsequent review with a caustic summation, calling the *Massenfestspiel* "[e]ine Kartoffel- und Gemüsesuppe, für die Menge ganz pikant zusammengekocht aus literarhistorischen Erinnerungen, Filmreminiszenzen und einer Lichterprozession; ein Massengulasch mit einer ätheistisch paprizierten Soße abgelöscht" (a potato-and-vegetable soup for the masses, cooked up all piquant from literary-historical remembrances, film reminiscences and a procession of lights; a mass-goulash deglazed with an atheistically spiced hot paprika sauce).[68] Birk concedes that the choreography of the masses leaves a strong visual impression, one he admiringly compares to Fritz Lang's silent masterpiece *Metropolis* (1927). Most of his attention is devoted, though, not to identifying what is aesthetically innovative about the performance, but to peering under the cloak of purportedly new dramatic techniques. He finds that "trotz alles Neuheidentums" (despite all neo-heathenism), the Social Democrats' constant reference points for festival culture are the "Kultgebräuche" (cultic customs) of

---

65 "Schauspiel der Masse im Stadion"; Stephan Hock, "Das große Festspiel im Stadion," *Arbeiter-Zeitung*, July 18, 1931, 5; Ehrenzweig, "Das Theater der Massen."
66 "Schauspiel der Masse im Stadion."
67 "Das Spiel der Viertausend im Stadion: Parteipolitischer Unfug in der städtischen Sportanlage," *Reichspost*, July 10, 1931, 7.
68 Dr. [Bernhard] Birk, "Das 'Spiel der Viertausend,'" *Reichspost*, August 4, 1931, 7.

Christian, primarily Catholic, ceremonial. Here, Birk cites numerous elements of the *Massenfestspiel*: the heaven-hell symbolism, the torch procession reminiscent of how the sacramental vows of First Communion and Confirmation are spoken solemnly with candle in hand, the battle scenes suggestive of those in Shrove Tuesday and Easter plays. Even the stage architecture, with its multi-tiered tower, reminds Birk of the upper and lower stages used in Easter festivals of yore.[69] Although the festival performance's content obviously demonized religion by yoking it to capitalism, its form nevertheless was reliant on a clerical template, as Birk demonstrates. His critique above all lays bare the two aesthetic poles between which the SDAPÖ's *Massenfestspiel* sought to navigate: liturgical celebration and popular culture.

IV

Audience participation was a crucial aesthetic component of the festival performances in Salzburg and Vienna, as was a contentiously debated ideal of public inclusivity. In the Prater stadium, the apex of dramatic action on the field—the *Massenfestspiel's* depiction of a successful proletarian revolution in the concluding scene—also signaled the final collapse of the fourth wall of the performance. An anonymous journalist from the *Arbeiter-Zeitung* referred directly to the dissolution of the boundary between actors and audience:

> das Gewaltige [war], daß es weder Schauspieler gab, noch das, was man Publikum nennt, daß die Fünftausend in der Riesenarena das eigene Schicksal darstellen und das eigene Bekenntnis sprachen, daß die Sechzigtausend rings im ungeheuren Kreis einbezogen waren in dieses Spiel, in diese Wirklichkeit.

> (the powerful aspect was that there were neither actors nor what is usually referred to as an audience, that the five thousand in the giant arena acted out their own destiny and spoke their own creed, that the sixty thousand in a vast circle were incorporated in this performance, this reality.)[70]

Further underscoring this effect was the erasure of the border between the stadium-theater and the surrounding city: the political energy created by the participatory festival performance was disseminated into

---

69 Dr. [Bernhard] Birk, "Das 'Spiel der Viertausend,'" *Reichspost*, August 4, 1931, 7.
70 "Schauspiel der Masse im Stadion," 8.

Vienna's very center. At the close of the *Massenfestspiel*, the performers—audience and actors alike—streamed out into the city night. The torch procession that had begun in the stadium made its way through the Prater, along the Danube Canal and around the Ringstraße, finally ending on the monumental square before City Hall. This parade, too, was staged; each detail was planned in advance, and instructions about the action were pre-circulated through pamphlets and newspapers.[71] It demonstrates how thoroughly the choreography of the masses permeated each aspect of socialist festival culture, and also makes clear a central conception of the festival organizers: despite the party's careful choreography, the masses were conceived of not as passive recipients, but ideally as actors themselves—protagonists and agents in their own political and aesthetic development.[72]

At the Salzburg Festival, too, the permeability of the boundary between stage and surrounding city was key to *Jedermann*'s effect. Like the Social Democrats, Hofmannsthal and Reinhardt utilized a multi-tiered tower, but the Salzburg structure was embedded within the audience. They availed themselves of a staging technique that derived from popular theatrical traditions. Hofmannsthal, citing Ludwig Tieck and Karl Immermann, believed that rooting part of the dramatic action spatially within the audience allowed viewers to identify more immediately and urgently with the plot—to see the allegorical drama not as directed *towards* them, but as stemming *from* the universality of their workaday struggles.[73] As in Vienna, the ideal Salzburg audience would mirror the stage action. At the Salzburg Festival, Michael Steinberg notes,

> The actual spectators were to serve as a paradigm for the nation as a whole. They were to see themselves – their "passion" – mirrored onstage. […] [O]ne can describe the onstage action as the symbol, the spectators as the symbolized, one the mirror of the other. The symbol, though, has the instrumental value of creating the symbolized.[74]

The grand aspiration underlying the Salzburg Festival was that Hofmannsthal's morality plays, modernized for the contemporary age, would awaken audiences to their shared Austrian heritage. Through a spectacular theatrical experience, viewers were to be immersed in a

---

71 Finkler, ed., *Festführer*, 33; K[anitz], "Das Festspiel der Viertausend."
72 See Janke, *Politische Massenfestspiele*, 126.
73 Hofmannsthal, "Das Spiel vor der Menge," 105.
74 Steinberg, *Austria as Theater and Ideology*, 38.

staged ideal and real cityscape of Catholic baroque culture. There, it was hoped, they would feel the national, moral, spiritual, and social unity of their *Volk*.[75] While the ideological orientation was different, this collective was no less ideally coherent than in the Socialists' conception. Access for all to the healing and transformative power of performance was a pressing issue in both camps. Max Reinhardt was convinced that the First World War, specifically, had demonstrated "daß das Theater nicht entbehrlicher Luxus für die oberen Zehntausend, vielmehr ein unentbehrliches Lebensmittel für die Allgemeinheit ist" (that, rather than being an unnecessary luxury for the top ten thousand, theater is indispensable sustenance for the general public).[76] Hofmannsthal, too, argued for an inclusive national festival, whose repertoire was carefully curated for its relevance "für die *ganze* Nation, nicht nur für die unruhige einzelne Schicht der großstädtischen Intelligenz" (for the *entire* nation, not just for a single restless class, the urban intellectuals).[77] In order to envision an idealized community as the festival audience, Hofmannsthal conveniently dispensed with notions of class, cultural, or ethnic fragmentation. He appealed instead to a concept of a culturally and spiritually uniform audience, a *Volk* that transcended the distinction between "die Gebildeten" (the educated) and "die Massen" (the masses).[78] Despite all evidence to the contrary, Hofmannsthal, writing in 1928, proudly deemed the bridge between the *Volk* and an educated urban elite successfully realized in the Salzburg Festival's audiences.[79]

As critics were quick to note, Hofmannsthal's wealthy character *Jedermann* was hardly the interwar Everyman or -woman. The reality of the Salzburg Festival—with its dependence on patronage, foreign sponsorship, and moneyed cultural tourism—quickly belied the ideals outlined in its organizers' programmatic texts. The sentiments of Karl Kraus's scathing 1922 "Vom großen Welttheaterschwindel" (On the Great World Theater Swindle) were pre-empted by regional publications, such as the *Salzburger Chronik*.[80] "Festspiele und Volksnot" (Festivals and People's Hardship) puts a fine point on the disparity between the "ungeheure Prunkentfaltung" (colossal display of splendor) by

---

75 Steinberg, *Austria as Theater and Ideology*, 25, 114.
76 Reinhardt, letter to Künzelmann, July 21, 1918, qtd. from Holl, "Dokumente," 175.
77 Hofmannsthal, "Zum Programm der Salzburger Festspiele 1928," 187. Emphasis in original.
78 Hofmannsthal, "Die Salzburger Festspiele," 259. See also Hofmannsthal, "Das Publikum der Salzburger Festspiele," GW X, 183–6, and Steinberg, *Austria as Theater and Ideology*, 25.
79 Hofmannsthal, "Zum Programm der Salzburger Festspiele 1928," GW 3, 188.
80 Kraus, "Vom großen Welttheaterschwindel."

wealthy foreign tourists and Viennese city slickers on the one hand, and growing local impoverishment in the face of dramatic inflation on the other.[81] Particularly in light of the "fast völligen wirtschaftlichen Entnervung unseres Landes" (almost total economic enervation of our country), the author reminds the festival directorate of their primary responsibility to the local populace and demands that they—and the government—redress the imbalance. For how can a nation whose very air is saturated with "handgreiflicher Krisenstimmung" (a palpable mood of crisis) ethically sponsor such celebrations when so many are going hungry?[82] Perhaps in response, an alternative production of *Jedermann* was staged in nearby Mondsee as early as 1922. Hofmannsthal himself authorized Franz Loser's translation into dialect, and the wealthy Everyman was replaced by a humble peasant.[83]

In Vienna, the Socialist Olympiad likewise gave occasion for critics to note the contradiction between the *Festspiel*'s content and the city's reality. Whereas on the field, class struggles were acted out and capitalism was positioned as the greatest evil, Birk, for one, points out the gaping discrepancy between the six-million-Schilling "Stadionluxusbau" (luxury stadium construction) and the very real unemployment and inflation in the Social Democrat-ruled capital.[84] Although the stadium had been realized as a communal architectural project with wide consensus in the municipal council, even from the political opposition,[85] few Social Democrats acknowledged the broader situation. In the case of the SDAPÖ, impressive displays of power—including the stadium and the Olympiad—were often symbolic compensation for the relative paucity of concrete change.[86] While one commentator in the *Arbeiter-Zeitung* did explicitly acknowledge the many Olympiad visitors who found their way to Vienna "trotz allen Schwierigkeiten und Krisennot" (despite all the difficulties and hardship),[87] most preferred to focus instead on the dimensionality and success of the Olympics and the *Massenfestspiel*.

Back in Salzburg, the author of "Festspiele und Volksnot" appealed to the festival organizers to return, essentially, to their own founding tenets. His final call is for a festival that benefits the whole nation, not just a select few well-heeled tourists. For only when the Festival ceases

---

81 "Festspiele und Volksnot," *Salzburger Chronik*, August 12, 1922, 1.
82 "Festspiele und Volksnot," *Salzburger Chronik*, August 12, 1922, 1.
83 "Theater, Kunst und Musik," *Salzburger Volksblatt*, September 21, 1921, 4. The Mondseer Jedermann [Mondsee Everyman] has, like its Salzburg counterpart, since been performed annually with few exceptions.
84 Birk, "Das "Spiel der Viertausend."
85 See Hachleitner, "Das Wiener Praterstadium," 104–10.
86 See Maderthaner, "Austro-Marxism," 36.
87 "Heute kommen Dreißigtausend!," 5.

to amplify the divisions between rich and poor "wird sie eine Festzeit für *alle* sein und dann erst werden die tieferen Schätze an Kunst und Kultur, die sie doch zu heben und hegen berufen sind, einigendes und verbindendes Gesamtgut für alle werden" (will it be a festival time for *all*, and only then will the deeper treasures of art and culture, which the Festival is called on to elevate and preserve, become a uniting and unifying common possession for all).[88] Here, we are reminded of the SDAPÖ's repeated entreaty for "Feste der Festlosen." Both interwar festivals envisioned utopian, egalitarian "invented traditions" of cultural and political heritage, which, it was hoped, would provide ideological coherence for the future. Regardless of whether they were able to live up to their respective visions, or were merely palliative, these two projects demonstrate that the greater the real-world existential challenges, the more charged the task of self-definition and self-representation become—and the more urgent the need for celebration in times of crisis.

Bibliography

Bach, David Josef. "Das Recht auf Heiterkeit," *Kunst und Volk* 1(10) (November 1926), 13.
Bach, David Josef. "Feste der Festlosen." *Kunst und Volk* 4(3) (November 1929), 74–5.
Beniston, Judith. *Welttheater: Hofmannsthal, Richard van Kralik, and the Revival of Catholic Drama in Austria, 1890–1934*. London: Maney, 1998.
"Bericht über das Festspiel anläßlich der zweiten Arbeiterolympiade in Wien." In Ingeborg Weber-Kellermann, *Saure Wochen, frohe Feste: Fest und Alltag in der Sprache der Bräuche*, 726–32. Hohenembs: Bucher, 1985.
Birk, Dr. [Bernhard]. "Das 'Spiel der Viertausend'." *Reichspost*, August 4, 1931, 7.
Bloch, Ernst. *Das Prinzip Hoffnung*. Frankfurt/M: Suhrkamp, 1959.
Burri, Michael. "Austrian Festival Missions after 1918: The Vienna Music Festival and the Long Shadow of Salzburg." *Austrian History Yearbook* 47 (2016), 147–66.
Deutsch, Julius. "Die Olympiade." *Arbeiter-Zeitung*, July 19, 1931, 4.
Deutsch, Julius. "Die Bedeutung der Welt-Olympiade des Arbeitersports." *Die politische Bühne*, June 1932, 4–5.
Ehrenzweig, Robert. "Das Theater der Massen." *Die politische Bühne* (June 1932), n.p.
"Festspiele und Volksnot." *Salzburger Chronik*, August 12, 1922, 1.
Finkler, Alfred, ed. *Festführer Sonderausgabe Arbeiterolympiade Wien 19.–26. Juli 1931*. Vienna: Druck- und Verlagsanstalt "Vorwärts," 1931.
Fischer, Ernst. "Jedermann in Salzburg." *Arbeiterwille*, August 25, 1921, 1–2.

---

88 "Festspiele und Volksnot." Emphasis in original.

Fischer-Lichte, Erika. *Eine kurze Geschichte des deutschen Theaters*. 2nd ed. Tübingen: Francke/UTB, 1999.
Gruber, Helmut. *Red Vienna: Experiment in Working-Class Culture, 1919–1934*. Oxford: Oxford UP, 1991.
Hachleitner, Bernhard. "Das Wiener Praterstadion/Ernst-Happel-Stadion: Bedeutungen, Politik, Architektur und urbane Relevanz." PhD thesis, University of Vienna, 2010.
"Heute kommen Dreißigtausend!" *Arbeiter-Zeitung*, July 22, 1931, 5–6.
Hobsbawm, Eric, and Terence Ranger, eds. *The Invention of Tradition*. Cambridge: Cambridge UP, 1983.
Hock, Stephan. "Das große Festspiel im Stadion." *Arbeiter-Zeitung*, July 18, 1931, 5.
Hofmannsthal, Hugo von. "Das alte Spiel von Jedermann." In Bernd Schoeller, ed., *Dramen III (1893–1927). Gesammelte Werke in zehn Einzelbanden*, Bd. III, 89–100. Frankfurt/M: S. Fischer, 1986.
Hofmannsthal, Hugo von. "Festspiele in Salzburg." In Bernd Schoeller, ed., *Reden und Aufsätze II (1914–1924). Gesammelte Werke in zehn Einzelbanden*, Bd. IX, 264–8. Frankfurt/M: S. Fischer, 1979.
Hofmannsthal, Hugo von. "Die Salzburger Festspiele." In Bernd Schoeller, ed., *Reden und Aufsätze II (1914–1924). Gesammelte Werke in zehn Einzelbanden*, Bd. IX, 258–63. Frankfurt/M: S. Fischer, 1979.
Hofmannsthal, Hugo von. "Das Spiel vor der Menge." In Bernd Schoeller, ed., *Dramen III (1893–1927). Gesammelte Werke in zehn Einzelbanden*, Bd. III, 101–6. Frankfurt/M: S. Fischer, 1986.
Hofmannsthal, Hugo von. "Zum Programm der Salzburger Festspiele 1928." In Bernd Schoeller, ed., *Reden und Aufsätze III (1925–1929). Gesammelte Werke in zehn Einzelbanden*, Bd. X, 187–9. Frankfurt/M: S. Fischer, 1980.
Holl, Oskar. "Dokumente zur Entstehung der Salzburger Festspiele: Unveröffentlichtes aus der Korrespondenz der Gründer." *Maske und Kothurn* 13(2–3) (1967), 148–79.
Janke, Pia. *Politische Massenfestspiele in Österreich zwischen 1918 und 1938*. Vienna: Böhlau Verlag, 2010.
K. D. "Saure Wochen, frohe Feste." *Berichte zur Kultur- und Zeitgeschichte* 6(5) [B/102–115] (September 20, 1931), 699–743.
Kanitz, Felix [as FK]. "Das Festspiel der Viertausend im Stadion." *Arbeiter-Zeitung*, June 28, 1931, 10.
Kanitz, Felix. "Festspielepilog." *Arbeiter-Zeitung*, August 5, 1931, 6.
Kraus, Karl. "Vom großen Welttheaterschwindel." *Die Fackel* 601–7 (1922), 1–7.
Maderthaner, Wolfgang. "Austro-Marxism: Mass Culture and Anticipatory Socialism." *Austrian Studies* 14 (2006), 21–36.
McGrath, William J. *Dionysian Art and Populist Politics in Austria*. New Haven, CT: Yale UP, 1974.
Pfoser, Alfred. "Massenästhetik, Massenromantik, Massenspiel – Am Beispiel Osterreichs: Richard Wagner und die Folgen." *das pult* 14(66) (1982), 58–76.
Pyrah, Robert. "The 'Enemy Within'? The Social Democratic *Kunststelle* and the State Theatres in Red Vienna." *Austrian Studies* 14 (2006), 143–64.
Rásky, Béla. *Arbeiterfesttage: Die Fest- und Feierkultur der sozialdemokratischen Bewegung in der Ersten Republik Österreich 1918–1934*. Vienna: Europa Verlag, 1992.
Rathkolb, Oliver. "In Salzburg eine Triumphpforte österreichischer Kunst errichten: Der kulturpolitische Kontext der Gründungsphase der Salzburger Festspiele."

Reprint. ed. Generaldirektion des Österreichischen Staatsarchivs. *Beruf(ung): Archivar. Festschrift für Lorenz Mikoletzky*. (= Mitteilungen des österreichischen Staatsarchivs 55/1, 55/2), 575–97. Innsbruck: Studien Verlag, 2011.

Renner, Ursula. "Hofmannsthals *Jedermann*: 'Die Allegorie des Dieners Mammon' zwischen Tradition und Moderne." In Gernot Gruber Csobadi, Jürgen Kühnel, Ulrich Mueller, and Oswald Panagl, eds., *Welttheater, Mysterienspiel, rituelles Theater: "Vom Himmel durch die Welt zur Hölle,"Gesammelte Vorträge des Salzburger Symposions 1991*, 435–48. Salzburg: Müller-Speiser, 1992.

Rosenfeld, Fritz. "Gedanken zum Sprechchor." *Der Kampf* 19(2) (February 1926), 85–6.

Rossbacher, Karlheinz. "'Verse auf einer Banknote geschrieben': *Jedermann* und das Geld." *Salzburger Festspiele 1985 Offizielles Programm/Festspielalmanach*, 214–18. Salzburg: Residenz, 1985.

"Schauspiel der Masse im Stadion." *Arbeiter-Zeitung*, July 19, 1931, 8.

Schmidt-Dengler, Wendelin. "Bedürfnis nach Geschichte." In Franz Kadrnoska, ed., *Aufbruch und Untergang: Osterreichische Kultur zwischen 1918 und 1938*, 393–404. Vienna: Europa-Verlag, 1981.

Schmidt-Dengler, Wendelin. "The Ideology of the Salzburg Festival." In Ritchie Robertson and Edward Timms, eds., *Theatre and Performance in Austria: From Mozart to Jelinek. Austrian Studies* 4, 171–6. Edinburgh: Edinburgh University Press, 1993.

Schumann, Wolfgang. "Die Sprechchorbewegung," *Kunst und Volk* 2(6) (September 1927), 9–11.

"Das Spiel der Viertausend im Stadion: Parteipolitischer Unfug in der städtischen Sportanlage." *Reichspost*, July 10, 1931, 7.

Steinberg, Michael. *Austria as Theater and Ideology: The Meaning of the Salzburg Festival*. Ithaca, NY: Cornell UP, 2000.

Stern, Josef Luitpold. "Feste der Festlosen." *Kunst und Volk* 3(1) (September 1928), 22.

"Theater, Kunst und Musik." *Salzburger Volksblatt*, September 21, 1921, 4.

Unowsky, Daniel L. *The Pomp and Politics of Patriotism: Imperial Celebrations in Habsburg Austria, 1848–1916*. West Lafayette, IN: Purdue UP, 2005.

Wagner, Ernst. "Gesicht des Proletariats," *Kunst und Volk* 2(4) (April 1927), 10–11.

Weber-Kellermann, Ingeborg. *Saure Wochen, frohe Feste: Fest und Alltag in der Sprache der Bräuche*. Hohenembs: Bucher, 1985.

"Der weiße und der rote Umgang." *Arbeiter-Zeitung*, June 17, 1927, 5.

Wolf, Norbert Christian. *Eine Triumphpforte österreichischer Kunst: Hugo van Hofmannsthals Gründung der Salzburger Festspiele*. Salzburg: Jung und Jung, 2014.

Wolf, Norbert Christian. "Ordnungsutopie oder Welttheaterschwindel? Hofmannsthals Salzburger Festspielkonzepte in ihrem kultur- und ideologiegeschichtlichen Kontext." *Hofmannsthal Jahrbuch zur europäischen Moderne* 19 (2011), 217–54.

Zweig, Stefan. *Die Welt van Gestern: Erinnerungen eines Europäers*. Stockholm: Bermann-Fischer Verlag AB, 1946.

Eight In the Shadow of the Salzburg Festival?: The Mozarteum Foundation and Conservatory as Protagonists in Salzburg Music Culture Between the Wars

Julia Hinterberger

In the summer of 1910, with the programmatic words "To Honor Mozart, to Honor Salzburg, to Give Art its Place,"[1] the protector of the Foundation and the public Music School Mozarteum, Archduke Eugen, took part in the groundbreaking ceremonies for the Mozart House, striking three hammer blows to the newly laid cornerstone stone of the building now popularly known as the "Old Mozarteum." The outbreak of the First World War four years later made the music festival planned for the inauguration of this house impossible. This fact also symbolizes the development of the Mozarteum Foundation (Stiftung Mozarteum) and Music School, which after the end of the Habsburg monarchy had become completely different from what the people in charge had ever imagined it would be.

How this process developed internally in the school and what roles the Foundation and Music School took on in Salzburg's self-perception and external image will be shown in this chapter's three parts, illustrated by selected examples.

---

1   As qtd. in *Dreißigster Jahresbericht der [...] Internationalen Stiftung*, 23. The present author is responsible for all translations from German to English in this text. The author has already presented some of this material in the cited articles, most recently and recently in Julia Hinterberger, "Salzburg ist ein Leuchtturm in der Kultur gegenüber der Welt."

Part one of this article briefly outlines the development of the two "Mozarteums"—i.e., the Dommusikverein (Cathedral Music Association), Music School, and Conservatory Mozarteum on the one side, and the International Mozarteum Foundation on the other—from their beginnings to the collapse of the Habsburg monarchy. Part two turns to the history of the Mozarteum Conservatory and Mozarteum Foundation in the years 1918 to 1938. It traces central structural developments of the two institutions and their relationship to the cultural metropolis Vienna, their changes in personnel and concepts in the context of changing political systems, as well as questions of identity construction. Part three is dedicated to the role the Mozarteum Foundation played externally, in the construction of Salzburg as the city of Mozart, as a music city, and as a festival city.

Historical Development and Positioning of the Mozarteum

When the Dommusikverein, founded in 1841, launched a music school called the Mozarteum, its goals were clearly defined. Initially reserved for boys, the school was to train youth "in fine art."[2] At the same time, this association, situated in the contested arena between church and civil interests, was committed to "raising music in all its branches."[3] In practice, however, the school's first priority was de facto to ensure musical personnel for the cathedral. The opening of the music school was followed a year later by the inauguration of the Mozart monument as part of a multi-day music festival.

Both initiatives served to establish Salzburg locally and internationally as the city of Mozart. Naturally, this burgeoning competition was met with resentment in the cultural metropolis of Vienna, as historian Robert Hoffmann points out:

> Against the will of the Viennese authorities, who delayed their consent to the erection of the monument as far as possible, the German countries showed solidarity with the Salzburg project and made possible the implementation of the monument through generous donations. In comparison—according to the Viennese writer Ludwig August Frankl—the sum that "Old Austria and Vienna—then completely music crazy—contributed to the establishment of the statue of Mozart" was shamefully small.[4]

---

2 Dom-Musik-Verein und Mozarteum, *Erster Jahresbericht*, 10.
3 Dom-Musik-Verein und Mozarteum, *Erster Jahresbericht*, 4.
4 Hoffmann, "Salzburg und Wien im Spannungsfeld von Provinz und Metropole," 66.

In the end, however, the outward-directed efforts to maintain Salzburg's image as a city of Mozart receded noticeably—the needs of the internal music culture seemed too urgent, the interests were too regional, and the available financial means too modest to fulfill the ambitious plans originally made for the school.

It was not until the establishment of the Mozart-Stiftung (Mozart Foundation) in 1870 that a new era began. In contrast to the Dommusikverein, which had concentrated on local projects, this now purely bourgeois initiative focused on strengthening both Salzburg's internal music culture as well as its international profile as the city of Mozart and music. Between 1877 and 1910, Internationale Mozarttage (International Mozart Days) and Musikfeste (Music Festivals) were introduced to represent the Foundation's aspirations externally.[5] These festivals lasted several days each and are generally considered to be the forerunners of the Salzburg Festival.

Prior to this reorientation, Salzburg had primarily oriented itself toward Bavaria and Bohemia in invitations to performers, but now the Vienna Philharmonic Orchestra made guest appearances in these Music Festivals, as well. This laid an axis leading to the capital of the Habsburg Reich, and even more importantly: "The flourishing of Salzburg's 'Mozart cult' in the late 19th century would [...] have been unthinkable without the transfer of creative cultural potential from the capital of Vienna,"[6] Hoffmann assesses. Salzburg was thus caught between two imperatives: on the one hand, dependent, on Viennese resources, but on the other, trying to assert itself against the metropolis by reactivating its historical status as a city of Mozart and at the same time bolstering its image as a city of music.[7] Nonetheless, their constant points of reference were not just the metropolis of Vienna, but German cities, as was repeatedly expressed in the context of the Music Festivals organized by the Mozarteum Foundation.[8]

---

5   On the Salzburg Music Festivals and the role of the Mozarteum institutions, see Hinterberger, "'An diesen Namen knüpft sich nun aber auch alle Localeitelkeit der Salzburger.'"
6   Hoffmann, "Salzburg und Wien," 75.
7   On the development of Salzburg from Mozart city to festival city, see for instance Robert Hoffmann, "Vom Mozartdenkmal zur Festspielgründung." On Vienna as music city see also, Martina Nußbaumer, *Musikstadt Wien*.
8   Star conductor Hans Richter, for example, summed up for the Music Festival in 1887: "Under the aegis of Mozart, the Salzburg Music Festival should soon become an event for the musical world that will come to the city of Mozart, which has been coming to Bayreuth, Düsseldorf and the Rhenish Festival for years" (*Siebenter Jahresbericht der [...] Internationalen Stiftung*, 18).
    The president of the Foundation, Graf Kuenburg, also thought about "making Salzburg a second Bayreuth in the Mozartian sense," wherein the Mozarteum Foundation would be the central institution for the realization of this project (*Dreißigster Jahresbericht der [...] Internationalen Stiftung*, 25).

The most important internal innovation that the Foundation introduced into Salzburg's music culture was the separation of the school from church patronage. This was made all the easier since, over the prior few years, the bourgeois-liberal forces surrounding the Mozarteum had already gained influence and had fueled the school's emancipation from its Catholic umbrella organization. Already in 1880, the Music School Mozarteum was taken over by the organization which was called the Internationale Stiftung Mozarteum (International Mozarteum Foundation), an arrangement that went into effect the following year. While the school retained its illustrious name form the past, its concept was completely new.[9]

The year 1914 marked two milestones. The first was the long-awaited opening of the Mozarthaus on Schwarzstrasse. With office space for the Foundation and the Conservatory as well as two representative concert halls, it became the main venue for Salzburg's music culture in the first half of the century. However, the price for the realization of the Mozarthaus was high for the Foundation. Dependent on state subsidies, in return for the granting of funds, the Foundation had to agree to the terms and conditions of the Ministry of Education and Culture in Vienna, which in effect meant the abandonment of its autonomy.[10] In the years that followed, the ministry made several uses of its right to exert influence, be it with regard to the curriculum or the appointment of the head of the Conservatory, Bernhard Paumgartner from Vienna in 1917, who became one of the figureheads of the Salzburg music culture, but who from the beginning of his tenure massively polarized local circles.

The second, no less important milestone was the upgrading of the bourgeois Music School to a Conservatory, changing its status on the landscape of Austrian education. Yet the ministerial approval of the Conservatory title was de facto—it meant that although the institution was not forbidden from using this title, it was not officially granted. This omission was deliberately concealed in the printed documents seeking to boost the reputations of the Foundation and the Conservatory: that sonorous name consolidated a past and a present internal identity and enhanced the external impact of the music

---

9   The same names had and still have some pitfalls. When we talk about the Mozarteum in the following, I mean the Music School, and later the Conservatory. To make the necessary distinction, I refer to the Mozarteum Foundation either with that double term or only with the word Foundation.
10 Minister für Kultus und Unterricht to the Internationale Stiftung Mozarteum, July 9, 1912.

school, which were both considered important steps on its path out of provinciality.¹¹

In principle, the Salzburg institution had thus in concept come closer to the k.k. Academy for Music and Performing Arts Vienna—but the qualitative differences between the two institutions remained unmistakable and for a long time insurmountable. In addition, Viennese decision-makers sometimes thwarted plans that could have made the Mozarteum more competitive, such as supporting the formal affiliation of a church music department with the school. That project had no prospect of realization, as the Vienna Church Music Commission, which had to review such applications for approval and financing, decided to strengthen the institution in the imperial capital. The Church Music Department, which had only recently been established there, was not to experience competition from the federal provinces. A year earlier, a similar application submitted from Klagenfurt in Carinthia had been rejected on the same grounds.¹² There are no other sources on this case: the Foundation's annual report says succinctly: "As a result of the warlike events of the day, the plan from which we expected the music to be revived and raised in the Alpine countries had to be postponed to a better time."¹³

Mozarteum Times Two: A Look Inside the Institutional Constellation

1 Common Paths of the Foundation and Conservatory

The "better time" that the Viennese Commission identified would not occur for the Mozarteum institutions before the end of the First World War, it was quite the contrary, as history showed. Kaiser and Haus Habsburg united Austria until that time. With the removal of these central administrative forces, the Alpine provinces became more hostile than ever toward Vienna, which had shrunk to the *Wasserkopf* ("water head") of the unloved remains of the country. Depending on the political opinion one held in the provinces, the capital would have been considered "Jewish" or "red,"¹⁴ "exalted" or the city of "usurers, illicit traders, [...] war profiteers."¹⁵ Appealing to the "down-to-earth

---

11 Letter of the k. k. Landespräsident to the Internationale Stiftung Mozarteum on behalf of "the title Conservatory," June 6, 1914.
12 Rudolf von Lewicki to Franz Stibral, June 13, 1914.
13 *Vierunddreißigster Jahresbericht der [...] Internationalen Stiftung*, 7.
14 Ernst Hanisch, "Provinz und Metropole," 69.
15 Landtagsabgeordneter Johann Hasenauer im Rahmen der 18. Sitzung des Landtages der I. Session der I. Wahlperiode am 16. Dezember 1919 (Verhandlungen des Salzburger Landtages der I. Session der I. Wahlperiode 1919/1920, nach den stenographischen Berichten, Salzburg 1920, 1330), as qtd. in Alfred Höck, "Auf der Suche nach Identität," 98.

population of Upper Austria, Salzburg, Tyrol, Carinthia and Styria," certain parties even launched initiatives for the provinces to split from the capital Vienna.[16] The formation of the Republic also brought massive structural shifts in the region's geopolitics as Austria-Hungary's eastern and southern provinces were lost, from which Salzburg benefited the most, as Ernst Hanisch states: "Vienna moved from the center to the 'periphery,' while [...] Salzburg now moved more from the periphery to the 'center' and formed an important hub for the German Empire, especially Bavaria."[17] After the collapse of the Habsburg monarchy, the remainder of Austria as a whole, but also even the capital and the federal provinces, were forced at almost all levels to reinvent and reposition themselves both externally and internally.

As is generally the case in times of political crisis, the recourse to the *topoi Musikland* (music country) and *Musikstadt* (music city), and, in Salzburg specifically, to the *Mozartstadt* (Mozart city), played significant roles in these identity-finding processes.[18] The programmatic document "Eine musikalische Hochschule in Salzburg" (A Musical University in Salzburg)[19] by Bernhard Paumgartner, director of the Mozarteum Conservatory, offers an idealized sketch of how the institution should be repositioned in the new Republic, reflecting the mood of cultural change that prevailed in Salzburg immediately after the end of the First World War.

In spring 1919, Paumgartner accepted an invitation to present his visions for the cultural and educational future of Salzburg. His concept, defamed by one of his Viennese opponents as a "delusion of an immature dreamer,"[20] envisaged a program for a comprehensive system of education centered around music, with a focus on the combination of *Tonkunst* (sound art) and science. A tripartite faculty was to be created under one roof, consisting of preparatory courses for beginners, advanced classes in the sense of a middle school, and an academy— the university that actually would be founded. Paumgartner's plan was immense and included the *Konzertante Kunst* (concert art) as well as the *Darstellende Kunst* (performing arts), a church music department, teacher training courses, music theory and music science, courses for rhythmic gymnastics, but also the launch of a Mozart-style school focused on music practice, the enhancement of the Mozarteum

---

16 SLA, RehrlLk-74. Anonymer Aufruf, o. O., undatiert [1919/1929], as qtd. in Höck, "Auf der Suche nach Identität," 98.
17 Hanisch, "Provinz und Metropole," 70.
18 Cornelia Szabó-Knotik, "Musikland Österreich."
19 Bernhard Paumgartner, *Eine musikalische Hochschule in Salzburg*.
20 Rudolf von Lewicki to Ludwig Sedlitzky, June 10, 1919.

Orchestra, Mozarteum Choir, and City Theater with the addition of a permanent opera division. And ultimately, he wanted the fine arts to be considered, including the establishment of commercial and craft workshops to complement stage work.

With these suggestions, Paumgartner's manifesto went far beyond plans to found a music university. His real goal was to finally establish Salzburg as a cultural metropolis. The linchpin was to be the Mozarteum University, which would be unique in this form in Austria and Germany, an "institute of first rank with an international reputation [...], valued as much as the first-tier institutions in the music cities of Vienna, Munich or Berlin, but combined with the tempting appeal of the small, wonderful cosmopolitan city, in which Mozart's spirit is in the air and where a specific artistic life could develop, a real fountain of health for a new, more down-to-earth culture to a better future."[21] The proposed merging of competencies and the associated networking of institutions would have given the Mozarteum a heretofore unseen monopoly position in German-speaking countries. Paumgartner would have given himself the status of an autocratic music and arts director, and the new situation would gradually have dislodged the supremacy of the Vienna State Academy.

That state academy had never before been publicly questioned or challenged by Paumgartner's predecessors or the members of the Foundation's Kuratorium (Board of Trustees). The self-assessment of the Salzburg institutions seemed to be too clear to do so: the Mozarteum was nominally a Conservatory, but in fact was, in the best sense, a music middle school that could not compete with the "first leading music school in the Reich."[22] Paumgartner was nevertheless the first to assume that parity did or could exist between Vienna and Salzburg, but his plans proved to be utopian. Even the few aspects of that project that could be implemented were subject to meddling from Vienna, such as assuring the public status of the Conservatory and teacher training courses as credentialed courses of study—as enjoying "public status." That designation meant that privately managed institutions were allowed to issue certificates that were equivalent to those of schools run by the state and were therefore generally recognized for professional positions.

Yet while the Academy in Vienna automatically acquired the status of a public music institution due to its nationalization in 1909, the Mozarteum had to fight for its public status and make special applications to the ministry. Particularly affected were the teacher training

---

21 Paumgartner, *Eine musikalische Hochschule in Salzburg*, 18.
22 *Jahres-Bericht des [...] Konservatoriums des "Mozarteums"* (1916), 5.

In the Shadow of the Salzburg Festival? 229

courses installed after the end of the First World War. The completion of these courses allowed those who finished the courses "to lead private music schools as well as to give singing courses at middle schools and to teach piano, organ, and violin at teacher training institutions."[23] The case of the training courses clearly shows the balance of power between the two music institutions and the Austrian strategy for resolving the issue, which has always been followed in critical matters.

A request from the Salzburg Board of the Foundation in spring 1919 was followed by an inspection by representatives of the Vienna State Academy and a fundamentally positive opinion of the Ministry of Education, based on their observations. The granting of public status was slowed merely until a few improvements were made.[24] However, the directorate of the State Academy vetoed a follow-up application made in 1920—this time for a definitive award of public status:

> Given that the equivalence of the curriculum and teaching objective of the teacher training courses in Salzburg with those of the State Academy only exists on paper, [...] since the results of even excellently qualified candidates are not nearly at the same level as those of the State Academy, the definitive granting of public status cannot be advocated. There is no objection to the extension of the status, provided that the teacher training courses continue to be under the control of a specialist from the faculty of the State Academy.[25]

This clearly shows that Vienna wanted not only to be involved but also to have sovereignty over the most important musical education programs. Conservatory director Paumgartner, however, overruled these requirements in an elegant Austrian manner by ignoring them without further ado and taking over the chair in the 1921 exams. No consequences are known; the courses themselves were discontinued the following year as part of a general restructuring.[26]

If, on the one hand, the Mozarteum institutions were still looking for autonomy from the capital, the era, especially its economic developments, pushed Salzburg's institutions into dependence on Vienna to an ever greater degree. The Conservatory had survived the First World War unscathed, even expanding, but now it was threatened by decline.

---

23 Karl Wagner, *Das Mozarteum*, 177.
24 Ministerium für Unterricht to the Internationale Stiftung Mozarteum, July 14, 1919.
25 Statement by the Board of Directors of the State Academy, June 24, 1921, as qtd. in Wagner, *Das Mozarteum*, 178.
26 Wagner, *Das Mozarteum*, 178–9.

The only way out of the crisis was to remove it from the patronage of the Foundation through nationalization, thereby ceding local control to the central government, and so the first application for that change of status was made in Vienna in 1919.

As can be seen from newspaper reports, the Social Democrats Josef Witternigg and Robert Preussler argued in the spirit of the general process of identity formation for the central government supporting the institutions in Salzburg. They brought together Salzburg's international reputation as a city of music and Mozart, the importance of the city's "new" location "in the center of Germany and German Austria," as well as the financial and representational value of the tourist city and its music venue for the identity formation of the still young republic.[27] Aside from what he said to the public press, Preussler made another valid argument:

> In order to maintain and further develop the Mozarteum Conservatory at its artistic level, it seems urgent that this institute be freed from the sometimes not very favorable influences of a Board of Trustees, in which corporation [...] not all members always have that degree of artistic understanding which is an essential prerequisite for the further prosperity of such an institute.[28]

While the ministerial treatment of the initial application came to nothing, despite such support, the Foundation started small-scale actions to maintain its Conservatory, such as the sales of Haydn autographs.[29] The teachers, however, insisted on improvements in their employment conditions and a voice in the curriculum, or otherwise they would stop working.

In a unanimous written decision, which the teachers presented to the Board of the Foundation in July 1920, they unequivocally expressed their political stance, in addition to addressing their structural and monetary concerns: "Regarding the filling of the concertmaster position, the teaching staff desires to exert influence so that 1. no non-Aryan is appointed."[30] Multiple pledges of subsidies from different pots could

---

27 "Ein Antrag auf Verstaatlichung des Mozarteums," *Salzburger Chronik*, May 10, 1919.
28 Preußler to the Staatsamt, May 17, 1919, as qtd. in Wagner, *Das Mozarteum*, 183.
29 Rudolph Angermüller and Géza Rech, *Hundert Jahre Internationale Stiftung Mozarteum Salzburg*, 104.
30 Letter of the teaching staff of the Mozarteum Conservatory to the Board of the Mozarteum Foundation, July 10, 1920.

not offset the dilemma of anchoring the Conservatory privately. At the same time, given the general economic conditions, the state seemed unable to assume sole responsibility for the Conservatory. Press reports on a meeting of those responsible for the Conservatory and the Foundation together with the Salzburg State Parliament and the local Council in March 1921 illustrate, on the one hand, the precarious situation in which the Mozarteum institutions found themselves.

On the other hand, these press reports also capture the mood that prevailed in circles in close contact with cultural issues, mostly German nationally oriented ones speaking about "German Austria" and democracy: "One blushed when one heard all these statements, and one had to blame […] this noble, wicked time of a democracy for the shame that art is begging […]. [This democracy] that has a lot for many, for too many, and that let mental work and art go to the dogs. The Mozarteum is a victim of these times."[31] This kind of pessimism about democracy here stands in for a negative attitude of many Austrians towards a state forced to independence, which was only a shadow of itself, a "mutilated trunk, bleeding from all veins,"[32] as Stefan Zweig in *The World of Yesterday* concludes.

In view of this crisis, the value of music that creates identity both internally and externally was once again emphasized: "Director Paumgartner said it very clearly yesterday that for this failing (= insolvent) state, maintaining its art is still the only letter of credit that it can use for the future, that music is one of our few export articles."[33] In spite of the dependence on the decisions of the new government, then, the Salzburg powers-that-be still could not resist a swipe at the capital and the unequal treatment of the provinces in relation to the metropolis. For example, the First Deputy Governor, Robert Preussler, emphasized that, "although the country itself is poor, it will certainly do its duty. Only one should not completely ignore the state, which spends enormous amounts for the great Viennese theaters. It must therefore also have something for the Mozarteum. Salzburg builds its entire economic existence on ideas as its commodities. If we dropped the Mozarteum, we would sin against the future of Salzburg."[34]

In the end, galloping inflation forced the Conservatory to be detached from the Foundation's aegis, which, despite subsidies, could no longer meet the cost of maintaining the school. However, the Conservatory became part of the new Schulerhaltausschuss (School Committee),

---

31 "Das Mozarteum in Not," *Salzburger Volksblatt*, March 4, 1921.
32 Stefan Zweig, *Die Welt von gestern*, 199.
33 "Das Mozarteum in Not," *Salzburger Volksblatt*, March 4, 1921.
34 "Das Mozarteum in Not," *Salzburger Volksblatt*, March 4, 1921.

so that, when it was nationalized in July 1922, four contractual partners—state, province, city, and Foundation in a ratio of 5:1:1:2—then had jurisdiction over the school's economic-administrative issues. Pedagogical and didactic matters now lay within the director's area of competence, who was no longer subordinate to the Foundation but solely to the Federal Ministry of Education in Vienna. To be sure, those responsible in the Foundation and in the Conservatory strove to maintain relationships, reciprocal nominees were represented on the committees,[35] and—following a long tradition—advanced students continued to participate in events organized by the Foundation even after 1922. But the two Mozarteum institutions went their separate ways from now on.

2 Separate Paths: The Mozarteum Conservatory

The fact that the 1922 nationalization of the Conservatory was a far greater turning point than the First World War is clearly documented by the numbers of students.

Despite the war, the number of students had increased massively due to the new infrastructure possibilities and had reached a provisional high in the academic year 1918/19.[36] But it fell rapidly in the early 1920s in view of the economic situation and the public debates about the future of the Conservatory. Smaller upturns were recorded several times in the following years, but the number of students tended to decrease and experienced a massive slump with the first year under National Socialist rule, followed by an even more massive expansion.

The latter was the result of a National Socialist music policy that declared the Mozarteum an "institute of prestige." The former Conservatory became a university in 1939, and in 1941 it was raised to the status of the first Reichshochschule (Reich's University) in the Ostmark. Furthermore, the institution was expanded with a Musikschule für Jugend und Volk (Music School for Youth and Volk) for young beginners and with a university for professionals to be. These expansion measures are reminiscent of the school policy visions designed by Paumgartner in 1919; however, the project's ideology and objectives had changed fundamentally.

---

35 On the function and constellation of the School Committee, see Walter Hummel, *Marksteine der Geschichte*, 33–4.
36 It cannot be determined from the sources whether there were any calls to the front on the students' side. In the annual reports, only the teachers or employees called up (four in total) are listed. For student and subject statistics 1880–1922, see Susanne Prucher, "Musikschule/Konservatorium Mozarteum 1841–1922," in Hinterberger, ed., *Von der Musikschule zum Konservatorium*, 174–211.

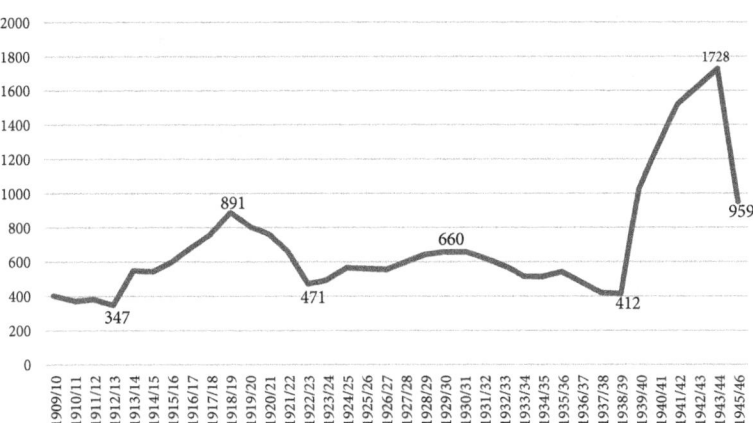

Figure 8.1 Number of students at the Mozarteum Conservatory, 1909/10–1945/46.

The countries of origin of the students documented in the annual reports require special attention as evidence of that new status meant. As the addition "comes from the place of birth" in the statistical charts already suggests, the student numbers are shown according to the place of their birth, not according to their current main residence. It remains to be seen whether this was a deliberate move by the Conservatory to list the widest possible range of countries of origin and thus to build the image of an international institution. In any case, it can be assumed that a large proportion of those students whose birthplace was outside what is now Austria had already moved to Salzburg and the surrounding area due to their family's relocation.

According to these figures, until the collapse of the monarchy, most of the students came from the city of Salzburg, followed by other Austrian crown lands, above all Upper and Lower Austria, Tyrol, Styria, and Bohemia. Another important recruitment area was Bavaria: the students from there predominated, compared to those from "the rest of Germany," as the differentiation in the annual reports record. Comparatively few students came from other regions of Salzburg, especially from the Pinzgau and Lungau; there, the infrastructure was probably too inadequate to provide preliminary training.

After the end of the First World War, the picture changed in that significantly fewer students came from the successor states of the Habsburg monarchy, i.e., from Czechoslovakia, the Kingdom of

Yugoslavia, Poland, or Italy with South Tyrol. The city and regions of Salzburg continued to dominate, followed by the Austrian federal provinces and Germany. Political measures and upheavals such as the 1,000 Mark ban imposed by Hitler in 1933, the proclamation of Austrofascism in 1934, or the annexation of Austria in 1938 were generally reflected in the number of students and especially in those from Germany. And although some of the students were born in more distant countries, such as the United States, Albania, Egypt, Brazil, China, or India, even in the years of the First Republic and Austrofascism, the school could hardly claim to be international in today's sense.

The Mozarteum was thus in the best sense still a music middle school which had to supply music education primarily for the Alpine countries, the other Austrian federal provinces, as well as neighboring Germany and above all Bavaria. In contrast to the Vienna Academy, the Conservatory in Salzburg with its dual system aimed both at music lovers, who made up the majority of the students, and at a manageable group of aspiring professional musicians. Although heavily criticized by the ministry, that guiding principle of fulfilling such an educational mandate and being a point of contact for all those interested in music remained in place under Paumgartner's leadership. However, he reversed the hierarchy in favor of educating professional musicians.[37]

That shift in emphasis brought other transformations. During the first years of the war, the teaching staff of the Conservatory expanded. The increase in personnel that had already begun before the war continued, with the first attempts to strike a balance in instructors between affordable teachers for the broad mass of students and internationally established personalities who were to bring their reputations to the institution. In contrast to those relatively optimistic emerging tendencies of the first years of the war, the situation for teachers deteriorated radically in the early 1920s. The financially precarious situation of the new nation and its uncertain future prospects prompted prominent lecturers, who were important for the Conservatory's increasingly professional and international image, to quit.[38] Others, on the other hand, saw themselves forced to continue their work even under gradually deteriorating conditions due to their personal situations.

Nationalization finally brought about a significant change and some relief. The ministerial decrees were restrictive, imposing, among other things, a reduction in the number of students in the lower grades, a

---

37 *Jahres-Bericht des Konservatoriums "Mozarteum"* (1919), 34.
38 Wagner states: "the star teachers Felix Petyrek [piano], Prasch-Cornet [vocals] and Willi Schweyda [violin] left the Mozarteum because of the dreary financial situation" (Wagner, *Das Mozarteum*, 195).

reduction in the numbers of some older teachers, and the cancelling of teacher training courses. The new personnel policy hit two teachers particularly hard, as the decree envisaged "removing them from their current duties as teachers of record. No objection will be raised against their possible further use as assistant teachers appointed by contract against hourly fees."[39] While one of the two affected could financially afford to reject their "re-use" on these untenable terms, the other colleague had to comply with the new demands.

In addition to financial hardship, this new contract also impacted this teacher's reputation as a musician, as the teaching staff stated in an intervention letter: "Mrs. Stögmüller is rightly afraid that she will not be able to dispel the concerns of the small-town population, who, assuming that she has been dismissed from the institute due to inability, would deprive her of all private lessons. So that in this case she actually will be left with nothing."[40] But none of the measures helped: Maria Stögmüller worked as an auxiliary teacher from the school year 1923/24 through 1941/42—with the same status—under the title of lecturer. It was only in 1943/44, in the last year of her activity, that she was declared a full teacher again and retired as such the following year.[41]

Beyond these individual fates, general reduction measures were imposed on the Conservatory due to its nationalization. The staff, consisting of a total of thirty-one persons in the school year 1920/21 (twenty-two full status teachers, six assistant teachers, two lecturers and one assistant) was reduced to fourteen federal teachers in the following years. A higher variance was shown by the number of much cheaper teaching assistants, which increased from two in the beginning to sometimes up to eleven.[42] After the annexation of Austria in 1938, with the exception of the director Bernhard Paumgartner, who was removed from office, the entire teaching staff was transferred to the new system. In addition, internationally renowned personalities such as the pianist Elly Ney, a convinced National Socialist, were engaged for the newly founded University, dedicated to the "cult of genius." The vacant positions in the newly installed Music School for Youth

---

39 Letter of the Salzburger Provincial Government to the "Verein Mozarteum," July 24, 1922.
40 Letter from the teachers of the Conservatory to the ministry, March 3, 1922, as qtd. in Wagner, *Das Mozarteum*, 196.
41 See Jahresberichte Konservatorium/Hochschule/Reichshochschule Mozarteum 1922–1943/44.
42 *Jahresberichte des Konservatoriums Mozarteum 1922–1938*.

and Volk, however, were mainly filled with local, system-compatible staff. Overall, the Mozarteum experienced a massive expansion, as up to ninety people were employed in the years of National Socialist rule, including the administrative staff.[43]

Wagner's assessment aligned with that the Conservatory, despite all the limits that were set as a result of the nationalization, had at least developed internally into a "real vocational school" in the years of the First Republic.[44] Its range of event formats and offerings was expanded significantly and now ranged from internal practice evenings for the pre-training classes, to public lectures for the training classes, orchestral concerts, and the large year-end concerts, during which the students performed some of the most demanding works in their repertoires. There were also commemorative concerts dedicated to certain composers.[45] The program also included repeated composition evenings that dealt with works by Salzburg composers from different eras—but little attention was paid to the current local composers. At the international level, on the other hand, representatives of moderate modernism, such as Debussy, Bartok, Ravel and comparatively often Richard Strauss, were sometimes considered. The Second Viennese School, however, had hardly any resonance in Salzburg.

In addition to regular teaching and events, the always polarizing director Bernhard Paumgartner set the tone from the beginning of his tenure about what was essential for the self-image of the institution internally and for its image externally. For example, he massively expanded the opera school that was founded in the academic year 1914/15. During the First World War, in June and July 1918, he managed to stage performances in the City Theater and in the Natural Theater in the Mirabell Gardens for around fourteen days. Earlier, that unit had performed just one evening a year.[46] To realize this initiative, he founded a cooperation project with the City Theater, which was initially met with broad approval: the Mozarteum Opera. Salzburg had

---

43 *Jahresberichte der Hochschule / Reichshochschule Mozarteum 1939–1944*. On the Mozarteum institutions during National Socialism, see Julia Hinterberger, "'Gottbegnadete Künstler' und 'volksverbundene Kunst'" in Kramml and Kühberger, eds., *Inszenierung der Macht*, 280–355.
44 Wagner, *Das Mozarteum*, 199.
45 The detailed event programs can be found in the annual reports of the Conservatory.
46 The detailed program can be found in *Jahres-Bericht des [...] Konservatoriums des "Mozarteums"* (1918), 68–72.

been without a permanent opera for decades,[47] so the venture of the Conservatory director initially turned out to be a win-win situation not only for the Mozarteum and the Theater, but for the Salzburg music culture in general. With opera as its "new project that has never been dared at any music school,"[48] the Conservatory acquired a unique selling point. It enabled students to do stage practice and teachers to gain additional income, while the Salzburg Theater was finally able to offer a permanent opera with little financial expense because it could employ students. Such cooperation was facilitated by Salzburg's image as a city of music and Mozart. The population, however, benefited: it no longer depended on the Theater's monthly opera or the operetta that was criticized as much as it was frequented. Paumgartner, who apparently wanted to secure the monopoly on the opera in Salzburg with his project, contractually committed himself to the "compilation and staging of a permanent opera guest performance, consisting of 80 performances"[49] for the season 1920/21.

While the response from the population and the press was positive, criticism from teachers and students as well as from members of the Board increased. Paumgartner was accused of neglecting school administration, his sole commitment to the opera, and overly careless handling of the voices and energy of the students.[50] Nonetheless, the dismissal of Paumgartner envisaged by some members of the Board did not occur. Instead, the director increasingly turned back to his core tasks. The Mozarteum Opera project, which was promising per se, however, became a brief entry into Salzburg's music culture. But the Conservatory's opera school remained. Paumgartner subsequently bought a portable stage for the Mozarteum, which made it possible to now perform opera productions in-house and thus gain autonomy vis-à-vis the City Theater.[51]

---

47 As in many theaters in the German-speaking area, the Salzburg Theater also concentrated for financial reasons on a two-branch company consisting of drama and operetta. Only once a year did an ensemble guest for four weeks. The fact that around fifteen different operas were shown in this short period of time meant an enormous effort for those involved, but also for the audience. On the concept, programming, and implementation of the monthly opera and its importance in Salzburg's music culture, see Hinterberger, "An diesen Namen," 13–114, primarily 101–4.
48 *Jahres-Bericht des Konservatoriums "Mozarteum" in Salzburg über das 40. Schuljahr 1920–1921*, 12.
49 *Jahres-Bericht des Konservatoriums "Mozarteum" in Salzburg über das 40. Schuljahr 1920–1921*, 12.
50 Copy of the Request for Removal to the Mozarteum Conservatory, September 1, 1921.
51 *Konservatorium Mozarteum in Salzburg, Jahresbericht* (1925), 19.

Paumgartner was also open to the new media. When the Salzburg broadcasting station of the Austrian broadcasting company RAVAG started operating in 1930, he saw the chance of a new performance opportunity for the Conservatory and of profiting from the new technology for educational purposes. With the help of sponsorship money, the Conservatory purchased appropriate equipment and a selection of gramophone records in the following years. The equipment also made it possible to integrate radio broadcasts such as the opera performances of the Vienna State Opera directly into the classroom. The Conservatory, in turn, was able to broadcast (and multiply rebroadcast) its own concerts across Austria, thereby presenting itself nationwide.[52] A few years later, Paumgartner responded to the tastes of the time by introducing into the curriculum subjects such as saxophone or tango harmonies[53]—both immediately removed from the course offerings with the Anschluss in 1938 as outflows of "Negro music."

The fact that recorder lessons were offered free of charge as a trial course in the school in 1937/38 is also a reflection of the times. On the one hand, it responded to the necessity of promoting interest of the "young musicians" whose number—according to the assistant teacher Wilhelm Domandl—"had experienced a catastrophic decline in recent years."[54] On the other hand, this instrument was especially suitable for such an initiative due to its low costs to purchasers. Coupled with free lessons, the offer was a particular draw for Salzburg children in view of the tense economic conditions. However, the recorder was also to be exploited ideologically around a year later, with the launch of the Music School for Youth and Volk in 1939: it served specifically to indoctrinate children in the National Socialist sensibilities about national community, as they made music together.

With the annexation, the concept of free tuition was again put into play, but now guided centrally, ideologically supported, and independent of institutional control. In the above-mentioned annual report of the Conservatory, one can read the text of a speech given by *Gauleiter* Josef Bürckel in Vienna in March 1938, under the heading "Emergency Aid." It was to be published as "decree of the school authorities, instructions of the H.J., in all newspapers, or in the films in the cinemas and adult education centers, on the radio." With the programmatic title "Bread and Work for Music Teachers in Need," the speech proposed two-months' free lessons for *Volksgenossen* (members of the national

---

52 *Konservatorium Mozarteum in Salzburg, Jahresbericht* (1932), 21–2.
53 The study of saxophone was introduced in the academic year 1930/31, that of the tango harmonica in 1936/37 (*Konservatorium Mozarteum in Salzburg, Jahresbericht* (1931]), 18, and *Konservatorium Mozarteum in Salzburg, Jahresbericht* (1937), 10).
54 *Konservatorium Mozarteum in Salzburg, Jahres-Bericht* (1938), 17–18, here 17.

community) to help people to help themselves, as a measure against the unemployment of music teachers. Such a program should be remunerated from the pot of emergency aid, and only subsequently paid for by the new students, when financial situations were stabilized. What at first glance looks like a win-win situation for both sides was, from the beginning of the Nazi regime on, a clever strategy for imposing a particular political culture through music. The new rulers wanted the lessons to be designed according to given guidelines, while at the same time aiming at unifying and indoctrinating the *Volksgemeinschaft* (national community) through the apparently non-political instrument of music and putting the unemployed music teachers into service—which also meant into the service of Nazi policy:

> We do not want to give degrading charity, but we want to create work! If you cannot pay, you free yourself through your own happy work in the service of the *Volksgemeinschaft*. Participation in *Jugend in Not* (Youth in Need), in school listening hours and school concerts, house music evenings for parents' associations, in open singing hours and company ceremonies, in individual and group lessons, for the Hitler Youth, in *Kraft durch Freude* (Strength through Joy), and in the *NS-Kulturgemeinde* (NS cultural community) gives tasks and challenges! Help and help yourself![55]

But it was not only with this mandatory "advertising" that politics entered the concerns of the Conservatory. The politicizing of music had a longer tradition.

Various examples of a dedication to the emperor can already be found during the First World War, for example in the form of concerts on the occasion of the emperor's birthdays. The fact that the Conservatory, which at that time was still associated with the largely German nationally oriented Foundation, set such Austrian-patriotic signals into place reflects the "double identity" that historian Ernst Hanisch claims especially for Salzburg.[56] The first days of the war were characterized by this German-Austrian attitude, in which a pronounced Austrian patriotism and a commitment to Germany were not mutually exclusive.[57]

---

55 *Konservatorium Mozarteum in Salzburg, Jahres-Bericht* (1938), 20.
56 Ernst Hanisch, *Der lange Schatten des Staates*, 154.
57 It also fits into this picture that (partial) proceeds from the concerts at the Conservatory were earmarked for war relief as a declaration of solidarity with the Habsburg House. This willingness to donate corresponded to the patriotic attitude generally observed in the population and—at least initially—also to a euphoric attitude of bourgeois society and intellectuals in particular towards war. See Ernst Hanisch, "Alltag im Krieg: Erfahrungen an der Heimatfront," particularly 40–3.

A further example of openly demonstrated commitment to politics took place in the Austrofascist years. For example, the annual report 1934/35 starts with a *Speech of Commemoration for Chancellor Dr. Dollfuss*.[58] Events such as the commemoration of the murder of the Federal Chancellor, at which the "official personalities of Salzburg" attended, or the musical framing of the start of the Salzburg State Parliament into its new session in 1934, bear witness to the increasing politicization of the Conservatory.[59] The fact that Bernhard Paumgartner had a close relationship with the state's governor, Franz Rehrl, and was positive about the *Ständestaat* may have fueled this turnaround, as well.

The final political incursion into the Conservatory took place immediately at the Anschluss. School-free days underlined the "holiday character" of this "permanent folk festival,"[60] as Ernst Hanisch describes those first weeks around the annexation. The following entry in the 1937/38 annual report documents the situation:

> From March 12 through March 16, 1938, no classes because the NSDAP assumed power. On March 24, 1938, school-free because all teachers were sworn in on the Fuehrer. On March 31, 1938, no classes in the morning because the Austrian Legion marched through Salzburg. On April 2, 1938, no classes, when *Generalfeldmarschall* Hermann Goering was passing through. April 6 and 7, classes cancelled due to the presence of the *Führer* in Salzburg. On April 20, 1938, no classes because of *Führer*'s birthday. A school ceremony at the Conservatory was dispensed with, given the fact that most of the students at the Conservatory were employed at the school ceremonies at other middle schools.[61]

The once-provincial Salzburg Conservatory, with its internationality aspirations and a predominantly cultural-German orientation, became a centrally directed "German" institution organized according to the state's leadership principles, which benefited—without too great own initiative—massively from the National Socialist cultural policy in structural terms.

Raised to a university in 1939 and two years later to the status of the first "Reich's University" in the Ostmark, the Mozarteum acted as a counterweight to the Vienna Academy. It was the upgrading of the

---

58 *Konservatorium Mozarteum in Salzburg, Jahres-Bericht* (1935), 3–5.
59 *Konservatorium Mozarteum in Salzburg, Jahres-Bericht* (1935), 21.
60 Ernst Hanisch, *Der lange Schatten des Staates*, 345.
61 *Konservatorium Mozarteum in Salzburg, Jahres-Bericht* (1938), 14–15.

province to the metropolis. A showdown between Salzburg and Vienna under new circumstances had thus begun.

3 Separate Paths: The Mozarteum Foundation

After the nationalization of 'its' Conservatory in 1922, the Foundation concentrated primarily on its other core missions. This was above all Mozart, consigned to the hands of three divisions, each of which had its own area of responsibility: memorials, research, and maintenance. The maintenance and care of the memorials have been one of the Foundation's most important tasks since its beginnings. The Mozart Birthplace (Mozarts Geburtshaus), which the Foundation had been able to buy in 1917 despite great financial difficulties and which housed the Mozart Museum, was under its care, as was the Zauberflötenhäuschen (Magic Flute House) on the Kapuzinerberg. Added to this—at least temporarily—was the Villa Bertramka in Prague, in which Mozart had completed his *Don Giovanni* in 1787. Contemporary statistics document the (tourist) influx that the cultural memorials experienced in the years 1923 to 1949, and at the same time they reflect economic developments and political breaks.

In addition to their economic importance, the memorials also had an identity-based significance. They identified vividly the Foundation as an institutional dedicated to Mozart and to Salzburg as a city of Mozart. This was comprehensible and understandable—both locally and internationally. In contrast, the research area was aimed at an international specialist audience. The Foundation sought to present itself as the world's leading Mozart research center with the establishment, gradual expansion, and continuous support of the archive and library, slowly beginning publication activities, the organization of scientific conferences and exhibitions such as the *Magic Flute* Exhibition in 1928 and the establishment of the Central Institute for Mozart Research in 1931.[62] However, sustainable steps towards the centralization of Mozart research would only take place in the time of National Socialism and thus under changed ideological conditions.[63]

---

62 The idea of founding the Central Institute for Mozart Research dates back to 1931, but according to the latest research results, the official constitution did not take place until autumn 1936 and thus under changed political conditions. Christoph Großpietsch, "Zur Selbstinszenierung von Erich Schenk in Salzburg und Wien," here 145–53.

63 But even during this period, despite the highest National Socialist protection and generously provided funds, many of the projects envisaged failed, such as the entire edition of W. A. Mozart's works. See Peter Danner, "'Weltanschauungsfreie Forschung [...] nicht einmal wünschenswert,'" in Veits-Falk and Hanisch, eds., *Herrschaft und Kultur*, 230–1 and recent research by Ulrich Leisinger, "Zwischen 'Führerauftrag' und Kriegswirklichkeit," Salzburg, November 22, 2019.

242 Interwar Salzburg

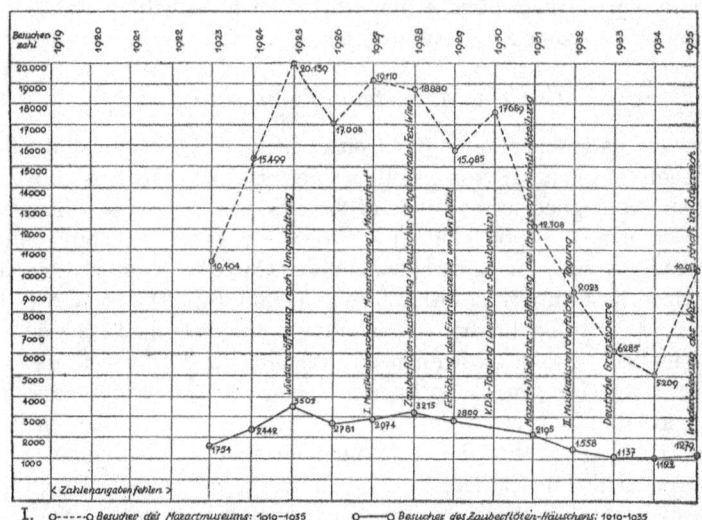

Figure 8.2 Visitors to the Mozart Museum and the *Zauberflötenhäuschen*, 1923–1935. Source: Hummel (1936), 50.

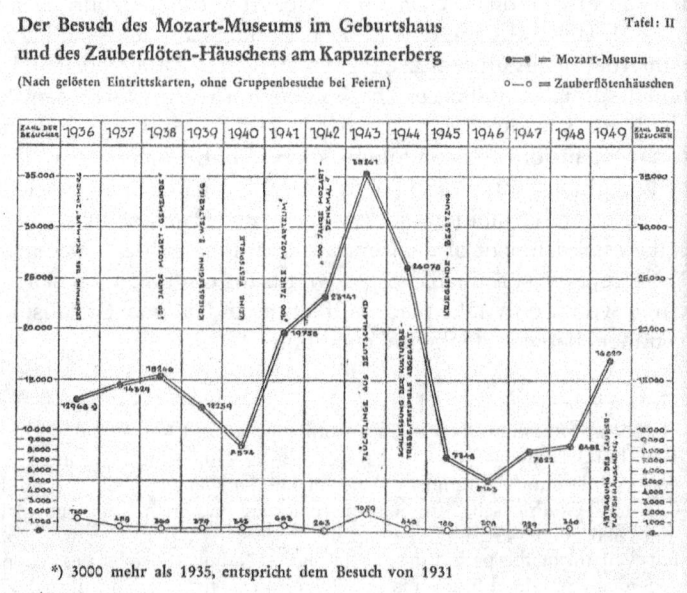

Figure 8.3 Visitors to the Mozart Museum and the *Zauberflötenhäuschen*, 1936–1949: by number of tickets sold (excluding group tours at special events). Source: Hummel (1951), 60.

However, the Foundation's most important area of responsibility for Salzburg's internal music culture was the preservation of Mozart's legacy and the organization of regular concerts and event-related festival concerts. But here, too, there was a significant change in status. While the Foundation was able to maintain its monopoly as a concert organizer even during the war years, it saw itself facing increasing difficulties in the early years of the First Republic, as is also stated in the annual report:

> Up until the post-war period, the International Mozarteum Foundation had the undisputed leadership in Salzburg's concert system, namely the Mozarteum was considered exclusively for the organization of festival concerts in the summer months and for regular concerts, either exclusively or as primary organizers. Now, however, the restructuring of the economic situation, the establishment of the *Festspielhausgemeinde* (Festival Hall Community), the start of the Salzburg Festival, and finally new concert office companies have brought about major changes in Salzburg's concert business.[64]

For example, the traditional *Vereins-Abonnementkonzerte* (club subscription concerts) could only be maintained until 1921. In the two subsequent seasons they had to be canceled due to the currency devaluation and the resulting lack of subscribers.

A new system was proposed and implemented, starting with the winter season 1923/24. The model was, as so often is the case, drawn from the musical culture of the metropolis, specifically from the format of the *Gesellschaft der Musikfreunde* in Vienna. *Gesellschaftskonzerte* (society concerts) were introduced in Salzburg. Internationally renowned artists and well-known conductors such as Hans Knappertsbusch or Clemens Krauss would be magnets for attracting a public and ensuring the recovery of the regular concert business.[65] The pricing of the events organized jointly by the concert offices of the Foundation and the Salzburg Festival Hall Community were adjusted to the economic conditions of the time, so that the concerts initially enjoyed great popularity. However, they were soon criticized as being too elitist, and, at the same time, their program design was criticized as too conservative.

The discussion also occupied the Salzburg press for several weeks. In letters to the editors and other statements, there were complaints, for example, about the lack of newer and the most contemporary music, the repetitive engagements of the same singers, the performance of a very limited pool of works, the general oversupply of events that had

---

64 Hummel, *Marksteine der Geschichte der Internationalen Stiftung Mozarteum*, 34.
65 Hummel, *Marksteine der Geschichte der Internationalen Stiftung Mozarteum*, 40.

no relation to the financial strength of the culture-interested population, the imbalance between song recitals and events with large orchestras, etc. In addition, the new format had to face the accusation of using the term "society" to address an audience that would not go to a concert out of musical interest, but because of the need to be part of an elite circle.[66] In addition, the Foundation had "backed the local artists up against the wall" through its "dangerous star system," which is why a critic of these events called for a return of "art to the people […], because they thirst more sincerely for emotional elevation than an audience in tuxedos and ball attire."[67]

In the winter of 1926/27, there was finally recourse for the complaints in the form of the "regular club concerts," which were now performed almost entirely by local forces with "reduced artistic standards."[68] A concert community was also set up, the committee of which not only influenced the programming, but also tried to raise funds

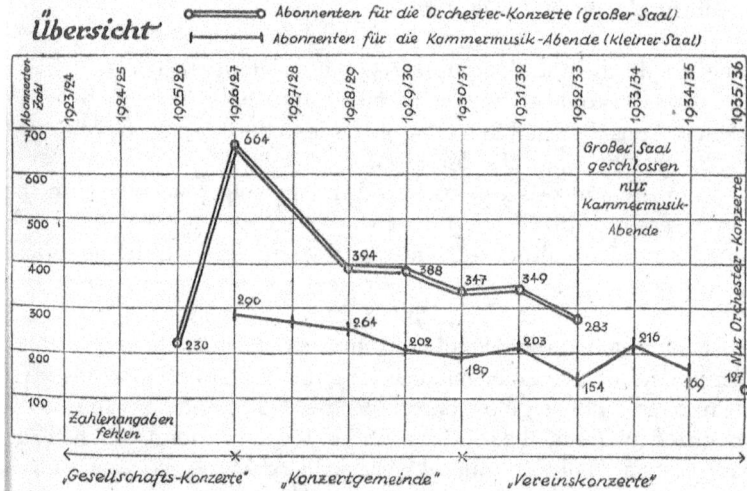

Figure 8.4 Concert attendance figures, 1925/26–1935/36. Source: Hummel (1936), 43.

---

66 See, among others, F.K. [= Franz Krotsch], "Salzburg und die Gesellschaftskonzerte," *Salzburger Volksblatt*, January 16, 1926; 4–5; "Salzburg und die Gesellschaftskonzerte," *Salzburger Volksblatt*, January 22, 1926, 3–4; "Salzburg und die Gesellschaftskonzerte," *Salzburger Volksblatt*, January 26, 1926, 3–4; "Salzburg und die Gesellschaftskonzerte," *Salzburger Volksblatt*, January 27, 1926, 3–4.
67 Eugen Müller, "Salzburg und die Gesellschaftskonzerte," *Salzburger Volksblatt*, February 2, 1926, 3–4, here 4.
68 Wagner, *Das Mozarteum*, 209.

and to increase attendance at the concerts. The main beneficiaries of this measure were the local musicians and especially the Mozarteum Orchestra. However, the general economic situation also took its toll here, as the following statistics document. The activities of the concert community also sank noticeably in numbers, so that the Foundation was the only one responsible for the events in the 1930/31 season but then had to avoid them in the following season. The Mozarteum Orchestra organized its concerts at its own risk. In the three years that followed, it concentrated on chamber music or orchestra concerts. The lack of attendance led to a further reduction in the number of orchestra evenings in the seasons 1936/37 and 1937/38.[69]

The National Socialist "reorganization" of Salzburg's cultural life finally provided for an expansion of the concert activities after a one-year hiatus due to the *Stillhaltemaßnahmen* (standstill measures), as well as a reactivation of the cooperation between the Conservatory respectively University and the Mozarteum Foundation. The once cosmopolitan Mozart now acquired a German-"ethnic" label, and the institutions dedicated to him were reorganized so that they could be used for an ideological indoctrination of large sections of the population.

Mozart City—Music City—Festival City: Positions of the Mozarteum Conservatory and Foundation

As the development sketched above shows, the Mozarteum Foundation and Conservatory were the central constituents of Salzburg's identity formation and the foundation of its lasting identity as a city of Mozart and music. For a long time, they held a kind of monopoly, and acted as the linchpins of the local and national music culture and, at the same time, as the figureheads for those images deemed essential for Salzburg's continued relevance in the arts.

When another facet was added to the identity of Salzburg's music culture, namely when it became the festival city, the position of the Foundation was shaken.[70] As early as 1913, the *Zentralvorsteher* (central head) of the Mozart community, Friedrich Gehmacher, who was mainly responsible for the construction of the Mozart House on *Schwarzstrasse*,

---

69 Hummel, *Marksteine der Geschichte der Internationalen Stiftung Mozarteum*, 41–3.
70 The Conservatory was less affected by this innovation in that its teachers as members of the Mozarteum Orchestra, the Mozart Orchestra or other ensembles, and its director as a conductor and composer were involved in the Festival, but the institution itself paused in the summer and so it had not appeared from the start.

approached the Foundation. However, the plans that he and Heinrich Damisch had to organize a festival in Salzburg were rejected. One of the main opponents of the new project was one of the most important patrons of the Mozarteum Foundation and music school, Lilli Lehmann. Salzburg's music culture owed much to her initiatives not only financially, but also artistically. Accordingly, the Board felt obliged to follow the assessment of the internationally known chamber singer who was also a member of the Board. However, the retrospective judgment that the Mozarteum alone "could not respond to the suggestions owing to the protests of its great sponsor [...]"[71] seems too short-sighted an explanation for the rejection.

Rather, their negative attitude was only one of several components leading to the turn-down. The ever-smoldering rivalry between Vienna and Salzburg, like the desire of Salzburg's cultural leadership to work outside Vienna's sphere of influence also played significant roles. In addition, Lehmann and like-minded members of the Board saw their priority projects, such as the purchase of the Mozart Birthplace, just as at risk as was purportedly the "patriarchal and dignified," "intimate"[72] character of this legacy as realized in the almost exclusive performances of Mozart's works, which had characterized the music festivals previously organized by the Foundation. And so, in 1917, the Festival Hall Community was founded, which was located outside the Foundation and whose main office was in Vienna.[73] Even a subsequent affiliation of the Festival Hall Community, as hoped for by Gehmacher, to the Salzburg Mozart Community and thus to the Foundation was not to be.[74] Though the Foundation—and with it, the Conservatory—paved the way for Salzburg as a city of Mozart and music, it had missed engaging the last entity in the Salzburg triad that controlled its identity: Salzburg became a festival city without the direct involvement of the Foundation.

With that omission, it was all the more important for the Foundation to retrospectively emphasize its pioneering role in this endeavor and at the same time to give a positive spin on its failure. The Foundation's

---

71 Hummel, *Marksteine der Geschichte der Internationalen Stiftung Mozarteum*, 26.
72 Letter from Friedrich Gehmacher to Heinrich Damisch, August 28, 1916, and letter from Friedrich Gehmacher to Heinrich Damisch, September 13, 1916, as qtd. in Oskar Holl, "Dokumente zur Entstehung der Salzburger Festspiele," 157–9 and 163.
73 Oswald Panagl, "Salzburger Festspiele," and letter from Heinrich Damisch to Friedrich Gehmacher, October 22, 1916, as qtd. in Holl, "Dokumente zur Entstehung der Salzburger Festspiele," 166–7.
74 Letters from Heinrich Damisch to Friedrich Gehmacher, September 16 and October 14, 1916, as qtd. in Holl, "Dokumente zur Entstehung der Salzburger Festspiele," 163–4 and 166.

In the Shadow of the Salzburg Festival? 247

40th annual report, for example, first recalled the glamorous Mozart festivals of the late nineteenth and early twentieth centuries, for which the Foundation was responsible, and then the text overtly claims a direct causal connection between these undertakings and the contemporary festival:

> The whole city of Salzburg was captivated by this festive mood. Everything to do with business was put in the background, and members of society [...] made themselves available free of charge [...]. But this gave the ceremonies a noteworthy hint of Salzburg society. [...] The festivals described here [...] will never return in that form. But they have done their job: They prepared the ground for the events of the Salzburg Festival Hall Community. Without the music festivals of the Mozarteum, the powerful commitment and the encouraging development of this Association, which is so important for Salzburg and Austria, would be unthinkable. In having done so, the International Mozarteum Foundation can be pleased that the very first suggestions for and driving force behind the foundation of a Festival Hall was born from its womb.[75]

A look into history shows, however, that the Foundation initially did not intend to accept the new competitive situation without any pushback.

In times of Salzburg's greatest financial hardships and despite the looming difficulties surrounding the nationalization of the Conservatory, the Foundation organized a Mozart week in summer 1921 as a counterpoint to the Salzburg Festival. Planned in the spirit of a backlash, this series of events was conceived on the models of the pre-war music festivals. Consisting of seven orchestral and chamber concerts in the Mozarthaus, a serenade in the courtyard of the Residenz, and a concert of sacred music in the cathedral, it offered a program comprising only works by Mozart—and it preceded the actual Festival.[76]

After the great success of its debut the previous year, the Festival Committee had had envisaged massive expansions of the programming—i.e., a festival in the sense of a new beginning, an opening of the concept that had previously focused on Mozart. The idea was to win over the "first forces of the Vienna State Opera" and the "artists of the Vienna Burgtheater"[77] for opera productions such as *Così fan tutte* or *Don Giovanni* and Molière's play *Le Bourgeois gentilhomme*. However,

---

75 Hummel, *Marksteine der Geschichte*, 25–6.
76 Hummel, *Marksteine der Geschichte*, 35.
77 Damisch and Kerber, "Festspiele 1921," *Mitteilungen der Salzburger Festspielhaus-Gemeinde* 1/2 (1921): 16.

the artists were not willing to perform in Salzburg "at their own risk,"[78] and, at the same time, the Ministry of Finance did not respond positively to the committee's application for a guarantee against such a failure.[79] So the Festival Hall Community had to deal with a very reduced "emergency program," which in the end could only be partially implemented.[80]

Not surprisingly, Richard Strauss was extremely annoyed by this "unauthorized programming by the Salzburgers,"[81] and the insufficiently transparent demarcation between the two series of events of the Mozart Week and Festival. At the end of June, he vented his anger in a letter to Franz Schalk:

> I find it outrageous that works from the program we have approved could not be performed, while without our approval, but still apparently as an event by the Festival Hall Community, some variety-like, some totally inferior amateur events sneaked onto the poster and almost under our oversight. I have absolutely no desire to hand over any protection for Mr. Paumgartner's artistic fraud. At least our approval had to be obtained for Ms. Bahr-Mildenburg's lust for directing. What is our common position on this, in my opinion, catastrophic matter for the reputation and renown of future, genuine Festival performances, and how can we ensure that the inescapably huge deficits of the Mozarteum are not incurred at the expense of the state or the Festival Hall Community?[82]

Despite these voices of doom and gloom, the Mozart Week project did not fail. On the contrary, the Mozarteum institutions, above all Conservatory director Paumgartner and the Foundation, established themselves as big players in that summer season. Not only could they come

---

78 Damisch and Kerber, "Festspiele 1921," *Mitteilungen der Salzburger Festspielhaus-Gemeinde* 5/6 (1921): 20.
79 Details on the problems surrounding the 1921 Festival can be found, among others, in Stephen Gallup, *Die Geschichte der Salzburger Festspiele*, 35–42.
80 The plan was to stage Mozart's early *Singspiel Bastien and Bastienne* in the Natural Theater of the Mirabell Gardens and in cooperation with the Salzburg Summer Course of the Dalcroze School, the ballet *Les petits riens*. The Singspiel performances, for which artistic director Anna Bahr-Mildenburg was to be responsible, as well as those of the ballet, were canceled due to "technical difficulties"—more detailed explanations are lacking—at short notice ("Salzburger Festspiele," *Salzburger Volksblatt*, August 29, 1921).
81 Edda Fuhrich and Gisela Prossnitz, *Die Salzburger Festspiele*, 29.
82 Letter from Richard Strauss to Franz Schalk, as qtd. in Fuhrich and Prossnitz, *Die Salzburger Festspiele*, 29–30.

In the Shadow of the Salzburg Festival? 249

up with a wide-ranging Mozart program, but they also had succeeded in doing something that the Festival Hall Community was for the time being still unable to carry off: in addition to its local staff, the Foundation won the Vienna State Opera Orchestra for its projects. With this successful Mozart Week, the Foundation once again claimed its role as the most important local (one might say local-patriotic) music organizers and thus tacitly also as a "domestic" rival of the Salzburg Festival, which was quite often deemed "foreign" and "Jewish."

At the same time, the Foundation also showed the native Salzburgers who were mostly critical of the Festival their ideas about what music festivals should look like—festivals that had grown out of the local structures and had already become traditional. The Foundation's festivals were presented as embodying the more promising concept, more appropriate to the city of Salzburg. The Foundation's summary of the event thus commented accordingly: "The project was approached with great trepidation, but it had an unexpected economic success [...], its artistic success provided the best basis for advertising for future events."[83]

But as so often was the case in this era, these ambitious plans for the future would be shattered. Due to the turmoil surrounding the nationalization of the Conservatory, no efforts were made to position the Foundation and the Conservatory in the Festival season in the following two years. It was only in 1924 that the Foundation, under the initiative of Paumgartner, succeeded in reactivating and gradually expanding their own successful concept of the Mozart serenades performed at historical sites, executed in the spirit of Hofmannsthal's idea of "City as Stage."

A closer cooperation between the Foundation and the Festival Hall Community only began in 1927. Representatives from each association were appointed to the Board of the other, previously competing institution. This gave the Foundation the opportunity to initiate so-called Mozart ceremonies, consisting of orchestral concerts, chamber music evenings and the performance of the C Minor Mass, which would become a tradition in the following years, and thus "to again have a more visible presence during the Festival."[84] At the same time, however, the Mozart ceremonies "had to be kept within a relatively narrow framework, because the Festival was broadened in scope,"[85] according to the laconic statement of the Foundation chronicler Hummel.

Such a change in the mutual contract hardly served the Foundation's image: from 1935 onwards, the Foundation held a few events as part of the Festival, but these were no longer referred to as Mozart ceremonies.[86] Finally, like the concerts of the Salzburg Cathedral Choir,

---

83 Hummel, *Marksteine der Geschichte der Internationalen Stiftung Mozarteum*, 35.
84 Hummel, *Marksteine der Geschichte der Internationalen Stiftung Mozarteum*, 36.
85 Hummel, *Marksteine der Geschichte der Internationalen Stiftung Mozarteum*, 39.
86 Hummel, *Marksteine der Geschichte der Internationalen Stiftung Mozarteum*, 39.

they were identified as external events, and their patronage named as a separate entity. Even in 1936 and 1937, the number of concerts that the Foundation organized as part of the Festival was very reduced. In addition to the obligatory C Minor Mass, the program included an orchestral concert with the Vienna Philharmonic and (church) concerts directed by Bernhard Paumgartner, with the participation of local music institutions. Finally, in the Anschluss year of annexation, the Foundation's participation was limited to the traditional performance of the C Minor Mass.

The conclusion of the Foundation's own history text reads a little like an attempt at self-consolation when it says:

> The International Mozarteum Foundation is pleased to note that the Festival continued on the path it [i.e., the Foundation] had shown before the war, particularly since Mozart's works were never missing from the opera schedule. [...] In the orchestral concerts, you can also see the expansion of the way the Foundation had pointed out before the war.[87]

All in all, the Mozarteum Foundation remained what it had been from the beginning of the Festival: the local, culture-conservative addition to the ever-increasing programming of a now cosmopolitan, thematically broad, and personnel-rich music festival.

After the loss of the Conservatory and its failure to play a major role at the Festival, the Foundation implemented another prestigious field of activity that again enabled the Foundation to reposition itself and to profile itself locally and internationally: the summer courses. Lilli Lehmann laid the foundation for this initiative in 1916 with singing courses, which she held privately at the Mozarteum until 1928 during the summer months. Contemporary reports illustrate the central importance of these "first master classes" for the identity of the Foundation and its international positioning.[88] They surrounded "the institute [...] with a new luster."[89]

However, the courses only came to be oriented towards a specific summer academy after the involvement of the American Julian Freedman.

---

87 Hummel, *Marksteine der Geschichte der Internationalen Stiftung Mozarteum*, 39.
88 For example, the 1916 annual report said: "If the past events have already enabled bustling life to unfold in the rooms of the *Mozarthaus*, the singing course of Ms. *Kammersängerin* Lilli Lehmann in July and August gave it a very significant reinforcement and a special sheen. [...] [She] accomplished a work that shone far into the whole musical world. With her singing courses, which were mainly devoted to Mozart's art, our great patron emphasized the destiny of the Mozarteum to be the focal point of the Mozart cult in an excellent way [...]" (*Sechsunddreißigster Jahres-Bericht des [...] "Mozarteums" in Salzburg 1916*, 10).
89 *Sechsunddreißigster Jahres-Bericht des [...] "Mozarteums" in Salzburg 1916*, 10.

In consultation with the Foundation, but, like Lehmann, negotiating on a purely private basis, he initiated "training courses for composition and orchestral conducting" for the first time in 1929, primarily aimed at American students. Freedman's basic concept, which was to be formative for the following years, provided for an offering of various, independent courses, each of which was led by international artists of "first order." Accordingly, teachers from the Conservatory were rarely on the list of course instructors, a list that, at least in the early years of the summer academy read like a who's who of the respective masterclass subject areas. Consequently, Freedman, former student of the former Mozarteum director Paul Graener who had studied in Austria and Germany, also pursued his ideal goal with a new concept in this framework, namely enabling "the English and Americans, who underwent their artistic studies in France during and after the war, to move back to Germany and Austria to bring this culture […] closer to its compatriots."[90]

The spectrum of students at the summer academy was broad, and its ideal and economic success was great, which is why the Foundation decided not only to provide resources for the project in the future, but also to take over responsibility for the summer courses. International first-tier artists and an attractive, continuously expanding range of courses met with a broad response in 1931: "These [75 participants] came from three continents – respectively, from 14 states – to Salzburg and had also brought their relatives and friends with them, which was of economic benefit to the Festival and the city."[91] The teachers of the Conservatory, however, only in individual cases, where the passage "members of the teaching staff of the Mozarteum Conservatory teach during the summer course (individual instrumental subjects)"[92] was noted in the program. Yet the organizers sought to connect the academy to the Festival from the beginning on. For instance, the more famous name was used on the 1929 program flyer, when it noted that the event dates were "Festival season July–August." The result was, instead, cooperation in the form of rehearsal visits or lectures by Festival actors as part of the summer courses.[93]

---

90 "Der Konflikt im Mozarteum," *Salzburger Volksblatt*, January 24, 1933.
91 Hummel, *Marksteine der Geschichte der Internationalen Stiftung Mozarteum*, 66.
92 Internationale Stiftung Mozarteum, *Broschüre Ausbildungskurse für Komposition und Orchesterleitung*, n.p.
93 However, these plans could not be sufficiently implemented, as documented by the report on the course in 1937: "The occasional visit to festival rehearsals announced in the prospectus could not be achieved to the desired extent in the year under review […]. It is to be hoped that […] the participants in the conducting course will be offered an expanded opportunity to further improve their artistic training using the example of the great conductors (Toscanini, Bruno Walter, Knappertsbusch, Furtwängler)" (*Bericht der Internationalen Stiftung Mozarteum über die Mozarteum Sommer-Akademie* [1937]), 7.

Übersicht über die Entwicklung der Kurse

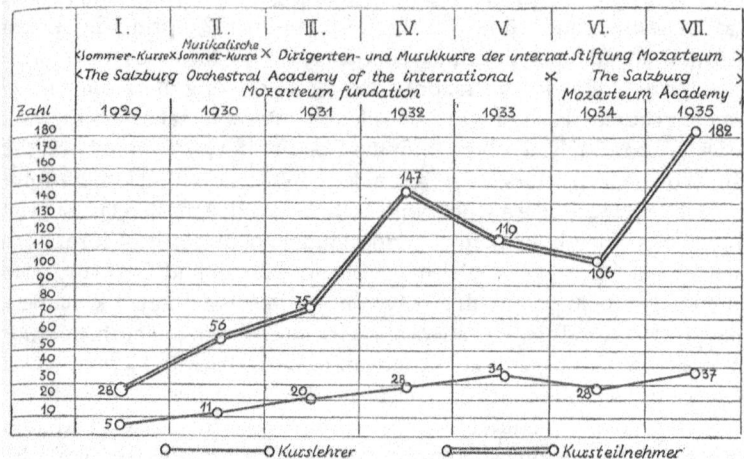

Figure 8.5 Students and teachers at the Mozarteum summer courses, 1929–1935. Source: Hummel (1936), 69.

The number of courses, and with them that of teachers and students, increased in the academy's early years, but experienced a slump in 1933, as is shown by contemporaneous statistics.

The reasons for this were first and foremost the poor dollar exchange rate and Hitler's economic blockade against expenditures in Austria. The course management tried to counter the latter by putting the character of the courses in a system-compliant light, in a letter to the German consulate and emphasizing the intention of a worldwide distribution of "German music": "Originally intended primarily as a summer school for Americans, as a result of a complete reorganization in the past winter, the conducting courses and music courses have become a consciously German art institution that has set itself the goal of promoting to artists from all over the world especially German works of art and the German concept of art."[94]

Despite the fundamentally positive reaction of the German Reichsstelle, the 1,000 Mark ban was reflected in the number of participants as well as the massively polarizing "affair Freedman," which had been covered by the local and national press and had led to the above mentioned "reorganization" of the summer academy. To what extent the

---

94 As qtd. in Wagner, *Das Mozarteum*, 213.

conflicts over the American initiator of the summer courses, who was allegedly guilty of currency evasion, were motivated by antisemitism can hardly be judged from the available sources. In any matter, the case was also used as an opportunity to publicly discuss the fields of activity and the ideological orientation of the Foundation. For example, the *Salzburger Volksblatt* printed the following letter:

> Such facts are factually very sad and indicate that the "internationalization" of the Mozarteum with the personality of Julian Freedman, with international music and conducting courses, which now follow up on an international American "school" with presumably even more "international" art groups should actually be seen as proof of the Mozarteum's poverty, of how it neglected and consciously abandoned its own intended purposes, its practical school and educational task, its role as a concert company, and its role in promoting the strength of native and Austrian art, that it can now only justify its current existence with such "international" tricks. […] Poor Mozarteum, where did you go? You have become a simple property manager, museum manager, and guest house manager with rather sad material and moral deficits. You have become a propagandist for dollar-bangling tourism, you are overgrown by an international music agency, with international music courses and you are now getting an internationally organized "school"–but by no means will you get your own school, which you lost to the federal government, back again.[95]

Despite all the criticism, the Foundation stuck to its international music courses. Once again, it had to accept a drop in the number of participants, as the political upheavals in Austria in 1933/34 were added to the factors already mentioned. It was not until the summer of 1935 that the statistics showed a massive increase—both the number of students from a total of twenty-one countries and that of the teachers reached a provisional peak. Success was maintained in the two following years before the courses experienced a radical slump in 1938 due to the political upheavals, the associated ideological realignments, and the resulting delayed advertising activities.

The Foundation's report on the 1938 courses explicitly refers to the changed official attitude of the now Ostmark towards the USA, which had previously been the summer academy's main clientele: "A corresponding visit to the courses from overseas could not be expected from the outset, especially since the American audience

---

95 "Der Konflikt im Mozarteum," *Salzburger Volksblatt*, January 24, 1933.

KURSTEILNEHMER NACH HERKUNFTSLÄNDERN

	1932	1933	1934	1935	1936	1937	1938	1939
Argentinien	–	1	–	1	–	1	–	–
Australien	2	1	–	–	1	–	1	–
Belgien	1	–	–	–	–	–	–	–
Bulgarien	–	–	–	–	–	1	1	1
Canada	1	–	3	1	2	4	2	–
China	–	–	–	–	–	1	1	–
ČSR	3	5	5	5	8	13	3	2
Dänemark	1	–	–	5	1	1	1	–
Deutsches Reich	35	16	6	6	9	12	16	38
Estland	–	1	–	–	–	1	–	–
Finnland	–	–	1	1	2	–	–	–
Frankreich	4	2	2	4	6	3	–	–
Griechenland	–	1	5	6	6	5	–	–
Großbritannien	12	10	11	14	12	18	3	–
Holland	1	2	7	7	4	6	4	1
Italien	–	–	1	5	14	1	1	–
Japan	–	1	–	–	1	–	–	–
Java	–	–	–	1	–	–	–	–
Jugoslawien	1	–	2	5	5	3	3	1
Lettland	–	–	–	–	–	1	–	–
Litauen	–	–	1	–	–	–	–	–
Norwegen	–	–	1	3	4	4	1	–
Österreich	15	16	24	31	27	31	–	–
Palästina	–	–	–	–	–	1	–	–
Polen	2	–	4	4	2	–	1	–
Rumänien	1	4	3	4	–	4	2	–
Rußland	1	–	1	–	1	–	–	–
Schottland	–	–	–	–	–	2	–	–
Schweden	–	1	2	2	8	2	3	2
Schweiz	4	4	1	6	14	5	1	1
Ungarn	–	2	2	1	1	1	–	0
USA	63	52	24	70	56	59	20	3
	147	119	106	182	184	180	64	49

Figure 8.6 Students at the Mozarteum summer courses, country of origin, 1932–1939. Source: Hummel (1951), 81.

already prepared their summer plans in February—not to mention the anti-German propaganda wave in America that had started particularly violently following the incorporation of the Ostmark into the German motherland."[96] With the political breaks, not only had the student numbers changed, but also the countries of origin of the participants, as the

---

96 Bericht der Internationalen Stiftung Mozarteum in Salzburg über die Mozarteum Sommer-Akademie (1938), 4–5.

following statistics illustrate. (Austria was also nominally and statistically integrated into the German Reich in that contemporary source and was not specifically shown as the Ostmark.)

In 1939, the Mozarteum Foundation was responsible for the summer academy for the last time—and here, too, only partially. An organizational cooperation with the "German Music Institute for Foreigners" Berlin-Potsdam was initiated that year, and the following year all responsibility for the conception and implementation of the courses was assigned to the Berlin office. Only in 1947 was the "International Summer Academy of the Mozarteum in Salzburg" reactivated.[97] Mozarteum by then no longer meant the Foundation, but the University-Conservatory, which from now on were responsible for the courses. They once again became a genuine Salzburg project, which was fed ideologically by the image of Salzburg, the city of Mozart, music and festival that was now deliberately proclaimed to be Austrian.

Bibliography

Archival Sources:

Universität Mozarteum, Kunst-ARCHIV-Raum, Ordner Archiv der Internationalen Stiftung Mozarteum 1841–1947.
Minister für Kultus und Unterricht to the Internationale Stiftung Mozarteum, July 9, 1912.
Letter of the k. k. Landespräsident to the Internationale Stiftung Mozarteum on behalf of "the title Conservatory," June 6, 1914.
Rudolf von Lewicki to Franz Stibral, June 13, 1914.
Rudolf von Lewicki to Ludwig Sedlitzky, June 10, 1919.
Ministerium für Unterricht to the Internationale Stiftung Mozarteum, July 14, 1919.
Letter of the teaching staff of the Mozarteum Conservatory to the Board of the Mozarteum Foundation, July 10, 1920.
Letter of the Salzburger Provincial Government to the "Verein Mozarteum," July 24, 1922.
Copy of the Request for Removal to the Mozarteum Conservatory, September 1, 1921.

Annual Reports

Bericht der Internationalen Stiftung Mozarteum in Salzburg über die Mozarteum Sommer-Akademie für Musik, Theater und Tanz, X. Kursjahr 1938. Salzburg: Eigenverlag der Internationalen Stiftung Mozarteum, 1938.

---

97 Broschüre *Internationale Sommer-Akademie des Mozarteums in Salzburg: Dirigenten- und Musik-Kurse.*

Bericht der Internationalen Stiftung Mozarteum über die Mozarteum Sommer-Akademie für Musik, Theater und Tanz, IX. Kursjahr 1937. Salzburg: Eigenverlag der Internationalen Stiftung Mozarteum, 1937.

Dom-Musik-Verein und Mozarteum, Salzburg. Erster Jahresbericht, vorgetragen bei der Plenarversammlung des Dom-Musik-Vereines und Mozarteums zu Salzburg. Salzburg: Duyle, 1843.

Dreißigster Jahresbericht der [...] Internationalen Stiftung: Mozarteum in Salzburg 1910. Salzburg: Selbstverlag der Internationalen Stiftung Mozarteum, 1911.

Hummel, Walter. Chronik der Internationalen Stiftung Mozarteum in Salzburg zugleich einundvierzigster Jahresbericht über die Jahre 1936–1950. Salzburg: Selbstverlag der Internationalen Stiftung Mozarteum, 1951.

Hummel, Walter. Marksteine der Geschichte der Internationalen Stiftung Mozarteum in Salzburg und vierzigster Jahresbericht (über die Jahre 1918–1935). Salzburg: Selbstverlag der Internationalen Stiftung Mozarteum, 1936.

Jahres-Bericht des [...] Konservatoriums des "Mozarteums" in Salzburg über das XXXVI. Schuljahr 1915–16, erstattet von der Direktion. Salzburg: Verlag des Konservatoriums des "Mozarteums" in Salzburg, 1916.

Jahres-Bericht des [...] Konservatoriums des "Mozarteums" in Salzburg über das 38. Schuljahr 1917–18, erstattet von der Direktion. Salzburg: Verlag des Konservatoriums des "Mozarteums" in Salzburg, 1918.

Jahres-Bericht des Konservatoriums "Mozarteum" in Salzburg über das 39. Schuljahr 1918–19, erstattet von der Direktion. Salzburg: Verlag des Konservatoriums "Mozarteum" in Salzburg, 1919.

Jahres-Bericht des Konservatoriums "Mozarteum" in Salzburg über das 40. Schuljahr 1920–1921, erstattet von der Direktion Salzburg: Verlag des Konservatoriums "Mozarteum" in Salzburg, 1921.

Jahresberichte Konservatorium/Hochschule/Reichshochschule Mozarteum 1922–1943/44.

Jahresberichte des Konservatoriums Mozarteum 1922–1938.

Jahresberichte der Hochschule/Reichshochschule Mozarteum 1939–1944.

Konservatorium Mozarteum in Salzburg, Jahresbericht über das 45. Schuljahr 1924/25, erstattet von der Direktion. [Salzburg]: o. V., 1925.

Konservatorium Mozarteum in Salzburg, Jahresbericht über das 51. Schuljahr 1930/31, erstattet von der Direktion. [Salzburg]: o. V., 1931.

Konservatorium Mozarteum in Salzburg, Jahresbericht über das 52. Schuljahr 1931/32, erstattet von der Direktion. [Salzburg]: o. V., 1932.

Konservatorium Mozarteum in Salzburg, Jahresbericht über das 57. Schuljahr 1936/37, erstattet von der Direktion. [Salzburg]: o. V., 1937.

Konservatorium Mozarteum in Salzburg, Jahres-Bericht über das 58. Studienjahr 1937/38, erstattet von der Direktion. Salzburg: Konservatorium Mozarteum Salzburg, 1938.

Konservatorium Mozarteum in Salzburg, Jahres-Bericht über das 55. Schuljahr 1934/35, erstattet von der Direktion. Salzburg: Konservatorium Mozarteum, 1935.

Paumgartner, Bernhard. Eine musikalische Hochschule in Salzburg, Vortrag, gehalten in der "Akademischen Arbeitsgemeinschaft" am 23. März 1919. Salzburg: n.p., 1919.

Sechsunddreißigster Jahres-Bericht des [...] "Mozarteums" in Salzburg 1916. Salzburg: Selbstverlag des Mozarteums, 1917.

Siebenter Jahresbericht der [...] Internationalen Stiftung: Mozarteum in Salzburg 1887. Salzburg: Selbstverlag der Internationalen Stiftung: Mozarteum, [1888].

Vierunddreißigster Jahresbericht der [...] Internationalen Stiftung: Mozarteum in Salzburg 1914. Salzburg: Selbstverlag der Internationalen Stiftung: Mozarteum, 1915.

In the Shadow of the Salzburg Festival? 257

Other Primary Sources

"Ein Antrag auf Verstaatlichung des Mozarteums." *Salzburger Chronik*, May 10, 1919.
Broschüre *Internationale Sommer-Akademie des Mozarteums in Salzburg: Dirigenten- und Musik-Kurse*. Salzburg: o. V., 1947.
Damisch, Heinrich, and Erwin Kerber. "Festspiele 1921." *Mitteilungen der Salzburger Festspielhaus-Gemeinde* 1/2 (1921a), 15–16.
Damisch, Heinrich, and Erwin Kerber. "Festspiele 1921." *Mitteilungen der Salzburger Festspielhaus-Gemeinde* 5/6 (1921b), 20–1.
F.K. [= Franz Krotsch]. "Salzburg und die Gesellschaftskonzerte." *Salzburger Volksblatt*, January 16, 1926, 4–5.
Internationale Stiftung Mozarteum, *Broschüre Ausbildungskurse für Komposition und Orchesterleitung*, unpag., Archiv der Internationalen Stiftung Mozarteum.
"Der Konflikt im Mozarteum." *Salzburger Volksblatt*, January 24, 1933.
Leisinger, Ulrich. "Zwischen 'Führerauftrag' und Kriegswirklichkeit."
Unpublished lecture on the occasion of the colloquium "Geschichte der (Internationalen) Stiftung Mozarteum vor, während und nach der NS-Zeit (History of the (International) Mozarteum Foundation before, during and after National Socialism)" Mozarteum Foundation, Salzburg, November 22, 2019.
"Das Mozarteum in Not." *Salzburger Volksblatt*, March 4, 1921.
Müller, Eugen. "Salzburg und die Gesellschaftskonzerte." *Salzburger Volksblatt*, February 2, 1926, 3–4.
"Salzburg und die Gesellschaftskonzerte." *Salzburger Volksblatt*, January 22, 1926, 3–4.
"Salzburg und die Gesellschaftskonzerte." *Salzburger Volksblatt*, January 26, 1926, 3–4.
"Salzburg und die Gesellschaftskonzerte." *Salzburger Volksblatt*, January 27, 1926, 3–4.

Secondary Literature

Angermüller, Rudolph, and Géza Rech. *Hundert Jahre Internationale Stiftung Mozarteum Salzburg 1880–1980: Eine Chronik*. Kassel: Bärenreiter-Verlag, 1980.
Danner, Peter. "'Weltanschauungsfreie Forschung ... nicht einmal wünschenswert': Wissenschaft in Salzburg während der NS-Zeit." In Veits-Falk and Hanisch, eds., *Herrschaft und Kultur*, 198–267.
Fuhrich, Edda, and Gisela Prossnitz. *Die Salzburger Festspiele: Ihre Geschichte in Daten, Zeitzeugnissen und Bildern*, vol. I 1920–1945. Salzburg: Residenz Verlag, 1990.
Gallup, Stephen. *Die Geschichte der Salzburger Festspiele*. Wien: Orac, 1989.
Gföllner, Karin, Oskar Dohle, and Franz Wieser, eds. *Salzburg – Wien, Eine späte Liebe: 200 Jahre Salzburg bei Österreich*. Salzburg: Samson Druck, 2016. 63–78.
Großpietsch, Christoph. "Zur Selbstinszenierung von Erich Schenk in Salzburg und Wien – Die Idee einer Zentralisierung der Mozart-Forschung." In Pinwinkler and Rathkolb, eds., *Die Internationale Stiftung Mozarteum und der Nationalsozialismus*, 133–63.
Hanisch, Ernst. "Alltag im Krieg: Erfahrungen an der Heimatfront." In Oskar Dohle and Thomas Mitterecker, eds., *Salzburg im Ersten Weltkrieg: Fernab der Front – dennoch im Krieg*, 33–45. Vienna-Cologne-Weimar: Böhlau, 2014.
Hanisch, Ernst. *Der lange Schatten des Staates: Österreichische Gesellschaftsgeschichte im 20. Jahrhundert*. Vienna: Ueberreuter, 2004.
Hanisch, Ernst. "Provinz und Metropole: Gesellschaftsgeschichtliche Perspektiven der Beziehungen des Bundeslandes zu Wien (1918–1934)." In Alfred Edelmayer,

Friedrich Koja, and Ernst Hanisch, eds., *Beiträge zur Föderalismusdiskussion*, 67–105. Salzburg: Landespressebüro, 1981.

Hinterberger, Julia. "'An diesen Namen knüpft sich nun aber auch alle Localeitelkeit der Salzburger': Das Mozarteum im Spiegel der Salzburger Musikkultur des 19. und frühen 20. Jahrhunderts." In Julia Hinterberger, ed., *Von der Musikschule zum Konservatorium: Das Mozarteum 1841–1922*, 13–114. Vienna: Hollitzer Verlag, 2017.

Hinterberger, Julia. "'Gottbegnadete Künstler' und 'volksverbundene Kunst': Musikkultur in Salzburg zur Zeit des Nationalsozialismus." In Peter F. Kramml and Christoph Kühberger, eds., *Inszenierung der Macht*, 280–355.

Hinterberger, Julia. "Salzburg ist ein Leuchtturm in der Kultur gegenüber der Welt: Schlaglichter auf die säkulare Salzburger Musikkultur der 1920er bis 1950er Jahre." In Julia Hinterberger, ed., *Vom Konservatorium zur Akademie: Das Mozarteum 1922–1953*, 14–129. Vienna: Hollitzer Verlag, 2022.

Höck, Alfred. "Auf der Suche nach Identität: Salzburg in der Ersten Republik." In Gföllner, Dohle, and Wieser, eds., *Salzburg – Wien, Eine späte Liebe*, 89–116.

Hoffmann, Robert. "Salzburg und Wien im Spannungsfeld von Provinz und Metropole: Die Zeit von 1816 bis 1918." In Gföllner, Dohle, and Wieser, eds., *Salzburg – Wien, Eine späte Liebe*, 63–78.

Hoffmann, Robert. "Vom Mozartdenkmal zur Festspielgründung." In Clemens Hellsberg and the Salzburger Festival Fonds, eds., *Eine glückhafte Symbiose: Die Wiener Philharmoniker und die Salzburger Festspiele*, 17–26. Salzburg: Residenz Verlag, 2017.

Holl, Oskar. "Dokumente zur Entstehung der Salzburger Festspiele: Unveröffentlichtes aus der Korrespondenz der Gründer." *Maske und Kothurn* 13 (1967), 148–79.

Kramml, Peter F., and Christoph Kühberger, eds. *Inszenierung der Macht: Alltag – Kultur – Propaganda*. Salzburg: Stadtarchiv und Statistik der Stadt Salzburg, 2011.

Nußbaumer, Martina. *Musikstadt Wien: Die Konstruktion eines Images*. Freiburg i.Br.-Berlin-Vienna: Rombach, 2007.

Panagl, Oswald. "Salzburger Festspiele." *Österreichisches Musiklexikon online*. Available online: www.musiklexikon.ac.at/ml/musik_S/Salzburger_Festspiele.xml (accessed October 10, 2019).

Pinwinkler, Alexander, and Oliver Rathkolb, eds. *Die Internationale Stiftung Mozarteum und der Nationalsozialismus: Politische Einflüsse auf Organisation, Mozart-Forschung, Museum und Bibliothek*. Salzburg: Verlag Anton Pustet, 2022.

Prucher, Susanne. "Musikschule/Konservatorium Mozarteum 1841–1922: Strukturen und Wirkungsfelder." In Hinterberger, ed., *Von der Musikschule zum Konservatorium*, 174–211.

Szabó-Knotik, Cornelia. "Musikland Österreich." *Oesterreichisches Musiklexikon online*. Available online: https://www.musiklexikon.ac.at/ml/musik_M/Musikland.xml (accessed September 15, 2019).

Veits-Falk, Sabine, and Ernst Hanisch, eds. *Herrschaft und Kultur: Instrumentalisierung – Anpassung – Resistenz*. Salzburg: Stadtarchiv und Statistik der Stadt Salzburg, 2013.

Wagner, Karl. *Das Mozarteum: Geschichte und Entwicklung einer kulturellen Institution*. Innsbruck: Helbling, 1993.

Zweig, Stefan. *Die Welt von gestern: Erinnerungen eines Europäers*. Göttingen: LIWI, 2018 [1942].

Nine Shadow Sides of Modernism: Poldi Wojtek's Designs for the Salzburg Festival and Austria's Conservative Modernity

Julia Secklehner

One of Austria's most established cultural highlights each summer is the Salzburg Festival of music and drama.[1] Taking place annually since 1920, the Festival was the brainchild of the poet Hugo von Hofmannsthal (1874–1929) and the director Max Reinhardt (1973–1943), who sought to give a new lease of life to Austrian culture after the collapse of the Habsburg Empire. In his ground-breaking analysis of the Festival's early days, the historian Michael P. Steinberg showed that Hofmannsthal conceived the event as an affirmation of a new Austrian identity, which aimed to merge a cosmopolitan outlook with a deep Catholicism and sense of greater German identity. This sense of "national cosmopolitanism" as a new Austrian culture was also anchored away from the old imperial capital Vienna—it located Austrian identity instead in Salzburg, a former independent prince-archbishopric and Baroque city in the Austrian Alps. The Festival thus manifested a different kind of modernity in Austrian interwar culture—one that embraced conservatism and nationalism as a significant part of its postimperial identity.

---

1 This article is part of a project that has received funding from the European Research Council (ERC) under the European Union's Horizon 2020 research and innovation programme (grant agreement No. 786314). Steinberg, *Austria as Theater and Ideology: The Meaning of the Salzburg Festival*.

Recent years have seen a growing critical engagement with the legacy of Salzburg's modernism.[2] In relation to art and visual culture, this interest was manifested by the 2016 exhibition *Anti:modern: Salzburg in the Heart of Europe Between Tradition and Renewal*, on view at the city's Museum der Moderne. The essays in the accompanying catalog addressed the tensions between "modern and anti-modern world views" in Salzburg culture between the wars, emphasizing the contradictory ways in which modernity was understood.[3] A central point of reference for their assessment of the contradictions within Salzburg modernism was, thus, Henri Lefebvre's definition of modernity:

> Modernity, in the shadow of the Revolution, absent here and incomplete there, no longer functions without crisis. Contradictions move through it and it constitutes their work in default of a radically revolutionary negativity which, according to the initial Marxist project, would have metamorphosed life itself. More: these crises multiply, grow closer together and become the general rule, the norm [...] Multiple and multifarious, despite all denials, these crises seem to constitute our Modernity. They are integral to its consciousness, to its image, to its apologetic project.[4]

This notion of crisis in relation to modern art in Salzburg is, perhaps, best encapsulated by the controversies surrounding the logo of the Salzburg Festival. When the Festival celebrated its centenary in 2020, debates about the reactionary sides of the event found new heights.

Following an initiative by the artist Konstanze Sailer, whose virtual project *Memory Gaps* remembers forgotten artists murdered by the National Socialist regime and calls out the NS past of others, discussions focused on the Festival's central visual identity: its logo, designed by Leopoldine (Poldi) Wojtek (1903–1978) in 1928 (Figure 9.1).[5]

As Wojtek became an ardent national socialist in the succeeding years, a historical commission, headed by eminent Austrian historian

---

2 See Nikolaus Schaffer, "Weltkrieg und Künstlerfehden Salzburger Kunst und Erster Weltkrieg – eine nüchterne Bilanz"; Stefanie Habsburg-Halbgebauer, "Aufbruch zu neuen Ufern: Umbruch von Tradition zur Moderne in der Kunst."
3 Sabine Breitwieser, "How Modern or Anti-modern is (was) Europe?," 218.
4 Henri Lefebvre, "Theses on Modernity," 11, qtd. in Breitwieser, "How Modern or Anti-modern is (was) Europe?," 17.
5 "Poldi Wojtek: Chronologie einer Erinnerungslücke." *Memory Gaps*. Available online: https://www.memorygaps.eu (accessed July 31, 2023).

Shadow Sides of Modernism 261

Figure 9.1 Poldi Wojtek, *Salzburger Festspiele 1928*, poster. Archive of the Salzburg Festival, © Salzburg Museum, Salzburg. Leopoldine Wojtek © OOA-S 2023. Photo: Salzburg Museum.

Oliver Rathkolb and the design historian Anita Kern, was set up to assess whether it was still appropriate to use the logo, concluding:

> The poster for the Salzburg Festival is a graphic product typical of its time and was probably created under the influence of the Vienna *Kunstgewerbeschule*, where Wojtek had completed her studies two years previously. The emblem was not used between 1938 and 1945, as it did not fit with the aesthetic of the Third Reich and was too closely linked to the Max Reinhardt era.[6]

---

6   Oliver Rathkolb, Anita Kern, and Margarethe Lasinger, *The Salzburg Festival's Logo and Its Designer Poldi Wojtek*, 114.

Thus, because the artistic origins of the design were rooted in the artist's education at Vienna's School of Applied Arts (Kunstgewerbeschule), an institution tied to progressive art movements such as Viennese Kinetism in the interwar period, the commission distinguished between the logo and the artist's later political convictions. Based on this line of argumentation, the poster could be separated from Poldi Wojtek as a national socialist and, instead, was tied to a cultural environment— that of the School of Applied Arts—which has long been positioned as one of Austria's most forward-looking institutions in the interwar period.[7] The assessment was further bolstered by the fact that Wojtek's work completed during the years of national socialism, including illustrations for the anonymously published children's book *A True Story: Words and Images from Two Germans in a Foreign Country* (1937, Figure 9.2) and a tapestry design with a swastika, had departed from her modernist working mode from earlier years.[8]

Locating the logo in a different period, which could be distinguished on the basis of a stylistic rupture, the report established that the logo could continue to be used with the promise that the artist's "uncomfortable past" would be addressed. As a further step of engaging with this topic, a public discussion took place as part of the program of the Salzburg Festival in 2021, focusing broadly on the topic of "Art and Ethos."[9]

This essay is prompted by the debates surrounding Wojtek's work. It focuses on Wojtek's design in the broader context of modern art in Salzburg and revisits some of the points raised in the report of the historical commission. Yet where the latter sought to differentiate Wojtek's earlier commitment to modernism from her subsequent turn to reactionary politics, this chapter argues that these two aspects were more entwined than is often acknowledged. Indeed, I suggest that the example of Wojtek's design for the Festival is symptomatic of much wider entanglements between conservatism and reactionary politics in the environment of the Salzburg Festival and interwar Austria more generally.

Branding the Salzburg Festival: A Modern Visual Identity

In 1928, the commission of the Salzburg Festival opened a competition to find a new poster design for its advertisement. Wojtek's entry was part of a group of late submissions by former students of Vienna's

---

7 Wolfgang Born, "Nachwuchs im Kunstgewerbe," 18.
8 Karl Springenschmied and Poldi Wojtek, *Eine wahre Geschichte: Worte und Bilder von zwei Deutschen aus dem Auslande*.
9 The panel discussion "Art & Ethos" took place at the Great Hall of Salzburg University on August 12, 2021. Available online: https://www.salzburgerfestspiele.at/en/p/panel-discussion-art-ethos (accessed July 31, 2023).

Figure 9.2 Karl Springenschmied and Poldi Mühlmann, *Eine wahre Geschichte. Worte und Bilder von zwei Deutschen aus dem Auslande.* Stuttgart: Frank'sche Verlagsbuchhandlung, 1937. Austrian National Library. Karl Springenschmied and Leopldine Wojtek-Mühlmann © OOA-S 2023.

School of Applied Arts, encouraged to take part by the commission. Her design was ranked second after a (now lost) work by Hanns Erich Köhler (1905–1983), but through personal intervention by the head of the Festival's marketing bureau and, later, Wojtek's husband, Kajetan Mühlmann (1898–1958), her entry emerged as the winning design.[10] The poster in question was a simple graphic composition, which combines key elements of the Festival's identity: on the top left, a red and white flag represents the colors of the federal state of Salzburg. The Flag also functions as a stage curtain, behind which a classical theater mask emerges. Finally, at the front of the picture, Salzburg's historical

---

10 Rathkolb et al., *The Salzburg Festival*, 12–13.

landmark, the Fortress Hohensalzburg, anchors the poster geographically in the town and its long history.

Anita Kern pointed out in her report on Wojtek and the design that the transformation of the poster into a logo was an unusual practice, but that its simple design lent itself to easy adjustment to forge a coherent visual identity for the Festival.[11] By the late 1920s, the Festival had gained growing international publicity. In 1926, the conductor Peter Bechert noted in an extended review of the event for the *Musical Times*, for example, that "what began modestly under the name of the Salzburg Festival five years ago [...] has since developed into a big and apparently firmly established summer institution."[12] As part of this international attention, it became increasingly important to give the Festival a recognizable brand, which could stand in for a new Austrian identity overall as modern, yet that was also rooted in tradition.[13]

Wojtek's design encompassed these aspects and provided a layout that could easily be adapted for wider use, offering a sense of coherence that the Festival has drawn on up to the present: in 2013, the Innsbruck design company Circus remodeled the poster so that the white lines intersecting the golden background at the top, initially used as a text line, came to represent staves in reference to music as another significant aspect of the Festival.[14] Such easy adjustments, enabled by a pared-down visual language, allowed a smooth transition from a poster to a logo when Wojtek's work was announced as the winning design: as the original gold background was too expensive for printing, for example, it was replaced by a matte ochre, while the shading and text from the original were reduced to emphasize the design's main elements. As the other entries to the poster competition have been lost, it is impossible to compare them. When asked about her competitors in an interview in 1978, Wojtek said that the other entries were "overly Salzburgian motifs. Mine was not so Alpine, it was [...] the most austere and therefore also the most effective and as a motif it was quite neutral."[15] Aside from the artist's personal connections to the selection committee, which seems to have had some influence on her success, Wojtek's comment indicates that the Festival's marketing bureau also chose her entry

---

11 Rathkolb et al., *The Salzburg Festival*, 114. See also Anita Kern, *Österreichisches Grafikdesign im 20. Jahrhundert*.
12 Peter Bechert, "The Salzburg Festival," 941.
13 On nation branding in Austria, see Oliver Kühschelm, "Promoting the Nation in Austria and Switzerland"; also Steinberg, *Austria as Theater and Ideology*.
14 Rathkolb et al., *The Salzburg Festival*, 38.
15 Interview with Wojtek, *Informationen* 11 (May 1978), 21, qtd. in Rathkolb et al., *The Salzburg Festival*, 115.

because it paid equal attention to modern design as to Salzburg's historical roots. This approach was not only central to Wojtek's work, but also reflective of the development of an independent scene of Salzburg art and design, which was closely tied to the Salzburg Festival throughout the interwar years.

Modernism, Opportunism, Artistic Networks

A key figure in this respect was Wojtek's future husband, Kajetan, or Kai, Mühlmann, as well as the artist's association *Der Sonderbund*, which had close ties to the Salzburg Festival. An art historian and prolific writer about Salzburg art and architecture, Mühlmann became the head of the Festival's marketing bureau in 1927.[16] Today, Mühlmann is mainly known for the crimes he committed under National Socialism: as an SS officer, he was involved in the looting of art in Poland and the Netherlands, including the Mannheimer collection, which was to become part of Adolf Hitler's Führermuseum in the Upper Austrian town Linz.[17] When exactly he became a party member is uncertain, but Rathkolb notes that when Mühlmann gained his position with the Salzburg Festival, he was known as a well-connected Social Democrat.[18] Indeed, this turn from Social Democracy to National Socialism was far from unusual in early 1930s Austria. Especially after the crushing of the February Uprising in 1934, many supporters of the Social Democratic Party became radicalized and turned to the illegal Communist and National Socialist parties.[19] In Wojtek and Mühlmann's case, the report of the Historical Commission implies that political opportunism played a significant role in their support for National Socialism, even though Mühlmann had already made contact with the party when it still operated clandestinely in Austria before the country's annexation to the Third Reich in 1938.

It should briefly be noted at this point that support for National Socialism was well established in the environment of the Salzburg Festival by the early 1930s. On Adolf Hitler's birthday in April 1933, for example, Deutsche Weihestunde ("German Hour of Consecration") celebrations were held in the Great Festival Hall, organized by the Kampfbund für

---

16 For example, see Kai Mühlmann, "Neue Kunst in Salzburg," or Kai Mühlmann, "Anton Faistauers neue Fresken in St Peter."
17 Jonathan Petropoulos, "Art Historians and Nazi Plunder"; Birgit Schwarz, *Hitlers Museum: Die Fotoalben Gemäldegalerie Linz*, 57.
18 Rathkolb et al., *The Salzburg Festival*, 19.
19 Helmut Wohnout, "Dreieck der Gewalt," 86; Rudolf Ardelt and Hans Hautmann, *Arbeiterschaft und Nationalsozialismus in Österreich*, 52.

Deutsche Kultur.[20] After the National Socialist Party was prohibited by the authoritarian government of Engelbert Dollfuß and his Fatherland Front party in June 1933, the National Socialists continued as a clandestine organization who actively worked against the Austrian state. The Salzburg Festival's strong presentation as a bastion of *Austrian* German culture led to an official boycott by cultural figures who openly supported the National Socialists, but several others, like Mühlmann, toed the line between the two factions. Thus, Nationalist Socialist supporters operated on multiple levels in 1930s Salzburg. On a personal level, the line between official "anti-Austrian" proclamations and other conservative views was much more blurred and explains how opportunists in the cultural sector, such as Mühlmann—but also Wojtek—could move between the seemingly oppositional National Socialist and Fatherland Front parties. This "flexibility," in turn, allowed them to build careers that began in the 1920s and seamlessly continued throughout the political frictions of the 1930s until the Anschluss.[21]

When Mühlmann took up his post as the head of the Salzburg Festival's marketing bureau in 1927, he was a committed defender of a historically rooted modernism—precisely in keeping with the ideals of the Salzburg Festival. Together with his stepbrother Josef, twenty years Kajetan's senior and an established art historian in his own right, Mühlmann had previously encouraged attempts of bringing modern art to Salzburg. Considering the wider networks their aims built on and the way Wojtek was implied within them sheds light on the wider Salzburg art scene in the interwar years, whose modernity was intrinsically tied to conservative and religious thought in line with the town's history.

In 1919, the painters Felix Albrecht Harta (1884–1967) and Anton Faistauer (1887–1930) founded the artistic group Der Wassermann ("Aquarius"), which focused on a consolidation of Salzburg's identity in the visual arts. One of the group's main aims was to establish a de-centralized Austrian culture in reaction to the collapse of the empire and focused on reclaiming a national identity. Seeing Vienna as an overbearing Habsburg remnant, the group's main figures were convinced that renewal could only take place outside it.[22]

---

20 Gert Kerschbaumer, "Kunst im Getriebe der Politik, 1933–1938–1945," 145.
21 On the role of continuity in Austrian culture, see Matthias Boeckl, "'Kulturnation Österreich': Bemerkungen zu ausgewählten Kunstereignissen 1934 bis 1948."
22 I discuss this process in greater detail in "Beyond the Provincial: Entanglements of Regional Modernism in Interwar Central Europe."

In the catalog of Der Wassermann's first exhibition in 1919, Josef Mühlmann explained, "the intention of this artist's association is not to cling on to a small country narrow-mindedly, but to forge links with artists in foreign countries. Contemporary art is a cosmopolitan art, directed towards all of humanity rather than just one people."[23] Following this lead in his own way, Mühlmann's proclamations of the group's cosmopolitanism were closely tied to Salzburg's identity as a baroque city deeply tied to Catholicism. A highlight of the exhibition was the juxtaposition between medieval sculptures and contemporary works, forging continuation on the basis of Christian iconography, including juxtapositions between Faistauer's votive altar, commissioned by the regional government.[24] Eva Michel has suggested that this was part of a legitimization process achieved by a visible genealogy to historical precedents.[25] Yet, the focus on Christian subject matter also defined the specific function of Salzburg as an alternative modern art. "Cosmopolitanism" in line with the exhibition set-up suggests affinity to Hofmannsthal's definition of the term, which he principally understood as a "German virtue" and conceived of in German-nationalist terms.[26] By extension, Der Wassermann promoted a modern art as embedded in the nationalist cosmopolitanism that the Salzburg Festival embodied as the locus for a new Austrian culture.

When the Wassermann dissolved after Harta's return to Vienna, Faistauer followed up in July 1925 with the founding of the Sonderbund Österreichischer Künstler in Salzburg (Special Association of Austrian Artists in Salzburg). This new association continued aims to promote contemporary art and modern culture in Salzburg with an even closer link to tradition and Catholicism, based on Faistauer's ideals.[27] The group laid particular emphasis on supporting young artists and designers "both in moral as in material terms."[28] With personal connections to figures such as Kajetan Mühlmann, it began to work more closely with the Salzburg Festival, which, after all, had already manifested a strong (Austrian) identity between modernity and tradition in music and theater. This offered a range of opportunities for Sonderbund artists to become involved in the consolidation of the Festival's ideals in arts, design, and architecture. Aside from former Wassermann members,

---

23 Josef Mühlmann, "Introduction to the exhibition," 5.
24 Josef Mühlmann, "Wassermannausstellung: Geistige Auffassung der Malerei," 2; Michel, "Inventing Tradition," 100.
25 Michel, "Inventing Tradition," 100.
26 Steinberg, *Austria as Theatre and Ideology*, 23.
27 Anton Faistauer, *Neue Malerei in Österreich*.
28 "Sonderbund Österreichischer Künstler in Salzburg," *Salzburger Wacht*, July 28, 1925, 4.

including Emma Schlangenhausen, Georg Jung, Maria Cyrenius, and Franz Schrempf, the new group, and its collaboration with the organizers of the Salzburg Festival, also included a number of new aspiring, conservative modernists: the writer Karl Heinrich Waggerl (1897–1973), the ceramicist Hilde Heger (1899–1998), and a young student of Vienna's School of Applied Arts, Poldi Wojtek.[29]

A Modern Salzburg Designer

Born into a German nationalist family in Brno/Brünn, today the Czech Republic, Wojtek attended a school for girls in Salzburg and, after training at the Professional School of Ceramics in Znojmo/Znaim (1919–1922), in what was then Czechoslovakia, went on to study at the School of Applied Arts in Vienna, which she completed in 1926. Whilst a student there, Wojtek studied the theory of ornamental form with Franz Čižek (1865–1946) and attended architecture classes taught by Josef Hoffmann (1870–1956). At this point in time, the School of Applied Arts had close ties to commercial luxury design with the Viennese Workshops (Wiener Werkstätte) and was home to experimental teaching practices and painting, through Čižek's efforts. In both branches, several of the school's female students, such as Erika Giovanna Klien (1900–1957), Vally Wieselthier (1895–1945), and Mathilde Flögl (1893–1958), became successful artists and designers and were counted among the most progressive representatives of Viennese modernism at the time.[30] While the careers and fate of these women, many of whom were of Jewish origin, seem a world away from that of Wojtek, they not only had the same artistic education, but also developed their careers in parallel.

Klien, for example, who studied at the school at the same time as Wojtek, was a prominent representative of the short-lived art movement known as Viennese Kinetism.[31] Like Wojtek, she moved to Salzburg after graduating, where she taught at the Elizabeth Duncan School until emigrating to New York in 1929. Klien had quickly become frustrated with life in Salzburg, complaining about its conservatism. A particularly telling example of the artist's negative experiences in the city can be found in the *Kleßheim Courier*—drawn diaries, which Klien would send to her

---

29 Nikolaus Schaffer, "Kurzer Höhenflug und langsames Stranden."
30 See *Die Frauen der Wiener Werkstätte / Women Artists of the Wiener Werkstätte*, eds. Christoph Thun-Hohenstein, Anne-Katrin Rossberg, and Elisabeth Schmuttermeier.
31 See *Viennese Kineticism: Modernism in Motion*, eds. Gerald Bast, Agnes Husslein-Arco, Harald Krejci, and Patrick Werkner.

Shadow Sides of Modernism 269

Figure 9.3 Erika Giovanna Klien, *Kleßheim Courier: Skandal-Nachrichten, Salzburg, 12 February 1927*. © Wien Museum, Vienna. Photo: Birgit and Peter Kainz.

friends in Vienna (Figure 9.3).[32] In a letter dated February 12, 1927, her readers are informed that "the editor of the *Kleßheim Courier* has joined the Union of Fine Artists in Salzburg and attends weekly nude drawing classes." Below, the letter shows one of these lessons, Klien sitting at the front, drawing a nude in the Kinetist style she developed in Vienna, while another student, himself having drawn a traditional nude, looks at her work incredulously. Fading out behind them, a group of figures hail insults at the artist and her work: "Defilement of Art!," "Idiocy!," "Bogus!" In Klien's experience, then, Salzburg undoubtedly represented a place hostile to modernist art.

Indeed, as one of Austria's more progressive artists, Klien's experimental style would have been met with reservations, especially after

---

32 Birgit Kirchmayer, "'Entwurzelt in diesem steinernen Meer von Wolkenkratzern.'"

the dissolution of the Wassermann. Art historian Nikolaus Schaffer has noted, after Harta's departure from Salzburg, the Sonderbund took a rather more "dogmatic" direction under Faistauer's lead, championed by Kajetan Mühlmann.[33]

In contrast to Klien's struggles with a growing conservatism in Salzburg, Wojtek's career flourished in the city from the mid-1920s onwards. While still a student in Vienna, Wojtek joined the Sonderbund, which—in line with its promise to support budding young artists—launched her career as a modern Salzburg artist working within the orbit of the Salzburg Festival. The wide-ranging training the artist received in Vienna thus formed the basis of a career which spanned different facets of artistic production. In this light, too, Wojtek's success as a graduate of the Academy of Applied Arts adds significantly more nuance to the established image of the *Kunstgewerblerin* (modern craftswoman) as a progressive figure challenging established conventions.[34] For even though Wojtek had the same training as her more progressive peers, followed by her successful career, the artist's politics could not have differed more from that of her fellow students, such as Klien. The example of Wojtek thus sheds new light on the complexities of Austrian interwar design, the story of which rarely considers how the education artists received in the capital was adjusted and redeveloped in response to different local conditions—and political ideals. Wojtek's poster design for the Festival, in line with a range of other works she produced in the 1920s and 1930s, shows how the artist adjusted her training as a modern designer to fit the specific conditions she found in Salzburg.

Becoming a member of the Sonderbund was essential to Wojtek's career as an artist deeply involved with the Salzburg Festival. Already in 1926, the year of her graduation, she was part of a group of artists that helped to execute a monumental fresco for the entry hall of the House for Mozart (formerly known as the Small Festival Hall), designed by Faistauer. The building itself had been remodeled in 1926 by the architect Clemens Holzmeister (1886–1983), a leading figure of Austrian interwar architecture who worked closely with Faistauer and his associates on several projects related to the Festival.[35] Wojtek participated in the realization of several of these different projects, all related to the public fashioning of the Festival—and Salzburg—as a representative of a new Austrian culture.

One such project was the above-mentioned fresco, which covered over 300 square meters of the foyer, including scenes from the Festival's

---

33 Schaffer, "Kurzer Höhenflug und langsames Stranden," 142.
34 See *Die Frauen der Wiener Werkstätte / Women Artists of the Wiener Werkstätte*.
35 Matthew Rampley, "Modernism and Cultural Politics in Inter-war Austria."

most prominent play, *Der Jedermann*, and religious scenes, as well as portraits by prominent figures related to the Festival, including Holzmeister, Faistauer himself, as well as the governor of Salzburg, Franz Rehrl. Wojtek was one of forty assistants who helped to realize this monumental project in a sgraffito technique, which the artist would later use for several other fresco designs of her own.[36] In 1930 she decorated Mühlmann's Salzburg apartment with dainty ornaments, for example, photographs of which were published in the arts magazine *Österreichische Kunst*.[37]

While fresco painting would be one of Wojtek's most successful trades, she also contributed to numerous other design projects. For example, she designed plant and flower ornaments for the tapestries in the Festival Hall, assisting Kolig and Robin Christian Andersen.[38] Thanks to Mühlmann, Wojtek's contributions were frequently mentioned in the press, even when she only took on a supporting role, as in the case of the frescos and the tapestries. In the subsequent years, Wojtek accepted numerous commissions in Salzburg, including several fresco paintings, such as the columns for the city's new postal hall (1930), which have now been lost.[39] Aside from architectural decoration, Wojtek was also an active in the Gewerbeförderungsinstitut (Institute for the Promotion of the Industrial Arts), where she designed exhibition posters and decorative souvenirs in the 1930s.[40]

Modern Design, the Salzburg Festival, and Tourism

Through the links to the Sonderbund and the press office of the Salzburg Festival, therefore, Wojtek became a prolific member of Salzburg's cultural scene. As a designer, artist, and art teacher, she would continue her manifold activities throughout the 1930s, as well as the years of the Second World War, featuring regularly in newspaper reports.[41] From the late 1920s until the Anschluss in 1938, reports and essays in different magazines also give a clear indication that the art and design practices she developed in relation to the Salzburg Festival closely related to the marketing of Salzburg as a touristic region. The conservative modernism she represented thereby stands in relation to a much wider—and barely

---

36 *Österreichische Kunst: Monatsheft für bildende Kunst* 1(9) (July 1930), 19.
37 *Österreichische Kunst: Monatsheft für bildende Kunst* 1(9) (July 1930), 19.
38 Kai Mühlmann, "Die Gobelins im Salzburger Festspielhaus," 12.
39 Julius Leisching, "Salzburg's derzeitige Kunst," 21.
40 "Geschmackvolle Reiseandenken."
41 For example, Kunz, "Reiseandenken und Fremdenartikel"; *Österreichische Kunst* 5 (1938), 6; *Österreichische Kunst* 8 (1933), 31; *Volksfreund* (January 9, 1932), 6; "Keramisches Schaffen in Oberdonau," *Oberdonau-Zeitung*, April 3, 1943, 4.

explored—phenomenon in interwar Austrian culture: the connection between modern design and tourism, and their importance in the manifestation of Austrian identity. Wojtek's logo for the Festival represents one example of this; her design for a Festival guide in 1928, another.

Aside from supporting the poster competition from which Wojtek's logo originated, Mühlmann also introduced elaborate guides to the Festival, which tied the event to Austrian tourism. In fact, Mühlmann also represented Salzburg in meetings of the national tourist board in the 1930s, showing how his—and by extension Wojtek's—role in the promotion of conservative modernism even went beyond the context of the Festival.[42] In the same year that she won the competition, Wojtek was responsible for the guide's layout and graphic design (Figure 9.4).

Figure 9.4 Kajetan Mühlmann and Poldi Wojtek, *Salzburger Festspielführer*. Salzburg: Salzburger Festspielhausgemeinde, 1928. Austrian National Library. Karl Springenschmied and Leopldine Wojtek-Mühlmann. © OOA-S 2023.

---

42 "Tagesneuigkeiten – Fremdenverkehrstagung in Vöcklabruck," 4.

Shadow Sides of Modernism 273

The guide opens with a quote by Hofmannsthal, which emphasizes Austrian tradition rather than modernity:

The state of Salzburg is the heart of the heart of Europe. It is situated halfway between Switzerland and the Slavic countries, halfway between northern Germany and Lombardian Italy; it is in the middle of South and North, between mountain and lowlands, between the heroic and the idyllic, its architecture lies between the urban and the rural, the ancient and the contemporary, Baroque nobility and the lovely, eternal vernacular: Mozart is the precise expression of all of that. The middle of Europe has no more beautiful space, and this is where Mozart had to be born.[43]

The following pages in the Festival guide visualize this "Salzburg charm" with numerous photographs and prints of artworks by Sonderbund members, including Faistauer and Waggerl. The content of the publication is strikingly conservative. It focuses on historical Salzburg and its sacral architecture, its untouched rural landscapes, as well as touristic information to emphasize Salzburg's excellent connection to other holiday destinations in Austria, Bavaria, and Italy. Wojtek's layout, however, frames the guide in a modern light, emphasizing the interplay between modernity and tradition so central to the ideology of the Festival.

On the cover, Wojtek used a capitalized serif-font type in a simple design, in which thick red lines in an otherwise black-and white layout appear as variations on the Salzburg flag, which also features on the logo. At the center of the page, a photograph by Bruno Reiffenstein (1868–1951) depicts the famous *Felsenreitschule* (literally, "rock riding school") theater venue. The square on the photograph is empty, framed by a rounded archway. Adding symbolic significance to the location itself by incorporating this photograph, Wojtek applied a similar approach to the guide's design as for the poster/logo. As the two closely correspond with each other in style, they underline the aim of giving a specific—modern—visual identity to the Festival without resorting to Alpine "kitsch." At the same time, the images and advertising materials used for the guide stand in tension with this modernity, instead forging an image of a rural Austria as an untouched archaic place, whose modernity lies only in comfortable amenities of the hotel industry and accessible transport links.

---

43 Hofmannsthal, "Salzburg die Festspielstadt."

Moving beyond Wojtek's poster/logo design as a single instance in which she supported the branding efforts for the Festival, the guide overall shows the integrative efforts that arose from a collaboration between Mühlmann and the Sonderbund artists. Given the various projects she was involved in, Wojtek represents a model example for a different kind of modernity in Austrian interwar art within this nexus, which merged a growing political conservatism with aims for artistic renewal. Not least, the guide to the Festival indicates that the moderate form of modernism artists such as Wojtek constructed also offered a marketable image for tourism, which helped to tie the Festival to this important source of income for Austria's interwar economy.

Facets of Austrian Modern Art and Design

The diverse nature of Wojtek's contributions to art and design illustrates the Salzburg cultural scene, which straddled modernity and tradition: though Wojtek was clearly aware of contemporary developments, referencing, as Kern has pointed out, elements of the New Objectivity and Marie and Otto and Neurath's Isotype signage system, even her most experimental work, such as the *Posthalle* frescos and the logo for the Festival, only does so in an attenuated manner. Yet rather than seeing this as an augury of her later work under National Socialism, this kind of modernism—"moderately modern through and through," as one reviewer called it at the time—was prevalent among most Salzburg artists at the time.[44] Even Faistauer and the architect Clemens Holzmeister, the most eminent figures associated with modern art and architecture in Salzburg, embraced a conservative form of modernism, whose main aim was to reconnect with tradition and spirituality.

As for Wojtek, both her training and her diverse work from the 1920s resemble that of many other female designers who trained at the School of Applied Arts, even though her politics distinguish her from more progressive women artists, such as Klien, who are usually the focus of research today. Simultaneously a modern artist who trained alongside some of Austria's most progressive cultural figures at the time and a reactionary figure who, after 1938, capitalized on the persecution of former colleagues, Wojtek and her work highlight some of the contradictions of modern Austrian art and design between the wars.[45] In relation to the circumstances under which the logo of the Salzburg Festival

---

44 -ei-, "Ein neuer deutschösterreichischer Künstlerbund."
45 Wojtek took over the studio of the Jewish artist Helene von Taussig (1879–1942), who was murdered in the Izbica Ghetto in 1942.

was created and selected, Wojtek's diverse artistic engagements and her wide networks in interwar Salzburg emphasize once more that the relationship between modernist-progressive and conservative-reactionary factions in interwar Austria was rather more complicated than one might like to admit.

There is no doubt that the logo represents the most important aspect of the Festival's visual identity. Not only that: tied to Wojtek's design for the Festival guide, it was part of an effort to construct a distinct image of the Festival in line with modern advertising strategies. Rather fittingly, the logo and its continued use also stand for the conflicted histories of Austrian modern art and design and the complex narratives behind them. Beyond asking whether the logo should still be in use today, therefore, it also raises the question what further blind spots and misconceptions of Austrian interwar art ought to be addressed in order to forge a more nuanced picture.

Bibliography

Ardelt, Rudolf, and Hans Hautmann. *Arbeiterschaft und Nationalsozialismus in Österreich*. Vienna and Zürich: Europaverlag, 1990.
Bast, Gerald, Agnes Husslein-Arco, Harald Krejci, and Patrick Werkner, eds. *Viennese Kineticism: Modernism in Motion*. Vienna: Edition Angewandte, 2011.
Bechert, Peter. "The Salzburg Festival." *The Musical Times* 67(1004) (1926), 941.
Boeckl, Matthias. "'Kulturnation Österreich': Bemerkungen zu ausgewählten Kunstereignissen 1934 bis 1948." In Patrick Werkner, ed., *Kunst in Österreich 1945–1995*, 32–42. Vienna: WUV Universitätsverlag, 1996.
Born, Wolfgang. "Nachwuchs im Kunstgewerbe." *Die Bühne* 239 (1929), 18–19.
Breitwieser, Sabine. "How Modern or Anti-Modern Is (Was) Europe?" In *Anti:modern: Salzburg inmitten von Europa zwischen Tradition und Erneuerung*, 217–25. Salzburg: Museum der Moderne; München: Hirmer Verlag, 2016.
-ei-. "Ein neuer deutschösterreichischer Künstlerbund." *Neue Freie Presse*, September 15, 1919, 2.
Faistauer, Anton. *Neue Malerei in Österreich: Betrachtungen eines Malers*. Vienna: Amalthea, 1923.
"Geschmackvolle Reiseandenken." *Profil: Österreichische Monatsschrift für bildende Kunst* 6 (1935), 281–3.
Habsburg-Halbgebauer, Stefanie. "Aufbruch zu neuen Ufern: Umbruch von Tradition zur Moderne in der Kunst." In Oskar Dohle and Thomas Mitterecker, eds., *Salzburg 1918–1919: Vom Kronland zum Bundesland*, 425–40. Vienna: Böhlau, 2018.
Hofmannsthal, Hugo von. "Salzburg die Festspielstadt." *Salzburger Festspielführer* (1928), n.p.
"Keramisches Schaffen in Oberdonau." *Oberdonau-Zeitung*, April 3, 1943, 4.
Kern, Anita. *Österreichisches Grafikdesign im 20. Jahrhundert*. Salzburg: Pustet, 2008.
Kerschbaumer, Gert. "Kunst im Getriebe der Politik, 1933–1938–1945." In Salzburger Kunstverein, ed., *150 Jahre Salzburger Kunstverein: Kunst und Öffentlichkeit 1844–1994*, 145–69. Salzburg: Salzburger Kunstverein, 1994.

Kirchmayer, Birgit. "'Entwurzelt in diesem steinernen Meer von Wolkenkratzern': Die österreichische Künstlerin Erika Giovanna Klien und ihre Briefe aus Amerika in den 1920er und 1930er Jahren als auto/biographische Quelle." *L'Homme Zeitschrift für feministische Geschichtswissenschaft* 26(2) (2015), 85–101.

Kühschelm, Oliver. "Promoting the Nation in Austria and Switzerland: A Pre-History of Nation Branding." In Ulrich Ermann and Klaus-Jürgen Hermanik, eds., *Branding the Nation, the Place, the Product*, 143–60. New York: Routledge, 2018.

Kunz, Otto. "Reiseandenken und Fremdenartikel." *WBS – Vierteljahrschrift des Werkbund Salzburg* (April 1935), 16–26.

Lefebvre, Henri. "Theses on Modernity." In Benjamin H. D. Buchloh, Serge Gilbaut, and David Solkin, eds., *Modernism and Modernity: The Vancouver Conference Papers*, 6. Halifax: The Press of Nova Scotia College of Art and Design, 2004.

Leisching, Julius. "Salzburg's derzeitige Kunst." *Österreichische Kunst* 1(9) (July 1930), 21.

Michel, Eva. *Inventing Tradition: Die Rezeption der Alten Meister und das "Barocke" in der österreichischen Malerei des 20. Jahrhunderts – Topos und künstlerische Strategie*. Disssertation, U of Vienna, 2009.

Mühlmann, Josef. "Einführung in die Ausstellung." *1. Ausstellung der Neuen Vereinigung Bildender Künstler Salzburgs "Der Wasserman": Künstlerhaus Salzburg im August 1919a*. Salzburg: Kiesel, 1919. 5–8.

Mühlmann, Josef. "Wassermannausstellung: Geistige Auffassung der Malerei." *Salzburger Chronik*, August 24, 1919b, 2.

Mühlmann, Kai. "Anton Faistauers neue Fresken in St Peter." *Salzburger Chronik für Stadt und Land*, October 8, 1926a, 2.

Mühlmann, Kai. "Die Gobelins im Salzburger Festspielhaus." *Die Bühne* 95 (1926b), 12.

Mühlmann, Kai. "Neue Kunst in Salzburg: Architektur und Kunstgewerbe." *Österreichische Kunst* 9 (1930), 12–31.

Petropoulos, Jonathan. "Art Historians and Nazi Plunder." *New England Review* 21(1) (2000), 5–30.

"Poldi Wojtek: Chronologie einer Erinnerungslücke." *Memory Gaps*. Available online: https://www.memorygaps.eu (accessed June 16, 2023).

Rampley, Matthew. "Modernism and Cultural Politics in Inter-war Austria: The Case of Clemens Holzmeister." *Architectural History* 64 (2021), 347–78.

Rathkolb, Oliver, Anita Kern, and Margarethe Lasinger. *The Salzburg Festival's Logo and Its Designer Poldi Wojtek*. Salzburg: Salzburger Festspielfonds, 2020. Available online: https://www.salzburgerfestspiele.at/cms/wp-content/uploads/2020/11/das-logo-der-salzburger-festspiele-und-seine-gestalterin-poldi-wojtek.pdf (accessed June 16, 2023).

Salzburger Kunstverein, ed. *150 Jahre Salzburger Kunstverein: Kunst und Öffentlichkeit 1844–1994*. Salzburg, 1994.

Schaffer, Nikolaus. "Kurzer Höhenflug und langsames Stranden: Oppositionen innerhalb des Kunstvereins: 'Wassermann' und 'Sonderbund'." In Salzburger Kunstverein, ed., *150 Jahre Salzburger Kunstverein*, 115–43.

Schaffer, Nikolaus. "Weltkrieg und Künstlerfehden Salzburger Kunst und Erster Weltkrieg – eine nüchterne Bilanz." *Mitt(h)eilungen der Gesellschaft für Salzburger Landeskunde*. Salzburg, 2014/15. 541–69.

Schwarz, Birgit. *Hitlers Museum: Die Fotoalben Gemäldegalerie Linz – Dokumente zum "Führermuseum."* Vienna, Cologne, Weimar: Böhlau, 2004.

Secklehner, Julia. "Beyond the Provincial: Entanglements of Regional Modernism in Interwar Central Europe." In Shona Kallestrup, Magdalena Kunińska, Mihnea Alexandru Mihail, Anna Adashinskaya, and Cosmin Minea, eds, *Periodisation in the Art Historiographies of Central and Eastern Europe*, 214–29. London and New York: Routledge, 2022.

"Sonderbund Österreichischer Künstler in Salzburg." *Salzburger Wacht*, July 28, 1925, 4.

Springenschmied, Karl, and Poldi Wojtek (Mühlmann). *Eine wahre Geschichte: Worte und Bilder von zwei Deutschen aus dem Auslande*. Stuttgart: Frank'sche Verlagsbuchhandlung, 1937.

Steinberg, Michael P. *Austria as Theater and Ideology: The Meaning of the Salzburg Festival*. Cornell: Ithaca UP, 1990.

"Tagesneuigkeiten – Fremdenverkehrstagung in Vöcklabruck." *Salzburger Chronik für Stadt und Land*, December 15, 1927, 4.

Thun-Hohenstein, Christoph, Anne-Katrin Rossberg, and Elisabeth Schmuttermeier, eds. *Die Frauen der Wiener Werkstätte/Women Artists of the Wiener Werkstätte*. Basel: Birkhäuser: 2020.

Wohnout, Helmut. "Dreieck der Gewalt." In Günther Schefbeck, ed., *Österreich 1934: Vorgeschichte–Ereignisse–Wirkungen*, 78–90. Vienna: Verlag für Geschichte und Politik, 2004.

Part IV

Eyes on Salzburg: Salzburg as Other

Ten Jewish Identities and Antisemitism in Salzburg after 1918

Helga Embacher

"If I wanted my sons to get a very religious education, I would not have moved to Salzburg." With these words, Daniel Bonyhadi—born in 1861 in Hungary, where he himself got a very religious education—justified his new Jewish tradition, whereas his visiting brother was shocked that the Bonyhadi boys were eating without wearing a yarmulke. Indeed, Jews came to Salzburg in search of new economic opportunities and did not expect an Orthodox community, which many regarded as old fashioned anyway. They made the effort to assimilate into their bourgeois environment and the bourgeois lifestyle became an important part of their identity.

Based on interviews with a number of Jews who were expelled from Salzburg in 1938,[1] I will concentrate on the question how it was possible to live a Jewish life as a tiny minority in a non-Jewish society in an increasingly antisemitic political climate. Thus, it is necessary to give a short overview of the history of the economically successful Jewish community as well as the history of modern antisemitism and its Salzburg specifics. It also must be emphasized that the Jewish population of Salzburg (the city; only a very few lived in the state) never numbered more than 0.1 percent of the entire population, as compared to 9 percent in Vienna. Although a few families were very successful, the Jewish

---

1   When the City and Province of Salzburg invited former Salzburg Jews to visit in 1993, Albert Lichtblau and I conducted numerous interviews, collected some autobiographies, and got new addresses for expelled Jews who refused to visit Austria or were too old to travel. Hans Pasch (born in 1908 and living in Denver, CO), Erwin Bonyhadi, who lived in San Francisco, and Nina Lieberman and her sister Gabriella Margules (both USA) could be interviewed over the following years. Most of the interviews have been published in Ellmauer, Embacher, and Lichtblau, eds., *Geduldet, geschmäht und vertrieben*.

minority as a whole played only an insignificant role in Salzburg's economic and political life.

The Founding of the Salzburg Jewish Community in the Late Nineteenth Century[2]

In 1498, Archbishop Leonard von Keutschach had expelled the Jews from Salzburg. After that time, no Jew was permitted to settle in the province for almost four hundred years.[3] After the constitution (*Staatsgrundgesetz*) was passed in 1867, however, Jews could no longer be prevented from settling. In 1873, as an upshot of liberalism, Albert Pollak was the first Jew to be accorded civil rights.[4] As was typical of the Jewish migration pattern in the Austro-Hungarian monarchy, the first wave of Jews that reached Salzburg migrated from the border area of Austria and West Hungary, from Bohemia and Moravia. They were already accustomed to the German language and had abandoned Orthodox Jewish tradition. It was not until the end of the century that Jews arrived from Eastern Europe. Though they came from poor families, most of them were already familiar with German culture and had decided to give up Orthodoxy. Not only in Salzburg but also in Linz, Graz, and Innsbruck, family networks formed the basis for Jewish migration and the founding of a Jewish community; as soon as the founders could make a living, relatives followed. As a result of this family migration, the family's network stretched across Austria, Bohemia, as well as Germany.[5] The Schwarz family, for example, not only owned the largest department store in Salzburg but was also co-owner of important department stores in Linz, Graz, and Vienna. Relatives owned a department store in Innsbruck.[6]

At the turn of the century, the majority of Salzburg Jews was able to live a bourgeois lifestyle. As for their overall social structure, most

---

2 See Embacher, "Jewish Identities and Acculturation in the Province of Salzburg in the Shadow of Antisemtism"; and Embacher, "Die Salzburger jüdische Gemeinde von ihrer Neugründung im Liberalismus bis zur Gegenwart."
3 See Altmann, *Geschichte der Juden in Stadt und Land Salzburg*.
4 Haas and Koller, "Jüdisches Gemeinschaftsleben in Salzburg," 33.
5 Friedrich Pasch, for example, had worked as a shoe salesman in Prague and Vienna. Since Salzburg still did not have a modern shoe store, he saw it as the ideal place to go into business for himself. As soon as he became successful, his brother opened his own shoe store in Innsbruck. Both were supplied by the shoe factory of their relatives in Bohemia. See video interview with Hans Pasch, conducted by Helga Embacher, Albert Lichtblau, and Karl Rothauer, Denver CO, 2002.
6 Embacher, "Exil als neue Heimat," 439–45.

of them were small merchants and retailers. An exception was Ignaz Glaser, who bought the assets of a bankrupt glass factory in Bürmoos in 1881. Thanks to his investment, the small village experienced an economic boom.[7] In 1900, the Jewish community included 199 members; by 1910, the number had grown to 285.

With the growth of the Jewish community, religious facilities were established to enable members to lead a Jewish life. In 1892, a Jewish cemetery could be built in Aigen despite the protests of local residents. In 1901, the synagogue on Lasserstraße was dedicated, although it had been difficult to find a Christian builder to do the job, and the municipal building department had also initially tried to prevent this project. Dr. Adolf Altmann, the city's first rabbi, was installed in 1907. Altmann was born in 1879 in Zips, Hungary, a linguistic enclave of the German language. As well as finishing rabbinical school, he also studied philosophy, history, and German literature, and thus also became the community chronicler.[8] His successor (and last rabbi before the Holocaust), Dr. David Margules, also represented a liberal Jewish tradition. He fled his Orthodox Jewish Community in Galicia to get a secular education at the University of Vienna and tried very hard to combine the practice of Jewish religion with German culture and his love for theater, opera, and the graphic arts.[9]

Despite the economic success and integration of the Jewish community into *German Kultur*, Jews were confronted with antisemitism long before the Anschluss. After the long depression of the 1870s, liberalism in Austria was displaced by an aggressive German nationalism after the 1880s. In places like Linz, Graz, and Salzburg, young German Nationalists took over the city council, as well as the liberal clubs, and dominated cultural life.[10] Antisemitism was the lowest common dominator that united the very heterogeneous Salzburg bourgeoisie, which also displayed strong anti-Czech feelings. In the 1890s, many new German Nationalist clubs, such as Verein Südmark and the Deutsche

---

7   Haas, "Die Bürmooser Fabrikantenfamilie Glaser – Industrielle-Bürger-Juden," 53–72.
8   Adolf Altmann published the first (1913) and second (1930) volume of the book *The History of the Jews in the City and Province of Salzburg up to 1913*.
9   Video interview with Nina Lieberman, Woodstock, NY, April, 2002, conducted by Helga Embacher, Albert Lichtblau, and Karl Rothauer. Also see Lieberman, "*Lost and Found: A Life*," unpublished memoir, LBI, 23. 49.
10 Haas, "Vom Liberalismus zum Deutschnationalismus"; Tweraser, "Der Linzer Gemeinderat 1880–1914: Glanz und Elend bürgerlicher Herrschaft"; Embacher, "Von liberal zu national: Das Linzer Vereinswesen 1848–1938." Concerning other Austrian cities, see Enderle-Burcel and Reiter-Zatloukal, *Antisemitismus in Österreich 1933–1938*.

Schulverein, were founded, and Jews were excluded from all of them by the so-called Arierparagraph.

In 1887, Albert Süß, the only male Jewish member of the famous Salzburger Turnverein, was thrown out of that gymnastics association; in 1891, three Jewish girls had to leave the women's section of the *Turnverein*. By the end of the First World War at the very latest, no Jewish members were left in formerly liberal clubs such as the Deutscher und Österreichischer Alpenverein or the Salzburger Liedertafel. Thus, Jews were excluded from major elements of social as well as of political live in the city—participation in many sports events, staying in certain mountain huts operated by the Alpenverein, as well as dancing at clubs or balls.[11] While Albert Pollak had found a political home in the liberal movement consisting of the Liberal party as well as by many liberal bourgeois clubs, Salzburg Jewry became politically homeless at the end of the nineteenth century.

Antisemitism During the First World War

A large number of Salzburg Jews served as soldiers in the First World War; some of them gave their lives or were seriously wounded. Rabbi Adolf Altmann came out as a fervent Habsburg patriot. During the First World War, he served as a military chaplain in Italy; after the war he became rabbi in Germany. When he began to experience antisemitism against Jewish soldiers during the war, he started to collect testimonies from commanding officers of Jewish soldiers to prove that Jews were brave fighters and loyal Austrians.[12]

While the Jews in Salzburg were proving their patriotism, antisemitism was assuming a new dimension in Salzburg, as was the case all over Austria during the First World War. As the Christian Social newspaper *Salzburger Chronik* commented on May 26, 1914: "People outside of Austria are often amazed that every respectable person in Austria is an antisemite." During the war, Jewish refugees became the target of antisemitism.[13] In Salzburg, many such refugees were housed in barracks in camps in Niederalm and Grödig. Although Jewish refugees

---

11 Haas and Koller, "Jüdisches Gemeinschaftsleben in Salzburg," 37–43.
12 Ironically, in 1934 Altmann was honored for his bravery with the medal for soldiers who served at the front; the accompanying certificate was signed by Adolf Hitler. In 1942, he and his wife were killed in Auschwitz. See Altmann, "K.u.k. Feldrabbiner Dr. Adolf Altmann an der Kriegsfront (1915–1918) in Begegnung mit Feldmarschall Conrad von Hötzendorf."
13 Hoffmann-Holter, "Abreisendmachung": Jüdische Kriegsflüchtlinge in Wien 1914 bis 1923.

never made up more than a sixth of all refugees present in Salzburg,[14] the hate campaign focused on highly conspicuous Eastern European Jews. Not only in Salzburg, the term *Ostjude* also became virtually synonymous with "black market dealer" and "profiteer."
The Jewish community did indeed provide the new arrivals with support, but many Salzburg Jews nevertheless distanced themselves from the Jewish refugees. They were ashamed of their "Shtetl mentality," their clothing, and their Yiddish language. But behind this was also the fear that antisemitism directed against the refugees and Orthodox Jews in general could ultimately turn against them, as well. "My family wasn't the only one that looked down on them. They were considered Polacks and not Jews," recalled Paul Neuwirth. As Hans Pasch expressed it: "The Polish Jews were very unpopular among the established locals—first of all, because they spoke Yiddish, and secondly because they did not look Western European. They destroyed what assimilation might have been able to help." Even when Eastern European Jews became successful in Salzburg, they still met with a certain amount of mistrust. When Hans Pasch's aunt thought that he was considering marrying the daughter of a well-to-do Jewish lawyer in Salzburg, she was shocked and said: "How can you marry the daughter of this Polish man!"[15] But this conflict between assimilated local Jews and immigrant *Ostjuden* was by no means unique to Salzburg; the same could also be observed in Vienna, New York, and even in Tel Aviv.

Everything Was Better Before the War

The Austrian First Republic was marked by economic instability, unemployment, and political street battles that climaxed in the Civil War of 1934, and an Austrofascist government. Few believed in Austria's ability to survive as an independent nation. The First World War is also considered a caesura in Jewish history.[16] The Austrian defeat triggered a new wave of antisemitism, and all German nationalist associations had introduced "Aryan paragraphs" into their by-laws by the end of the war. German nationalism had previously been primarily a bourgeois phenomenon, but during the First Republic in Salzburg, its character clearly transcended class boundaries.[17] The Christian Socials openly

---

14   Of a total of 13,831 refugees counted on May 1, 1917, 1,915 were Jews; by the summer of 1918, this number had declined to six. See Fellner, *Antisemitismus in Salzburg 1918–1938*, 85–90.
15   Video interview with Hans Pasch.
16   See Lichtblau, "Antisemitismus – Rahmenbedingungen und Wirkungen auf das Zusammenleben von Juden und Nichtjuden."
17   See Fellner, *Antisemitismus in Salzburg*.

denied that the Jewish population belonged to the German nation. "Jewry is the enemy of the people, and all those who support it are too," concluded the *Salzburger Chronik* on January 26, 1919. During the first postwar election campaign, inflammatory antisemitic articles filled the pages of this daily paper, which had the highest circulation in Salzburg. It was suggested that the Jews would "suck the economic life blood" out of the helpless "German Volk." To turn back this threat, the Christian Social Party's 1918 platform demanded the "exclusion of all non-Germans from the civil service, public office and representative bodies, and stipulated that the Jews were a non-German nation."[18]

A special feature of this provincial antisemitism was that it was instrumentalized in conjunction with the periphery-metropolis conflict. There were warnings of the danger posed by the "Jewish stronghold" of "Red Vienna," a reference to the many Jewish leaders of the Social Democratic Party in Vienna. It was said that Austria's "Christian-German" alpine states should defend themselves against Jewish-Socialist Vienna's efforts to achieve domination.[19] Special warnings were directed to women, who were being permitted to vote for the first time. In order to turn them away from the "Jewified" Socialists, the Social Democrats were accused of destroying Austria morally by means of a marriage reform, by which civil marriage (*Zivilehe*) was meant.[20]

From July 1920, Austria was governed solely by political parties that propagated antisemitism in their platforms. For the first time, government agencies permitted direct antisemitic propaganda and organizational activities.[21] In 1919, the Deutsch-österreichische Schutzverein Antisemiten-Bund was founded; by 1921, its Salzburg chapter already had 446 members. The *Eiserner Besen* (iron broom, published in Salzburg from 1923 to 1932), the magazine of the Salzburg Antisemitenbund, was already in the 1920s anticipating in words what the National Socialists later carried out in practice: Jews were called "vermin" who should be "mucked out" and "destroyed." A "Jewish directory" published by the Antisemitenbund was a precursor to the Nazis' boycotts of Jewish stores. Individual Salzburg Jews were repeatedly targets of the attacks printed in this political smear-sheet. The *Eiserner Besen* also regarded mixed marriages as a danger for the "German Volk" and prominently reported the names of German girls "who shamelessly run around with the racially destructive Jews."[22]

---

18 *Salzburger Chronik*, December 7, 1918; see as well *Salzburger Chronik*, December 6, 1918, January 25, 1919, January 31, 1919.
19 See Fellner, *Antisemitismus in Salzburg*, 89.
20 Embacher, "Das Frauenwahlrecht als Belohnung für die Kriegsarbeit."
21 See Albrich, "Vom Antijudaismus zum Antisemitismus in Österreich."
22 See for example *Der Eiserne Besen*, March 6, 1925 and May 8, 1925.

Jewish Identities and Antisemitism in Salzburg after 1918   287

The miserable economic situation during the First Republic also led to a general rejection of all that was "foreign." The touristic city of Salzburg protested against tourism—most of all against Jewish summer guests. There were complaints that they would "make themselves comfortable" in restaurants and eat the hungry Salzburgers out of house and home.[23] As in other Austrian tourism regions, "summer vacation antisemitism" could be observed in Salzburg as well after the First World War. Already in the 1920s, Mattsee, Oberndorf, St. Johann in Pongau, Seeham, Neumarkt am Wallersee, and other towns declared themselves off-limits to Jews.[24] Many in Salzburg also were put off by Jewish guests attending the Salzburg Festival, and especially those who liked to wear *Dirndlkleider* and *Lederhosen*. Nevertheless, numerous Jewish families did not let this spoil their enjoyment of spending their summer vacation in Salzburg, attending the Festival and wearing *Trachten*.[25]

Not even the protest movement carried on by large segments of the population against the founding of the Salzburg Festival "amidst the postwar hunger"[26] was free of antisemitic resentment. The Festival was considered "Jewified" and many took exception to Jewish or purportedly Jewish artists like Max Reinhardt and his wife, actress Helene Thimig,[27] Hugo von Hofmannsthal, both of whom were baptized, and Alexander Moissi, an Albanian who was not the least bit Jewish.[28] On the other hand, the Jews who founded the Salzburg Festival (Salzburger Festspiele), as well as Jewish artists and writers, showed little or no interest in the Salzburg Jewish community.[29] Rabbi David Margules complained that only a handful would ever make their way to the synagogue.[30] As early as the 1920s, Rabbi Altmann remarked: "When *Everyman* is going to the Festival, who's left to go to synagogue?"[31] Famous writer Stefan Zweig, who lived with his wife Friderike in a house on Kapuzinerberg, also maintained only casual contact with the Jewish

---

23 Fellner, *Antisemitismus in Salzburg*, 97; *Eiserner Besen*, March 15, 1924.
24 See Kriechbaumer, *Jüdische Sommerfrische in Salzburg*.
25 Kammerhofer-Aggermann, "Von der Trachtenmode zur heiligen ererbten Vätertracht – Volk in Tracht ist Macht," 183–90.
26 Steinberg, *The Meaning of the Salzburg Festival*; Hofinger, *Die Akte Leopoldskron: Max Reinhardt, Das Schloss, Arisierung & Restitution*.
27 Embacher, "Pendlerinnen zwischen Konventionen und Welten: Verhinderte große Salzburgerinnen."
28 See Kerschbauer, "Festspielstadt Salzburg: Weltoffen und antisemitisch," 931–42.
29 Thimig-Reinhardt, *Wie Max Reinhardt lebte*, 105.
30 Margules, "Jüdisches aus der Festspielstadt Salzburg," 7; see as well Strasser, *Carl Zuckmayer: Deutsche Künstler im Salzburger Exil 1933–1938*.
31 Altmann, "Einführung zum Kriegserinnerungsbuch von Adolf Altmann," 528.

community. At least he apologized for not being able to attend a speech entitled "German Jewry's Struggle for Equal Rights."[32]

Despite increasing antisemitism, Salzburg became a refuge for Jewish artists who fled Germany after Hitler came to power in 1933. The Wiesmühle in Henndorf, owned by Alice and Carl Zuckmayer, who had been living there since 1926 and had turned the place in a cultural center, provided an important gathering place. Some even spoke of a "branch office of the Salzburg Festival."[33]

Excluded from all bourgeois and Catholic associations and political parties, Salzburg Jewry was politically homeless. Most voted Social Democratic, a party which was by no means free of antisemitism but did not exclude Jews according to racial or religious criteria and had many Jewish members and leaders. If Jews liked to do gymnastics or go hiking, their only choice was to join a Social Democratic club. In contrast to Vienna, there were no Jews among the leadership or functionaries of the Salzburg Social Democratic Party, and the intellectual element that was also typical of the Viennese party was largely absent in Salzburg. Due to its social structure, the party could not offer any prospects for advancement to bourgeois Salzburg Jews. Henry Berkowitz was the only Jew who was active in the Socialist Youth Group. Nevertheless, it was made clear to him that, as a Jew, he did not completely belong.

As Hans Pasch pointed out, most of the economically successful Jews in Salzburg distanced themselves from the working class. Their concept of assimilation was to become part of the leading class in town: the successful non-Jewish businessmen. Being able to afford a bourgeois lifestyle, they wanted to be integrated into the non-Jewish middle and upper classes, which unfortunately had found a new identity in German Nationalism and antisemitism.[34]

Jewish Identities and Traditions in Salzburg

To settle in Salzburg, Jews had to be ready to modify their Jewishness and adapt to a non-Jewish society. But here we have to ask what assimilation actually meant and how far this process could go in an antisemitic climate.

Becoming a businessman meant first of all giving up one's Jewish name: Avraham Pollak was changed to Albert Pollak, Isidor Neuwirth to Julius Neuwirth, and Luser Nissen Ornstein to Ludwig Ornstein.

---

32 See *Die Wahrheit: Jüdische Wochenschrift*, 5. Also see Dr. Margules, "Stefan Zweig – der Jude," 4–6.
33 Scope, "Das Ambiente der Salzburger Festspiele," 191–5.
34 Video interview with Hans Pasch.

Others also changed their last names: Abeles became Anninger, and Kohn turned into Köhler. Ludwig Ornstein's daughter Heller assumes that, in the Catholic atmosphere of Salzburg, it would have been impossible to do business under a Jewish name.[35] They closed their stores on Christian holidays and worked on the Jewish Sabbath. The German language was not only spoken in public and while doing business, but in private life as well. The children were no longer taught Hungarian, Czech, Yiddish, or Polish. Daniel Bonyhadi, for example, was upset that Hungarian visitors were speaking Hungarian in the famous Café Bazar. Though he himself was born in Hungary in 1861, he advised them to speak German because "people here don't like to listen to the Hungarian language." Rabbi David Margules, who was born in Galicia, was very proud of his "perfect High German" and never spoke a word of Yiddish, the language he had learned in his childhood.[36]

Salzburg Jews also preferred to wear *Trachten*—not like Viennese Jews who did so only during *Sommerfrische* (vacation in the country) or while visiting the Festival in summer,[37] but in everyday life. The Ornstein family became famous for their *Trachten* wares, especially their Wetterfest brand loden coat that was sold in their store on the Getreidegasse. As early as 1911, the clothing store Zum Matrosen on Salzburg's Mirabell Square had its own department for *volkstümliche* goods, in which they offered mountaineering and *Trachten* outfits.[38]

Whereas the Jews of Salzburg adapted to the business world and developed a special love for the German language (especially the dialect of the city of Salzburg), at home, they lived according to their own individual Jewish traditions, of which we can find a variety of forms. Nina Lieberman, the daughter of Rabbi Margules, remembered:

> The Jewish congregation in Salzburg practiced their religion in varying degrees, from Orthodox to non-observant. However, there was only one congregation and that was traditional. Women sat separately from men, but only a minority kept the dietary laws and was Sabbath-observant.[39]

Because religious institutions necessary to guarantee an orthodox Jewish life did not exist in Salzburg, keeping kosher was complicated. For Nina Margules, a piece of kosher salami or a hot dog was a rare treat. It

---

35 Neuwirth, Private Family Chronicle (unpublished).
36 Video interview with Nina Lieberman.
37 See Reinhard Kriechbaumer, *Jüdische Sommerfrische in Salzburg*.
38 Kammerhofer-Aggermann, "Von der Trachtenmode zur heiligen ererbten Vätertracht," 179.
39 Lieberman, *Lost and Found*, 28.

was either sent by relatives from Poland or ordered from Vienna. Having grown up in the 1920s and 1930s, she remembered that the cantor was also the ritual slaughterer and carried out these duties once a week. You placed your order, and it was sent to you from the slaughterhouse.[40] Bertha Reichenthal remembered that her mother bought a live chicken and brought it to the cantor to be slaughtered in the religious manner. Others ordered their meat from a kosher butcher in Vienna.[41] Nina Lieberman also described how her family prepared for the High Holidays and especially for Pesach, which meant hard work for the women. While in Vienna or other cities with a larger Jewish community, traditional Jewish foods like gefilte fish, chicken fat, or horseradish could be bought in stores, in Salzburg everything had to be prepared at home, where the Jewish wives were assisted by Christian maids. During Pesach, the Margules had their own milk pail and went to the farmer to have milk milked directly into a pail that was made kosher for Pesach.[42]

Though only a few Jewish families kept kosher, the children got a religious education from the rabbi, and the boys had a Bar Mitzvah. Most of the Salzburg Jews went to the synagogue at least on the High Holidays and closed their shops, even if they occurred on a regular weekday. After visiting the synagogue, they celebrated at home with their families and relatives. Because they were broadly excluded from non-Jewish society and forced to integrate into a very small Jewish community, relatives became very important for their social life.

It is very interesting that—not only in Salzburg—some Jews had Christmas trees and celebrated Christmas, but, as they emphasized, without any religious context. To adopt Christmas as a non-religious custom was possible because Christmas had, for many, lost its religious character in the nineteenth century and had turned into a sort of folk festival.[43] Especially so that children could take part in Christmas, some Jewish families also used a little trick or subterfuge. Hugo Schwarz described how his mother, one of the leading Zionists in Salzburg, would have never accepted a Christmas tree. But Hugo got his Christmas presents under their maid's Christmas tree.[44]

With a very few exceptions, none of the interviewed former Salzburg Jews could recall non-Jewish friends coming to their homes. Some even

---

40 Lieberman, *Lost and Found*, 136.
41 Bonyhadi and Bertha, "Interview," 123 and 244.
42 Lieberman, *Lost and Found*, 120.
43 Embacher, "Weihnukka: Zwischen Assimilation und Vertreibung – Erinnerungen deutscher und österreichischer Juden an Weihnachten und Chanukka."
44 Schwarz in Ellmauer, Embacher, and Lichtblau, *Geduldet, geschmäht und vertrieben*, 275.

remembered that, when their parents visited the prominent Café Bazar, they were sitting together only with Jews. Hans Pasch described how his father used to play cards in a café, but the only non-Jewish partner he could find was a politician from the Social Democratic Party. Also the Schwarz family, who ran the biggest and most modern department store in Salzburg, was friendly with leading Social Democrats. What seems interesting is that religious Jews like insurance agent Daniel Bonyhadi and Rabbi David Margules met with the archbishop. When Gabriella, the younger daughter of the rabbi, was thrown out of public school in 1938, the archbishop offered her the opportunity to continue in a private Catholic school run by the Ursuline Order.[45]

In the words of Ludwig Löwy, the Jewish minority was accepted and supported by the local government authorities, but the only contacts Jews and non-Jews maintained in Salzburg was the conduct of business.[46] On the other hand, the founders of the community were successful in business life—a major success from their perspective. Still remembering the fight to be officially accepted as a religious community, they appreciated that they were at least tolerated.

Memories of Isolation in the Second and Third Generations

Members of the older generation, many of whom had fought for Austria in the First World War, also tended to ignore antisemitism in a sort of self-defense reaction, concentrating instead on their work and withdrawing into private life. The handful of Salzburg Jews "would anxiously avoid attracting attention or provoking enmity in any way," Rabbi Altmann concluded.[18] While the founder generation identified with liberalism and the next generation could still identify with the Monarchy and the Emperor, the generation born after 1900 often felt politically homeless. While their parents tried to ignore antisemitism, they were much more sensitive and suffered from their isolation amidst non-Jewish society.

The limits to the coexistence between Jews and non-Jews were already being set down in school. In contrast to several Viennese municipal districts in which Jews comprised up to 50 percent of the pupils in some classes, there were only a few Jewish children in Salzburg.[47] Even in elementary school, Jewish children experienced antisemitism directed

---

45 Video interview with Gabriella Margules, conducted by Helga Embacher, Albert Lichtblau and Karl Rothauer, Woodstock NY, 2002.
46 Ludwig Löwy, "Erinnerungen eines Salzburger Juden," 17.
47 Historian Gert Kerschbaumer documented that in Salzburg 153 Jewish children were born in the Austrian Hungarian Monarchy and only 38 in the First Republic. See Kerschbauer, "Festspielstadt Salzburg," 1939.

against them personally. Their social contacts were usually limited to their few Jewish fellow-pupils. "It was always the Jewish friends who went out together, and I don't recall ever having been invited to go out with anyone else," Louis Fox recalled sadly.[48]

Nina Lieberman, born in 1921, remembered how difficult it was for a Jewish girl to take part in a dance course. To make sure that she had a partner, her parents tried to arrange for her to attend a class with another Jewish boy:

> A week before we were to start, my parents received a telephone call from the director of the dancing school informing them that the other boys and girls had threatened to withdraw – or rather their parents had threatened to pull them out – if Jews were part of the group. Regretfully, therefore, the director asked my parents and those of the young boy to withdraw us. He quickly added that he would be very happy to give us private lessons, thus showing his liberal attitude and probably also his underlying thinking that the Jews could pay for them.[49]

Nina again felt caught up in the web of prejudice when she was looking for a tennis partner. As a properly brought-up, middle-class girl, she had to learn tennis, but none of the daughters or sons of doctors, lawyers, or teachers would consider a Jewish partner.[50] Not only antisemitism excluded her from middle-class Salzburg society; due to her religion, she knew that she was different from a very young age on but learned how to deal with it:

> Even when I was invited to the home of one or the other schoolmate, I had to be careful about what I could eat. Milk, cocoa, chocolate, sodas were permitted, but with every cake or cookie, I had to be reassured that no animal fat had been used in the baking. Even when I was invited, I stuck out by being different. This in itself was not perceived as a hardship by me; I felt special.[51]

As the daughter of a liberal and well-educated rabbi, she felt a strong Jewish identity and was proud of her Jewish heritage, whereas other interviewees with a weaker Jewish identity were ashamed of being Jewish.

Bertha Reichenthal is one of the few who has fond recollections of her school days. Although her family was strictly religious, she had

---

48 Interview with Louis Fox, Salzburg 1993.
49 Lieberman, *Lost and Found*, 184.
50 Lieberman, *Lost and Found*, 188.
51 Lieberman, *Lost and Found*, 160.

many non-Jewish girlfriends. One reason for this might be that Bertha's family, refugees in the First World War, was very poor, and thus the social barriers between her and her classmates were absent. In high school, Jewish students were confronted by children of the Salzburg bourgeoisie, which was most vehement in refusing contacts with the Jewish minority.

Generational Conflicts

The generation born after 1900 not only felt isolated from non-Jewish society; they also in many instances felt that they were under pressure from old-fashioned and traditional-minded parents. These elders had indeed made it possible for their families to enjoy comfortable, middle-class lives, but showed little interest in politics and culture. Their expectations were often that their sons would join the business and that their daughters would marry a Jewish businessman. But many of the children had other dreams—attending college, living the life of an artist, or becoming a farmer in Palestine.

Rudolf Ornstein wanted to escape from the career path of a businessman that his father had determined; against his father's will, he went to work for a farmer in Germany, which he, as a staunch Zionist, saw as preparation for a life in Palestine. But when his father became severely ill, he returned to Salzburg to run the business. Nevertheless, he continued to dream of making *Aliyah*, emigration to Palestine, which he had already visited in the 1920s.[52] Hans Pasch, on the other hand, had been ready to join his father's business, but the conflicts between the two became more and more frequent. For Hans, his father represented the "world of yesterday":

> I just couldn't exist in Salzburg working side-by-side with my father. He was from the old school, in which you addressed the clientele indirectly. You know what I mean? "What would madam like? How may I help the gentleman?" We spoke to the customers directly. And I had another way of life too. He just couldn't understand that.[53]

The Pasch family came up with a solution: the son was sent to manage the branch in Linz, where Hans found the political climate considerably more pleasant than in bourgeois Salzburg.[54]

---

52 See Helga Embacher, "Exile," 451.
53 Video Interview with Hans Pasch.
54 Video Interview with Hans Pasch.

The children and grandchildren of the founding generation reacted to antisemitism not only more sensitively but also in some cases more defensively. They also displayed receptiveness to new political currents. During the years immediately after the First World War, some sons of Jewish bourgeois families like Hans Pasch were not unfavorably disposed to communism. "There was the revolution, the great upheaval, everything that had been there before no longer existed, and we were very impressed by Russia and the revolution. As a Jew, you couldn't be a pan-German, so you just became a communist."[55] In his nineties, having lived in Denver, USA, for many years, he still had in his possession the books by Lenin, Ernst Troller, and George Grosz that he purchased in a "leftist" bookshop in Salzburg during his brief revolutionary phase. Thereafter, he became a follower of Vladimir Jabotinsky, the right-wing Zionist leader who advocated establishing a Jewish state on both banks of the Jordan. In the early 1920s, he made a trip to Palestine, though he never considered making *Aliyah*. The land was too primitive and, he pointed out, "at this time my life was still too comfortable in Austria. We supported a state for Jews, which definitely was not meant for us."[56]

The acts of discrimination in everyday life and the almost total exclusion from bourgeois society made above all young males receptive to Zionism. As in Vienna and Linz, there were also Zionist associations in Salzburg, like the rather moderate *Blau Weiss* (blue-white) that attracted many Jewish youths during the time of the First Republic. Besides providing a forum for political discussions, they organized group outings. To youngsters who were ashamed of being Jewish, Zionism imparted a positive Jewish identity and, among other things, an introduction to self-defense. For them, it was very important to no longer have to accept antisemitic slurs, to take a stand against such insults and to gain respect thereby. According to Erwin Bonyhadi's account, young people had to work out their aggressions that had been built up by the humiliations experienced in everyday life. Fistfights were also occasionally provoked to prove their strength and bravery and thus impress antisemites.[57]

The younger generation's turn to socialism and Zionism, however, also led to fierce conflicts within their families. Aside from Walter Schwarz's wife Dora, who had already emigrated to Palestine in the 1930s and set up a hotel for nutritional therapy in Sichron Yakov, the older generation was mostly opposed to Zionism. They considered

---

55 Video Interview with Hans Pasch.
56 Video interview with Hans Pasch.
57 For details, see Embacher, "Lenin oder Jabotinsky?," 181–93. See as well interviews with Erwin Bonyhadi, Paul Neuwirth and Hugo Schwarz, conducted by Helga Embacher and Albert Lichtblau, Salzburg 1993.

themselves loyal Austrians and perceived Zionism as a threat. The Pollak family was shocked when their son Ernst emigrated to Palestine, and the father tried very hard to convince him to return to Salzburg. Ernst tragically died of malaria there.[58]

Whereas Zionism supplied young people with a strategy to fight against antisemitism in their homeland, parents regarded Zionism as a danger to the future they had imagined for their children. These generational and social conflicts, as well as the pressure to find Jewish partners, help to explain the decline in membership of the Jewish community from 285 in 1910 to 239 in 1934.

1938: The End of the Jewish Community

Despite the antisemitism in everyday life and their isolation, never in their wildest dreams did the Jews of Salzburg imagine what would happen after March 12, 1938. Since there had been no prominent left-wing Jews in Salzburg, the Civil War and the end of the Social Democratic Party had left scant traces in their memory. For them, the persecution began suddenly. Between March and September 1938, a total of 250 laws were enacted to rob the Jews of their freedom, deprive them of their human rights, and take over their property. Immediately after the Anschluss and during the Reichskristallnacht on November 9, 1938, many Jewish men were arrested and deported to Dachau, though most of them were released, often with the help of their wives.[59] On November 12, Salzburg declared itself as having been *"judenrein"* (cleansed of Jews). All Jewish men and women who were still living in Salzburg had to move to Vienna; more than a hundred were killed during the Holocaust.[60] But Salzburg was never completely *judenrein*; a few Jews survived in hiding and in mixed marriages.[61] There were also Jewish forced laborers working in Kaprun and in the Stubach Valley on a hydroelectric plant project.

Many of those who escaped and found refuge in the US, Great Britain, Palestine/Israel, Australia, and the Netherlands recall the persecution as a very traumatic experience; some were unable to ever visit Salzburg again. Nevertheless, many also have positive memories of

---

58 See Kraft, *Portrait of a Pioneer*.
59 Lichtblau, "'*Arisierungen*,' beschlagnahmte Vermögen, Rückstellungen und Entschädigungen in Salzburg"; Hofinger, *Nationalsozialismus in Salzburg*.
60 See *Stolpersteine Salzburg* (Stumbling Blocks): An Art Project for Europe by Gunter Demnig. Available online: https://www.stolpersteine-salzburg.at (accessed July 31, 2023).
61 See Bäumer, *Die Geschichte eines Kindes von 1932 bis 1945*.

Salzburg. Numerous former Salzburg Jews stated that being Jewish was only one facet of their identity; they also regarded themselves as members of the German *Kulturkreis*, and, in a regional sense, as Salzburgers. Hans Pasch assumed that if the Jews in Salzburg had been permitted to do so, they would have totally assimilated.[62]

Bibliography

Interviews

Bertha Reichenthal. In Ellmauer, Embacher, and Lichtblau, eds., *Geduldet, geschmäht und vertrieben*, 244.

Erwin Bonyhadi. In Ellmauer, Embacher, and Lichtblau, eds., *Geduldet, geschmäht und vertrieben*, 123.

Erwin Bonyhadi, Paul Neuwirth and Hugo Schwarz, conducted by Helga Embacher and Albert Lichtblau, Salzburg, 1993.

Hugo Schwarz. In Ellmauer, Embacher, and Lichtblau, eds., *Geduldet, geschmäht und vertrieben*, 275.

Video interview with Hans Pasch, conducted by Helga Embacher, Albert Lichtblau, and Karl Rothauer, Denver, CO, 2002.

Video interview with Nina Lieberman, Woodstock, NY, April 2002, conducted by Helga Embacher, Albert Lichtblau, and Karl Rothauer, Woodstock, NY, April 2002.

Secondary Literature

Albrich, Thomas. "Vom Antijudaismus zum Antisemitismus in Österreich." In Enderle-Burcel and Reiter-Zatloukal, eds., *Antisemitismus in Österreich*, 37–60.

Altmann, Adolf. *Geschichte der Juden in Stadt und Land Salzburg von den frühesten Zeiten bis auf die Gegenwart*. Vol. 1 (1913), vol. 2 (1930); continued to 1988 by Günter Fellner and Helga Embacher. Salzburg: Otto-Müller-Verlag, 1990.

Altmann, Manfred. "K.u.k. Feldrabbiner Dr. Adolf Altmann an der Kriegsfront (1915–1918) in Begegnung mit Feldmarschall Conrad von Hötzendorf und anderen Armeekommandanten" (erstmalige Veröffentlichung seines Kriegserinnerungsbuches mit einer Einführung von Manfred Altmann). In Feingold, ed., *Ein ewiges Dennoch*, 189–572.

Bäumer, Angelica. *Die Geschichte eines Kindes von 1932 bis 1945*. Wien: Verlag der Theodor Kramer Gesellschaft, 2022.

Bonyhadi, Erwin, and Bertha Reichenthal, "Interview." In Ellmauer, Embacher, and Lichtblau, eds., *Geduldet, geschmäht und vertrieben*, 118–20.

Ellmauer, Daniela, Helga Embacher, and Albert Lichtblau, eds. *Geduldet, geschmäht und vertrieben: Salzburger Juden erzählen*. Salzburg: Otto-Müller-Verlag, 1998.

Embacher, Helga. "Exil als neue Heimat." In Feingold, ed., *Ein ewiges Dennoch*, 439–45.

Embacher, Helga. "Das Frauenwahlrecht als Belohnung für die Kriegsarbeit." In Mazohl-Wallnig, ed., *Die andere Geschichte*, 311–34.

---

62 Video interview with Hans Pasch.

Embacher, Helga. "Jewish Identities and Acculturation in the Province of Salzburg in the Shadow of Antisemtism." In Liedtke and Rechter, eds., *Towards Normality? Acculturation and Modern German Jewry*, 291–308.

Embacher, Helga. *Juden in Salzburg: History – Cultures – Fates*. Salzburg: Verlag Anton Pustet, 2002.

Embacher, Helga. "Lenin oder Jabotinsky? Jüdische Identitätssuche in Salzburg nach dem Ersten Weltkrieg." In Yotam Hotam, ed., *Deutsch-Jüdische Jugendliche im "Zeitalter der Jugend,"* 181–92. Göttingen: V&R unipress, 2009.

Embacher, Helga. "Pendlerinnen zwischen Konventionen und Welten: Verhinderte große Salzburgerinnen." In Thurner and Stranzinger, eds., *Die andere Geschichte* 2, 71–94.

Embacher, Helga. "Die Salzburger jüdische Gemeinde von ihrer Neugründung im Liberalismus bis zur Gegenwart." In Embacher, *Juden in Salzburg: History – Cultures – Fates*, 38–66.

Embacher, Helga. "Von liberal zu national: Das Linzer Vereinswesen 1848–1938." *Historisches Jahrbuch der Stadt Linz 1991* (1992), 71–80.

Embacher, Helga. "Weihnukka: Zwischen Assimilation und Vertreibung – Erinnerungen deutscher und österreichischer Juden an Weihnachten und Chanukka." In Esther Gajek and Richard Faber, eds., *Politische Weihnachten in Antike und Moderne*, 287–305. Würzburg: Verlag Königshausen & Neumann, 1997.

Enderle-Burcel, Gertrude, and Ilse Reiter-Zatloukal, eds. *Antisemitismus in Österreich 1933–1938*. Vienna-Cologne-Weimar: Böhlau Verlag, 2018.

Feingold, Marko M., ed. *Ein ewiges Dennoch: 125 Jahre Juden in Salzburg*. Vienna: Böhlau Verlag, 1993.

Fellner, Günter. *Antisemitismus in Salzburg 1918–1938*. Vienna-Salzburg: Veröffentlichungen des Historischen Instituts der Universität Salzburg, 1979. 85–90.

Haas, Hanns. "Die Bürmooser Fabrikantenfamilie Glaser – Industrielle-Bürger-Juden." In Feingold, ed., *Ein ewiges Dennoch*, 53–72.

Haas, Hanns. "Vom Liberalismus zum Deutschnationalismus." In Heinz Dopsch, ed., *Geschichte Salzburgs*, vol. II, 833–906. Salzburg: Anton Pustet Verlag, 1988.

Haas, Hanns, and Monika Koller. "Jüdisches Gemeinschaftsleben in Salzburg: Von der Neuansiedlung zum Ersten Weltkrieg." In Feingold, ed., *Ein ewiges Dennoch*, 31–52.

Hoffmann-Holter, Beatrix. *"Abreisendmachung": Jüdische Kriegsflüchtlinge in Wien 1914 bis 1923*. Vienna-Cologne-Weimar: Böhlau Verlag, 1995.

Hofinger, Johannes. *Die Akte Leopoldskron: Max Reinhardt, Das Schloss, Arisierung & Restitution*. Salzburg: Verlag Anton Pustet, 2005.

Hofinger, Johannes. *Nationalsozialismus in Salzburg: Opfer. Täter. Gegner*. Innsbruck: Studienverlag, 2016 (2nd ed., 2018).

Kammerhofer-Aggermann, Ulrike. "Von der Trachtenmode zur heiligen ererbten Vätertracht – 'Volk in Tracht ist Macht.'" In Feingold, ed., *Ein ewiges Dennoch*, 183–90.

Kerschbauer, Gert. "Festspielstadt Salburg: Weltoffen und antisemitisch." In Enderle-Burcel and Reiter-Zatloukal, eds., *Antisemitismus in Österreich*, 931–42.

Kraft, Dina. *Portrait of a Pioneer: The Spiritual Odyssey of Ernst Pollak (1901–1920)*. Senior Thesis, Department of History, University of Wisconsin, Madison (unpublished).

Kriechbaumer, Reinhard, ed. *Jüdische Sommerfrische in Salzburg*. Vienna-Cologne-Weimar: Böhlau-Verlag, 2002.

Lichtblau, Albert, "Antisemitismus – Rahmenbedingungen und Wirkungen auf das Zusammenleben von Juden und Nichtjuden." In Tálos et al., eds., *Handbuch des politischen Systems Österreich: Erste Republik 1918–1933*, 454–71.

Lichtblau, Albert. "'Arisierungen,' beschlagnahmte Vermögen, Rückstellungen und Entschädigungen in Salzburg." *Vermögensentzug wä-2rend der NS-Zeit sowie Rückstellungen und Entschädigungen seit 1945 in Österreich*. Veröffentlichungen der Österreichischen Historikerkommission, Bd. 17/2. Wien-München, 2004.

Lieberman, Nina. *Lost and Found: A Life*. Unpublished memoir. Leo Baeck Institute, 23.

Liedtke, Rainer, and David Rechter. *Towards Normality? Acculturation and Modern German Jewry*. Schriftenreihe wissenschaftlicher Abhandlungen des Leo-Baeck-Instituts 68. Tübingen: Mohr Siebeck, 2003.

Löwy, Ludwig. "Erinnerungen eines Salzburger Juden." In Mendel Karin-Karger, ed., *Salzburgs wiederaufgebaute Synagoge: Festschrift zur Einweihung*, 17–20. Salzburg: Judaica Verlag, 1968.

Margules, Rabbi Dr. D. S. "Jüdisches aus der Festspielstadt Salzburg." *Die Wahrheit: Jüdische Wochenschrift* 41 (October 10, 1930), 7.

Margules, Rabbi Dr. D. S. "Stefan Zweig – der Jude." *Die Wahrheit: Jüdische Wochenschrift* 49 (December 4, 1931), 4–6.

Mazohl-Wallnig, Brigitte, ed. *Die andere Geschichte: Eine Salzburger Frauengeschichte von der ersten Mädchenschule (1695) bis zum Frauenwahlrecht 1918*. Salzburg: Verlag Anton Pustet, 1995.

Neuwirth, Hella. Private Family Chronicle (unpublished).

Scope, Alma. "Das Ambiente der Salzburger Festspiele." In Feingold, ed., *Ein ewiges Dennoch*, 191–5.

Steinberg, Michael P. *The Meaning of the Salzburg Festival: Austria as Theater and Ideology, 1890–1938*. Ithaca: Cornell UP, 1990.

Strasser, Christian. *Carl Zuckmayer: Deutsche Künstler im Salzburger Exil 1933–1938*. Vienna-Cologne-Weimar: Böhlau-Verlag, 1996.

Stolpersteine Salzburg (Stumbling Blocks): An Art Project for Europe by Gunter Demnig. Available online: https://www.stolpersteine-salzburg.at (accessed June 18, 2023).

Tálos, Emmerich, Anton Staudinger, Herbert Dachs, and Ernst Hanisch, eds. *Handbuch des politischen Systems Österreich: Erste Republik 1918–1933*. Vienna: Manz Verlag, 1995.

Thimig-Reinhardt, Helene. *Wie Max Reinhardt lebte*. Percha am Starnberger See: Verlag R. S. Schulz, 1973.

Thurner, Erika, and Dagmar Stranzinger, eds. *Die andere Geschichte 2: Eine Salzburger Frauengeschichte*. Salzburg: Anton Pusted Verlag, 1996.

Tweraser, Kurt. "Der Linzer Gemeinderat 1880–1914: Glanz und Elend bürgerlicher Herrschaft." In *Historisches Jahrbuch der Stadt Linz 1979* (1980), 300–10.

Eleven

Hungarian Salzburgs: Salzburg and the Salzburg Idea as Inspiration for Mozart Concerts, Urban Tourism Development, and Festivals in Interwar Hungary

Alexander Vari

Commenting on the Calderon-inspired performance of Hugo von Hofmannsthal's "Grosses Welttheater" in the *Collegienkirche* at the third edition of the Salzburg Festival in 1922, the Budapest mainstream daily *Pesti Napló* (Pest Courier) noted appreciatively that

> Reinhardt had directed [set designer Alfred] Roller to build a red mystery stage, onto which the angels descended from the top of the altar. Reinhardt's lighting effects were so distinctive that the church-like atmosphere of the mystery never devolved into comedy at any moment. Among the actors, Moissi in the role of the beggar, Helene Thimig as the personification of Wisdom, with Madame Wohlgemuth in the role of the Beauty and Rainer in that of the Death, all made a great impression on the spectators.[1]

The attention that this festival (and others like it) attracted in Hungary during the 1920s was due to Salzburg's emergence onto the postwar Austrian public stage as a new cultural center with a distinctive

---

1   "A 'Világszínház' kulisszái mögött," *Pesti Napló*, August 20, 1922, 11; translations by the present author.

national and increasingly international reach.² Due to its popularity in Austria and abroad, between 1925 and 1933, the Salzburger Festspiele attracted annually between sixty and seventy thousand visitors, a figure which, together with the exciting artistic program that the festival organizers offered, enabled Salzburg to become a "European cultural capital for the duration of the summer," as one of the historians of the interwar history of the event called it.³

The rise of Salzburg as a *Kulturstadt* (a "city of culture") had a noticeable impact not just on First Republic Austria but also on neighboring Hungary. Post-imperial Hungary was fertile ground for cultural transfer between the two postwar countries, given its historical connections to the Austrian lands through their common Habsburg history reaching back several centuries, including more than a half century of Austro-Hungarian dualism after the 1867 Compromise (Ausglsich). However, as I argue here, it is remarkable that, instead of the Vienna that had been at the core of Hungarian-Austrian cultural exchanges for centuries, it was the former "provincial city" of Salzburg that became an important reference point for Hungarian music, urban, and cultural policy makers after the dissolution of the Dual Monarchy. Indeed, during the interwar period, the Hungarian press started to report regularly on the Salzburger Festspiele.

Notwithstanding this interest during the early 1920s, it was not the Salzburg Festival that first triggered a desire among Hungarians to imitate Salzburg, but rather the more established Mozarteum, which in 1925 inspired the creation of a Hungarian Mozart Society aiming to spread knowledge of Mozart's music in Hungarian society. In a similar vein, it was the fortress of Hohensalzburg that intrepid Hungarian businessmen wanted to recreate during the mid-1920s, in order to establish a tourist attraction on Budapest's own Gellérthegy (Gellért Hill), yielding plans that at this point still trumped the initial interest that had been raised by the early seasons of the Festpiele.

By the late 1920s, however, as the Salzburg Festival proved its long-term viability, the festival idea itself finally claimed precedence, becoming a craze that swept through Hungary. Inspired by the original Festival's success, town after town wanted to appropriate for itself the rubric of being a "Hungarian Salzburg" in the making. Sopron, Eger, Pécs, and Szeged all claimed that they had something that was as equally deserving of celebration. They had the historical reference points that would make such claims plausible.

For instance, Sopron touted its geographic proximity to Esterháza, where Haydn was for his lifetime employed by the princely Esterházy

---

2   Steinberg, *The Meaning of the Salzburg Festival*, 70–1.
3   See Charnay, "Le public du festival de Salzbourg 1920–1950."

family as a musician, and Liszt's birthplace in Burgenland at Doborján/Raiding. By contrast, Eger touted its picturesque baroque cityscape which included a medieval fortress, numerous Catholic churches, and a minaret. A strong theater scene and many distinguished urban landmarks were claimed by Pécs, while Szeged highlighted a recently built neo-gothic square that juxtaposed a cathedral with new university buildings. All hoped that festivals could help them acquire symbolic cultural capital like Salzburg's, which would, in turn, stimulate their economic growth through tourism.

While all these towns were well positioned in one sense or another to become a "Hungarian Salzburg," the one that succeeded in the end in monopolizing this identity was the city of Szeged, the country's second largest city, situated in the southeast corner of post-Trianon Hungary. Championed by Count Kuno Klebersberg, Hungary's Minister of Religion and Public Education (and a former Szeged MP in the Hungarian Parliament), the city of Szeged had received governmental support in 1931 to start an outdoor festival on its recently completed Cathedral Square. Although the initial goal of the government-sponsored festival was to serve Hungary's post-Trianon revisionist cultural policies by positioning the country as an extended outpost of European civilization, in later years, once its management was taken over by the municipality and the owner of a local newspaper, the festival's focus followed the Salzburg model, stressing more on how Szeged could become a regional attraction through the quality of its cultural programming. Thus, by the 1930s, Salzburg had acquired not only a Hungarian epigone but also a cultural competitor in a Hungary that was trying to carve out its own sphere of influence and visibility in the European festival world so that it would attract both domestic and foreign visitors.

This essay focuses on the extraordinary influence that Salzburg had on the development of a variety of music, urban tourism, and festival policy initiatives in interwar Hungary. To document the different phases of this influence, I will look first at the early 1920s representations of postwar Salzburg in the Hungarian press, then turn in the next sections to a discussion of the different musical, urban, and cultural contexts in which the Salzburg cultural model was influential in the Hungarian context.

Representations of Postwar Salzburg in the Hungarian Press in the Early 1920s

During the interwar period, the international press was a major conduit for the flow of information about Salzburg's emergence as an important cultural center. Like their English, American, French, and

Italian counterparts, Hungarian newspapers also provided ample coverage of the annual Festspiel events. In its early reporting on the Salzburg Festival, the Hungarian press often reproduced to a great extent the festival founders' own claims, presenting it as a combination of the German and Italian artistic spirit and thus as a quintessentially Austrian product. Another dominant representation emerging during these years offered Hungarian readers an image of Salzburg as a source of beauty and serenity (both natural and musical) that also inspired Mozart's music.[4]

Reflecting such convictions, the author of a journalistic piece titled "Salzburg: The Most Beautiful Austrian City" declared that, "from the perspective of beauty and culture, Salzburg lives up to its reputation not only in Europe, but throughout the whole world."[5] Most importantly, however, as the leaders of the democratic and then communist revolutions that occurred in Hungary in 1918 and 1919 were replaced by the Christian conservative regime of Miklós Horthy (the country's regent between 1920 and 1944), the fact that Salzburg was a conservative city, Catholic, Baroque, and mired in the past turned it into an appealing place for supporters of Hungary's recent conservative turn. In a world defined by a frenzy of new cultural fashion, Salzburg was seen as a haven of tradition. For instance, the author of a press notice published in 1921 emphasized the postwar cosmopolitan effervescence of Paris and Berlin, but then pointed out that phenomena like American dance crazes enjoyed a considerably more muted reception in places like Salzburg which comfortingly featured classical ballet rather than emulating the latest transatlantic dance styles that had taken Paris and Berlin by storm.[6]

Music also figured prominently in the Hungarian press reports on Salzburg.[7] In fact, the series of modern chamber music concerts that took place in Salzburg's Mozarteum in 1922, 1923, and 1924 elicited even more attention than did Reinhardt's productions. The summer 1922 concerts in the Mozarteum featured composers like Richard Strauss, Darius Milhaud, Joseph Marx, Béla Bartók, Francis Poulenc, and Igor Stravinsky, with many performing their own works. This series was presented to Hungarian readers as an important cultural event which allowed Hungarian music, through Bartók's works, to gain more

---

4   Spur, "Az ünneplő Mozart-város," *Szózat*, August 20, 1922.
5   "Salzburg Ausztria legszebb városa," *Esti Kurir*, August 29, 1925.
6   N. T., "Páris-Berlin-Salzburg," *Pesti Hírlap*, September 8, 1921.
7   See, among others, "Jedermann," *Világ*, August 24,1920; "Reinhardt Jeder-mann-előadása a Salzburg Dóm-téren," *Az Est*, August 26, 1920.

international recognition.⁸ The 1923 edition of the Mozarteum's concert series, organized this time by Salzburg's Internationale Gesellschaft für neue Musik (founded just the previous year), again included a wide array of contemporary compositions, ranging from those by Ravel and Stravinsky to Bartók and Kodály. In 1924, the festival brought together twenty-eight composers from eleven countries, allowing Kodály's music to shine once more.⁹

These concerts, at which—according to Hungarian press reports—the public showed the greatest appreciation for the works of Bartók and Kodály, made many music lovers in Hungary think of Salzburg both as a mecca of modern music and as a place of sacred cultural pilgrimage.¹⁰ However, for this audience, Salzburg was not yet a place that emerged with a distinct identity apart from other urban centers. As the international programming of the Festival's contemporary music concerts made clear (both in terms of the works performed and the performers represented), Salzburg simply connected Hungary to a transnational network of musicians who were also regulars on the stages of Vienna, Berlin, Paris, London, and New York, as well as those of other music festivals.

The Salzburger Festspiele which debuted in Salzburg in 1920 were also initially seen through the lenses of a broader festival circuit. However, soon after its inception, the Salzburg Festival also came to be deemed a fresher cultural event in the world of Central European festivals—a festival which was, in many ways, more inspirational to high culture aficionados than the older Wagner-inspired opera festivals held in Munich and Bayreuth. Moreover, the Salzburg festival was perceived as being different from Bayreuth's because it distinguished itself through its outdoor theatrical performances. Due to its staging of modern passion plays, some Hungarian commentators also emphasized the connections between the festival and the region's strong Catholic cultural traditions, something that placed Salzburg in the company of Oberammergau.

Yet, while awareness of these cultural differences and connections, and of the role of Salzburg as an international theater marketplace for concluding business agreements and making PR for artists increased year by year, Hungarian journalists and visitors occasionally also voiced their criticism by describing Reinhardt and Hofmannsthal's Salzburger

---

8   "Megkezdődtek a salzburgi ünnepi játékok. Bartók Béla nagy sikere az első matinén," *Pesti Hírlap*, August 10, 1922.
9   Bence Szabolcsi, "Salzburg," *Világ*, August 30, 1924, and "Zeneünnepély Salzburgban: Modern kamarazene a Mozarteumban – Kodály Zoltán az ünnepély hőse," *Pesti Napló*, August 19, 1924.
10 "Bartók Béla és Kodály Zoltán salzburgi diadala. Levél a modern zene Mekkájából," *Az Est*, August 19, 1923.

Festpiele as an artistic humbug and a money-making enterprise that felt more like a fair than a festival.[11] Moreover, reflecting the wave of postwar antisemitism which swept Hungary in the early 1920s, Hungarian commentators also described the Festival as being dominated by Jewish artists and foreigners, who together reveled in the staging and consumption of Catholic mystery plays. With the opening of the Salzburg Casino in 1923, the city was even seen as giving up the conservative moral stance for which it had earlier been praised.[12]

Notwithstanding some of these racist, xenophobic, and moralistic attacks aimed at the modern music events presented at the Mozarteum and the plays and operas featured in the program of the Salzburger Festspiele, Salzburg was nonetheless celebrated as a rising cultural center. While press reports sometimes presented Salzburg as a place of conflict and discontent between locals and foreigners, on the one hand, and working-class versus upper-class people, on the other, what actually dominated the news in Hungary in the early to the mid-1920s was *not* information about the Festival program, but rather information about the Mozarteum's role in raising the city's international visibility and triggering a thriving tourism industry. Not surprisingly, then, the early impacts of Salzburg in Hungary were felt mainly in these two areas.

Salzburg's Mozarteum and its Hungarian Connections

Hungarian interest in Salzburg's Mozarteum predated by several decades the founding of the Salzburger Festpiele. The "Cathedral Music Association and Mozarteum" was founded in Salzburg in 1841 by a group of "committed citizens";[13] the Salzburg Mozarteum Foundation was added in 1870 (with the Mozarteum Orchestra becoming a third and separate institution in 1880). Through their organization of classical concerts and commemorative events, these three institutions were instrumental not just in preserving Mozart's musical heritage locally,[14] but also in making it better known elsewhere. For instance, as early as 1870, Julius Blau, the first violinist of the Mozarteum Orchestra, had already received great acclaim for his musical performances in Budapest,[15] while the Hungarian press often mentioned the Mozarteum for

---

11 Gusztáv Rab, "A dobverős halál," *Világ*, August 19, 1925.
12 "Játékbank," *Szózat*, January 25, 1922.
13 See Mozarteum, "History." Available online: https://mozarteum.at/en/history/ (accessed November 25, 2018).
14 For more on the history of these institutions, see the essays in Julia Hinterberger, *Von der Musikschule Zum Konservatoriums: Das Mozarteum, 1841–1922*.
15 "Színpadi concert," *Fővárosi Lapok*, May 6, 1870.

the role it played in organizing concerts such as those commemorating the 1887 centennial of Mozart's *Don Giovanni* opera[16] or that of the 1888 anniversary celebration for the 40th year of the reign of the sovereign shared by Austria and Hungary, Franz Joseph.[17] The 1914 opening of the Mozarteum's new Concert Hall in Salzburg and the institution's subsequent role in promoting modern music, together with the inclusion of its concerts and venue in the offerings of the Salzburger Festpiele, further enhanced Hungarian observers' esteem for this institution.

Such visible successes probably led to the birth in the early 1920s of these observers' desire to promote Mozart's music in Hungary. Thus, after a successful series of Mozart concerts presented to Budapest audiences during the 1923–1924 concert season by pianist Margit Weisz, a group comprising Weisz together with her husband, Dr. György Bárdos (a lawyer by profession), Dr. Antal Szebeny (a medical doctor), and Dezső Demény (a composer and concert maestro of St. Stephen's Basilica in Budapest) took the initiative and founded a Hungarian Mozart Association in December 1924.[18] Receiving official permission from Hungary's ministry of interior six months later, the association set as its goal to "make better known, popularize, and promote especially Mozart's lesser known and rarely performed works."[19] In addition, the association wanted to bring Mozart's music to the poorer classes through free or low-priced concert tickets, while providing music education to promising talents without economic means, and promoting interest in Mozart's works through awards given to talented music school pupils.[20]

Another rationale that the founders offered for creating this association at the time was that, as they put it, "during the last few years everywhere in Europe there has been an enhanced interest in Mozart's music, and therefore there is reason to hope" that through their action, they will be able "to turn Budapest into a musical Salzburg"[21]—a direct reference to their high appreciation of Salzburg's early postwar music scene. As Bárdos pointed out in a public presentation in September 1925, after Salzburg, Dresden, Berlin, and Vienna, Budapest was the fifth city to start its own Mozart Association, joining thus a transnational network of cities dedicated to the promotion of Mozart's music.[22]

---

16 "'Don Juan' díszelőadása," *Fővárosi Lapok*, July 17, 1887.
17 "Jubiláns díszhangversenyek," *Fővárosi Lapok*, July 15, 1888.
18 See Imre Molnár, *A magyar muzsika könyve*, 206.
19 "Mozart-kultusz Budapesten," *Az Ujság*, May 28, 1925.
20 "Mozart-kultusz Budapesten," *Az Ujság*, May 28, 1925.
21 "Mozart-kultusz Budapesten,"*Szózat*, June 20, 1925.
22 "Mozart-kultusz Budapesten," *Pesti Napló*, September 17, 1925.

Despite acknowledgment of such a network's existence, however, the association's most frequently recurring international reference point was neither Vienna nor Berlin, but Salzburg. As Bárdos put it in another one of his public statements: "if we want to present our goals in a nutshell: what we want to do is create the Hungarian Salzburg."[23] Such frequent references to Salzburg in the public pronouncements of the Hungarian Mozart Association clearly confirm that by the mid-1920s Salzburg and its Mozarteum had acquired a cultural aura that people in places such as Budapest were trying to replicate for their own benefit.

Indeed, the Hungarian Mozart Association started working on its project to turn Budapest into a Hungarian Salzburg by organizing in the fall of 1925 a diverse panel of cultural events, including several afternoon presentations featuring short musical pieces by Mozart.[24] A larger concert was organized in the hall of Budapest's Music Academy in January 1926, intended to celebrate 170 years since Mozart's birth (a concert that was attended, among other musical notables, by the then-current vice-president of Salzburg's Mozarteum).[25] With the latter event, the association also hoped to attract to Budapest a certain percentage of the foreign visitors who made their annual pilgrimages to Salzburg.[26] These concerts were followed in the spring of 1926 by a guest concert tour of the Mozart Association to Székesfehérvár, a county seat an hour away from Budapest.[27]

However strong the Hungarian Mozart Association's plans to catch up with Salzburg may have been in 1925 and 1926, public interest in importing Salzburg's symbolic cultural capital to Budapest fizzled out during subsequent years. During the next decade, except for its annual concerts held each spring (for which the musicians involved received mixed reviews) and the association's participation in celebrating the Mozarteum-initiated and Austrian Ministry of Education-financed international Mozart Year in 1931,[28] supporters of the Hungarian Mozart Association could turn little else into building blocks for elevating Budapest to the status of a Hungarian Salzburg.

---

23 "Mozart-kultusz Budapesten," *Világ*, October 11, 1925.
24 See "Tegnap tartotta első zenés kulturdélutánját tagjai számára a Budapesti Mozart-Egyesület," *Ujság*, October 27, 1925 and "A Budapesti Mozart Egyesület ma tartotta harmadik zenésdélutánját," *Pesti Hírlap*, December 16, 1925.
25 See "A Mozart Egyesület ma este Mozart születésének 170. évforduló napján kitünően sikerült hangversenyt rendezett a Zeneakadémia nagytermében," *Világ*, January 28, 1926.
26 "Nemzetközi Mozart-ünnep Budapesten," *Ujság*, December 6, 1925.
27 "A Budapesti Mozart Egyesület Székesfehérvárott," *Ujság*, March 23, 1926.
28 "Mozart-ünnepségek 1931-ben," *Budapesti Hírlap*, October 14, 1930 and "Mozart-est," *Pesti Napló*, April 14, 1931.

Plans for Creating a Hohensalzburg in Budapest

Although by the mid-1920s the Mozarteum had turned into an important component in Salzburg's cultural appeal in Hungary, there was another, much older layer of Salzburg history that played a role in Hungarians' desire to create their own analogue to Salzburg. Salzburg's medieval fortifications, baroque urban heritage, and natural setting in a valley surrounded by the Alps, had provided impetus for the creation of a local tourist industry as early as the nineteenth century.[29] That Salzburg's natural beauty had been envied by Hungarians decades earlier is demonstrated by the commonplace claim circulating in the 1880s, according to which the distant Transylvanian city of Brassó/Kronstadt (today Brașov in Romania) was, through the scenic beauty of its own cityscape and natural surroundings, simply another Salzburg.[30]

Visiting Salzburg in person, however, proved that the original still eclipsed its Hungarian epigones. Turn-of-the-century Salzburg had been visited by numerous Hungarian travelers, some of whom published their impressions of the place in various dailies. They extolled the natural beauties of the Salzach River valley and of the hills overlooking Salzburg, as well as the city proper for its notable cultural life and iconic status as Mozart's birthplace.[31] The start of the Salzburger Festpiele in 1920 also played an important role in enhancing the city's touristic appeal.

What fascinated many observers was the continuous growth of Salzburg tourism and how the city was turning into a cosmopolitan place. The sound of French, German, Italian, and English (both in its British and American variants) spoken on Salzburg's streets, with Hungarian also occasionally mixing in, was becoming by the mid-1920s another recurring trope in many Salzburg Festival reports published in the Hungarian press.[32]

It was within this context, that in 1926, just a year after Budapest was singled out as a place that had to be turned into a Hungarian Salzburg through the efforts of its Mozart Association, yet another plan was born to follow in Salzburg's footsteps. This plan grew out of the municipality's strong interest in attracting more tourists to the Hungarian capital; it focused on the Gellérthegy, a barren hill centrally overlooking the

---

29 See the section "Die 'Schöne Stadt': Romantische Entdeckung und früher Tourismus," in Dopsch and Hoffmann, *Salzburg – die Geschichte einer Stadt*, 413–22.
30 See the reference to this on p. 103 in Kovách, "Közegészségügyünk állapotáról," *Nemzetgazdasági Szemle*, 98–132.
31 "Úti és fürdői rajzok. I. (Bécsből Salzburgig)," *Fővárosi Lapok*, July 3, 1870.
32 See, for instance, Ferenc Herczeg, "Uj vagyon és régi művészet (Salzburgi levél)," *Uj Idők*, September 10, 1922, and Sándor Galamb, "Iphigénia a sziklák közt," *Szózat*, August 19, 1924.

Danube and downtown Pest, which local tourism promoters and urban developers wanted to turn into a Hungarian Hohensalzburg.[33] In March 1926, Jenő Berczel, the head of the urban planning unit of the Municipality of Budapest announced that, in preparation for the international Spa Towns Association's Congress to be held in Budapest in 1927, the Gellérthegy was to be re-landscaped through a combination of funds provided by the Budapest Spa Association, the Budapest municipality, and a number of private investors. According to the plans of the Budapest municipality, the hill was to "have, on the model of Hohensalzburg, either a lift or a cogwheel track built leading to its top." In addition, the Gellérthegy, rebranded by Berczel as a future Hungarian Hohensalzburg, was described as a place that would acquire many "luxury hotels and extremely gorgeous restaurants" surrounded by parks to be lit at night, while the Danube-facing hillside would have many spotlights installed to attract the viewer's attention from afar.[34] In Berczel's vision, the Gellérthegy was destined to become part of a larger touristic complex which included the nearby Rudas, Rácz, and Gellért Baths (the latter with its modern luxury hotel built in 1918 around the Hungária mineral water source). It was also projected that the hillside of the Gellérthegy would be outfitted with viaducts, artesian fountains, colonnades, and a Japanese garden, so as to make the area through its multiple attractions and amenities even more attractive than the actual Hohensalzburg was.[35]

Berczel's project, however, soon found its detractors and was criticized by Rusztem Vámbéry, a councilor from the ranks of the municipal opposition, for its grandiosity and pompousness—and not least for the exorbitant financial investment that it would require. In a direct swipe against Berczel's boasting about the many leisure amenities that his project would provide for the area, Vámbéry argued that the only commonality between the Gellérthegy and Hohensalzburg was that "both were hills, and neither there nor there would one find an artesian fountain or a viaduct." He considered the whole plan of recreating Hohensalzburg in Budapest nothing more than a fantasy born out of the desire to mimic things that were foreign and transplanted from abroad—just like "the hat of the German fraternity students and the Darwinian theory."[36]

---

33 On pre-war municipal efforts to increase Budapest's urban tourism figures, see Sipos, "'Világváros' Nyugat és Kelet határán? Várospolitikai törekvések Budapest nemzetközi vonzerejének erősitésere, 1870–1918," while for a discussion of international sources of inspiration in their development, see my chapter "From 'Paris of the East' to 'Queen of Danube': Transnational Models in the Promotion of Budapest Tourism, 1885–1940."
34 "Hohen-Salzburg a Gellérthegyen," *Magyarország*, March 4, 1926.
35 "Hohen-Salzburg Budán," *Ujság*, March 4, 1926.
36 "A beruházóprogram a főváros közgyűlésén," *Világ*, April 22, 1926.

Given that one could think of so many other foreign sources of inspiration for developing the hill, ranging from Edinburgh's Hollyrood Palace and Heidelberg's Schlossberg to Prague's Hradčin, Vámbéry also wondered why it was specifically Hohensalzburg that Berczel took up as a model for the redevelopment of the Gellérthegy. He considered it simply wrong to build a simulacrum of Hohensalzburg in Budapest, instead of creating something more authentic to the city. Moreover, if one wanted to attract tourists to Budapest, Vámbéry pointed out, one should not attract them there through the promise of a fake Hohensalzburg, but through better and cheaper hotel and restaurant fares, better public transportation, and much more moderate local expectations for tips.

Vámbéry brought up other important considerations to counter turning the hill into an attraction for foreign visitors, especially the use of municipal funds not for city beautification but rather the building of public housing for the economically distressed urban population and keeping the Gellérthegy available as a space for the recreation of the poorer social classes. Nonetheless, at the conclusion of a speech that he addressed to the plenary meeting of the Budapest Municipal council, he admitted that importing the cosmopolitan spirit of Salzburg or Berlin to Budapest was something that the Hungarian capital could benefit from. If these cities could stage theatrical productions in English or Italian and thus set aside their wartime animosity towards the countries in which these languages were spoken, then there was no reason to persist in the century-old push to nationalize Budapest's theatrical life and resist having theatrical productions presented in English or French to Budapest audiences.[37]

Ultimately, though, it wasn't Vámbéry's opposition that sank Berczel's project (and implicitly, that of the investors that he represented) to model the Gellért Hill after Hohensalzburg, but a set of other, more practical, concerns. Already in February, the Hungarian Geological Institute publicly expressed its worry that tunneling a lift shaft on the Danube-facing side of the Gellérthegy might cause structural problems due to the hill's porous geological structure and affect the water quality of the underground springs feeding the Rudas and Gellért Baths.[38] Later in the course of these discussions, another voice joining the public debate regarding the future of Gellérthegy was that of Károly Kaán, a well-known economist and forestry specialist, and a

---

37 For the full text of Vámbery's interpellation, see the minutes of the April 21, 1926 meeting of the Budapest Municipal Council, published in *Fővárosi Közlöny*, April 23, 1926.
38 "A Földtani Intézet nem enged alagutat vagy liftaknát fúrni a Gellérthegyben," *Az Est*, February 19, 1926.

corresponding member of the Hungarian Academy of Sciences. Kaán argued that through its location in the middle of the city and as a witness of centuries of Hungarian history, the hill was part of the national patrimony, and as such, it had to be preserved in its natural state, together with the Austrian-built military fortress on top of it. The only minimal modification to the original natural ensemble of the hill (one that he had also proposed in a separate memorandum that he had submitted earlier to the municipality) that he could approve of was the building of a scenic overlook that would allow visitors to enjoy panoramic views of Budapest and the Danube River. As for publicly accessing the hill, he recommended building a serpentine road (that could be used equally by private motor cars and charabancs for tourists), inspired not by Hohensalzburg's example, but rather by the scenic road that led down from the heights of the neighboring Saint-Nizier village to the French city of Grenoble.[39]

Odd as it might seem, Kaán was able to settle the debate in his favor, and as the subsequent redevelopment of the Gellérthegy area during the late 1920s and 1930s showed, instead of following in the footsteps of Salzburg, which was geographically much closer to Budapest, the hill's redevelopment followed the example provided by the natural and man-made surroundings of a geographically more distant and relatively unknown French regional center.

Hungarian Participation and Successes at the 1926 and 1927 Salzburger Festspiele

By the mid-1920s initiatives such as the creation of the Mozart Association in Budapest and (despite its failure) the project to develop the Gellérthegy as a Hungarian Hohensalzburg had cemented Salzburg's image among Hungarians as a city possessing considerable cultural, architectural, and natural capital. What added a new layer of meaning to this representation was the large participation and considerable success of Hungarian artists at the 1926 edition of the Salzburg Festival. By comparison with previous years, when the presence of Hungarian artists in the Festival program was thin, in 1926 Max Reinhardt cast up-and-coming Hungarian actress Lili Darvas in the role of the main character's mother in the Festival flagship production of *Jedermann*, a role in which she excelled, while Mária Németh sang to great acclaim in the role of Donna Anna in Mozart's *Don Giovanni*. Piroska (aka Rosette) Anday's mezzo-soprano performance as Prince Orlovsky in Johann Strauss's

---

39 Károly Kaán, "A Szent Gellért-Hegy," *Budapesti Hírlap*, May 23, 1926.

Hungarian Salzburgs 311

Fledermaus also received good reviews.[40] The Hungarian press also highlighted the Festival participation of Rózsi Várady, a Hungarian violoncellist living in New York, who successfully played several of Mozart's and Kodály's cello sonatas for the international public.[41] Ferenc Molnár, the internationally celebrated Hungarian novelist and playwright (who had recently married Lily Darvas, and who was an intimate friend of Max Reinhardt) was also in Salzburg after spending several weeks together with his own wife, Reinhardt, and the latter's spouse, Helene Thimig, at the Excelsior Hotel on Venice's Lido.[42] There were also other Hungarian musicians playing minor roles in the program of that year's Festival. Newspaper reports singled out János Koncz who closed the Mozarteum's program with a solo recital which included compositions by Hubay, Paganini, Mozart, and Brahms, as well as Győző (aka Viktor) Madin, a singer at the Vienna State Opera born in pre-war Hungary, performing together with Mária Németh in the opera *Don Giovanni*.[43]

In 1926 as in no earlier edition of the Salzburg Festival, the inclusion and presence of so many Hungarians made it stand out in the cultural news section of Hungarian newspapers. To emphasize even more Hungarian connections to the Salzburger Festspiele, the Hungarian press always referred to Max Reinhardt using the Hungarian spelling (Miksa) of his first name, also describing him as a Hungarian national, on account of the frequent pre- and postwar theatrical performances that he directed in Budapest,[44] and his alleged Hungarian citizenship.[45]

---

40 Jób Paál, "Magyarok diadala Salzburgban az idei nagy ünnepi játékokon." *Színházi Élet*, 1926, 34.
41 Erzsébet Pünkösti, "Várady Rózsi Salzburgban is sikert aratott Kodály Zoltán csellóra irt magyar táncaival," *Ujság*, August 25, 1926.
42 "A megsoványodott Molnár Ferenc és az elegáns Darvas Lili délelőtt fürdőruhában nyaralnak a Lidón, esténkint pedig pezsgő mellett táncolnak Reinhardtékkal," *Esti Kurir*, August 6, 1926.
43 See Paál, "Magyarok diadala ... "
44 While between 1899 and 1904 and 1907 and 1914, Reinhardt performed, either as an actor or director, every year in Budapest, he continued to also do so in 1916, and then intermittently between 1926 and 1935. For the extremely wide range of classic and modern plays that Reinhardt brought to Hungarian audiences, see Geza Staud, "Max Reinhardt in Ungarn."
45 Although according to the accounts published in English and German sources, Max Reinhardt was born in Baden-bei-Wien in 1873, moving to Vienna when he was four years old, Hungarian encyclopedias of the interwar period identified him alternately as having been born either in Bazin (Bösing in German and Pezinok in Slovak) or Stomfa (Stumpfen in German; Stupava in Slovak), two small towns located in pre-war Hungary in the immediate vicinity of Pozsony (Bratislava), the latter being also the birthplace of Reinhardt's father. See the entries "Reinhardt Miksa" in Újvári, *Magyar Zsidó Lexikon*, and "Reinhardt Max" in Schöpflin, *Magyar Színművészeti Lexikon*.

Reinhardt was a familiar figure on the Hungarian stage, someone whose work received constant coverage in the press because of the formative influence that he had on many Hungarian theater directors before the First World War.[46] Such coverage clearly helped many readers familiar with Reinhardt's work to see the Festival as a joint Austrian and Hungarian undertaking.

The strong impression on Hungarians made by that year's festival was also reinforced by a local staging of *Jedermann* by the young director of a Hungarian theater troupe based in Miskolc, Mihály Sebestyén, just a couple of months after the closing of Reinhardt's Salzburg production. Translated as *Akárki* (literally *Jedermann* in Hungarian), Hofmannsthal's mystery play premiered in Budapest's Operetta Theater on October 2, 1926.[47] Although it opened to mixed reviews,[48] the theater responded to the heightened public interest for the production by extending the initially scheduled run of five performance to include two more;[49] after debuting in Budapest, *Akárki* was also taken on a tour of the provinces.[50]

The 1927 edition of the Salzburger Festpiele had noteworthy Hungarian participation once more. Lili Darvas and Mária Németh were again invited to perform.[51] After spending the month of July in his favorite resort on Venice's Lido, Molnár also headed for Salzburg. That year, the city's performance venues, hotels, and streets were filled with scores of other Hungarian celebrities and the cream of Hungary's aristocracy. The reporter of the flagship theater publication, *Színházi Élet* (Theatrical Life), read by every person of a certain economic and cultural status in Hungary, interviewed Molnár in Salzburg. The playwright offered a who's who listing of his Hungarian entourage:

> Look around on the *Domplatz* [Dome Square] – see how many Hungarians [are here]. To mention just ones whom I know: the Gyula Andrássy clan is here, as are the Odescalchi princes, the Csáky family, almost all the Eszterházys (who came to Salzburg

---

46 See Pór, "Max Reinhardt, figure budapestoise."
47 "'Akárki' ('Jedermann') a Fővárosi Operettszínházban," *8 Órai Ujság*, October 2, 1926.
48 See "A magyar 'Jedermann'," *Az Est*, October 2, 1926; Kürti, "Jedermann a Fővárosi Operettszínházban"; Ödön Marjay, "Művészeti Szemle," *Napkelet*, November 1, 1926; and "Nemcsak a salzburgi ünnepi játékokon a Fővárosi Operettszínházban is sikert aratott a Jedermann." *Színházi Élet*, 1926, 41.
49 "Meghosszabbították a Jedermann előadásait," *Magyarság*, October 10, 1926.
50 "A mostanában divatos turnék után, mint értesülünk, rövidesen aktuális lesz a Jedermann-turné," *Magyarország*, October 5, 1926, and "A miskolci színház megnyitása," *Budapesti Hírlap*, October 10, 1926.
51 "Németh Mária és Darvas Lili a salzburgi ünnepi Játékokon," *Pesti Hírlap*, July 29, 1927.

Hungarian Salzburgs 313

with four motor cars), the counts Bánffy, the Rudnyánszky family, Andor Miklós and Frida Gombaszögi, Henrik Fellner, Dr. Aurél Egry, Ödön Beniczky with his wife, the Bettelheims, then Franci Gál with her husband, Sándor Lestyán, Jenő Faludi, Géza Raskó, Géza Feleki, Gyuri Marton, the Góth clan, Irén Gombaszögi, Lili Hatvany, Jenő Nádor with his wife, Ödön Lázár, Miklós Lázár and his wife, Dr. Pauker, Tessza Madarassy-Beck, not to mention hundreds of others whom I don't know, but who are Hungarian and belong to the social circles that constitute the best public for every theatrical event. The thought springs unbidden to mind: wouldn't it be possible to organize similar *Festspiele* in some Hungarian provincial city? And wouldn't it be a fine thing if this Hungarian public, which traversed hundreds of kilometers to come here, could visit Hungarian productions with the same fervor?[52]

At the festival, Darvas excelled again in her new role as Lady Milford in Reinhardt's production of Schiller's *Kabale und Liebe* (Intrigue and Love).[53] As journalists reported, after the performance, Max Reinhardt gave a Hungarian dinner in Darvas's honor and invited select Festival guests to come to his summer residence at Leopoldskron to celebrate her. As many Hungarian publications noted with delight, the highlight of the menu that evening was "*gulyás* [hearty Hungarian beef soup] served in gold and silver dishes."[54]

All this commotion in the Hungarian press about Hungary's artistic, aristocratic, and culinary participation in the Salzburger Festpiele naturally propelled the event into the forefront of everyone's attention for a second time. The 1926 clamor around the Festival had led in the autumn of that year to the staging of *Jedermann* in Budapest and several provincial cities. Now, the 1927 hullaballoo about the prime place reserved for *gulyás* on the menu of Reinhardt's Leopoldskron dinner, together with Molnár's call for the creation of a Hungarian counterpart to the Festspiele, quite naturally spawned ambitious plans in the minds not just of stage directors but also of politicians, city officials, and venue promoters all over Hungary, who jumped at the opportunity and started talking about the need to create Salzburg-like events in several Hungarian towns and cities.

---

52 "Molnár Ferenc elmondja: kik voltak idén magyarok a salzburgi Festspielen?" *Színházi Élet*, 1926, 36.
53 Sándor Lestyán, "Ünnepi játékok, Ármány és szerelem, Reinhardt és Darvas Lily," *Ujság*, August 24, 1926.
54 "Schiller tragédiájának salzburgi előadása után Reinhardt gulyásra hívta meg a Festspiele vendégeit," *Színházi Élet*, 1926, 36, and "Reinhardt gulyás-bankettje Salzburgban," *Pesti Napló*, September 1, 1926.

Salzburg and the Emerging Arts Festival Field in Hungary

In 1929, following up on this nationwide infatuation with Salzburg and responding to Molnár's 1927 prompt about what a wonderful thing a Hungarian festival could be for domestic theater audiences, three Hungarian provincial cities, Szeged, Eger, and Sopron (followed a few years later by Pécs), made bids to follow in the footsteps of the Salzburger Festspiele. The scarce Hungarian representation in the program of the 1928 Salzburg festival might have also been a motivating element, given that the Hungarian triumphs of previous years had not produced a sequel.

Szeged, a university city and county seat of slightly over a hundred thousand inhabitants in the southeast of Hungary, about 180 kilometers from Budapest, was first to express public interest in starting its own festival. The call was raised by a young Hungarian theater director, Ferenc Hont, who had worked during the mid-1920s as assistant director of the Odéon Theater in Paris under the direction of Firmin Gémier. Like Reinhardt, Gémier was famous for his large open-air theatrical productions which included hundreds of actors watched by thousands of spectators.[55] Due to his close connections with Hont, Gémier was already familiar with the Hungarian theatrical scene: in an interview given to the Hungarian director in Paris, the text of which was published in May 1927 in one of Szeged's main dailies, Gémier even hinted that starting a theater festival might be the right path for Szeged to overcome its cultural marginalization by Budapest and to connect itself to the European theatrical scene by staging avant-garde works.[56]

Later, however, and perhaps also influenced by Molnár's prompt, Hont dropped Gémier's earlier suggestion in order to propose a plan of action more in line with the expectations and tastes of a Hungarian theater public fascinated with the example set by Salzburg. Therefore, in April 1929, Hont came out strongly in favor of staging mystery plays "on the model of the Salzburger Festspiele in an open area, specifically on the decorative plaza in front of Szeged's so-called Alsóvárosi Church."[57] Looking for ways to boost local tourism, Szeged's

---

55 For an informed discussion of Gémier's career in the world of French and European theater, see Faivre-Zellner, *Firmin Gémier: Héraut du théâtre populaire*, while for the influence that Reinhardt's mass theatrical productions had on Gémier, see Baron, "Max Reinhardt, Firmin Gémier, Jacques Copeau: influences et analogies."
56 Ferenc Hont, "Gémier a szegedi színházról. A Színházi Világszövetség elnökének nyilatkozata a Délmagyarország számára," *Délmagyarország*, May 11, 1927.
57 Ferenc Hont, "Ünnepi játékok Szegeden," *Ujság*, April 23, 1929.

municipality readily embraced Hont's project,[58] and Hont, together with local theater intendant Pállfy, presented it for approval to Hungary's Ministry of Religion and Public Culture.[59] Instead of a permit, however, their submission only yielded a programmatic cultural policy article written by Minister Count Kuno Klebelsberg, published in July 1929 in the Budapest daily *Pesti Napló*. A leader in matters of cultural policy in Hungary, Klebelsberg dangled the possibility of staging passion plays in Szeged once its new square, surrounded with arcades overlooking the still unfinished Votive Church, was completed. However, he also bowed to upholding the capital city's cultural primacy by considering at the same time the possibility of opening an outdoor theater for summer theater productions on Budapest's Margaret Island.[60]

While Klebelsberg's hesitation to grant immediate permission for Hont's festival stalled the idea of Szeged following in Salzburg's footsteps, other public figures still pushed the festival idea forward as a profitable option for other cities. For instance, in an article published in May 1929, just a few weeks after Hont's proposal to stage mystery plays in Szeged, Andor Pünkösti, the theater critic of *Ujság* (News), a liberal daily published in Budapest, declared Eger to be the leading candidate to become a Hungarian Salzburg. According to Pünkösti, the suitability of Eger for such a role, a town of 31,000 inhabitants located in the foothills of the Bükk Mountains about 110 kilometers northeast of Budapest, was based on the fact that the city had "a bishopric founded by St. Stephen," that it was "a county seat" with "an organized municipal council," and that it had "a courthouse, a finance office, and a state-managed urban planning board." Pünkösti also drew attention to the city's educational institutions, listing them as "law and theology faculties, a public notary course, and numerous impressive boys' and girls' schools." In addition, Eger also sported "a dozen famous churches" and a "fortress, which was built before [the era of] St. Stephen, and which was carved into Hungarian history by the heroism of István Dobó" as part of the Hungarians' resistance against a sixteenth-century Turkish military onslaught. Moreover, Eger also had "[writer Geza] Gárdonyi's house and tomb. Warm springs and wonderful spas, [and] *last but not least* [as Pünkösti emphasized in English], Eger wines."[61]

Most importantly, just like Salzburg, Eger offered tourists a baroque cityscape. As they could in its Austrian counterpart, they were able to

---

58 "A magyar Salzburg: Ünnepi játékok Szeged környékén szabad ég alatt," *Magyarország*, April 23, 1929.
59 "Magyar ünnepi játékok Szegeden," *Magyarság*, April 23, 1929.
60 Gróf Kuno Klebelsberg, "Munka, tudás és tőke," *Pesti Napló*, July 28, 1929.
61 Gróf Kuno Klebelsberg, "Munka, tudás és tőke," *Pesti Napló*, July 28, 1929. Gárdonyi was the author of *Egri csillagok* (*Eger Stars*), an important historical novel and children's book bestseller in Hungary.

stroll on its cobbled streets and listen to the bells tolling from the towers of its numerous churches. Moreover, Eger had a minaret (dating back to the years of its Turkish occupation), so that someone on a stroll might even imagine hearing the voice of the muezzin calling Muslims to their ritual prayer, an element of Eastern exoticism that—as Pünkösti believed—could trump Salzburg's appeal for foreign visitors. What is more, Eger was not just baroque, but modern as well. Walking its streets, one could not just be transported into the past, but then also miraculously be brought back to the present by the sight of "men in trench-coats and short-skirted women sporting [contemporary] bob-style hairdos."

There were other cultural amenities, as well. In 1785 a member of the Esterházy family had built the Eger Lyceum, an institution "originally meant to become a university," which had "eighty thousand precious books bound in leather." In the 1830s, Bishop Pyrker had built the city's Metropolitan Cathedral Basilica of St. John the Apostle, a building that, even if not as old as Salzburg's Cathedral, was bigger and more imposing. As Pünkösti pointed out in a rhetorical climax: the Basilica's set of majestic colonnades "was beyond every Hungarian's imagination," and so this building and the spacious area in front of it clamored "for a new Reinhardt, who would stage on its wonderful front steps the Hungarian *Jedermann*."[62] How could a "dream city" such as Eger not become a Hungarian Salzburg?

In spite of all its rhetorical bombast, what Pünkösti's boosterism left unsaid was that turning the city into a replica of Salzburg required not only baroque buildings, an appealing natural setting, modern people, libraries with old books, and cathedrals with appropriate staging areas for mystery plays, but also a festival ideology, artistic talent, money, institutional support, crowds of tourists, and a reserve of symbolic cultural capital to build on—the kind of long-term precedents that Salzburg already had and that Eger was far from having acquired by that point. To be sure, in 1929, Eger's municipal government had opened a few new administrative buildings and made some moves in the direction of attracting tourists to come visit the city to discover its natural setting and baroque cityscape.[63] Yet for lack of public support, Eger's momentum faltered. Years later, in 1938, the celebrated journalist and novelist Sándor Márai, an important figure in interwar public life, relaunched the campaign to turn Eger into a Hungarian Salzburg, but it was too late.[64] By then, the advances that Sopron, Pécs, and most importantly Szeged had made in starting their own cultural events turned Márai's PR campaign for Eger into a futile enterprise.

---

62 Andor Pünkösti, "Magyar Salzburg," *Ujság*, May 26, 1929.
63 "Eger példája a helyes idegenforgalmi propagandára," *Városok Lapja*, June 1, 1929.
64 Sándor Márai, "Ünnepi játék," *Pesti Hírlap*, April 7, 1938.

Szeged's initial stalling and Eger's failure to take up this role in 1929, however, facilitated the efforts of another provincial city, Sopron, to become a Hungarian Salzburg, through a set of initiatives that at the beginning turned out to be much more effective. Situated on the western border of Hungary, directly adjoining Austria, and thus located geographically much closer to Vienna (only 60 kilometers away) than to Budapest, Sopron's hinterland had over the centuries acquired its own place in European musical history. In the immediate vicinity of Sopron are both the Esterházy Palace in nearby Kismarton (since 1918, Eisenstadt in Austria's Burgenland), together with another palace at Esterháza built in the 1760s, where Joseph Haydn had lived and composed while in the employment of the Esterházy princes. Even more importantly, Doborján/Raiding, the village where Franz (Ferenc) Liszt was born in 1811, lies just a few kilometers south of Sopron. Even more critically, the Choral and Musical Association of Sopron, which was proud to have had Karl (Károly) Goldmark (1830–1915) as a pupil during the 1840s, was also turning a hundred years old in 1929, the year when the association decided to celebrate its centennial by organizing a three-day music festival in the city.

What made this initiative competitive to the point where Sopron suddenly actually began to be comparable to Salzburg was the simple fact that such well-known composers as Bartók, Hubay, Dohnányi, and Kodály, who had already been celebrated for their musical achievements in Salzburg and many other European musical centers, lent their names and physical presences to the event. Moreover, just as in the case of the Salzburger Festpiele, which relied to a great extent on the participation of conductors, musicians, and actors from the Vienna Opera and the Burgtheater, the organizers of Sopron's 1929 musical festival were able to secure the participation of many musicians and singers from the Budapest Philharmonic and Opera. In an additional attempt to enhance its reputable historical genealogy as a city of music, organizers of the event cleverly associated names from contemporary Hungarian music with the more famous names of Sopron's musical past: Haydn, Liszt, and Goldmark. In doing so, they hoped that the centennial celebration of the founding of Sopron's musical association would be the prologue for an "annual recurring musical event that will turn Sopron into a Hungarian Salzburg."[65]

---

65 "Október húszadikán magyar Salzburggá változik Sopron," *Ujság*, September 29, 1929. It is interesting to note that both Liszt and Goldmark had disputed legacies, with Liszt being also seen as a German composer, and Goldmark as an Austrian one. For more on this, see Quinn, *Franz Liszt* and Brodbeck, "Heimat Is Where the Heart Is; or, What Kind of Hungarian was Goldmark?"

The Hungarian Minister of the Interior's decision to waive the visa fee for foreign visitors (mostly Austrians) attending the event[66] and Hungarian radio's willingness to broadcast the Sopron Festival's concert program showed that important governmental and media support had already been secured by the organizers, offering a significant guarantee that Sopron would be able to measure up in time to Salzburg's appeal. The fact that Sopron's musical program would be available not just to listeners in Budapest but also to German audiences in a broadcast by Radio Munich was another important step in this direction.[67] To support Sopron's claim as a venerable musical center, the commentary in the Budapest press about the Sopron concert broadcasts also emphasized the important connections between the city and Liszt, highlighting that an eight-year-old Liszt had appeared for the first time on stage in Sopron, thereby launching his subsequent European career.[68] The implication that such commentary drew was obvious: if Salzburg was Mozart's city, then Sopron was Liszt's.[69]

Aside from Liszt's music, the inclusion in the festival's program of concerti and sonatas by Weber and Bach also showed that Sopron, just like Salzburg, was open to the idea of internationalism in music.[70] What made Sopron's bid to become a Hungarian Salzburg even more promising was that the festival idea was not dropped after the completion of the 1929 series of concerts. Although in 1930 the city flirted mostly with the idea of turning the popular fair held in late September into an event more like Munich's Oktoberfest,[71] in 1932, Sopron's comparison to Salzburg was back in the news because the city had decided to organize its own week-long Haydn festival.[72] Once again, to provide the event more public exposure, the Budapest radio broadcast the Festival program's concluding highlight, Haydn's *Creation* oratorio, while festival organizers arranged for discounted fare trains to run to Sopron from Vienna and Budapest throughout the duration of the event.[73] Indeed, more than two thousand tourists from these two cities flocked to Sopron on the

---

66 "Zenei ünnep Sopronban," *Budapesti Hírlap*, October 10, 1929.
67 "Rádióközlemények," *Népszava*, October 17, 1929.
68 "Rádió-zene," *Magyarság*, October 22, 1929.
69 "Zenei életünkből," *Magyarság*, November 9, 1929.
70 "Zenei ünnepségek Sopronban. A százesztendős zeneegyesület," *Pesti Hírlap*, October 22, 1929.
71 "Sopron legyen a magyar Salzburg," *Városok Lapja*, September 1, 1930. On the origins and history of Munich's own Oktoberfest, see Gaab, *Munich: Hofbräuhaus & History*, 17–27, *passim*, and Krauss-Meyl, *Das Oktoberfest*.
72 "A külföld is érdeklődik a soproni ünnepi játékok iránt," *8 Órai Ujság*, August 28, 1932.
73 "A soproni ünnepi játékok," *Pesti Hírlap*, September 4, 1929.

second day of the festival, Sunday, September 4, only to be frustrated and blocked from enjoying the outdoor performance of Haydn's *Creation* by the sudden downpour that drove everyone away from the city's main square.[74] Although Haydn's famous oratorio had been enjoyed by many other spectators the day before, the weather's adversity the next day showed that, unlike Salzburg, where, with the exception of *Jedermann*, the majority of performances were held indoors, Sopron did not have enough indoor venues where other musical and theatrical events could be performed in case of bad weather.

Unfortunately for Sopron, it was not just the lack of indoor festival venues and tourist amenities such as Salzburg's luxurious hotels and restaurants that set back its attempt to compete with Salzburg, but the fact that, after organizing Liszt-centered and Haydn festivals, local boosters simply ran out of creative ideas and gave up on the idea of organizing more music festivals. Although from the mid- to the late 1930s, another provincial city, Pécs, located in the south of the country, also intermittently joined the emerging field of Hungarian festival cities, trying to capitalize both on its cityscape, musical heritage and theatrical institutions to acquire a notable place in it, the city that succeeded during those years in earning for itself the Hungarian Salzburg moniker was not Pécs, but the aforementioned Szeged.[75]

It was in Szeged where, after the initial stalling of its festival preparations at the end of the 1920s, a summer arts festival was opened in 1931 that was able to prove its viability in the long term. Large monetary investments, strong governmental support, the involvement of Budapest artists, skillful marketing campaigns, and the participation of notable artistic talent, enabled this event to be repeated annually throughout the 1930s, and to continue operating in Hungary both under communism and during the post-communist period, a development that ultimately undermined the efforts of other Hungarian cities to become epigones of Salzburg at their turn.

The Festival Cultures of Salzburg and Szeged during the 1930s

By the 1930s, after a decade marked by the accumulation of success after success, the Salzburger Festspiele had become a venerable institution on the Festival circuit, enjoying both European and North American

---

74 "Ünnepi játékok Sopronban. A vasárnapi szabadtéri előadást elmosta az eső," *Pesti Hírlap*, September 6, 1932.
75 For more on the artistic aims of and the different types of performances that the Pécs festival included, see the collection of press articles included in Kerekes, Kindl, and Szabó, *Post Festum*, esp. 139–84, 347–82 and 495–553.

fame. Salzburg also thrived on the Austrian interwar cultural scene as a counterpart and complement to Vienna's offerings.

According to Michael Steinberg, a reason for the Salzburg Festival's domestic significance was that it presented a neo-baroque cultural construct to postimperial Austria, one that reconnected Austrians with the roots of a widely shared baroque Catholic cosmopolitanism. In the interwar period, in consequence, the Salzburger Festpiele became an important laboratory for the construction of an Austrian identity. For the outside world, as Steinberg put it, "the tact and success of the pan-European Salzburg propaganda came from the fact that this nationalist program could be expressed as a cosmopolitan ideal that it would in turn seem like pure internationalism to the English and the French."[76]

While "the French and the English" might well have appreciated the Salzburger Festspiele for the event's perceived internationalism, Hungarians found the Festival's greatest appeal in Reinhardt's and Hofmannsthal's nationalist cosmopolitanism. According to many historians, during the interwar period the Horthy Regime's national and Christian political program[77] had produced a neo-baroque society in Hungary, with a mindset defined by "copying and imitation."[78] The conservative and nationalist ideology of the Salzburg Festival, together with its veneer of Christian universalism and baroque cosmopolitanism, were therefore seen sympathetically and were eagerly embraced by an older generation of Hungary's political and cultural elite.

The best example proving this point is the inclusion of Hont's proposed Szeged festival into the Hungarian government's revisionist cultural offensive. After stalling the proposal in 1929, Count Kuno Klebelsberg, as Szeged's MP in the Hungarian Parliament and Hungary's Minister of Religion and Public Education between 1922 and 1931, tied it to the neo-nationalist ideological platform that he developed in the mid-1920s as the framework for a more coherent Hungarian cultural diplomacy. With revisionist goals in mind, he aimed to present Hungary to foreign audiences as a *Kulturnation* (nation of culture)

---

76 Steinberg, *The Meaning of the Salzburg Festival*, 69.
77 For an overview, see Hanebrink, *In Defense of Christian Hungary*.
78 For this observation and the original formulation of the concept of the neo-baroque society as a heuristic device to understand the mentality of interwar Hungary, see Szekfü, *Három nemzedék és ami utána következik*, 401–505 and esp. 410 for the quote; while for the role of a generational cohort of prominent Hungarian cultural agents in propagandistically framing the cultural values of their country's neo-baroque society, see Ujváry, *A Harmincharmadik Nemzedék: Politika, kultúra és történettudomány a "neo-barokk társadalomban."*

belonging to the west, one that was unjustly sacrificed at Trianon,[79] and so, at the beginning of the 1930s, he jumped at the opportunity to create a cultural event that would replicate the ideology of the Salzburg Festival, while at the same time emphasizing its own Hungarian identity. To achieve this goal, Klebelsberg sidelined the initially more internationalist and populist festival ideas of Gémier and Hont. Instead, after the consecration in 1930 of the newly built Szeged Cathedral (an architectural symbol of Hungary's post-Trianon grievances), in 1931 Klebelsberg gave his blessing to an outdoor festival in the neo-gothic square that had been created around the cathedral, framed by the buildings of the new Szeged university. The cornerstone for that university was laid in 1919 with the relocation to Szeged of the personnel and archival holdings of the University of Kolozsvár, which had been located in a Transylvanian city lost in 1918 to Greater Romania.[80] Due to this relocation, Szeged was seen in the interwar Hungarian public mind as the city that preserved Transylvania's cultural heritage, a part of Hungary that Hungarian revisionists hope to recover in the future. Moreover, as another gesture of deep political significance, the festival was opened by Klebelsberg in Szeged, a city that after the First World War had also briefly served as the provisional capital and rallying point for the counter-revolutionary government that came to power in Budapest with the help of the Allies in the summer of 1919. Thus Szeged was a place that had an important symbolic value in the eyes of Hungary's conservative and nationalist elites, a position that the festival was expected to further enhance.

Klebelsberg's selection of the play *Hungarian Passion* by Géza Voinovich to open the Szeged festival in mid-June 1931 was also devised to provide symbolic service for the Hungarian revisionist cause. The plot of *Hungarian Passion* drew parallels between the sufferings of Christ and the arduous construction of the Kassa (Košice) Cathedral during the fifteenth-century reign of Hungarian King Matthias Corvinus; it was staged in a metaphorical *mise en abyme*, using the metaphor of church construction in front of a recently built cathedral dedicated to redeeming the wounded beliefs and national cause of a betrayed country. A contemporary reviewer of the Szeged staging of Voinovich's *Hungarian Passion* pointedly emphasized the close connections between the two. He commented on how the play excelled at using "artistic tact to unite the religious idea with the national one, the

---

79   See Klebelsberg's programmatic collection of essays, *Neonacionalizmus*, Budapest, Athenaeum, 1928, while for an analysis of the cultural policy implementation of this program, see Nagy, *Great Expectations and Interwar Realities*.
80   For more on this, see Marjanucz, "A kolozsvári egyetem Szegeden."

betrayal of the Redeemer and his triumphant resurrection with the fall of the Hungarian nation and its hoped resurrection" in "a place that could not have ever been better chosen."[81]

While in Salzburg's case, the Festival aimed at forging a common Austrian and Bavarian Catholic identity under the aegis of their shared cosmopolitan baroque spirit, and at strengthening Salzburg's role as a cultural mediator across the Austrian and German border, Szeged, as a border city close to the new frontiers of Yugoslavia and Romania, was equally well positioned for such a mediating role. Indeed, the Szeged Festival was conceived as an event that would attract an audience made up not just of domestic visitors, but also of members of the new Hungarian minorities living in the neighboring states. Mirroring Salzburg's attempt to bring together Germans and Austrians, the Szeged Festival, as Klebelsberg hoped, would turn into a successful cross-border identity-building tool that would symbolically make up for Hungary's postwar territorial losses.[82]

An additional parallel can be made between the political orientations of Szeged and Salzburg festivals in the 1930s. In 1933, the rise of Nazism in Germany and the subsequent Nazi press attacks and economic restrictions that Hitler placed on the Salzburg Festival[83] led the Salzburg Festival to shift its focus. That shift has been described in the 1930s and the immediate Second World War period as the Festival's anti-Bayreuth phase, when Salzburg hoped to act as a place of "refuge for German culture,"[84] symbolized by the coming together in Salzburg after 1933 of prominent anti-Nazis like Marlene Dietrich, Erich Maria Remarque, Thomas Mann, and H. G. Wells, as well as Jewish exiles from Germany like Bruno Frank and Carl Zuckmayer.

The year 1933 was the beginning of important changes in Szeged, as well. Significantly, when the Szeged Festival was restarted in 1933 by the owners of several Szeged newspapers after a year's hiatus caused by Klebelsberg's premature death in 1932, the *Hungarian Passion* was

---

81 Galamb, "A 'Magyar Passio' Szegeden," 137.
82 For more on this, see the preface of Kerekes et al., *Post Festum*, esp. 14–15.
83 For Hitler's attempts to hurt Salzburg's tourist industry, see Otruba, *Hitler's "Tausend-Mark-Sperre" und die Folgen für Österreichs Fremdenverkehr*.
84 The formulation is that of François Mauriac in 1934, cited by Amélie Charnay in her chapter "Au coeur de la construction de l'identité autrichienne: le festival de Salzbourg, 1917–1950." For other recent discussions of the post-1933 Austrian corporatist orientation of the festival, which included a desire to draw a line between Dollfuß/Schuschnigg's Austria and Hitler's Germany, see Novak, *"Salzburg hört Hitler atmen": Die Salzburger Festpiele, 1933–1934*, 27–76, and Kriechbaumer, *Zwischen Österreich und Großdeutschland: Eine Politische Geschichte der Salzburger Festspiele*, esp. 17–204.

Hungarian Salzburgs 323

replaced as the Festival's signature piece. Already in 1931, local journalists had called for *The Tragedy of Man*, a nineteenth-century play by Imre Madách, to be staged under Reinhardt's direction[85] (a suggestion countered by Klebelsberg's preference). With Klebelsberg gone and its governmental links weakened, in 1933, Madách's play did replace the *Hungarian Passion* in the festival's program. With their choice of the *Tragedy of Man*, the new organizers were trying to put the Szeged Festival on the map of European festivals by staging a play with universal meaning, much like that attributed to Reinhardt's staging of *Jedermann*, and possibly under his direction. This play had the necessary scope to fulfill that ambition: it illustrated the challenges to human spirit's triumph in different biblical and historical epochs through the characters of Lucifer and Adam and Eve, and then in a quick succession of stage tableaus set in Heaven, the Garden of Eden, ancient Egypt, Athens and Rome, medieval Constantinople, Renaissance Prague, the French Revolution's Paris, London's Industrial Revolution, an imaginary socialist phalanstery community, and a dystopian ice age society located at the North Pole in a distant future.

After being approached in Salzburg in August 1931, however, Reinhardt politely declined to take charge as Szeged's artistic director,[86] but other directors were eager to follow in his footsteps. Still, none of the quick succession of directors who staged the *Tragedy of Man* in Szeged in the 1930s (Ferenc Hont in 1933, with Gémier also listed as artistic director in the festival program; Count Miklós Bánffy in 1934; Gusztáv Oláh in 1935; Jenő Janovics in 1936; and Hont again in 1937) ever succeeded in creating a Reinhardtian image for this event abroad.[87] Nonetheless, the continuous references to Salzburg in the Szeged and Budapest press showed that Szeged continued to see Salzburg as its main model, which it committed itself to doggedly follow during these years.

As another reflection of the closeness in the political orientation of the two festivals, and in the spirit of solidarity with Austria and its resistance to Nazi Germany, Szeged welcomed the visit of Austrian

---

85 "Jaték a szabadtéren," *Délmagyarország*, May 16, 1931. According to István Nikolényi (see his "Az ember tragédiája a szabadtérin: Reinhardt üzenete," *Délmagyarország*, July 11, 1976), it was József Pásztor, the chief editor of *Délmagyarország*, who expressed the desire to have Reinhardt direct the Szeged festival.
86 As a sign of the continuing interest in Reinhardt's work, soon after the closing of the 1931 edition of the Szeged festival, he was interviewed in Salzburg by Szeged journalist Jób Paál, who invited him to direct Madách's play in Szeged in 1932, but Reinhardt politely declined. See Jób Paál, "Reinhardt és a szegedi ünnepi játekok," *Délmagyarország*, September 3, 1933, and István Nikolényi, "Az ember tragédiája a szabadtérin: Reinhardt üzenete," *Délmagyarország*, July 11, 1976.
87 Lugosi, *A szegedi szabadtéri játékok története, 1931–1937*.

Chancellor Kurt Schuschnigg in 1934. Schuschnigg arrived in the city to attend the Festival only days after that summer's assassination of his predecessor, Chancellor Dollfuß by Austrian Nazis, and the outlawing of the Nazi party in Austria.[88] The visit was not only ceremonial: after that visit, Schuschnigg conferred with Prime Minister Gyula Gömbös and Regent Horthy in Budapest about ways to consolidate the tripartite Austro-Italian-Hungarian political rapprochement, which he intended to turn into a bulwark against the Nazi threat.[89] As in Salzburg, where the Festival disassociated itself from what was going on in Germany in 1933 by choosing the Italian Arturo Toscanini, well known for his anti-Nazi views, as the permanent conductor of the Salzburg orchestra, during the mid-1930s the Szeged Festival also added an Italian component to its program.

Indeed, after Schuschnigg's visit in 1934, it was Italy's turn to make an appearance at the Szeged festival, as the Hungarian government celebrated the renewed Hungarian-Italian friendship by inviting composer Pietro Mascagni to come to Szeged in 1935 to join Horthy in watching the performance of his famous opera *Cavalleria Rusticana* (*Parasztbecsület* in Hungarian).[90]

In these years, the Salzburger Festpiele also again welcomed Hungarian artists to celebrate together with its own. The success of the Hungarian-born Attila Hörbiger's first casting in the role of *Jedermann* at the 1935 edition of the Festspiele,[91] followed two years later by a performance of Ernst (Ernő) von Dohnányi's *Szeged Mass* in Salzburg's Cathedral,[92] together with Richard Strauss's premiere of his *Elektra* in the Festpielhaus, were indeed declared by the Hungarian press to be the two most important highlights of the 1937 Salzburg Festival.[93]

Conclusion

In spite of the important ideological correlations between Salzburg and Szeged's founding as neo-baroque festivals and the mid-1930s political alignment between Austria, Hungary, and Italy which left their imprint

---

88 See "Schuschnigg kancellár Szegeden," *Budapesti Hírlap*, August 9, 1934.
89 "A nézetek teljes összhangja, a legszorosabb barátság és együttműködés: Hivatalos közlés a két kormányfő tanácskozásáról," *Budapesti Hírlap*, August 11, 1934.
90 Lugosi, *A szegedi szabadtéri játékok története*, 45, 48–9.
91 See "A salzburgi játékok hőse: Hörbiger Attila," *Magyarság*, July 31, 1935.
92 Dohnányi was already familiar to Salzburg audiences through his conducting of the guest appearance of the Budapest Philharmonic Orchestra which opened the 1930 Festspiele; see "Magyar kompozíciókat játszik Salzburgban a pesti filharmónia," *Ujság*, November 23, 1930.
93 "Dohnányi Ernő ünneplése és az 'Elektra' premierje Salzburgban," *Ujság*, August 10, 1937.

on these festivals' programming, contemporaries believed that by 1937, the Szeged Festival had matured into an event with a distinct Hungarian flavor. Organizers even added ethnographic elements such as specially designed ticket counters and festival tents that reproduced the shape of village houses in the vicinity of Szeged and festival ushers and waiters dressed up in Hungarian costumes—touches that they hoped could be further enhanced in the future.[94]

As the Festival thrived during the 1930s, those who have written about it have generally analyzed it from the perspective of a domestic context to emphasize its role as the premier summer festival of interwar Hungary and, after its relaunching in 1959, as central to socialist and post-socialist Hungary, as well.[95] Yet when considered from the perspective of the impact that Salzburg's rise as a *Kulturstadt* had on neighboring Hungary during the interwar period, one must see the Szeged Festival in a new light. Szeged's success came at the end of a series of attempts that Budapest, Eger, Sopron, Pécs, and a few other Hungarian cities[96] had made to copy and turn Salzburg's natural, cultural, and symbolic capital into their own local currency. As part of an arts festival field that would emerge domestically, Szeged was the first city to publicly proclaim its desire to become a Hungarian Salzburg. Although such hopes had initially been challenged by other competitors and slowed down by Klebelsberg's emphasis on national Hungarian cultural policy imperatives in building a favorable image for Hungary abroad, it was this southeastern Hungarian city (second in size only to Budapest) that during the mid-1930s created for itself the most consistent profile as a festival city in Hungary—one not only influenced by but walking in tandem with the Salzburger Festspiele.

These developments have not been recognized in the dominant historiography about the Salzburg Festival, which has remained Austria-centric, focused on its connections to the more familiar German contexts of Munich, Oberammergau, and Bayreuth, or contrasted

---

94 Lugosi, *A szegedi szabadtéri játékok története*, 88.
95 For in-house works looking at the interwar and postwar history of the Szeged Festival, see the already cited Lugosi, *A szegedi szabadtéri játékok története*; Pásztor, *A szegedi szabadtéri játékok története: Három év monográfiája*; Sz. Simon, *A játékok krónikája*; Kovács, Nikolényi, and Pollner, *A szegedi szabadtéri játékok kézikönyve*; Bátyai, Herczeg, and Kesselyák, *A szegedi szabadtéri játékok története*; Herczeg, *A szegedi szabadtéri játékok 85 éve*.
96 Among others, one could mention Miskolc and Tatatóváros, two cities that had organized cultural events in the 1930s with the similar aim of labeling themselves as Hungarian Salzburgs. See Mihály Hajós, "Jöjjetek a magyar Salzburgba!," *Magyar Festőipar*, July 1, 1932, and "Magyar Salzburgot és Haydn-operát tervez a tatai gróf," *Pesti Hírlap*, June 14, 1933.

Salzburg's festival culture with that of social democratic Vienna.[97] By contrast, if one reverses that dominant optic and looks across Austria's eastern border, Hungary's festival plans document how Salzburg's Festspiele created a much broader map of Central European festivals which included smaller non-Germanic festivals that emerged in its orbit.

In a similar vein, the impact that Salzburg's touristic image, with its Mozarteum, fortress, and Festival had on Hungarian music life, cultural policy initiatives, urban boosterism, and city marketing in Hungary documents another important dimension of the transnational and international influence that this western Austrian city had attained during the interwar years. Indeed, Salzburg was not just a *Kulturstadt* but a paradigmatic *Tourismusstadt* for the region that provided Hungarian cities with immediate cues on how Salzburg's tourism industry promoted urban and economic growth.[98]

Most importantly, however, as this brief excursus into the history of cultural transfers between Salzburg and interwar Hungary illustrates, there were many ways in which Salzburg, stimulated the cultural imagination of Hungarians during the 1920s and 1930s. Based on the evidence presented here, one must conclude that there were many imaginary Salzburgs that were constructed in Hungary during this time period knowledge of which enables us to better understand the significance of the original.

Bibliography

Secondary Literature

Baron, Phillippe. "Max Reinhardt, Firmin Gémier, Jacques Copeau: influences et analogies." Special issue: "Modes intellectuelles et capitales mitteleuropéennes autour de 1900: échanges et transferts." *Germanica* 43 (2008), 161–72.

Bátyai, Edina, Tamás Herczeg, and Gergely Kesselyák. *A szegedi szabadtéri játékok története, 2004–2009*. Szeged: Szegedi Szabadtéri Játékok és Fesztivál Szervező Kht., 2010.

Brodbeck, David. "Heimat Is Where the Heart Is; or, What Kind of Hungarian was Goldmark?" *Austrian History Yearbook* 48 (April 2017), 235–54.

---

97 See Janke, *Politische Massenfestspiele in Österreich zwischen 1918 und 1938*, and Alys X. George, "Everyman and the New Man: Festival Culture in Interwar Austria" (reprinted in the present volume).

98 For an elaboration on the close connections between such iconic figures as Mozart and the rise of Salzburg's tourism industry, see Hoffmann, "Mozart and the Image of Salzburg." For other approaches on the growth and general significance of Salzburg's tourism industry, see the essays in Haas, Hoffmann, and Luger, *Weltbühne und Naturkulisse: Zwei Jahrhunderte Salzburg-Tourismus*.

Charnay, Amélie. "Au coeur de la construction de l'identité autrichienne: le festival de Salzbourg, 1917–1950." In Anaïs Fléchet, Pascal Goetschel, Patricia Hidiroglou, Sophie Jacotot, Caroline Moine, and Julie Verlaine, eds., *Une histoire des festivals: XXe–XXIe siècle*, 203–16. Paris: Publications de la Sorbonne, 2013a.

Charnay, Amélie. "Le public du festival de Salzbourg 1920–1950." In *Festivals et sociétés en Europe XIXe–XXIe siècles*, sous la direction de Philippe Poirrier. *Territoires contemporains, nouvelle série* 3 (2013b), posted January 15, 2013. Available online: http://tristan.u-bourgogne.fr/CGC/publications/Festivals_societes/A_Charnay.html (accessed October 18, 2018).

Dopsch, Heinz, and Robert Hoffmann. "Die 'Schöne Stadt': Romantische Entdeckung und früher Tourismus." In *Salzburg – die Geschichte einer Stadt*, 413–22. Salzburg: Pustet, 2008.

Faivre-Zellner, Catherine. *Firmin Gémier: Héraut du théâtre populaire*. Rennes: Presses universitaire de Rennes, 2006.

Gaab, Jeffrey S. *Munich: Hofbräuhaus and History – Beer, Culture and Politics*. New York: Peter Lang, 2006.

George, Alys X. "Everyman and the New Man: Festival Culture in Interwar Austria." *Austrian Studies* 25 (2017), 198–215.

Haas, Hans, Robert Hoffmann, and Kurt Luger, eds. *Weltbühne und Naturkulisse: Zwei Jahrhunderte Salzburg-Tourismus*. Salzburg: Pustet, 1994.

Hanebrink, Paul. *In Defense of Christian Hungary: Religion, Nationalism and Antisemitism, 1890–1944*. Ithaca: Cornell University Press, 2006.

Herczeg, Tamás. *A szegedi szabadtéri játékok 85 éve*. Szeged: Szegedi Szabadtéri, 2016.

Hinterberger, Julia, ed. *Von der Musikschule Zum Konservatoriums: Das Mozarteum, 1841–1922*. Vienna: Hollitzer, 2017.

Hoffmann, Robert. "Mozart and the Image of Salzburg." In Reinhold Wagnleitner, ed., *Satchmo Meets Amadeus*, 111–18. Innsbruck: Studien Verlag, 2006.

Janke, Pia. *Politische Massenfestspiele in Österreich zwischen 1918 und 1938*. Vienna: Böhlau, 2010.

Kerekes, Amália, Melinda Kindl, and Judit Szabó, eds. *Post Festum: Szabadtéri játékok a két vilagháború között Salzburgban, Szegeden és Pécsett*. Budapest: Gondolat, 2009.

Kovács, Ágnes, István Nikolényi, and Zoltán Pollner. *A szegedi szabadtéri játekok kézikönyve 1931–1991*. Szeged: Szegedi Szabadtéri Játékok Igazgatósága, 1991.

Krauss-Meyl, Sylvia. *Das Oktoberfest: Zwei Jahrhunderte Spiegel des Zeitgeists*. Regensburg: Verlag Friedrich Pustet, 2015.

Kriechbaumer, Robert. *Zwischen Österreich und Großdeutschland: Eine politische Geschichte der Salzburger Festspiele, 1933–1944*. Wien: Böhlau, 2013.

Marjanucz, László. "A kolozsvári egyetem Szegeden." *Tiszatáj* 62(3) (2008), 77–83.

Mozarteum. "History." Available online: https://mozarteum.at/en/history/ (accessed November 25, 2018).

Nagy, Zsolt. *Great Expectations and Interwar Realities: Hungarian Cultural Diplomacy, 1918–1941*. Budapest: Central European University Press, 2017.

Nikolényi, István. "Az ember tragédiája a szabadtérin: Reinhardt üzenete," *Délmagyarország* 66(166) (July 11, 1976), 5.

Novak, Andreas. *"Salzburg hört Hitler atmen": Die Salzburger Festpiele, 1933–1934*. München: Deutsche Verlags-Anstalt, 2005.

Otruba, Gustav. *Hitler's "Tausend-Mark-Sperre" und die Folgen für Österreichs Fremdenverkehr (1933–1938)*. Linz: Trauner, 1983.

Pór, Katalin. "Max Reinhardt, figure budapestoise." Special issue: "Modes intellectuelles et capitales mitteleuropéennes autour de 1900: échanges et transferts." *Germanica* 43 (2008), 151–60.
Quinn, Erika. *Franz Liszt: A Story of Central European Subjectivity*. Leiden: Brill, 2014.
"Reinhardt, Max." In Aladár Schöpflin, ed., *Magyar Színművészeti Lexikon* (1929–1931). Available online: http://mek.oszk.hu/08700/08756/html/szocikk/w/30/30488.htm (accessed November 29, 2018).
"Reinhardt, Miksa." In Péter Újvári, ed., *Magyar Zsidó Lexikon* (1929). Available online: http://mek-oszk.uz.ua/04000/04093/html/szocikk/14082.htm (accessed November 29, 2018).
Sipos, András. "'Világváros' Nyugat és Kelet határán? Várospolitikai törekvések Budapest nemzetközi vonzerejének erősitésere, 1870–1918." In Györgyi Barta, Krisztina Keresztély, and András Sipos, *A "Világváros" Budapest két századfordulón*, 309–31. Budapest: Napvilág, 2010.
Staud, Geza. "Max Reinhardt in Ungarn." In Edda Leisler and Gisela Prosnitz, eds., *Max Reinhardt in Europa*, 7–31 and 312–19. Salzburg: Otto Müller Verlag, 1973.
Steinberg, Michael P. *The Meaning of the Salzburg Festival: Austria as Theater and Ideology*. Ithaca: Cornell University Press, 2000 (1st ed., 1990).
Szekfü, Gyula. *Három nemzedék és ami utána következik*. Budapest: Magyar Egyetemi Nyomda, 1934. 401–505.
Sz. Simon, István. *A játékok kronikája*. Szeged, 1983.
Ujváry, Gábor. *A Harmincharmadik Nemzedék: Politika, kultúra és történettudomány a "neo-barokk társadalomban."* Budapest: Ráció Kiadó, 2010.
Vari, Alexander. "From 'Paris of the East' to 'Queen of Danube': Transnational Models in the Promotion of Budapest Tourism, 1885–1940." In Eric G. E. Zuelow, ed., *Touring Beyond the Nation: A Transnational Approach to European Tourism History*, 103–25. Farnham, UK: Ashgate, 2011.

Contemporaneous Sources

Galamb, Sándor. "A 'Magyar Passio' Szegeden." *Budapesti Szemle* 222 (1931), 136–9.
Galamb, Sándor. "Iphigénia a sziklák közt." *Szózat*, August 19, 1924.
Hajós, Mihály. "Jöjjetek a magyar Salzburgba!" *Magyar Festőipar*, July 1, 1932.
Herczeg, Ferenc. "Uj vagyon és régi művészet (Salzburgi levél)." *Uj Idők*, September 10, 1922.
Hont, Ferenc. "Gémier a szegedi színházról: A Színházi Világszövetség elnökének nyilatkozata a Délmagyarország számára." *Délmagyarország*, May 11, 1927.
Hont, Ferenc. "Ünnepi játékok Szegeden." *Ujság*, April 23, 1929.
Kaán, Károly. "A Szent Gellért-Hegy." *Budapesti Hírlap*, May 23, 1926.
Klebelsberg, (Count) Kuno. *Neonacionalizmus*. Budapest: Athenaeum, 1928.
Klebelsberg, (Count) Kuno. "Munka, tudás és tőke." *Pesti Napló*, July 28, 1929.
Kovách, Imre. "Közegészségügyünk állapotáról." *Nemzetgazdasági Szemle* I (1885), 98–132.
Kürti, Pál. "Jedermann a Fővárosi Operettszínházban." *Nyugat*, 1926, 20.
Lestyán, Sándor. "Ünnepi játékok, Ármány és szerelem, Reinhardt és Darvas Lily." *Ujság*, August 24, 1926.
Lugosi, Döme. *A szegedi szabadtéri játékok története, 1931–1937*. Budapest: Színpad, 1938.
Márai, Sándor. "Ünnepi játék." *Pesti Hírlap*, April 7, 1938.
Marjay, Ödön. "Művészeti Szemle." *Napkelet*, November 1, 1926.
Molnár, Imre, ed. *A magyar muzsika könyve*. Budapest: Havas, 1936.

Hungarian Salzburgs 329

N. T., "Páris-Berlin-Salzburg." *Pesti Hírlap*, September 8, 1921.

Paál, Jób. "Reinhardt és a szegedi ünnepi játékok." *Délmagyarország*, September 3, 1933.

Paál, Jób. "Magyarok diadala Salzburgban az idei nagy ünnepi játékokon." *Színházi Élet*, 1926, 34.

Pásztor, József. *A szegedi szabadtéri játékok története: Három év monográfiája*. Szeged: Városi Nyomda, 1938.

Pünkösti, Andor. "Magyar Salzburg." *Ujság*, May 26, 1929.

Pünkösti, Erzsébet. "Várady Rózsi Salzburgban is sikert aratott Kodály Zoltán csellóra irt magyar táncaival." *Ujság*, August 25, 1926.

Rab, Gusztáv. "A dobverős halál." *Világ*, August 19, 1925.

Spur, Endre. "Az ünneplő Mozart-város." *Szózat*, August 20, 1922.

Szabolcsi, Bence. "Salzburg." *Világ*, August 30, 1924.

Anonymous Contemporaneous Sources

"'Akárki' ('Jedermann') a Fővárosi Operettszínházban." *8 Órai Ujság*, October 2 1926.

"Bartók Béla és Kodály Zoltán salzburgi diadala: Levél a modern zene Mekkájából." *Az Est*, August 19, 1923.

"A beruházóprogram a főváros közgyűlésén." *Világ*, April 22, 1926.

"A Budapesti Mozart Egyesület ma tartotta harmadik zenésdélutánját." *Pesti Hírlap*, December 16, 1925.

"A Budapesti Mozart Egyesület Székesfehérvárott." *Ujság*, March 23, 1926.

"Dohnányi Ernő ünneplése és az 'Elektra' premierje Salzburgban." *Ujság*, August 10, 1937.

"'Don Juan' díszelőadása." *Fővárosi Lapok*, July 17, 1887.

"Eger példája a helyes idegenforgalmi propagandára." *Városok Lapja*, June 1, 1929.

"A Földtani Intézet nem enged alagutat vagy liftaknát fúrni a Gellérthegyben." *Az Est*, February 19, 1926.

"Hohen-Salzburg a Gellérthegyen." *Magyarország*, March 4, 1926.

"Hohen-Salzburg Budán." *Ujság*, March 4, 1926.

"Jaték a szabadtéren." *Délmagyarország*, May 16, 1931.

"Játékbank." *Szózat*, January 25, 1922.

"Jedermann." *Világ*, August 24, 1920.

"Jubiláns díszhangversenyek." *Fővárosi Lapok*, July 15, 1888.

"A külföld is érdeklődik a soproni ünnepi játékok iránt." *8 Órai Ujság*, August 28, 1932.

"A magyar 'Jedermann.'" *Az Est*, October 2, 1926.

"Magyar kompozíciókat játszik Salzburgban a pesti filharmónia." *Ujság*, November 23, 1930.

"A magyar Salzburg: Ünnepi játékok Szeged környékén szabad ég alatt." *Magyarország*, April 23, 1929.

"Magyar Salzburgot és Haydn-operát tervez a tatai gróf." *Pesti Hírlap*, June 14, 1933.

"Magyar ünnepi játékok Szegeden." *Magyarság*, April 23, 1929.

"Meghosszabbították a *Jedermann* előadásait." *Magyarság*, October 10, 1926.

"Megkezdődtek a salzburgi ünnepi játékok: Bartók Béla nagy sikere az első matinén." *Pesti Hírlap*, August 10, 1922.

"A megsoványodott Molnár Ferenc és az elegáns Darvas Lili délelőtt fürdőruhában nyaralnak a Lidón, esténkint pedig pezsgő mellett táncolnak Reinhardtékkal." *Esti Kurir*, August 6, 1926.

330 Interwar Salzburg

"Minutes of the 21 April 1926 meeting of the Budapest Municipal Council." *Fővárosi Közlöny*, April 23, 1926.
"A miskolci színház megnyitása." *Budapesti Hírlap*, October 10, 1926.
"Molnár Ferenc elmondja: kik voltak idén magyarok a salzburgi Festspielen?" *Színházi Élet*, 1926, 36.
"A mostanában divatos turnék után, mint értesülünk, rövidesen aktuális lesz a Jedermann-turné." *Magyarország*, October 5, 1926.
"A Mozart Egyesület ma este Mozart születésének 170. évforduló napján kitünően sikerült hangversenyt rendezett a Zeneakadémia nagytermében." *Világ*, January 28, 1926.
"Mozart-est." *Pesti Napló*, April 14, 1931.
"Mozart-kultusz Budapesten" *Az Ujság*, May 28, 1925.
"Mozart-kultusz Budapesten." *Pesti Napló*, September 17, 1925.
"Mozart-kultusz Budapesten."*Szózat*, June 20, 1925.
"Mozart-kultusz Budapesten." *Világ*, October 11, 1925.
"Mozart-ünnepségek 1931-ben." *Budapesti Hírlap*, October 14, 1930.
"Nemcsak a salzburgi ünnepi játékokon a Fővárosi Operettszínházban is sikert aratott a Jedermann." *Színházi Élet*, 1926, 41.
"Németh Mária és Darvas Lili a salzburgi ünnepi Játékokon." *Pesti Hírlap*, July 29, 1927.
"Nemzetközi Mozart-ünnep Budapesten." *Ujság*, December 6, 1925.
"A nézetek teljes összhangja, a legszorosabb barátság és együttműködés: Hivatalos közlés a két kormányfő tanácskozásáról." *Budapesti Hírlap*, August 11, 1934.
"Október húszadikán magyar Salzburggá változik Sopron." *Ujság*, September 29, 1929.
"Rádióközlemények." *Népszava*, October 17, 1929.
"Rádió-zene." *Magyarság*, October 22, 1929.
"Reinhardt gulyás-bankettje Salzburgban." *Pesti Napló*, September 1, 1926.
"Reinhardt Jedermann-előadása a Salzburg Dóm-téren." *Az Est*, August 26, 1920.
"Salzburg Ausztria legszebb városa." *Esti Kurir*, August 29, 1925.
"A salzburgi játékok hőse: Hörbiger Attila." *Magyarság*, July 31, 1935.
"Schiller tragédiájának salzburgi előadása után Reinhardt gulyásra hivta meg a Festspiele vendégeit." *Színházi Élet*, 1926, 36.
"Schuschnigg kancellár Szegeden." *Budapesti Hírlap*, August 9, 1934.
"Sopron legyen a magyar Salzburg." *Városok Lapja*, September 1, 1930.
"A soproni ünnepi játékok." *Pesti Hírlap*, September 4, 1929.
"Színpadi concert." *Fővárosi Lapok*, May 6, 1870.
"Tegnap tartotta első zenés kultúrdélutánját tagjai számára a Budapesti Mozart-Egyesület." *Ujság*, October 27, 1925.
"Ünnepi játékok Sopronban: A vasárnapi szabadtéri előadást elmosta az eső." *Pesti Hírlap*, September 6, 1932.
"Úti és fürdői rajzok: I. (Bécsből Salzburgig)." *Fővárosi Lapok*, July 3, 1870.
"A "Világszínház" kulisszái mögött." *Pesti Napló*, August 20, 1922, 11.
"Zenei ünnep Sopronban." *Budapesti Hírlap*, October 10, 1929.
"Zenei életünkből." *Magyarság*, November 9, 1929.
"Zenei ünnepségek Sopronban: A százesztendős zeneegyesület." *Pesti Hírlap*, October 22, 1929.
"Zeneünnepély Salzburgban: Modern kamarazene a Mozarteumban – Kodály Zoltán az ünnepély hőse." *Pesti Napló*, August 19, 1924.

Contributors

Katherine Arens is Professor of Germanic Studies, Comparative Literature, and Women's and Gender Studies at the University of Texas at Austin, USA. A former President of the Austrian Studies Association, she has published widely on Austrian and German cultural and intellectual history since 1750, especially in comparative contexts. Her most recent monographs are *Vienna's Dreams of Europe*, *Belle Necropolis: Ghosts of Imperial Vienna* (both 2015), and *Other Kantianisms: Experiments in Embodied Knowledge* (with Carlos Amador, forthcoming).

Robert Dassanowsky was CU Distinguished Professor of Film and Austrian Studies at the University of Colorado, Colorado Springs, USA. He worked as an independent film producer, and was a former President of the Austrian Studies Association. His recent books include *Austrian Cinema: A History* (2005); *New Austrian Film* (editor, 2011); *The Nameable and the Unnameable: Hofmannsthal's* Der Schwierige *Revisited* (editor, 2011); *Quentin Tarantino's* Inglourious Basterds (editor, 2012); *World Film Locations: Vienna* (editor, 2012); and *Screening Transcendence: Film under Austrofascism and the Hollywood Hope 1933–1938* (2018).

Christopher Dietz is active in publishing in Vienna. After German Studies in Vienna and Paris (Sorbonne) and his PhD work at Vienna, he has published on Heimito von Doderer, Alexander Lernet-Holenia, and Adolf Loos, as well as a volume on *Die berühmten Gräber Wiens* (Wien–München: Deuticke Verlag 2000; Kindle eBook 2011). He has also trained as a public speaker at the *Schule des Sprechens* (Wien), moderates conferences, and gives public recitations from literary works.

Helga Embacher is Professor for Contemporary History at the University of Salzburg. She was a visiting professor at the University of Minnesota, USA (1997), the University of Pennsylvania, USA (2003–2004) and at the University Haifa, Israel (2022). She is the author of

A New Beginning without Illusions: Jews in Austria after 1945 (1995) and co-author of *The Relationship of Austria and Israel in the Shadow of the Holocaust* (1998). Her most recent monograph (with Bernadette Edtmaier and Alexandra Preitschopf) is *Antisemitisms in Europa: Fallbeispiele eines globalen Phänomens im 21. Jahrhundert* (2019).

Alys X. George is Assistant Professor of German Studies at Stanford University, USA, where she specializes in interdisciplinary approaches to modern Austrian and German culture and cultural history. She is the author of the multiple-award-winning book *The Naked Truth: Viennese Modernism and the Body* (2020).

Julia Hinterberger is Assistant Professor at the University Mozarteum in Salzburg. Her research interests are in Salzburg music history, among other areas, and she is the editor of the four-volume series *Geschichte der Universität Mozarteum Salzburg: Von der Musikschule zum Konservatorium. Das Mozarteum 1841–1922* (volume 1, 2017).

Vincent Kling is a translator and scholar of German literature who teaches at La Salle University in Philadelphia, Pennsylvania, USA. He has translated fiction, poetry, and criticism by Heimito von Doderer, Heimrad Bäcker, Andreas Pittler, Gert Jonke, Gerhard Fritsch, Hugo von Hofmannsthal, and Aglaja Veteranyi. He was awarded the Schlegel-Tieck Prize in 2013 for his translation of Veteranyi's *Why the Child Is Cooking in the Polenta*, and the Helen and Kurt Wolff Prize in 2022 for his translation of Heimito von Doderer's *The Strudlhof Steps*.

Andreas Praher is Postdoc Researcher and Lecturer at the University of Salzburg and is currently holding a scholarship at the Botstiber Institute for Austrian-American Studies. His research focuses on Contemporary Austrian History, Sport and Migration History. The former editor at the *Salzburger Nachrichten* works as Exhibition Curator and is co-editor of *Migrationsstadt Salzburg. Arbeit, Alltag und Migration 1960–2010* (2018), *Zwischenräume. Macht, Ausgrenzung und Inklusion im Fußball* (2019), and the author of numerous articles on the history of sport in Austria, including *Der jüdische Sport im Salzburg der Zwischenkriegszeit* (2017). He is the author of the award-winning book *Österreichs Skisport im Nationalsozialismus. Anpassung – Verfolgung – Kollaboration* (2021).

Julia Secklehner is a Research Fellow at the Department of Art History at Masaryk University in Brno, Czech Republic. As part of a collaborative grant project "Continuity/Rupture: Art and Architecture in Central Europe, 1918–1939 (CRAACE)," her research focuses on regional and rural aspects of modern art, design, and visual culture in Central Europe. Her publications have appeared in *The Austrian History Yearbook*, *Austrian Studies*, and the *Leo Baeck Institute Yearbook*.

Alexander Vari is Professor of History and Former Chair of the Department of Social Sciences at Marywood University in Scranton, Pennsylvania, USA. He has published on topics ranging from the history of urban tourism and neighborhood preservation to the history of nightlife and popular entertainment. He is also a co-editor of *Socialist Escapes: Breaking Away from Ideology and Everyday Routine in Eastern Europe, 1945–1989* (2013) and *Urban Popular Culture and Entertainment: Experiences from Northern, East Central and Southern Europe, 1870s–1930s* (2022), as well as the author of a forthcoming book with Bloomsbury Academic on twentieth-century European arts festivals.

Index

Italic numbers indicate figures.

Age of Aquarius, Salzburg's 92–4
  see also Der Wassermann
  (Aquarius) artist group
Alt, Rudolf von 83–4
Altmann, Adolf 283, 284, 284n12,
  287, 291
*Anti:modern: Salzburg in the Heart
  of Europe Between Tradition
  and Renewal* exhibition 260
antisemitism
  after First World War 285–8
  conflict between locals and
    immigrants 285
  education 291–3
  during First World War 284–5
  gymnastics (*Turner*) movement
    189, 190
  isolation due to 291–3
  Jewish footballers and 187–8
  prior to First World War 283–4
  Reinhardt, Max 149–50
  sports culture/clubs 178
  Zionism and 294
  Zuckermayer and Zweig 148
  see also Jewish community
architecture 47
arts, commitment to in Salzburg
  art public, building of 70–1
  "back to nature" paintings 55
  civic awareness, growth of 51
  civic education, art as part of 62
  contexts for art 51–7
  domination of Vienna in art
    history 52–3
  framework for art revival 50
  growth of 51
  material ground of the arts
    63–71
  modernization of public sphere
    51
  post-WWI 65
  refuge, Salzburg as place of 67
  Salzburger Kunstverein (KV)
    52, 56–63
  Salzburg Museum 51–2, 55
  success of 71
  viewership, changes in 54–5
  see also Der Wassermann
    (Aquarius) artist group
ASKÖ (workers' sports
  association) 186
ATSV Grödig-Fürstenbrunn
  (workers' sport group) 185
Austrian Football Association
  (ÖFB) 181, 182
Austrian-Hungarian Film
  Company 105

Bacher, Ernst 182
Bahr, Hermann 67
Bárdos, György 305, 306
Bayreuth Festival 36

Beck, Eduard 183
Beller, Steven 19
Berczel, Jenö 308
Bernhard, Thomas 139–40
Billinger, Richard 165–6
Bloch, Ernst 205, 211
bourgeoisie as art patrons 54
Bradl, Josef 193–4
British historiography 16

Cartellieri, Carmen 107
cinema in Salzburg
  1921 as significant year for 106
  Alpentragödie/Alpine Tragedy 106, 107
  appearance of Salzburg in films 103–4
  Austrian-Hungarian Film Company 105
  Casta Diva (Gallone) 129
  culture films 105
  Der Pfarrer von Kirchfeld/The Pastor of Kirchfeld (Kolm-Fleck) 123–9
  Der Schwierige/The Difficult Gentleman (Hofmannsthal) 113–14
  Der weisse Tod/The White Death 106, 107
  Die Festspiele 1921/The Festival 1921 107
  Die Tragödie des Carlo Pinetti/The Tragedy of Carlo Pinetti 108
  earliest surviving film 103
  early status 103
  film studios, first 104
  film theory, Hofmannsthal on 112–13
  first films produced in 106
  Hochzeit am Wolfgangsee/ Wedding at Lake Wolfgang (Behrend) 109
  Hofmannsthal, Hugo von 104–5, 111–19
  Im weissen Rössl/In the White Horse Inn (Blumenthal and Kadelburg) 108, 109, 110
  Italian-Austrian film co-production scheme 129
  Lasset die Kleinen zu mir kommen/Let the Little Children Come Unto Me (Neufeld) 107
  Liebling der Götter/Darling of the Gods (Schwarz) 108–9
  Mozarts Leben, Lieben und Leiden/Mozart's Life, Loves and Sorrows (Kreisler) 107
  official birth of 105–6
  pre-technology of film, contributions to 102–3
  as propaganda vehicle 113–14, 119–23
  Reinhardt, Max 104–5
  rural culture in documentaries 117
  Saison in Salzburg (A Season in Salzburg) (Raymond) 110
  Salzburger Kunstfilm-Industrie-A.G. 106, 107–8
  Salzburg Festival and 100–1
  setting, Salzburg as 108–9
  Singende Jugend/An Orphan Boy of Vienna (Neufeld) 119–23
  testing ground, Salzburg as 108
  two film industries in Austria 109–10
  Unsterbliches Lied/Silent Night (Marr) 119
  Vienna-Hollywood co-production initiative 130–4
  Wolfgangsee films 109
  Zell am See 103
class struggles in football 184–7
conservative modernism of Wojtek 271–5
consumption of art, changes in 54–5
Csokor, Franz Theodore 160–1

336 Index

Dachinger, Johann (Isak) 188
Der Pfarrer von Kirchfeld/The Pastor of Kirchfeld (Kolm-Fleck) 123–9
Der Rosenkavalier (Wiene), Hofmannsthal and 111–12
Der Schwierige/The Difficult Gentleman (Hofmannsthal) 113–14
Der Wassermann (Aquarius) artist group
   aims 66, 266–7
   artist's voice in 77–92
   art school 69
   audience's relationship to the artwork 79
   contexts for 266–7
   education of art public 69
   end of 69–70
   first exhibit 1919 68, 72–6, 78
   founding 67–8
   Internationale Schwarz-Weiß-Ausstellung 69
   international networks of artists 77–8
   meaning of Aquarius 65–6
   Mühlmann on 72–6
   Salzburg's *Age of Aquarius* 92–4
   second exhibit 1920 68–9, 76–7
   self-presentation 72–7
   third exhibit 1921 76–8
   women artists 68
Der weisse Tod/The White Death 106, 107
Die Festspiele 1921/The Festival 1921 107
Dommusikverein Music School *see* Mozarteum

Eger, Hungary 315–16
Ehrenzweig, Robert 213
Ein Künstlerleben/An Artist's Life (Kreisler) 107
Emigrantenfilm 110
exhibitions, Faistauer on 90

Faistauer, Anton 66, 67, 69, 70, 77–9, 80, 81–92, 93–4, 266–7
"Fantasy in Salzburg" (Bahr) 39–43
   cultural strains, amalgamation of in Salzburg 34
   as fantasy 35
   as *feuilleton* 33–4
   Kling on 33–7
   as parody of literary dialogue 34
   spoofing of beliefs on finance 36–7
   twisting meanings of original writings 35–6
festival culture
   audience participation 215–18
   emotional identification as goal 213
   events included in 202
   invented traditions as basis for 203
   Massenfestspiele 210–15
   need for 201–2
   purpose of 201–2, 205–6
   reality/content contradiction 218–19
   religion as inspiration source for 204–5
   Salzburg Festival 206–9
   workers' 210–15
   see also Salzburg Festival
film industry in Salzburg *see* cinema in Salzburg
film theory, Hofmannsthal on 112–13
Fischer, Ernst 208, 209
football 178, 179–88
Freedman, Julian 250–1, 252–3
French historiography 15
Freumbichler, Johannes 166–7

galleries, opening to the public 54–5
Gémier, Firmin 315

gender representation
  skiing 196–7
  Turner movement 189–90
  women artists 60–1, 68
  generational conflicts in Jewish
    community 293–5
  German language usage in Jewish
    community 289
  glocal network, Salzburg as part
    of 14
  gymnastics *(Turner)* movement
    189–91

Habsburg-Halbgebauer, Stefanie 62
Habsburg myth 143–4
Hanisch, Ernst 227
Haringer, Jakob 167–8
Harta, Felix Albrecht 66, 67, 68,
  69–70, 266–7
Hauser, Hans 193, 195, 196
Hauser, Max 193, 195
Hebbel, Friedrich 139, 140
Heimkehrerstück (Hofmannsthal)
  114–15
Henndorf circle
  Billinger, Richard 165–6
  Csokor, Franz Theodore 160–1
  disparate members 141
  Freumbichler, Johannes 166–7
  Haringer, Jakob 167–8
  Herdan-Zuckmayer, Alice
    141–2, 166–7, 168–70
  Horch, Franz 159–60
  Horváth, Ödön von 161–3, 170
  house guests 157–64
  Ibach, Alfred 163–4
  Jannings, Emil 147, 155–7
  Joseph, Albrecht 157–9
  Krauß, Werner 147, 153–5
  Lernet-Holenia, Alexander 147,
    150–3
  local residents 147–57
  personal, emphasis on the
    170–1

Reinhardt, Max 147, 149–50
Schiebelhuth, Hans 164
sources of information on
  140–1
Zuckermayer as centre 141
Zweig, Stefan 147–9
Henndorf village as laboratory of
  historical development 139
Henz, Rudolf 115
Herdan-Zuckmayer, Alice 141–2,
  166–7, 168–70
historiography
  British 16
  conventions of and alternative
    approaches to 8–9
  different versions of Salzburg's
    20
  essentialization of terminology
    21–2
  French 15
  materialist base in Austria
    16–18
  revisions to Austria's histories
    18–19
  Salzburg as challenge to
    Austrian and Habsburg
    13–20
Hobsbawn, Eric 203
*Hochzeit am Wolfgangsee/Wedding
  at Lake Wolfgang* (Behrend)
  109
Hock, Stephan 213
Hoffman, Robert 223, 224
Hofmannsthal, Hugo von 34, 35,
  104–5, 111–19, 202, 206–9,
  217, 267, 273
Hogan, Jimmy 181
Hohensalzburg, ambitions for
  307–10
Höllbacher, Roman 60
Hollywood-Vienna film
  co-production initiative
  130–4
Hont, Ferenc 314, 315

Horch, Franz 159–60
Horváth, Ödön von 161–3, 170
Hungarian Passion (Voinovich) 321–2
Hungary, Salzburg Festival and
1926 and 1927 festivals 310–13
1930s festival culture 320–4
appeal of 320
attention given to festival 299
Eger 315–16
emerging arts festival field in Hungary 314–19
Gellérthegy, ambitions for 307–10
impact on Hungary 300
Mozart Association 305, 306
Mozarteum, connections with Hungary 304–6
perception of the festival 303–4
press reports of post-war Salzburg 301–4
Sopron 317–19
Szeged 301, 314–15, 319, 320–5
tourism, ambitions for 307–10
towns in as Hungarian Salzburgs 300–1

Ibach, Alfred 163–4
Im weissen Rössl/In the White Horse Inn (Blumenthal and Kadelburg) 108, 109, 110
Internationale Schwarz-Weiß-Ausstellung 69
Italian-Austrian film co-production scheme 129

Janik, Allan 17
Jannings, Emil 147, 155–7
Jedermann/Everyman (Hofmansthal) 107, 108, 111, 206–9, 217–18, 312
Jewish community
bourgeois lifestyle 282–3, 288
Christmas, celebration of 288–90
creative, Salzburg as haven for 117–18
education 290
end of in 1938 295–6
families, importance of 290
footballers 187–8
generational conflicts 293–5
German language usage 289
identity and traditions 288–91
kosher, keeping 289–90
migration to Salzburg 282
political parties 288
population size in Salzburg 281
rabbis 283
refuge, Salzburg as 288
religious facilities 283
Social Democratic Party 288
socialising within 290–1
Trachten, wearing of 289
Zionism 294–5
see also antisemitism
Johnston, William 17
Joseph, Albrecht 157–9
Judson, Pieter 18

Kaán, Károly 309–10
Kern, Anita 261, 264
Klebelsberg, Kuno 315, 320–1
Kleßheim Courier—drawn diaries (Klien) 268–269, 269
Klien, Erika Giovanna 268–270, 269
Klimt, Gustav, Faistauer on 83–7
Kokoschka, Oskar, Faistauer on 90–1
Kolig, Anton, Faistauer on 90
Kolm, Anton 105
Kolm, Louise 105
Krauß, Werner 147, 150, 153–5
Kunstwillen (Faistauer) / *Kunstwollen* (Riegl) 80

Lang, Otto 195
Lasset die Kleinen zu mir kommen/ Let the Little Children Come Unto Me (Neufeld) 107

Index 339

Lefebvre, Henri 260
Lehmann, Lilli 246, 250
Lernet-Holenia, Alexander 147, 150–3
Liebling der Götter/Darling of the Gods (Schwarz) 108–9
Lodron, Paris Graf von 47–8
Lucidor (Hofmannsthal) 114

Madách, Imre 323
Manners, Diana *102*
Margules, David 283, 287, 289
Massenfestspiele
   audience participation 215–16
   common theme with Salzburg Festival 207–8
   festival culture and 202, 210–15
   purpose of 204
   religion as inspiration source for 204–5
materialist-based concepts of historiography 16–18
Melnitz, Curt *101*
Michel, Adolf 190–1
Michel, Eva 267
migrations, internal 2
modernism, Salzburg's
   conservative modernism of Wojtek 271–5
   Der Wassermann 266–7
   engagement with legacy of 260
   logo for Salzburg Festival, continued use of 261–2
   Sonderbund Österreichischer Künstler in Salzburg (Special Association of Austrian Artists in Salzburg) 267–8
   see also Wojtek, Leopoldine (Poldi)
modernity defined 260
Morawetz, Ferdinand 183, 187–8
Mozart, Wolfgang Amadeus 4

Mozarteum
   common paths with Mozarteum Foundation 226–32
   free tuition 238–9
   goals 223
   historical development and positioning 223–6
   Hungarian connections 304–6
   music lovers/professional musicians 234
   nationalization, impact of 234–6
   new media, use of 238
   number of students 232, *233*
   opera school, expansion of 236–7
   Paumgartner's proposals 227–8
   place of birth of students 233–4
   politicizing of music 239–40
   public status, fight for 228–9
   recorder lessons 238
   separate paths from Mozarteum Foundation 232–41, *233*
   separation from Mozarteum Foundation 229–32
   teacher training courses 228–9
   teaching staff 234, 235
   upgrading to Conservatory 225
Mozarteum Foundation
   autonomy, abandonment of 225
   common paths with Mozarteum 226–32
   as concert organizer 243–5, *244*
   focus of on establishment 224
   memorials, maintenance and care of 241
   Mozart week 1921 247–9
   research 241, *242*
   Salzburg Festival and 245–50
   school/church separation 225
   separate paths from Mozarteum 241–5, *242*, *244*
   summer courses 250–5, *252*, *254*

Mozarthaus 222, 225
Mozarts Leben, Lieben und Leiden/ Mozart's Life, Loves and Sorrows (Kreisler) 107
Mühlmann, Josef 72–6, 78, 266, 267
Mühlmann, Kajetan 75, 265, 272, 272
Müllner, Rudolf 191
Museum Salzburg 51–2
Musulin, Janko 169

Nazarene Movement painters 53–4
Neufeld, Max 107
New Painting in Austria (Faistauer) 79–80, 81–92
Nochlin, Linda 61

Oksiloff, Assenka 113
Olympic Games 1936 181–2
Opernring/Thank You, Madame (Gallone) 129
Oppelt, Rudolf 103

Paumgartner, Bernhard 67, 227–8, 229, 236–8, 240
political parties in Jewish community 288
Preussler, Robert 230, 231
professionalism in sports 184
propaganda vehicle, film as 113–14, 119
Pünkösti, Andor 315

rabbis in Salzburg 283
Rainer, Friedrich 191, 193
Rathkolb, Oliver 261
Reigl, Alois 78–9, 80–1, 93
Reinhardt, Max 67, *101, 102*, 104–5, 133–4, 140, 147, 149–50, 201–2, 209, 217, 311–12, 323
religious facilities in Salzburg, Jewish 283
rural culture in documentaries 117

Saison in Salzburg (A Season in Salzburg) (Raymond) 110
Salzburg
 architecture 47
 as Austria's other 46–71
 beyond revisionisms 2–25
 as challenge to Austrian and Habsburg historiography 13–20
 critical and nuanced vision of 9
 geographical alignment 2–3
 history 3–4, 46–51
 industrialization as limited in 3
 international roots 46–47
 materialist-based concepts of historiography 17, 19
 national identity and 4–6
 as place of exile from Nazi regime 146
 as second city 4
 see also arts, commitment to in Salzburg
Salzburger Athlethiksportklub 1914 179–80
Salzburger Kunstfilm-Industrie-A.G. 106
Salzburger Kunstverein (KV) 52
 first exhibits 58
 funding 59
 Künstlerhaus 59, 60–3
 membership 57–8
 mission of 56–63
 modern painters, exhibition of 67
 origin and founding of 56–7
 outreach 59
 setbacks 60
 women artists 60–1
Salzburg Festival
 1930s success 319–20
 antisemitism in Salzburg 288
 audience participation 216–18
 choice of Salzburg 143–5

common theme with
  Massenfestspiele 207–8
concern over foreign visitors
  145
Europe-wide interest in
  299–300
festival culture and 202, 206–9
forerunners of 224
goals of 259
Habsburg myth 143–4
hopes for 99–100
ideology of 145
inaugural performance 206–8
Jedermann performances 206–9
logo for, continued use of 261–2
modernity and 259
Mozarteum Foundation and
  245–50
National Socialism and 265–6
purpose of 204, 206
religion as inspiration source
  for 204–5
see also cinema in Salzburg;
  "Fantasy in Salzburg"
  (Bahr); Hungary,
  Salzburg Festival and;
  Wojtek, Leopoldine (Poldi)
Salzburg Museum 51–2, 55
Salzburg Sport Club (SSK 1919)
  183
Sannen, Saskia 14
Schaffer, Nikolaus 65, 70, 270
Schiebelhuth, Hans 164
Schiele, Egon 86, 87
Schmalzhofer, Albin 185–6
Schorske, Carl 17–18
Second International Workers'
  Socialist Olympiad 210–15
Silverman, Lisa 118
Singende Jugend/An Orphan Boy of
  Vienna (Neufeld) 119–23
Skiclub Zell am See 192, 194
SK Kaufhaus Schwarz (Ski club) 188

Social Democratic Party, Jewish
  community and 288
socialist festival culture 210–15
Sonderbund Österreichischer
  Künstler in Salzburg
  (Special Association of
  Austrian Artists in Salzburg)
  267–8, 270
Sopron, Hungary 317–19
Spector, Scott 19
sports culture/clubs
  amateur players 182
  antisemitism 178, 180
  antisemitism, Jewish
    footballers and 187–8
  Catholic footballers 186
  class struggles 184–7
  football 178, 179–88
  gymnastics *(Turner)* movement
    189–91
  international stage 194–7
  Olympic Games 1936 181–2
  political forces, influence of
    177–8, 180, 183–7, 193–4
  professionalism 184
  regional differences 178
  Salzburger Athlethiksportklub
    1914 179–80
  skiing 191–7
  workers' sports movement
    183–7
Stampfer disk 102
Steinberg, Michael 118, 145, 216,
  259, 320
Strasser, Christian 140
Strauss, Richard 248
stroboscopic disk, first 102
style 80, 81
SV Horekan Salzburg 185
Svoboda, Christa 52, 55
Szeged, Hungary, Salzburg
  Festival and 301, 314–15,
  319, 320–5

Tandler, Julius 211
Toulmin, Stephen E. 17

Unsterbliches Lied/Silent Night
  (Marr) 119

Vámbéry, Rusztem 308–9
Van Gogh, Vincent, Faistauer on
  89–90
Vienna
  after First World War 2
  domination of in art history
    52–3
Vienna Academy 54
Vienna-Hollywood co-production
  initiative 130–4
Vogl, Fritz 194
Voinovich, Géza 321–2

Waldmüller, Ferdinand Georg
  54
Wiegele, Franz, Faistauer on 90
Wiesmühl circle *see* Henndorf
  circle
Wiesmühl estate 139–40
Wingfield, Nancy 19
winter sports 191–4
Wojtek, Leopoldine (Poldi)
  career in Salzburg 270–1
  complexities of Austrian
    interwar design 270
  conservative modernism of
    271–5
  continued use of logo for
    Salzburg Festival 261–2
  description of poster 263–4
  educational background 268
  National Socialism and 265
  Salzburger Festspeile 1928 poster
    261
  Salzburger Festspielführer
    (festival guide) 272, 272–4
  Sonderbund membership 270

  transition of poster to logo
    264–5
  *A True Story: Words and Images
    from Two Germans in a
    Foreign Country* illustrations
    262, 263
  winning of poster competition
    262–3
Wölfflin, Heinrich 93
Wolfgangsee films 109
women artists
  Der Wassermann (Aquarius)
    artistic group 68
  Salzburger Kunstverein (KV)
    60–1
workers' festival culture 210–15
Workers' Sports Clubs (VAFÖ) 184
workers' sports movement
  football 183–7
  skiing 192
Worringer, Wilhelm 93

Zeitgeist, Faistauer on 87
Zinkenbacher Malerkolonie 76
Zionism 294–5
Zuckmayer, Carl 139–40
  1970 visit to Henndorf 170
  autobiography 140, 142, 170
  autonomy and independence,
    importance of for 143
  Billinger and 165–6
  Csokor and 160–1
  exit from Austria 147
  Freumbichler and 166–7
  Haringer and 167–8
  Herdan-Zuckmayer, Alice
    168–70
  Horch and 159–60
  Horváth and 161–3, 170
  Jannings and 155–7
  Joseph and 157–9
  Krauß and 153–5
  Lernet-Holenia and 150–3

purchase and move to
 Henndorf 141–2
reaction to Zweig's suicide
 148–9
*Reichsverband Deutscher
 Schriftsteller* (RDS),
 membership of 146–7

Reinhardt and 149
Salzburg as place of exile
 146–7
Schiebelhuth and 164
see also Henndorf circle
Zweig, Stefan 7, 67,
 147–9

In Memory of Robert Dassanowsky

A Final Note from Katie Arens

Just as this volume was about to go to press, Robert Dassanowsky passed away, completely unexpectedly. This note is to acknowledge his contributions to this, likely his final publication. The vision behind this volume was Robert's, his challenge to us to re-center Austrian and Central European studies, and we were fortunate to have had him plan it and assemble its contributors. And as his co-editor, I want to acknowledge his unfailing eye for detail, which extended to every facet of the book (including a last tweak to a font color on the cover). As I did the very final proofreading and verification of the index, I'll claim any remaining errors as mine, not Robert's.

More importantly: we all want to remember Robert Dassanowsky as a transformative visionary in Austrian studies and film studies—a person who set an agenda into place and acted as a guiding light to many, many scholars, helping them to find voices outside older stereotypes. *Interwar Salzburg* will be his legacy, opening eyes and minds to new optics on how Austria and Central Europe continue to resonate on a scholarly landscape still overly dominated by the World Wars of the twentieth century. He hoped it would open up new connections between regions, disciplines, and evaluations of germanophone cultures and restore contemporary visions of Central Europe as a fraught but vibrant space of innovation. Let us celebrate Robert's estimable career by following his example.

Volumes in the series:

Vol. 1. *Improvisation as Art: Conceptual Challenges, Historical Perspectives*
by Edgar Landgraf

Vol. 2. *The German Pícaro and Modernity: Between Underdog and Shape-Shifter*
by Bernhard Malkmus

Vol. 3. *Citation and Precedent: Conjunctions and Disjunctions of German Law and Literature*
by Thomas O. Beebee

Vol. 4. *Beyond Discontent: 'Sublimation' from Goethe to Lacan*
by Eckart Goebel

Vol. 5. *From Kafka to Sebald: Modernism and Narrative Form*
edited by Sabine Wilke

Vol. 6. *Image in Outline: Reading Lou Andreas-Salomé*
by Gisela Brinker-Gabler

Vol. 7. *Out of Place: German Realism, Displacement, and Modernity*
by John B. Lyon

Vol. 8. *Thomas Mann in English: A Study in Literary Translation*
by David Horton

Vol. 9. *The Tragedy of Fatherhood: King Laius and the Politics of Paternity in the West*
by Silke-Maria Weineck

Vol. 10. *The Poet as Phenomenologist: Rilke and the New Poems*
by Luke Fischer

Vol. 11. *The Laughter of the Thracian Woman: A Protohistory of Theory*
by Hans Blumenberg, translated by Spencer Hawkins

Vol. 12. *Roma Voices in the German-Speaking World*
by Lorely French

Vol. 13. *Vienna's Dreams of Europe: Culture and Identity beyond the Nation-State*
by Katherine Arens

Vol. 14. *Thomas Mann and Shakespeare: Something Rich and Strange*
edited by Tobias Döring and Ewan Fernie

Vol. 15. *Goethe's Families of the Heart* by Susan E. Gustafson

Vol. 16. *German Aesthetics: Fundamental Concepts from Baumgarten to Adorno*
edited by J. D. Mininger and Jason Michael Peck

Vol. 17. *Figures of Natality: Reading the Political in the Age of Goethe*
by Joseph D. O'Neil

Vol. 18. *Readings in the Anthropocene: The Environmental Humanities, German Studies, and Beyond*
edited by Sabine Wilke and Japhet Johnstone

Vol. 19 *Building Socialism: Architecture and Urbanism in East German Literature, 1955–1973*
by Curtis Swope

Vol. 20. *Ghostwriting: W. G. Sebald's Poetics of History*
by Richard T. Gray

Vol. 21. *Stereotype and Destiny in Arthur Schnitzler's Prose: Five Psycho-Sociological Readings*
by Marie Kolkenbrock

Vol. 22. *Sissi's World: The Empress Elisabeth in Memory and Myth*
edited by Maura E. Hametz and Heidi Schlipphacke

Vol. 23. *Posthumanism in the Age of Humanism: Mind, Matter, and the Life Sciences after Kant*
edited by Edgar Landgraf, Gabriel Trop, and Leif Weatherby

Vol. 24. *Staging West German Democracy: Governmental PR Films and the Democratic Imaginary, 1953–1963*

by Jan Uelzmann

Vol. 25. *The Lever as Instrument of Reason: Technological Constructions of Knowledge around 1800*

by Jocelyn Holland

Vol. 26. *The Fontane Workshop: Manufacturing Realism in the Industrial Age of Print*

by Petra McGillen

Vol. 27. *Gender, Collaboration, and Authorship in German Culture: Literary Joint Ventures, 1750–1850*

edited by Laura Deiulio and John B. Lyon

Vol. 28. *Kafka's Stereoscopes: The Political Function of a Literary Style*

by Isak Winkel Holm

Vol. 29. *Ambiguous Aggression in German Realism and Beyond: Flirtation, Passive Aggression, Domestic Violence*

by Barbara N. Nagel

Vol. 30. *Thomas Bernhard's Afterlives*

edited by Stephen Dowden, Gregor Thuswaldner, and Olaf Berwald

Vol. 31. *Modernism in Trieste: The Habsburg Mediterranean and the Literary Invention of Europe, 1870–1945*

by Salvatore Pappalardo

Vol. 32. *Grotesque Visions: The Science of Berlin Dada*

by Thomas O. Haakenson

Vol. 33. *Theodor Fontane: Irony and Avowal in a Post-Truth Age*

by Brian Tucker

Vol. 34. *Jane Eyre in German Lands: The Import of Romance, 1848–1918*

by Lynne Tatlock

Vol. 35. *Weimar in Princeton: Thomas Mann and the Kahler Circle*

by Stanley Corngold

Vol. 36. *Authors and the World: Modes and Models of Literary Authorship in 20th and 21st Century Germany*

by Rebecca Braun

Vol. 37. *Germany from the Outside: Rethinking German Cultural History in an Age of Displacement*

edited by Laurie Johnson

Vol. 38. *France/Kafka: An Author in Theory*

by John T. Hamilton

Vol. 39. *Representing Social Precarity in German Literature and Film*

edited by Sophie Duvernoy, Karsten Olson, and Ulrich Plass

Vol. 40. *The "German Illusion": Germany and Jewish-German Motifs in Hélène Cixous's Late Work*

by Olivier Morel

Vol. 41. *Interwar Salzburg: Austrian Culture Beyond Vienna*

Edited by Robert Dassanowsky and Katherine Arens

www.ingramcontent.com/pod-product-compliance
Lightning Source LLC
Chambersburg PA
CBHW070011010526
44117CB00011B/1510